The Dynamics of Educational Effectiveness

After 40 years of research on educational effectiveness, the initial optimism with which it was greeted has begun to wane, perhaps because educational effectiveness research was insufficiently related to the changes that take place in education. In looking at the dynamic perspective of education, this book implies that the new, constantly changing goals of education and the associated changes in the teaching and learning strategies should be incorporated in the modelling of educational effectiveness. The dynamic model advocated in the book is a response to this demand and contributes to the establishment of a theoretical framework for the field that can be used by policy-makers and practitioners to improve practice through a theory-driven and an evidence-based approach.

After providing an overview of the development of the field and its main theoretical concepts and methodological tools, the authors present, in detail, a dynamic model of educational effectiveness which refers to factors at student, teacher, school and context level. This implies scrutinising and redefining traditional factors and introducing new overarching factors at each level. Specifically, the factors of the model and their functioning are used in analysing the current situation and to design policies and practices for improvement.

World renowned for his work in the field, Creemers now writes with Kyriakides to create a book that both elucidates current understandings of educational effectiveness and carries the discipline forward by proposing profound changes. The book provides empirical support that will help readers design their own research and evaluation studies, and so will be an invaluable resource for academics, researchers, and students in education, psychology and sociology.

Bert P. M. Creemers is Professor in Educational Sciences at the University of Groningen, the Netherlands. He is the founding editor of the journals *School Effectiveness and School Improvement* and *Educational Research and Evaluation*.

Leonidas Kyriakides is Assistant Professor of Educational Research and Evaluation at the University of Cyprus. He is a member of the editorial board and book review editor of *School Effectiveness and School Improvement*.

Contexts of Learning

Series editors:
Bert P. M. Creemers
David Reynold
Janet Chrispeels

The Dynamics of Educational Effectiveness

A contribution to policy, practice and theory in contemporary schools

Bert P. M. Creemers and Leonidas Kyriakides

Routledge
Taylor & Francis Group

LONDON AND NEW YORK

First published 2008
by Routledge
2 Park Square, Milton Park, Abingdon, Oxon OX14 4RN

Simultaneously published in the USA and Canada
by Routledge
270 Madison Ave, New York, NY 10016

Routledge is an imprint of the Taylor & Francis Group, an informa business

© 2008 Bert P. M. Creemers and Leonidas Kyriakides

Typeset in Times New Roman
by Keystroke, 28 High Street, Tettenhall, Wolverhampton
Printed and bound in Great Britain
by Antony Rowe Ltd, Chippenham, Wiltshire

British Library Cataloguing in Publication Data
A catalogue record for this book is available from the British Library

Library of Congress Cataloging in Publication Data
A catalog record has been requested for this book

ISBN10: 0–415–38951–8 (hbk)
ISBN10: 0–415–39953–X (pbk)
ISBN10: 0–203–93918–2 (ebk)

ISBN13: 978–0–415–38951–8 (hbk)
ISBN13: 978–0–415–39953–1 (pbk)
ISBN13: 978–0–203–93918–5 (ebk)

March 3, 2008

Contents

Figures

Tables

Preface

More than ten years ago, one of us wrote a book on what the effective classroom looks like and how such a classroom can be established. Educational effectiveness theory and research provided an overarching conceptual framework for this attempt, with a clear focus on different types of outcomes of schooling. The learning and teaching level were emphasised. After years of research into curriculum development, evaluation of educational innovations and, especially, teacher behaviour in the classroom, a comprehensive model of educational effectiveness was developed. The other one of us, with a background in educational research and evaluation, began his research journey by looking at issues associated with effective assessment in the classroom and moved via research on baseline and value added assessment to a broader perspective concerning the evaluation of educational effectiveness, whether of teachers, schools, or educational systems. At this stage he was concentrated on testing empirically the comprehensive model and generating ideas for expanding the model.

The publications on the comprehensive model brought us together and helped us discover that we share similar ideas about the ways to address problems associated with the development of the field. And problems there are many: the use of different criteria for measuring effectiveness, the conceptualisation of effectiveness factors and their relation with input variables, the relationship between effectiveness and improvement, and the quality of research and evaluation. In our view, a more theoretical orientation together with a research programme could guide our attempt to solve these problems and increase the contribution of the field to policy and practice.

In this publication we present the first results of our joint efforts towards the development of a dynamic perspective on educational effectiveness. The book is divided into four parts. Part I presents an overview of the current status of theory and research on educational effectiveness and improvement. It helps us identify the main problems that we would like to address in the development of the field through the establishment of a dynamic perspective. Part II presents our effort to establish a dynamic model of educational effectiveness research which is able to address these problems and expand the contribution of the field to policy and practice. The essential characteristics of the model are presented. We also provide a description of our perspective of what effective classrooms, schools, and contexts could look like. Part III illustrates in detail our efforts to test the validity of the proposed dynamic model through both an empirical study and a quantitative meta-evaluation of effectiveness studies. These studies, and especially the results and their implications, are informative concerning the empirical support the model is able to command at the current stage. Part III also suggests how researchers might design studies and conduct meta-analyses focused on the dynamic perspective of effectiveness. Finally, Part IV explores the implications and gives suggestions for research and evaluation, educational policy, and improvement of practice.

While writing this book we received support from many colleagues, policy-makers, and practitioners, as well as from our families. We would like to mention some of them in particular. Our colleague and friend Professor David Reynolds provided us with constructive feedback on an early draft of the book and challenged us to sharpen our arguments. Our friend Dr Gerry Reezigt gave us her comments from the perspective of both a former researcher in the field and a current evaluator within the inspectorate. Her comments helped us to clarify our position and draw further implications for research and policy. Our friend Ioannis Yiannakis, who is currently an inspector but was a teacher for many years, gave us comments that helped us identify the extent to which our work could contribute to the improvement of policy and practice. We also thank him for helping us to draft figures of the proposed model. The research assistants of our team, and especially our PhD students Demetris Demetriou and Panayiotis Antoniou, gave us comments about the proposed model from the perspective of both a researcher and teacher. We also thank them for their support in our effort to design and carry out the empirical study and the meta-analysis. Britanny Hijlkema, Conny Lenderink, and Cathrynke Dijkstra helped us in the production of the book and supported us in its linguistic editing. Moreover, they have helped not merely from a strictly linguistic perspective; they were also critical in helping us clarify the book's meaning. Our respective universities were also supportive by facilitating our effort to write the book and conduct the empirical study. Finally, we are grateful to the Ministry of Education of Cyprus for permission to conduct the empirical study reported in Part III of this book, and to the teachers and students who participated in it. We should like to thank them all for their help and we hope that they will be pleased with the final product. Of course, any mistakes left are ours.

As mentioned, the book is a report of our journey to study educational effectiveness from different perspectives and to propose a dynamic one. We welcome comments, criticisms, and contributions towards further development and research from readers with different perspectives on education. To facilitate further comparative research into the dynamic model, we are preparing a manual that hopefully will be available on request as soon as the book is published. We hope that you will join our journey towards the establishment of a theoretical framework for educational effectiveness research.

Part I

Background to educational effectiveness research

Towards the development of the theoretical framework of educational effectiveness research

Introduction

This introductory chapter offers a definition of educational effectiveness. We also refer to theory and research in educational effectiveness and especially to the importance of establishing a new theoretical framework which, among other things, takes into account the new goals for education, the existence of differential effects of education upon students, and the dynamic relations between the multiple factors of effectiveness. It will be argued that the development of this framework will contribute to the improvement of research, evaluation and practice. Finally, the aims of the book and its structure will be outlined.

Stringfield (1994) defines effectiveness research as the process of differentiating existing ideas and methods of schooling along dimensions deemed to be of value. Educational effectiveness research (EER) does not attempt to invent new ideas or programmes; rather, it aims to concentrate on understanding the lessons to be drawn from existing practices. In this way, EER attempts to establish and test theories that explain why and how some schools and teachers are more effective than others. It is important to note here that three terms – school effectiveness, teacher effectiveness, and educational effectiveness – are used inconsistently in the literature but are interrelated. We are taking school effectiveness to mean the impact that school-wide factors, such as school policy for teaching, school climate, and the school's perceived mission, have on students' cognitive and affective performance. On the other hand, teacher effectiveness refers to the impact that classroom factors, such as teacher behaviour, teacher expectations, classroom organisation, and use of classroom resources, have on student performance.

Teddlie (1994) argued that most teacher effectiveness studies have been concerned only with processes that occur within the classrooms, to the exclusion of school-wide factors, whereas most school effectiveness studies have involved phenomena that occur throughout the school with little emphasis on particular teaching behaviours within individual classrooms. Only a few of them have looked at both school and classroom effectiveness simultaneously (e.g. Mortimore et al., 1988; Teddlie and Stringfield, 1993), but this weakness is being addressed in recent studies (e.g. de Jong et al., 2004; Kyriakides, 2005a; Reynolds et al.,

2002; Opdenakker and Van Damme, 2000). This can be seen as a significant development in the field, since joint studies on school and teacher effectiveness revealed that neither level can be adequately studied without considering the other (Reynolds *et al.*, 2002). In this context, we are using the term 'educational effectiveness' rather than the terms 'teacher' and/or 'school effectiveness' to emphasise the importance of conducting joint school and teacher effectiveness research which can help us identify the interactions between the school, classroom, and individual student levels, and their contributions to student performance. Finally, it is important to note that EER refers to the functioning of the system as a whole, and can therefore be used to develop models of effectiveness (e.g. Creemers, 1994; Scheerens, 1992; Stringfield and Slavin, 1992) that ultimately explain why educational systems perform differently.

The origins of EER stem from reactions to the work on equality of opportunity undertaken by Coleman *et al.* (1966) and Jencks *et al.* (1972). These two studies from two different disciplinary backgrounds – sociological and psychological, respectively – came to almost the same conclusion in relation to the amount of variance that can be explained by educational factors. After taking into consideration student background characteristics, such as ability and family background, not much variance in student achievement was left. This pessimistic feeling of not knowing what, if anything, education could contribute to society was also fed by the failure of large-scale educational compensatory programmes, such as 'Head Start' and 'Follow Through', both conducted in the United States, which were based on the idea that education in schools would compensate for initial differences between students. Similar results have been reported for the effects of compensatory programmes conducted in other countries (e.g. Driessen and Mulder, 1999; MacDonald, 1991; Schon, 1971; Taggart and Sammons, 1999).

Thus, the first two effectiveness studies, undertaken independently by Edmonds (1979) and Rutter *et al.* (1979) during the 1970s, were concerned with examining evidence and making an argument about the potential power of schooling to make a difference to students' life chances. This was an optimistic point of view, because many studies published in that period showed that teachers, schools, and maybe even education in general did not make much of a difference at all. The early existence of two independent research projects in different countries asking similar questions and drawing, to a certain extent, on similar quantitative methodologies demonstrated the potential for establishing a scientific domain dealing with effectiveness in education (Kyriakides, 2006a). Thus, the publications by Brookover *et al.* (1979) and Rutter *et al.* (1979) were followed by numerous studies in different countries on school effectiveness (Teddlie and Reynolds, 2000). During the same period, based on expectations that effective knowledge can be used to improve education, studies on school improvement efforts were conducted (Edmonds, 1979), and contributed to the establishment of links between school effectiveness and school improvement research (Townsend *et al.*, 1999).

In the past 25 years, EER has improved considerably by responding to the criticisms on research design, the sampling, and statistical techniques. Methodological advances have enabled more efficient estimates of teacher and school differences in student achievement to be obtained (Goldstein, 2003). Anyone now attempting to measure the effects of educational systems, schools, and teachers has already encountered two methodological imperatives: 'collect longitudinal data' and 'pay attention to the multilevel organisational structure' in which education occurs. This can be attributed to the fact that school and teacher effects are dynamic things that occur within multilevel, hierarchical organisational structures. Their dynamic character is essential both because school effects modify children's growth and because the schools that produce them are changing (Kyriakides and Creemers, 2006a). Longitudinal data are, therefore, needed to measure the effect of schools and teachers on student achievement gains. Longitudinal data also enhance the validity of causal inferences in non-experimental research by providing a basis for assessing the direction of causation between two variables and by making possible some control over selection effects (Cook and Campbell, 1979). The multilevel, hierarchical character of school and teacher effects is crucial, because such effects occur only when policies and practices implemented at the school and/or teacher level affect learning measured at the student level. Incorporating multilevel effects into statistical analyses helps the researcher avoid a variety of errors of statistical inference, discussed in more detail in Chapter 2 (see also Aitkin and Longford, 1986; DeLeeuw and Kreft, 1986; Goldstein, 2003; Kyriakides and Charalambous, 2005; Raudenbush and Bryk, 1986). Finally, there is substantial agreement regarding appropriate methods for estimating school or teacher differences or effects and the kinds of data required for valid comparisons to be made (Teddlie *et al.*, 2000; Gray *et al.*, 1995; Goldstein, 1997).

As far as the theoretical aspects of the field are concerned, progress was made by more precisely defining the concepts used and the relations between the concepts (e.g. Creemers, 1994; Levine and Lezotte, 1990; Mortimore *et al.*, 1988; Scheerens, 1992; Slavin, 1987a). However, there is a shortage of well-developed theoretical models from which researchers in the area of effectiveness can build theory. The problem is aggravated by the infrequent use of existing models (Scheerens and Bosker, 1997). As a consequence, most of the studies on educational effectiveness are atheoretical and are concerned with the establishment of statistical relationships between variables rather than with the generation and testing of theories that could explain those relationships (Creemers, 2002). There are several reasons to argue for the need to develop and test models of effectiveness that could help us explain differences in student learning results by specifying the relationships between the components in the models and student outcomes. First, a model serves to explain previous empirical research parsimoniously. Second, the establishment and testing of models of educational effectiveness could help us generate a guide to the field to prevent new entrants from reinventing the wheel by repeating existing research. It also maps a series of avenues for future research that may help us expand our knowledge base of educational effectiveness. Finally, a model may provide a useful road map for practitioners, and indeed there are hints that, in part, it has been the absence of educational effectiveness theory that has hindered the uptake of effectiveness knowledge by practitioners in schools (Creemers *et al.*, 2000). It is therefore argued in this book that the next step of EER is to establish models that can be used in policy and practice for improvement.

Characteristics of the proposed theoretical framework of educational effectiveness research

The first part of this section is therefore concerned with the importance of generating a theoretical framework for EER that is able to establish stronger links between EER and improvement practice. A critical review of the main findings and of the theoretical models of educational effectiveness is also provided and helps us identify what the essential characteristics of this new theoretical framework of EER should be.

First of all, it is important to mention that researchers in the 1990s attempted to develop models of educational effectiveness by integrating the findings of school effectiveness research (SER), teacher effectiveness research (TER) and the early input–output studies (e.g. Creemers, 1994; Scheerens, 1992; Stringfield and Slavin, 1992). The studies conducted to test the validity of these models, and especially those studies that tested Creemers' model (i.e. de Jong *et al.*, 2004; Kyriakides *et al.*, 2000; Kyriakides, 2005a; Kyriakides and Tsangaridou, 2004), revealed that the influences on student achievement were multilevel. This finding is in line with the findings of most studies on educational effectiveness conducted in various countries during the past two decades (Teddlie and Reynolds, 2000), and provides support for the argument that models of educational effectiveness should be multilevel in nature. The analysis of the results of these studies also reveals that in addition to the multilevel nature of effectiveness, the relationship between factors at different levels might be more complex than is assumed in the integrated models of educational effectiveness. This is especially true for interaction effects among factors operating at the classroom and student levels, which reveal that effective teachers are expected to provide different learning support systems to different groups of students in order to help them achieve different types of objectives.

Second, one significant methodological criticism of EER is that most effectiveness studies have examined the magnitude of teacher and school effects overall and have paid very little attention to the extent to which teachers and schools perform consistently across different school groupings. Thus, the concepts of teacher and school effectiveness have been developed in a generic way by drawing up a 'one-size-fits-all' model, in which the assumption is that effective teachers and schools are effective with all students, in all contexts, in all aspects of their subjects, and so on. Such conceptualisation of effectiveness has led policy-makers and the general public to a simplistic dichotomy between effective and ineffective teachers or schools (e.g. the idea of schools falling behind) and has eschewed the possibility that teachers may have strengths and weaknesses in their professional practice and some schools may be more or less effective for some groups of students. One consequence is that it becomes difficult to use teacher or school effectiveness research findings to measure such strengths and weaknesses, and therefore difficult for the findings to become a source for conducting formative teacher or school evaluation (Kyriakides and Campbell, 2003). Another consequence is that researchers have attempted to develop generic models of educational effectiveness even though there is some evidence in support of differential educational effectiveness. It is important to acknowledge that the term 'differential effectiveness' is often used in the literature to indicate variation in effectiveness at teacher or school level for different groups of students (e.g. Jesson and Gray, 1991; Nuttall *et al.*, 1989). However, the term here is used in a broader sense to indicate that the effect of a factor may be different not only for different groups of students but also when effectiveness is measured through different outcomes of schooling or in different contexts (Kyriakides and Tsangaridou, 2004). Therefore, this concept is used to emphasise the importance of differentiation not only in teaching but also in the functioning of different types of schools and educational systems. This weakness of the current integrated models of educational effectiveness (e.g. Creemers, 1994; Scheerens, 1992; Stringfield and Slavin, 1992) is aggravated by the fact that there is some evidence that low- and high-ability students and students of low and high socio-economic status (SES) respond to different teacher behaviours and styles (e.g. Brophy, 1992; Walberg, 1986a). Although causal relations between teacher behaviour and student achievement have been demonstrated, resulting in a description of effective teaching practice, many of the characteristics of effective teaching vary according to student SES and ability, grade level, or teachers' objectives (see Campbell *et al.*, 2004; Kyriakides and Creemers, 2006b). Therefore, researchers should attempt to develop models of educational effectiveness that are not only multilevel in nature but also able to demonstrate the complexity of improving educational effectiveness by taking into account the major findings of research on differential effectiveness.

Third, there is a need to carefully examine the relationships between the various effectiveness factors in order to incorporate differential effectiveness in educational effectiveness modelling. It should be acknowledged that one model of educational effectiveness illustrates such relationships. Specifically, Walberg (1984) formulated an encompassing model of educational productivity which is based on the main factors of Carroll's (1963) model and includes an additional category of environmental variables. Aptitude, instruction, and the psychological environment are seen as major direct causes of learning. They also influence one another and are in turn influenced by feedback on the amount of learning that takes place. Walberg's model was tested as a structural equation model on science achievement, indicating more complex, indirect relationships (Reynolds and Walberg, 1990). This finding seems to provide support to our argument that there is a need to develop a model of effectiveness revealing the relationships between the factors of effectiveness which operate at the same level. Such an approach to modelling educational effectiveness might reveal optimal combinations of factors that make teachers and schools effective which could contribute to the establishing of strategies for improving effectiveness.

Fourth, most studies on educational effectiveness are exclusively focused on language or mathematics, and this is seen as one of the most significant weaknesses of EER. Researchers have not been able to monitor student progress across the full range of the school curriculum and did not examine educational effectiveness in relation to the new goals of education, such as the development of metacognitive skills (Campbell *et al.*, 2003). Thus, EER let itself fall under the suspicion of being solely interested in the cognitive domain and restricting itself further by focusing on basic knowledge and skills. As a consequence, EER has been criticised by opponents for having a narrow scope by reducing school learning to discrete, assessable, and comparable fragments of academic knowledge (Slee and Weiner, 1998, p. 2). For example, Lingard *et al.* (1998) state that educational effectiveness starts from an impoverished idea of what counts as achievement, since it is said to assume that the outcomes of schooling can be measured in conventional terms of skills, behaviour, knowledge, and competences. The arguments used by the critics of EER can be countered by referring to numerous studies that used multiple measures of schooling outcomes (e.g. Bosker, 1990; Knuver and Brandsma, 1993; Kyriakides, 2005a; Opdenakker and Van Damme, 2000). It becomes evident from these studies that it is possible to measure a broad range of outcomes in a valid and reliable way using conventional methods of assessment. A typical example is the Torrance Tests of Creative Thinking (TTCT), which have been translated into more than 35 languages and have become highly recommended in the educational field for measuring creativity (Clapham, 1998; Kim, 2006) and designing intervention programmes (e.g. Garaigordobil, 2006). It is therefore argued in this book that there is a need to develop a new theoretical framework of EER that takes into account the new goals of education and emphasises teaching for understanding and development of metacognitive skills rather than teaching based on the transmission of knowledge (Pines and West, 1986; Prawat, 1989a). Moreover, studies testing the validity of theoretical models in relation to the achievement of new goals of education should be conducted.

Fifth, the current models of effectiveness do not explicitly refer to the measurement of each effectiveness factor. On the contrary, it is often assumed that these factors represent unidimensional constructs. For example, the comprehensive model of educational effectiveness states that there should be control at the school level, meaning that goal attainment and the school climate should be evaluated (Creemers, 1994). In line with this assumption, studies investigating the validity of the model have revealed that schools with an assessment policy focused on the formative purposes of assessment are more effective (e.g. Kyriakides *et al.*, 2000; Kyriakides, 2005a). However, the examination of assessment policy at school level can be examined not only in terms of its focus on the formative purpose but also in terms of many other aspects of the functioning of assessment, such as the procedures used to design assessment instruments, the forms of record-keeping, and the policy on reporting results to parents and students. Therefore, the models of educational effectiveness should not only illustrate the various effectiveness factors but also identify the dimensions upon which each factor can be measured. Considering effectiveness factors as multidimensional constructs provides a better picture of what makes teachers and schools effective and helps us develop specific strategies for improving educational practice.

Finally, most quantitative studies in the area of EER concentrate on differences between schools in their effectiveness at a certain point in time – the so-called cross-sectional approach – or have collected data at only two time points (Teddlie and Reynolds, 2000). Modelling effectiveness or change in such circumstances typically involves fitting conditional models in which measures of student learning outcomes (adjusted for background characteristics such as SES, gender, and prior knowledge) are regressed on explanatory variables. However, measures of change based on only one or two time points are unreliable (Bryk and Raudenbush, 1987; Goldstein, 1997; Willett, 1988) and provide an inadequate basis for studying change (Bryk and Weisberg, 1977; Rogosa et al., 1982). Moreover, such an approach implies that the outcome variables in EER are mainly short-term outcomes of the immediate effect of schools and teachers on student achievement gains during a school year. One consequence of using this methodological approach in EER is that most effectiveness studies were primarily concerned with the stability of school and teacher effects rather than their converse, and did not help us develop models of effectiveness that illustrate the dynamic character of educational processes and effects (Kyriakides and Creemers, 2006a). The need for longitudinal research to study results of schools and classrooms and their functioning over a longer period is stressed in this book.

Teaching and learning are dynamic processes that are constantly adapting to changing needs and opportunities. Therefore, studies investigating the process of change in schools may have important implications for modelling educational effectiveness. Moreover, such studies may help us look at the functioning of each factor using a dynamic rather than an instrumental perspective. For example, researchers could examine each factor using not only strictly quantitative ways of measuring each factor, such as how frequently tasks associated with a factor take place, but also qualitative ways that can help us find out when and under what conditions the functioning of a factor improves learning. Furthermore, these studies will contribute significantly to the development of dynamic models of educational effectiveness, which could help us identify factors that not only are associated with student achievement at a certain period but also are able to explain changes in the effectiveness status of teachers, schools, and educational systems. In this context, this book is an attempt to promote the development of a dynamic model that is in line with the characteristics, mentioned earlier, that are considered to be essential for the development of the new theoretical framework of EER. The model not only concentrates on the current situation of schools and teachers but also illustrates the actions that have to be taken in order to improve their effectiveness. It is expected that all schools and teachers are able to improve their effectiveness but that the actions that have to be taken may vary according to their current situation and the context of the school (Datnow *et al.*, 2003; Stringfield, 1995). As a consequence, specific strategies for improving teaching could emerge from this model.

Aims and outline of the book

Aims of the book

The main aim of this book is to propose the development of a dynamic model of educational effectiveness which is in line with the six characteristics, discussed in the previous section, that are essential for generating the theoretical framework of EER and to contribute to establishing stronger links between EER and the improvement of policy and practice. A critical review of theories and empirical findings of research on effectiveness is also provided in the book and helps us justify the importance of the proposed dynamic model. Moreover, findings of a longitudinal study designed to test the validity of the model are presented. Finally, the book illustrates different ways of using the model for improving educational policy and practice.

Nature and structure of the book

The book is divided into four parts. A summary of the main points of each part will be provided at the end of it. In the last chapter the main conclusions emerging from the book will be outlined.

Part I presents an overview of theory and research on educational effectiveness modelling which helps us draw out the main principles upon which the dynamic model of educational effectiveness should be based. After this introductory chapter, Chapter 2 will provide readers with a background on EER which helps them identify its essential characteristics and the progress that EER has made. Implications for establishing the theoretical framework of EER will also be drawn. Chapter 3 will present the comprehensive model of educational effectiveness (Creemers, 1994), on which we draw to build the dynamic model. In order to justify the significance of the comprehensive model, Chapter 4 will refer to the studies which were conducted in order to test parts of the model. The strengths and weaknesses of these studies will be discussed and the extent to which these studies provide empirical support for Creemers' model will be examined. Suggestions for expanding the model which arise from these studies are taken into account for the development of the dynamic model.

Part II will present the dynamic model of educational effectiveness. In connection with the essential characteristics of EER presented in Chapter 2 and the conclusions emerging from the empirical studies testing the comprehensive model of educational effectiveness presented in Chapter 4, we shall outline in Chapter 5 the characteristics and main assumptions upon which the dynamic model is based. A description of the proposed dynamic model at the student and classroom levels will be provided in Chapter 6. More emphasis is placed on teachers' contributions to student learning, which are considered to be the most important overarching factor associated with student achievement gains. In Chapter 7 the factors of the model that operate at the school and the context levels will be presented.

Part III is an attempt to justify the importance of the main principles and the effectiveness factors of the dynamic model. In Chapter 8 we shall illustrate the application of the model in a specific research project conducted to test the main aspects of the model. The extent to which this study provides empirical support for the validity of the dynamic model will be examined. The results of a quantitative synthesis of studies investigating the impact of school factors on student achievement gains will be presented in Chapter 9. The extent to which the findings of this review justify the importance of the school factors presented in the dynamic model will be identified. Moreover, conceptual and methodological issues associated with the main characteristics of the dynamic model are examined.

Part IV will explore the implications for research and evaluation, educational policy, and improvement of practice of the proposed dynamic model. Chapter 10 will examine the implications for research and evaluation, in so far as these can be discerned. Special emphasis will be given to the use of this model for evaluating reform policies. Chapter 11 will explore the implications of the dynamic model for educational policy. These include the development of an evidence-based model for building educational policy. Ways of using the dynamic model for improving educational practice will be illustrated in Chapter 12, and the possibilities of connecting EER with research on improvement discussed.

Chapter 2

Essential characteristics of educational effectiveness research

Introduction: a short history of educational effectiveness research

Based on an analysis of the progress that EER has made during the past three decades, some background on EER is provided in this chapter which reveals the essential characteristics of EER. These arise from analysing the disciplinary perspectives of EER, the development of the criteria of educational effectiveness, and the methodology of EER. It is also argued that EER has reached a stage where it is able to develop a theoretical framework that incorporates and integrates the various theoretical perspectives upon which the existing models of effectiveness have been based.

Educational effectiveness research can be seen as a conglomerate of research in different areas: research on teacher behaviour, curriculum, grouping procedures, school organisation, and educational policy. The main research question of EER is what factors in teaching, curriculum, and learning environment at different levels such as the classroom, the school, and the above-school levels can directly or indirectly explain the differences in the outcomes of students, taking into account background characteristics, such as ability, SES, and prior attainment. This research question has been pursued for many years, sometimes with an optimistic view about the contribution of education to student outcomes and sometimes with a societal feeling that education cannot contribute much to student outcomes, at least when adequate controls for student background characteristics such as ability, motivation, and socio-cultural background are applied.

As was mentioned in Chapter 1, one way to tell the story about EER is to start with the publications by Brookover *et al.* (1979) in the United States and Rutter *et al.* (1979) in the United Kingdom. These two effectiveness studies, undertaken independently, were concerned with examining evidence and making an argument about the potential power of schooling to make a difference to students' life chances. Since the initial effectiveness studies of Brookover *et al.* (1979) in the United States and Rutter *et al.* (1979) in the United Kingdom, a multitude of research studies have been published about factors that make a difference between more and less effective education. The results of the studies of the first phase of

EER revealed that teachers and schools differ among themselves in performance. How much they differ was the next question raised by researchers in the field, and a more refined and precise version of this question is how much schools differ when they are more or less equal as far as the innate abilities and socio-economic background of their students are concerned. A somewhat different statement of the principle of fair comparisons between teachers and schools is the aim of EER to assess the impact of schooling on student achievement gains that can be uniquely attributed to being taught by teacher A or at school X rather than by teacher B or at school Y, respectively. However, in EER, questions do not end by merely assessing the differences between schools and teachers in their effectiveness status. The main research question refers to the *reasons* why one school or teacher does better than another when the differences in their performance cannot be attributed to differences in the student population of the schools or classrooms. This implies that EER is ultimately searching for theory that can explain why some schools and teachers are more effective than others.

In respect to the main question of EER, which is concerned with the factors explaining differences in the effectiveness status of schools, the results of studies conducted during the past 25 years in different countries have been collected in recently published reviews by Teddlie and Reynolds (2000) and Scheerens and Bosker (1997). Like other reviewers (e.g. Levine and Lezotte, 1990; Sammons *et al.*, 1995), the authors found numerous correlates for effective classrooms, schools, and above-school levels (districts, states, country) which emphasise a more theoretical foundation of EER, including a combination of the correlates into categories. It is argued here that the reviews of literature in EER reveal the different disciplinary perspectives of the field, which are reflected in the different types of variables considered as effectiveness factors by different researchers. This argument is supported by a brief review of the main findings of effectiveness studies presented below.

It is first of all important to note that one of the first lists of effectiveness factors was concerned with the so-called 'five-factor model' (Edmonds, 1979). These five correlates of educational achievements were:

- strong educational leadership;
- high expectations of student achievement;
- an emphasis on basic skills;
- a safe and orderly climate;
- frequent evaluation of student progress.

This model has repeatedly been criticised on methodological grounds (see, for example, Ralph and Fennessey, 1983) and also conceptually (Scheerens and Creemers, 1989). Later on, more refined models of school effectiveness were developed (e.g. Clauset and Gaynor, 1982; Duckworth, 1983; Ellett and Walberg, 1979; Glasman and Biniaminov, 1981; Murphy *et al.*, 1982; Schmuck, 1980; Stringfield and Slavin, 1992; Squires *et al.*, 1983). The latter models elaborate

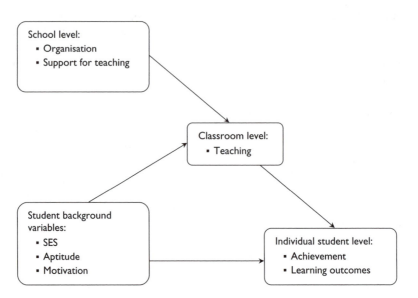

Figure 2.1 A contextual multilevel model of school effectiveness (adapted from Scheerens and Creemers, 1989).

on, or at least operate along the lines of, the framework for a causal model of educational effectiveness as developed by Scheerens and Creemers in 1989. An adapted version of this model is presented in Figure 2.1. The framework stresses the fact that various levels in education contribute to student performance. The characteristics of educational effectiveness found in the research can be placed at different levels, or in the blocks presented in the framework. However, it should be noted that the framework does not answer the question of why certain characteristics correlate positively with achievement. Later, several theoretical orientations were used to explain why certain characteristics might contribute to educational effectiveness. These will be presented in the next section of the chapter.

Disciplinary perspectives of EER

Generally speaking, there are three perspectives within EER that attempt to explain why and how certain characteristics contribute to educational effectiveness, and three relevant theoretical models have emerged from these approaches. First, economists have focused on variables concerned with resource inputs, such as per-student expenditure, to explain variation in the effectiveness status of teachers and schools. Specifically, the economic approach is focused on producing a function that reveals the relationship between the 'supply of selected purchased schooling inputs and educational outcomes controlling for the influence of various background features' (Monk, 1992, p. 308). The function may be linear, consisting of main effects and interaction effects, or non-linear (Brown and Saks, 1986). Thus, the emerging 'education production' models (e.g. Elberts and Stone, 1988; Brown and Saks, 1986) were based on the assumption that increased inputs will lead to increments in outcomes, and their main characteristics are concerned with: (1) the selection of resource inputs as the major type of selection of antecedent condition, (2) the measurement of direct effects, and (3) the use of data at only one level of aggregation (i.e. either at micro (e.g. student) level or aggregated (e.g. school) level). Second, the sociological perspective of EER is focused on factors that define the educational background of students, such as SES, gender, social capital, and peer group. This perspective examines not only student outcomes but also the extent to which schools manage to reduce the variance in student outcomes compared to prior achievement. Thus, two dimensions of measuring school effectiveness emerged from this perspective, concerning quality and equity respectively. Moreover, the sociological perspective calls attention to process variables that emerged from organisational theories – such as the school climate, culture, and structure – and to contextual variables. Finally, educational psychologists focused on student background factors such as 'learning aptitude' and 'motivation', and on variables measuring the learning processes that take place in classrooms. The main assumptions upon which each of these perspectives of EER are based will now be discussed.

Economic perspective on EER

In economics the effectiveness concept is seen as related to the production process of an organisation. The production process is summed up as a transformation of inputs into outputs. In the case of education, students with certain given characteristics and financial and material aids are seen as inputs, whereas outputs include student attainment at the end of schooling. Thus, the transformation process within a school or a school system can be seen as the instruction methods, curriculum choices, and organisational preconditions that make it possible for students to acquire knowledge (see Cheng, 1993). It is vitally important for the economic analysis of effectiveness that the values of inputs and outputs are expressed in terms of money. For example, unless input costs such as teaching materials and teachers' salaries are known, school effectiveness cannot be determined.

However, a strict implementation of the economic characterisation of educational effectiveness runs up against many problems. These already start with the question of how the 'desired outputs' of a school can be defined. For example, the production of a secondary school could be measured by the number of students who successfully manage to graduate from it. However, what if the units of production have to be established in a more sensitive way: do we have to look, for instance, at the grades achieved by students for various examination results? And if so, should only performance on basic skills be examined, or should measures of higher cognitive processes and/or measures of social and affective returns on education be established? Other problems related to the economic analysis of education are the difficulty in determining the monetary value of inputs and processes and the prevailing lack of clarity on how the production process operates. Moreover, research done using this approach has revealed that the relation between input and outcomes is more complex than was assumed. For example, studies by Hanushek and Hedges (e.g. Hanushek, 1986, 1989; Hedges *et al.*, 1994) show that reducing the student/teacher ratio and/or increasing the amount of funding of education per student does not necessarily result in better student outcomes. Therefore, the economic perspective of EER has so far not helped us to clearly understand what procedural and organisational measures are necessary to achieve maximum outputs.

Sociological perspective: organisational perspectives on effectiveness

The sociological perspective on EER addresses three issues. First, input factors concerned with the educational background of students, such as SES, gender, and social and cultural factors, are examined in an attempt to identify the effect of these factors on student achievement gains, as well as the ability of education to compensate for these differences by adapting education to the needs of different groups of students. Second, related to this, the sociological perspective has contributed to the discussion about the criteria of measuring effectiveness. Through their emphasis on the importance of reducing the variance in student outcomes compared to the educational gap in their prior achievement, two dimensions of measuring educational effectiveness concerning both quality and equity emerged. In this respect, studies on the effect of contextual factors (Opdenakker and Van Damme, 2006) and on the extent to which teachers and schools are equally effective with different groups of students (i.e. differential educational effectiveness) have been conducted (e.g. Campbell *et al.*, 2004; Kyriakides, 2004a). Third, process variables associated with sociological theories of organisation have been treated as school-level factors associated with student achievement. The main organisational theories that are taken into account by the sociological perspective will now be presented, and it is shown that school climate, culture, and structure have been treated as the most important effectiveness factors.

Organisational theories often adhere to the thesis that the effectiveness of organisations cannot be described in a straightforward manner. Instead, a pluralistic attitude is taken with respect to the interpretation of the concept in question. Thus, organisational approaches to effectiveness have indicated a range of models, each emphasising a different type of criterion by which to judge effectiveness. The major categories are as follows: productivity, adaptability, involvement, continuity, and responsiveness to external stakeholders. However, most empirical educational effectiveness studies are concerned with the productivity criterion. Scheerens (1992) argues that this position can be legitimised from the point of view of a means-to-an-end ordering of the criteria, with productivity taken as the ultimate criterion. However, other authors see the criteria as 'competing values' (see Fairman and Quinn, 1985) or claim that the predominance of any single criterion should depend on the organisation's stage of development (Cheng, 1993). This issue will be discussed further in the next main section.

It is also important to note that since educational effectiveness is a causal concept, not only the type of effects but also the dimension of the causes or means should be considered. In doing so, the question that is dealt with, from this perspective of EER, concerns the distinction of all the possible features of the functioning of schools that are malleable in order to reach the effects that are aimed for. According to Scheerens *et al.* (2003), the following six categories can be used as a core framework to further distinguish elements and aspects of school functioning: goals, the structure of authority positions or subunits, the structure of procedures, culture, the organisation's environment, and the organisation's primary process. Each of these main categories has been treated by researchers in the field as an area that can be influenced by the school or external change agents. However, the structure of procedures (particularly school management) and the culture have received the most emphasis in the practice of empirical effectiveness research, but the empirical basis for the importance of these factors still needs to be strengthened (Creemers and Reezigt, 1999a; Freiberg, 1999; Maslowski, 2003).

Psychological perspective of EER: investigating the process of learning

Studies on instructional effectiveness show the psychological point of view of EER with respect to the process of learning. Early research on educational effectiveness focused on the characteristics of effective education, mostly at school, but later focused also on classroom, level (Scheerens and Creemers, 1989). However, in educational research there is already a long tradition of research into teacher effects. The major contribution of Gage (1963) was that he stressed the fact that the characteristics of teachers and teaching activities (or teaching behaviour) should be related to student achievement gains. Gage's belief was the start of a vast amount of research on the effects of teaching, which was reviewed and summarised by Rosenshine (1976) and Brophy and Good (1986). This resulted in a list of teacher behaviours that were positively related, consistently over time, with student achievement. Brophy and Good (1986) mention the following list of teacher behaviours:

- quantity and pacing of instruction;
- whole class as opposed to small group instruction;
- structuring of information;
- questioning of students;
- reacting to students' responses;
- handling seatwork and homework assignments.

Combining the findings on time, content covered, work grouping, teacher questions, student responses, and teacher feedback, Rosenshine (1983) indicated a general pattern of results that he labelled the Direct Instruction Model of teaching, sometimes called a Structured Approach. A slightly different model called Active Teaching, with more emphasis put on the involvement of students in the learning and teaching process, was also developed. In active teaching there is a great deal of teacher talk, but most of it is academic rather than procedural or managerial, involving a lot of 'asking questions' and 'giving feedback' rather than extended lecturing (Brophy and Good, 1986, p. 361). In research on teaching, there was gradually less interest in teacher behaviour and the effect of teacher and instructional behaviour, and more interest in teacher cognition and teacher thinking. Within EER, attention was initially directed to the effects of schools; however, after the introduction of methods for multilevel analysis and a more theoretical orientation within EER, more emphasis was put on the learning and instructional level (see Teddlie and Reynolds, 2000).

Theoretically, it might be expected that student outcomes would be related to learning activities, which take place mostly at the learning/instructional level. This resulted in a reorientation, empirically and theoretically, within effectiveness research, on the processes taking place at the teaching–learning level. Factors at the classroom level or, in fact, the teaching and learning level are therefore seen as the primary effectiveness factors. This brings us back to the research, and its results, of teacher effectiveness into EER. When a better foundation for EER was sought, this also resulted in an orientation towards theories about learning in schools. These theories were seen as a possible bridge between learning outcomes, which are used as criteria for effectiveness, and processes at the classroom and school level.

It can be questioned, however, whether the models used in EER, such as the model developed by Carroll (1963), were empirically valid enough to be used as the foundation for a theory about educational effectiveness or as a point of departure for empirical research, indicating, as they did, the most important concepts at the process, input, and context levels. Walberg (1986b) states that although the theories about learning yield some good ideas, they are not sufficiently supported empirically.

A favourite model within EER was Carroll's model (1963) for learning in schools. It was popular because it related individual student characteristics important for learning to characteristics of education important for instruction. In addition, Carroll indicated the factors of time and the quantity and quality of instruction to be important concepts for learning in schools. These were also important characteristics for school effectiveness, as found in earlier effectiveness studies (Creemers, 1994).

The concepts of time/opportunity and quality are rather vague, but can be made more concrete by looking at other characteristics of effective instruction related to learning outcomes. The Carroll model states that the degree of student mastery is a function of the ratio of the amount of time spent on learning tasks to the total amount of time needed. Time actually spent on learning is defined as equal to the smallest of three variables: (1) opportunity (i.e. time allowed for learning), (2) perseverance (i.e. the amount of time in which students are willing to engage actively in learning), and (3) aptitude (i.e. the amount of time needed to learn, in the optimal instructional conditions). This last amount of time is possibly increased by poor-quality instruction and the lack of ability to understand less than optimal instruction (Carroll, 1963, p. 730). The Carroll model can be criticised for being more of an instructional than a teaching model since it does not provide information about how learning itself takes place. Rather, it emphasises that learning takes time and depends on multiple-level interrelated factors. The relationship between time, perseverance, aptitude, and quality of the instruction was further elaborated by Bloom, using Carroll's model to develop mastery learning. Because of the elaboration Bloom provided within a broadly instructional framework (although some writings of Carroll make clear that he thinks that this is a rather technical and mechanical elaboration of his original intentions), the influence of this learning theory on educational practice was substantial. A consistent line of reasoning was developed in models and theories of educational effectiveness between learning outcomes and learning theories relating instructional processes at classroom level and school and contextual conditions to the quality of the instructional level (see Creemers, 1994; Slavin, 1996; Scheerens, 1993; Slater and Teddlie, 1992).

These conceptual frameworks of educational effectiveness, especially the one focused on the instructional and learning processes at the classroom level, received some support from the results of empirical research. Factors discerned within the instructional process related to these theories about learning in schools found support from individual studies, although the picture was not always the same. Some factors related to structuring were supported by some studies but not all; however, evaluation and feedback gained support in the majority of studies. In addition, the reviews of research on effectiveness support the structural processes related to theories that put an emphasis on a mainly reproductive style of learning (see, for example, Creemers, 1994; Fraser *et al.* 1987; Scheerens, 1992; Teddlie and Reynolds, 2000).

Conclusions

Although the different attempts of researchers within the field of EER to identify factors associated with student achievement and to explain how and why these factors influence the effectiveness status of schools might start from different theoretical origins, the organisational, the structural, and the learning and teaching orientations of effectiveness are often combined. The organisational approach to educational effectiveness results in actions to be taken at the level of the teaching and learning process. Similarly, the effectiveness models, which are based on theories of learning (and teaching), also need the organisational approach, because education in schools is not the individual learning of individual students and/or individual teaching by one individual teacher. Effective learning and teaching requires schools to function as organisations. It will therefore be argued in the last section of this chapter that EER has reached a stage where it is able to develop a theoretical framework that incorporates and integrates the theoretical perspectives upon which the existing models of educational effectiveness have been based.

Educational objectives: the development of criteria for effectiveness

In EER, different indicators for effectiveness have been used at different points in time. In early research, school results such as the number of referrals for special education, transitions from primary to different kinds of secondary education or university education, and grade repetition were used as indicators of effectiveness. Later, it was argued that decisions about promotion and referrals are influenced by factors other than education in school and classrooms alone. Therefore, other criteria were advocated, such as achievements in school subjects like reading and mathematics. Further improvement included taking into account students' prior knowledge and background. Moreover, the majority of current studies collected data from national tests in subject areas like mathematics and languages.

However, the educational effectiveness movement came to be suspected of being solely interested in the cognitive domain, and indeed of restricting itself further by focusing, within the cognitive domain, on basic knowledge and skills. As a consequence, EER has been criticised by opponents for having a narrow scope, reducing school learning to discrete, assessable and comparable fragments of academic knowledge (Slee and Weiner, 1998, p. 2). These narrow conceptions are seen as historical artefacts of an industrial era, rather than as versions of schoolings and constructions of the modern human subject. More modernist conceptions of education suggest that effectiveness can be conceptualised and measured in terms of new kinds of citizens' sensibilities, moral and cultural practices, and indeed kinds of discourses. These cultural productions could be generative and redistributive, leading to new conditions rather than being simply reproductive of existing divisions of wealth, gender, and labour (Bage, 1997). But these rather vague modern conceptions of educational effectiveness reveal the importance of establishing clear criteria of effectiveness.

Student outcomes: the cognitive domain of learning

If we agree that student outcomes are the essential criteria for the effectiveness of education, the question remains about what kinds of outcomes, objectives, and goals can be achieved by schools. Especially in an era when other organisations in society cannot fulfil their functions, there is a danger that the school may be overstretched by formulating and emphasising more and more objectives. For example, at a time when families are no longer able to provide their children with agreed moral standards, schools are supposed to take over these responsibilities, even when it is clear that schools on their own cannot significantly alter the life chances of children (Karweit, 1994). The definition of the task of the school and the objectives that have to be pursued are based on an analysis of learning and instructional objectives (Sosniak, 1999). Sosniak (1994) argues that formulating very specific behavioural or performance objectives leads to a situation where we may lose sight of what, according to him, is really important in education. He suggests that the acquisition of subject matter knowledge and skills in the most effective and efficient manner is not the most important aim for public education. Probably virtually everybody agrees with the statement that schools are concerned with the learning of students, especially their cognitive learning, which means that schools are expected to help their students to learn, for example, mathematics and languages.

Thus, the first question connected to this is: how much knowledge and what kind of knowledge is important? Especially in times of economic recession, there is always a tendency to go back to a concern with 'the basics'. Basic skills initially stood as key outcomes within EER, especially because disadvantaged students did not succeed well enough in these skills (Brookover et al., 1979). However, when schools are actually pursuing these kinds of objectives, there is often criticism, especially concerning the teaching methods of basic skills, such as the methods of learning by rote facts and figures. There are often ideas that children should learn more than these things, which leads to objectives in the areas of higher-order learning such as knowledge transfer, evaluation, metacognition, and the learning of 'how to learn' (Bereiter and Scardamalia, 1989). As long as we do not deny the importance of basic knowledge and skills, more than basic knowledge should certainly be added to the objectives and the goals of education in schools. But on the basis of research on metacognition (Prawat, 1989b), and also according to Bloom's et al.'s taxonomy of educational objectives (1956), it is evident that for higher-order learning to take place, basic learning and basic knowledge are required firstly. Therefore, schools must ensure that a basic corpus of knowledge for all students is available so that students can subsequently acquire and develop other types of knowledge and skills (Creemers, 1994).

However, the problem we face is that it is quite easy to add numerous objectives and goals for education in schools, but it is more problematic to make choices between them. In the past, the most important task in curriculum development was the legitimisation and the formulation of educational objectives. It turns out – and it is a traditional problem in education – that most of the time there are many more objectives than can be reached within the constraints of the available time. There is a tendency for the available time for actual learning to decrease at the same time as the goals and objectives of education and schools increase. We clearly cannot go on endlessly adding more objectives and more content for schools and still expect schools to succeed. Schools have to restrict themselves to certain objectives. This also happens to be one of the conclusions of EER. In the past, it was found that schools which restricted themselves to a limited set of objectives and spent time on these objectives did better than other schools (Levine and Lezotte, 1990; Teddlie and Stringfield, 1993). An emphasis on certain objectives requires time and opportunity to learn for students, so schools have to find that time to secure their students' results. Fragmentation into all kinds of subjects, and into concentrating upon too many different kinds of objectives, may affect the achievements of students.

With respect to cognitive development and cognitive goals, we should conclude that there is more involved than just the acquisition of basic knowledge and skills. In order to make students more capable of acquiring knowledge in the future, it is important to pursue more objectives, especially in the areas of the transferability of knowledge, the evaluation of knowledge, the synthesising of knowledge, and the area of metacognitive knowledge. In this context, self-regulated learning and achievement of the so-called higher-order objectives (Bloom *et al.*, 1956) are the main focuses of the constructivist approach to learning (Boekaerts, 1999; Costa, 1984; Resnick, 1987) which should be taken into account in developing the theoretical framework of EER.

Student outcomes: beyond the cognitive domain of learning

So far we have restricted ourselves to the cognitive domain. No one, however, can deny that there is more to education than merely cognitive knowledge and cognitive skills. Schools also have to deal with objectives in the field of societal and democratic values, aesthetic skills, social skills, and attitudes, and in the areas of personal competences such as reflection and initiative-taking (Eisner, 1993; Oser, 1992, 1994; Raven, 1991). Thus, in several countries there is an emphasis on other types of goals apart from simply cognitive goals for education in schools. Sometimes, this is based on the expectation that schools have to compensate for deficient education by other educational institutions or on the recognition that social life is becoming more and more complicated and needs specific and systematic attention. This, for example, is one of the reasons that civic education receives attention in Western countries intending to promote good citizenship by providing cognitive knowledge and skills, value orientation, and social cognition and skills (Delors, 1996). Especially where the transition from school to work comes into focus, these goals are formulated and pursued. In other countries, such as the Pacific Rim countries, education is seen as a continuation of what happens in the society and families. Therefore, schools are expected to contribute to moral education and character-building (Cheng, 1996; Lewis and Tsuchida, 1997).

In times when other organisations in society do not fulfil their tasks properly or sufficiently, schools come under even more pressure to pursue more than just cognitive outcomes. The school is a place where students and teachers meet, interact with each other, and exchange experiences, so it is more than just a place for cognitive development (Oser, 1994). However, how much schools can teach and how many objectives students can achieve in all these domains depend on the time available and the possibility of actually teaching these domains in school. In general, there is a tendency across countries to expand their curricula in order to respond to the needs of their societies by including domains that are only marginally related to cognitive outcomes, but teaching time is not equally expanded. This makes it more difficult for the schools to achieve non-cognitive outcomes. However, schools can contribute to some extent to the achievement of outcomes in these domains. Nevertheless, research has shown that the impact of education in these domains is quite small (Haanstra, 1994). For example, studies investigating school effects on both cognitive and affective outcomes revealed that the school effect on affective outcomes is very small (sometimes less than 5 per cent) in comparison to that on cognitive outcomes (Knuver and Brandsma, 1993; Opdenakker and Van Damme, 2000).

When we take into account the fact that schools need a lot of time to fulfil their tasks properly in the cognitive domain, then probably all other goals can best be seen as welcome side effects and as non-intended outcomes of education. Apparently the influence of other social organisations is far more important than that of schools in this respect (van der Werf, 1995). Schools seem to achieve more in these affective areas when these follow on from cognitive development, as in the case of the cognitive component in social behaviour or in affective or aesthetic education. As research in the past has shown, there is no discrepancy between the achieving of objectives in the cognitive domain and the achieving of them in the area of students' well-being. Students can feel quite happy in schools where cognitive objectives are being pursued, and they can also acquire the cognitive knowledge that is important in the other domains as well (Kyriakides, 2005a). For example, the study by Knuver and Brandsma (1993) reveals a reciprocal relationship between cognitive and affective outcomes by showing that higher scores in the cognitive domain increase motivation and well-being, and this enables students to achieve cognitive goals thereafter.

In summary, this section is a plea for cognitive objectives, in a broad sense, as the criteria for the effectiveness of education in schools. This is a broader definition than EER has generated in the past, since research has mostly focused on a very narrow selection of cognitive outcomes. Curricular reforms have clearly added other objectives that transcend the cognitive domain. The minimal competence that needs to be achieved in these areas by schools is related to the cognitive substrata of these domains. Especially in relation to the time available for teaching and learning, schools have to make decisions on how much they can and will achieve in these areas.

Dimensions of effectiveness: quality and equity

So far, we have discussed schools' educational objectives related to different domains and subject areas. It is expected generally in society that education should achieve good results in those domains and subject areas. This means that the criteria for effectiveness will be at the level to be obtained by individual students, classes, and schools with respect to those objectives (excellence). However, it is also possible to look at the effectiveness of a school from a different angle, especially through investigating how far each school manages to reduce the variance between students (equity). This results in educational objectives and criteria for educational effectiveness which are not related to a specific objective and specific students, but related to different groups of students in relationship to each other. The idea behind this is that education can contribute to social justice and democracy by closing the gap between students with regard to their background, especially their abilities and the socio-cultural status of their family. As a consequence, the early school effectiveness research and school improvement projects had been determined, more or less, by the idea of creating effective schools for the urban poor (Edmonds, 1979). In the 1980s there was quite a lot of criticism of this kind of school improvement and research, with its conspicuous sampling biases (Firestone and Herriott, 1982; Good and Brophy, 1986; Purkey and Smith, 1983; Ralph and Fennessey, 1983; Rowan et al., 1983). As a result, EER is nowadays more realistic and modest in its beliefs about the contributions educational effectiveness can make in promoting equity. On the basis of the knowledge base concerning quality education, one may say that effective schools are able to promote the learning of their students but may not have a special impact on disadvantaged students (Kyriakides, 2004a). The research concerned with the influence of schools on different groups of students, so-called differential effectiveness research, results in the conclusion that those which achieve good results in terms of attaining educational objectives in general do so for specific groups, but they cannot significantly decrease the within-classroom variance of student achievement (Campbell et al., 2004; Teddlie and Reynolds, 2000). However, research into educational effectiveness reveals that teachers and schools matter most for underprivileged and/or initially low-achieving students (Kyriakides, 2004a; Scheerens and Bosker, 1997). This reveals the importance of using both dimensions for measuring effectiveness – excellence and equity – in building theoretical models of educational effectiveness. Moreover, the main findings of research on differential educational effectiveness should be incorporated into the models of effectiveness.

Decision-making about objectives: who defines the criteria for measuring effectiveness

In the previous section, the different types of criteria for measuring effectiveness in relation to the achievement of outcomes of schooling were discussed. A major question that arises from this discussion concerns the impact that EER should have on the discussion regarding the aims of education. In this section we argue that researchers and school improvers should not set and formulate objectives and criteria for measuring effectiveness. For example, the quality of the educational leadership introduced by change facilitators and attained by a specific school with the help of the facilitators can be the criterion for the effectiveness of their interventions but cannot be treated as a criterion for measuring the effectiveness of the school. The criteria for measuring teacher and school effects should be related to the aims, the goals, and the objectives of education that are supported, formulated, and legitimised in any specific society or community.

The position and the relationship of educational researchers and change facilitators towards the objectives of education are quite special. Sometimes researchers have mistakenly expected that they can formulate the objectives of education, and in that way set the criteria for effectiveness themselves, which happens especially when specific schools ask for help in their change process. The history of educational innovation in general shows quite a number of examples of educators who wrongly thought that they could make decisions about educational objectives, which is obviously a misguided idea (Hopkins *et al.*, 1994). Educational researchers, change agents, and facilitators always have to deal with objectives concerned with the quality of their own work, but they do not determine educational goals on their own. The ultimate decision about the aims and objectives of education is made at a national level and is the task of educational policy-makers. The quality of education is determined by the nation or the state and, based on that responsibility for the quality of education, more or less precise outlines for education can be formulated, like the national curriculum and inclusion policies for children with special needs in the United Kingdom (Reynolds, 1993). Indeed, precisely as a reaction to a situation in which educational researchers and change facilitators thought that they could determine the objectives and goals of education in the 1980s, educational professionals subsequently took no part at all in the discussion about educational objectives, and the discussion was taken away from them by educational policy-makers, educational practitioners, and politicians. However, even if educational researchers cannot determine or cannot make any ultimate decisions about the goals and objectives of education, they can usefully contribute to the discussion in several ways:

- They can offer different *possibilities for educational aims, goals, and objectives*. Especially when there is a choice between different kinds of objectives, they can make analyses about the pros and cons of these objectives.
- They can provide information about *what can be achieved by education* and what can be done in schools, given the time constraints. They can also formulate under what kinds of conditions objectives can be achieved by schools.
- They can carry out research on *how students can meet the objectives* or how they may even meet them already, given the pre-existing conditions.
- They can make *rational balances* between different kinds of objectives or between different kinds of subject areas, *relate* subject areas to each other, and *analyse* the relationships between the developmental states of children with respect to objectives and to subject areas.
- They can make an analysis about *educational needs in the future* and offer new formulations and new sets of possible objectives.

Even though researchers in the field of EER do not determine objectives, their influence in the formulation process, as well as in the determination and the decision-making processes, is very important. This is how it should be, because the influence of a professional organisation is necessary in all areas of society where decisions are taken at the political level.

In our discussion about the decision-making process, most emphasis has so far been put on the national or state level. The same notions hold for other levels, for example the 'intermediate' level of school districts or provinces, or even the school level. However, at these levels the decision-making process takes place within a framework of decisions already made by higher levels about the aims and objectives of education, which implies that change facilitators and educational researchers can have one additional function, that of translating the goals and processes of the national level to the other levels in education. In this respect there are differences between countries because in some countries the specification at the national level is so precise that it determines daily life in schools and even in classrooms and specific lessons (Kyriakides, 1999a). In other countries the aims and goals at the national level are mere guidelines, and it then requires an extensive transformation process for districts and schools to make these guidelines usable in educational practice. In these circumstances, support by educational researchers, curriculum developers, and change facilitators is even more important in making aims more concrete.

Conclusions

The purpose of the second section of this chapter has been to outline the improvement of EER in respect of its attempt to determine the criteria for effectiveness and improvement. It has been argued that there is a great deal of confusion when criteria concerning the nature of the system and the inputs and processes are confounded with criteria for the quality of the educational system. Ultimately, the criterion for success is the attainment of the aims, goals, and objectives of education. Since schools are primarily places where learning takes place, the objectives of education are primarily student learning outcomes. These can be found in the cognitive domain and also in other areas such as the affective, the social, and the aesthetic domains. We must conclude that student learning in non-cognitive areas is determined overwhelmingly by other actors in the society, whereas the cognitive domain is determined less by other social agents. This implies that schools have a specific role in the cognitive domain and that, consequently, objectives in this area are crucial for the educational system in general. Moreover, achievement of cognitive outcomes determines to some extent achievement in other domains, such as motivation and well-being. However, this does not mean that education should be restricted to cognitive objectives, since only a partial relationship between the achievement of cognitive and that of non-cognitive domains exists. Therefore, the cognitive basis for non-cognitive areas can be offered. Moreover, schools may act as social agents and, being a part of society, they can also contribute partially to these areas. They can provide a social and aesthetic environment in which social behaviour and aesthetic attitudes can be developed. Schools and teachers should be supported in such a way that objectives are reached and educational quality becomes a fact. In this context, research can offer insight into which factors and variables contribute to student results.

Educational professionals can and should contribute to the processes of formulating and deciding upon educational objectives, within the context of the determination of educational policy nationally. Although not every activity in educational research and school improvement is directly related to educational outcomes, in the end there should be a tradition of thinking that it establishes relationships between actions and activities within schools on the one hand, and achievement of educational objectives on the other. This provides direction to the activities of educational researchers and school improvers, a direction for what happens at different levels of education. It is also clear that we need evaluation of these activities to find out whether they contribute to the attainment of educational objectives.

In this book, when we refer to effectiveness we will use the term 'outcomes', but in a broader sense. The dimensions of quality and equity are both used as criteria for measuring effectiveness. In the case of quality, student achievement gains in both the cognitive domain as well as other domains can be examined. On the other hand, equity is measured by looking at the extent to which schools and teachers manage to reduce unjustifiable differences in outcomes of schooling. Figure 2.2 illustrates the way we conceptualise measures of effectiveness in relation to dimensions and domains of learning. In this section we referred to studies which show that interaction between the two dimensions as well as among

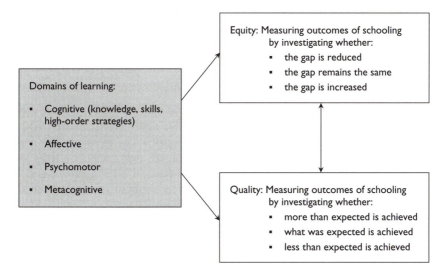

Figure 2.2 Dimensions of measuring effectiveness concerned with outcomes of schooling.

the domains of learning is expected to exist. Such interactions are illustrated in Figure 2.2. It is also assumed that interactions among dimensions and domains may also exist. Therefore, bear in mind that the term 'outcome' is used in a broader sense and refers to the impact of learning on student development (cognitive and non-cognitive) as well as to the impact of education on reducing the variance in achievement that can be attributed to student background characteristics that are not changeable, such as gender, ethnicity, and SES.

The methodology of educational effectiveness research

This last section of the chapter refers to the methodological advances that have taken place during the past 25 years in the field of EER. It is argued that EER has improved considerably, taking account of the criticism on research design, sampling, and statistical techniques. As a consequence, more valid estimates of teacher and school differences in student achievement are obtained nowadays (Goldstein, 2003).

Operational questions in the modelling of teacher and school effects

As has been claimed above, when one is trying to estimate school and teacher effects, a major research question that arises is concerned with the choice of a particular effectiveness criterion. However, the following two questions also need to be addressed by researchers measuring teacher and school effects:

• What definition of effectiveness should be applied?
• What kinds of statistical problems should be avoided when estimating teacher and school effects?

Implicit operational definitions of educational effectiveness

The different underlying definitions of teacher and school effectiveness are concerned with the use of unadjusted 'raw' or value added measures of student outcomes. More importantly, when one is using value added measures, different corrections are being made before the actual teacher and/or school effects are assessed. Schereens and Bosker (1997) refer to four different approaches that can be used by researchers to assess school effects: raw or unadjusted school effects, school effects based on unpredicted achievement, school effects based on learning gain, and school effects based on unpredicted learning gain.

RAW TEACHER OR SCHOOL EFFECTS

In this case the mean (unadjusted) achievement score of students in a certain class or school is used to measure the class or school effect. The value of this definition lies in its use within a criterion-referenced framework. Specifically, it is assumed that since standards are set, it is important for both accountability and research reasons to judge whether each school, on average, performs below or above the standard.

TEACHER OR SCHOOL EFFECTS BASED ON UNPREDICTED ACHIEVEMENT

In this case a prediction equation is estimated. Specifically, student background factors such as aptitude, SES, age, gender, and ethnicity status are used to predict student achievement. The reasoning behind this approach is that since schools differ in their student population and since student background variables are associated with student achievement, the effect of these variables, which are static, should be partialled out when school and teacher effects are measured. This implies that the measure of aptitude should ideally take place before or at school entry through use of information gathered from baseline assessment systems (Kyriakides, 1999b).

TEACHER OR SCHOOL EFFECTS BASED ON LEARNING GAIN

The third operational definition of effectiveness can be seen as a further development of the second one. In this case the difference between achievement at the end and at the beginning of a certain period (e.g. a school year) is used to assess the teacher or school effect. Thus, the teacher or school effect transforms into the effect of a school on its students within a certain time interval. This definition implies that researchers often measure the partial rather than the full school effect since longitudinal data on achievement gains during the whole of the period during which students are expected to attend a school are needed in order to measure the full school effect (see Kyriakides and Creemers, 2006a).

TEACHER OR SCHOOL EFFECTS BASED ON UNPREDICTED LEARNING GAIN

This last is the strictest definition and combines the previous two definitions. The score of the final measure of student outcomes is initially corrected by using a score of student prior achievement and is in turn corrected for other student background variables, such as SES, age, and gender, that are related to student achievement gains (Kyriakides, 2002).

In the literature on EER, teacher and school effects are usually measured through approaches that seek to assess value added. There is a broad consensus that 'fair' indicators of school performance need to measure the contribution of teaching to progress made by students at school (Fitz-Gibbon et al., 1990). Moreover, information gathered from assessment of value added is more valid in exploring the effectiveness of a school unit than using outcome data only, since variations in the final test results of schools reflect partly the educational attainment of students when they enter the school (Fitz-Gibbon, 1997). However, it is argued here that there are at least three different sets of value added-based school effects. Actually, the value added-based definition can be made stricter by correcting not only for the student-level effect of the covariates but also for the potential extra effects of their aggregates, or what was historically called 'balance' (Rutter *et al.*, 1979; Opdenakker and Van Damme, 2006). This approach is based on the fact that research investigating the effect of contextual factors reveals that being a student from a socially disadvantaged background has a negative effect on achievement, but being in a school with a majority of working-class students has a substantial additional negative effect on achievement as well.

Although researchers use value added approaches to measure school and teacher effects, and especially approaches that take into account the effect of SES on student achievement, it is important to acknowledge the difficulty of eliminating SES from the measures of school effectiveness. In many countries it is common for upper- or middle-class parents to send their children to places promising better schooling and often to lobby for the 'best' teachers for their children. As a result, low-SES children attend the schools deemed least attractive by upper-middle-class parents. Moreover, it is easier, and often more rewarding, to teach students of upper-middle-class parents since they have the cultural capital to support their children's learning and raise their motivation. Good teachers who feel under a lot of stress in teaching students of low-class parents are able to transfer to other areas. The consequence is that when attempting to identify the school effect, researchers tend to attribute most of the variance, which is 'multi-collinear' (Stringfield, 1994), to parental SES and thereby underestimate the effects of schooling. Although massive state control over the deployment of teachers and parental choice is not advocated, it is acknowledged that without this, the difficulty of measuring effectiveness remains a real one (Kyriakides *et al.*, 2000).

Statistical issues: the importance of using multilevel modelling techniques

The statistical techniques that can be used to estimate school and teacher effects are discussed below. It is first of all important to note that the selection of a certain statistical technique to estimate teacher and school effects is partly based on the type of operational definition of effectiveness that researchers adopt. Thus, the first definition, which is concerned with the gross school effect, implies the use of mean achievement, but it is actually averaged over all of the students within a school, with a correction for sampling error. This correction is crucial, especially since only a restricted number of students per school may participate in a study. Moreover, a multi-stage sampling procedure is usually employed. For example, a three-stage sample is employed to measure school and class effects by initially selecting schools, then choosing specific classrooms within each selected school, and finally choosing students within each selected classroom. Thus, in a multi-stage sample some variation will show up as between school variance by chance, and therefore correction for sampling error is necessary. This is based on the assumption that the less reliable the information for a certain school is, the more its effect is estimated using information from the rest of the sample (see Snijders and Bosker, 1999).

Given that the other three definitions use value added approaches to measure the teacher and school effects, we discuss below the importance of using multilevel modelling approaches in effectiveness studies, an approach that has been used by most researchers in the field during the past decade. Its importance arises mainly from the fact that clustered data are collected in order to measure the teacher and school effect. Thus, the use of multilevel analysis for analysing clustered data is recommended below. In the three-stage sampling procedure described above, students are nested within classrooms and classrooms are nested within schools. It is therefore important for research to take into account the hierarchical structure of the data. We shall now explain the importance of using multilevel techniques to identify the effect of factors operating at different levels on student achievement rather than aggregated data.

A common procedure in social research with two-level data is to aggregate the micro-level data to the macro level. The simplest way to do this is to work with the averages for each macro-unit. There is nothing wrong with aggregation when the researcher is only interested in macro-level relations, although the reliability of an aggregated variable depends, among other things, on the number of micro-level units in a macro-level unit. However, in cases where the researcher is interested in macro–micro or micro-level relations, aggregation may result in gross errors, such as the 'shift of meaning' (Huttner and van den Eeden, 1995) and the 'ecological fallacy' (Alker, 1969). These errors will now be explained.

The first potential error – 'shift of meaning' – arises from the fact that a variable being aggregated to the macro level refers to the macro-units and not directly to the micro-units. For instance, although student intelligence could be seen as an index of the extent to which students are able to perform a learning task, the classroom average of students' intelligence may be seen as an index of how demanding the intended curriculum could be in order to meet the learning needs of the classroom, which implies that we may have a shift of meaning of the variable. The second potential error – 'ecological fallacy' – has to do with the fact that a correlation between macro-level variables cannot be used to make assertions about micro-level relations. For example, the average classroom ability of students may be negatively related to the frequency of praise of students, because teachers tend to provide positive feedback more frequently to low-achieving students (Brophy, 1992). However, this does not reveal anything about the micro-level (i.e. student-level) relationship between the frequency of providing positive feedback and achievement. On the contrary, studies within educational psychology have shown that positive feedback may improve student achievement (Walberg, 1986a).

Aggregating data also prevents researchers from investigating cross-level interaction effects. For instance, aggregation does not allow us to find out whether the effect of aptitude on achievement varies according to the extent to which ability grouping of students within the classroom is used. It is also not possible to examine how variables measured at one level affect relations occurring at another (Bryk and Raudenbush, 1992).

However, the most significant statistical error is the neglect of the original data structure (Raudenbush and Bryk, 1986) (e.g. the fact that students are nested within classrooms and classrooms are nested within schools). Single-level analyses require the researcher to assume incorrectly that individuals within similar subunits share no common characteristics. Such an approach leads to the possibility of biased regression coefficients and associated standard errors. Specifically, the group (e.g. class) and its members (e.g. students) both influence and are influenced by the group membership. Students bring certain skills and attitudes with them; at the same time, they are clustered in classes and schools with certain characteristics. Therefore, treating students as if they were independent of the class and school group ignores the complexity in the data (Snijders and Bosker, 1999). To ignore this relationship risks overlooking the importance of group effects, and as a consequence we may overlook important relationships and draw erroneous conclusions (Heck and Thomas, 2000). This can be attributed to the fact that individuals in a group or context tend to be more similar on many important variables than individuals in different contexts.

Multilevel modelling techniques, a methodology for the analysis of data with complex patterns of variability, can meet the deficiencies of the single-level analysis mentioned above. Specifically, multilevel analysis explicitly models the manner in which students are grouped within classes or schools, and therefore has several advantages (Goldstein, 2003). First, multilevel analysis takes into account the existence of hierarchically structured data and the variability associated with each level. As has been argued above, erroneous conclusions may be drawn if any of these sources of variability is ignored (see also Snijders and Bosker, 1999; Opdenakker and Van Damme, 2000). Second, multilevel analysis provides a means of partitioning the outcome variables' variance into different levels (within and between units). This enables researchers in the area of EER to measure the teacher and school effects separately. Third, it yields better-calibrated estimates for the variance of standard errors. Fourth, it offers a single framework that combines the information within and across units to produce more accurate explanations and outcomes. Finally, clustering information provides correct standard error confidence intervals and significance tests, which are more conservative than the traditional ones that are obtained simply by ignoring the presence of clustering (Snijders and Bosker, 1999). By allowing the use of covariates measured at any of the levels of a hierarchy, the researcher is able to explore the extent to which the differences in average achievement results between schools can be accounted for by factors related either to the school, to class, or to student characteristics. For all of these reasons, a specific methodology of EER has been developed which is based on the use of value added and multilevel modelling techniques to measure effectiveness at different levels and identify relevant effectiveness factors.

The development of integrated models of educational effectiveness research

The previous sections of this chapter have revealed that over the past 25 years, EER has improved considerably by taking into account criticism of research design, sampling, and statistical techniques. Methodological advances have enabled more efficient estimates of teacher and school differences in student achievement to be obtained (Goldstein, 2003). As far as the theoretical component of the field is concerned, progress was made by defining more precisely the concepts used and the relations between the concepts (e.g. Mortimore *et al.*, 1988; Scheerens, 1992; Levine and Lezotte, 1990), and because of the development of different disciplinary perspectives on EER. However, during the past decade researchers have attempted to integrate the findings of research from the three disciplinary perspectives of EER and develop theoretical models (e.g. Stringfield and Slavin, 1992; Scheerens, 1992; Creemers, 1994) with a multilevel structure. Although the emerging integrated models of educational effectiveness make use of both organisational theories and theories of learning, and refer to multiple factors at different levels, each of them is focused on either the classroom or the school level. Depending on which is the case, more emphasis is given either to theories of learning (e.g. Creemers, 1994) or to organisational theories (e.g. Scheerens, 1992).

Studies investigating the validity of integrated models of effectiveness (e.g. de Jong *et al.*, 2004; Kyriakides, 2005a; Kyriakides *et al.*, 2000) have revealed that the influences on student achievement are multilevel. This finding is in line with the findings of most studies on educational effectiveness conducted in various countries (Teddlie and Reynolds, 2000) and provides support for the argument that models of effectiveness should be multilevel in nature. Analysis of the results of these studies also reveals that in addition to the multilevel nature of effectiveness, the relationship between factors at different levels might be more complex than is assumed in the integrated models. In this context, this book argues that EER has reached a stage at which it is able to develop a theoretical framework that:

- incorporates and integrates the various theoretical perspectives upon which the existing models of educational effectiveness have been based and which are described in the first section of this chapter;
- concentrates on the impact of schools and teachers on learning outcomes and searches for the functions of schools that induce learning by taking into account the broader views of learning outcomes as we discussed earlier;
- takes into account the methodological development of EER in respect of the operational definitions used to measure effectiveness and the use of value added and multilevel modelling techniques to measure teacher and school effects.

In order to achieve this purpose, a dynamic model of educational effectiveness is proposed in this book. The earlier comprehensive model of educational effectiveness (Creemers, 1994) is seen as the starting point for establishing the dynamic model. This is attributed to the fact that Creemers' model refers to factors at different levels (i.e. student, classroom, school, district, system) and at the same time is based on the assumption that there are direct and indirect relations between the levels and the outcomes. This comprehensive model of educational effectiveness is presented in the next chapter. Special emphasis in this chapter is given to the principles upon which the model is based and to the nature of the interactions between the factors presented in the model. The strengths and weaknesses of this model will be presented in Chapter 4 and the importance of establishing a dynamic model identified.

Chapter 3

The comprehensive model of educational effectiveness

Introduction

In Chapter 2 it was argued that the different attempts of researchers within the field of EER to identify factors associated with student achievement and to explain how and why these factors influence the effectiveness status of schools start from different theoretical origins. It was also claimed that the organisational structural tradition and the learning and teaching orientations of effectiveness research should be combined. This was attributed to the fact that the organisational approach of educational effectiveness promotes actions to be taken at the level of the teaching and learning process. Similarly, the effectiveness models which are based on theories on learning (and teaching) also need the organisational approach, because education in schools is not simply about the learning of individual students and/or teaching by one individual teacher. Effective learning and teaching require schools to be effective organisations. In this context, during the past decade researchers have attempted to integrate the findings of research on the three disciplinary perspectives of EER and to develop theoretical models (e.g. Creemers, 1994; Scheerens, 1992; Slater and Teddlie, 1992; Stringfield and Slavin, 1992) that have a multilevel structure.

This chapter refers to the comprehensive model of educational effectiveness (Creemers, 1994), which is considered one of the most influential theoretical constructs in the field (Teddlie and Reynolds, 2000). Moreover, the model is in line with two recommendations given in Chapter 2, concerned with the emphasis given to the impact of schools and teachers on learning outcomes and the importance of taking into account the multilevel nature of the factors affecting student achievement. Thus, Creemers' model can be considered the starting point for developing the proposed dynamic model of educational effectiveness. Specifically, in this chapter the relation of the comprehensive model of educational effectiveness to the Carroll model is provided and the factors included in the model are briefly presented. Finally, the main principles upon which the model is based are discussed.

The comprehensive model of educational effectiveness: general characteristics

A model specifies or visualises complex phenomena in a simplified or reduced manner. In a more abstract way, it is described in terms of a set of units (facts, concepts, variables) and a system of relationships among these units. The modelling approach to educational effectiveness is aimed at further clarification of the core elements and relationships of the more general concepts that were used in the second chapter. A distinction should also be made between conceptual and formal models. In the case of conceptual models, only verbal descriptions and diagrams are used, whereas formal models consist of mathematical equations. The comprehensive model of educational effectiveness belongs to the category of conceptual models and its main characteristics are described below.

First, Creemers' model distinguishes between levels in education (see also Scheerens, 1992; Slavin, 1996; Stringfield, 1994; Stringfield and Slavin, 1992), and is therefore multilevel in nature. Specifically, the model has four levels: the student level, the classroom level, the school level, and the context level. Higher levels are expected to provide conditions for the operation of lower levels. Therefore, outcomes are provided by the combined effects of levels. Second, the model is based on the Carroll model of school learning (Carroll, 1963), which was described in Chapter 2. The concept of time, central in Carroll's model, has been systematically complemented by the concept of opportunity to learn, and the only classroom factor in the Carroll model, quality of instruction, has been elaborated in more detail and put at the core of the comprehensive model of educational effectiveness. Combining the key concepts and the hierarchical structure of the levels, Creemers' model defines the key concepts at each educational level by outlining specific selected factors on the basis of a theoretical criterion – that these factors should have demonstrated their impact on outcomes. Most factors represent the alterable behaviours of teachers and school teams. The model shows how the levels influence student outcomes, but since the model places more emphasis on the classroom-level factors, the relation of the model to the various instructional theories will first of all be elaborated in the next subsection of this chapter.

Instructional theories as the basis for the development of Creemers' model

Theories about effective education that start at the classroom level focus on the instructional elements of learning theories. In fact these theories, taking into account the background characteristics at the student level, try to explain how the instructional factors can contribute to the outcomes of education – or, more precisely, how differences in educational outcomes can be explained by differences in instruction at the classroom level. These theories emphasise instructional factors that are changeable. In addition to the student background characteristics, instructional theories take into account elements or components of instruction at the classroom level such as the methods used at the classroom level, other learning methods, the learning environment, and especially the teacher's behaviour, in the classroom. By distinguishing between the different components of instruction at the classroom level, one can discover correlates that are associated with effectiveness in research, and indeed these correlates for effectiveness from past research are rearranged in a conceptual framework (Creemers and Reezigt, 1996). It is important to note that in various instructional theories developed during or prior to the 1970s (e.g. Bloom, 1976; Carroll, 1963; Cooley and Lohnes, 1976; Glaser, 1976; Harnischfeger and Wiley, 1976) the theoretical constructs are almost the same. Specifically, a distinction between 'the quality of instruction' and 'time on task and opportunity to learn' is often made. Like Carroll (1963), they merge time and opportunity to learn together. However, time and opportunity to learn can be discerned in several categories. For example, Harnischfeger and Wiley (1976) distinguish seven categories of time. In this context, Creemers (1994) made a distinction between time on task on the one hand and opportunity to learn on the other. Thus, Creemers (1994) developed Carroll's model of learning by adding to the general concept of opportunity the more specific notion of opportunity to learn. Moreover, in Creemers' model time and opportunity are discerned both at the classroom level and at the school level. In this way Creemers made a distinction between available, and actually used, time and opportunity.

Similarly, quality of instruction can be outlined in quite a lot of different elements, especially when quality is distinguished for different components within the instructional process such as curricula, grouping procedures and teacher behaviours (Creemers, 1994). Each of these three components of instruction can contribute to the quality of instruction and have characteristics that are correlated with the effectiveness of education at the classroom level (Kyriakides et al., 2000). Creemers (1994) claims that these components can influence learning outcomes directly but may also influence time and opportunity and therefore learning outcomes indirectly.

It is apparent that there is a difference between what is offered to students and the actual use students make of that offer. According to Creemers' model, that holds both for time and for opportunity. Therefore, the quality of instruction can influence the use that students make of time and opportunity, as well as the amount they need before they master the objectives of education. With respect to time, Creemers (1994) argues that the distinction between planned time and used time is obvious in terms of allocated and engaged time. With respect to opportunities, the distinction is rarer but it can provide a useful tool for explaining differences in student outcomes.

In summary, Creemers' model concentrates on the classroom level, the rationale being that most studies on educational effectiveness supported the idea of the predominance of classroom-level factors over school-level factors (Teddlie and Reynolds, 2000). Moreover, the classroom factors most directly related to time on task and opportunities to learn used at the student level are the corresponding factors used at the class level: 'time for learning' and 'opportunity to learn'.

Furthermore, Creemers (1994) distinguishes three components of the quality of classroom instruction: curriculum, grouping procedures, and teacher behaviours. However, teachers are considered to be the central component in instruction. They make use of curricular materials and they carry out grouping procedures (such as mastery learning, ability grouping, and cooperative learning). These three components of the quality of instruction are elaborated in specific effectiveness-related variables in the model. In curriculum and teacher behaviour similar kinds of variables are distinguished, such as clarity of goals, structuring of content, and evaluation and feedback to produce corrective instruction. Additional teacher behaviour characteristics refer to high expectations, homework, presentational skills, and class management (Creemers, 1994, p. 119). Finally, it could be claimed that the model in its concentration on education emphasises learning and instruction but, as is articulated below, the model is less developed in the organisational part of the school and the educational system.

Conditional role of the school level

Creemers took as his point for departure that student learning, and especially differences in learning outcomes, has to be explained by the primary processes at the classroom level. These primary processes directly influence time on task and opportunities to learn used by students, and indirectly influence student achievement. However, it is not expected that the school level directly contributes to time on task and opportunities used by the students, or to student achievement. Creemers (1994) claims that the school provides conditions for quality of instruction, time on task, and opportunity to learn at the classroom level. It is also postulated that at the school level the conditional factors can be related to the overarching categories mentioned above: quality, time, and opportunity. The conditional role of the school level is depicted in Figure 3.1, which illustrates the comprehensive model of educational effectiveness.

Quality, time and opportunity at the school level

Figure 3.1 shows that school-level factors are expected to directly influence the quality of instruction, time for learning, and opportunity to learn at the classroom level. Their influence on student achievement is mediated by time on task and by opportunities used at the student level. Therefore, school-level factors are categorised within the same conceptual notions of quality, time, and opportunity as the classroom-level factors. However, the school-level factors include the organisation of the school (teachers, students, parents), but also the educational system above the school level (i.e. the context, or national level). This relates to the curriculum of the school through effects on the textbooks and the time schedule. Thus, Creemers (1994) made a distinction between the school level as an organisational system and the school level as an educational system. The two systems are related to each other, but the first – the school level – can create and

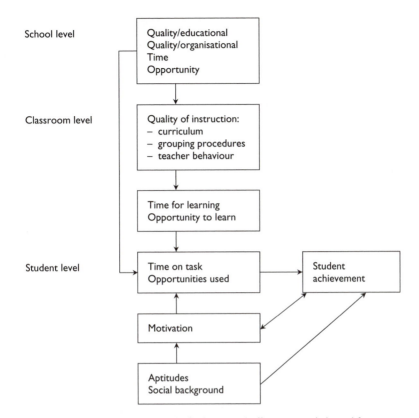

Figure 3.1 The comprehensive model of educational effectiveness (adapted from Creemers and Reezigt, 1996).

sustain the situation in which education takes place to some extent, comparable with what classroom management 'does' for instruction. It is also important to note that according to the comprehensive model of educational effectiveness, the factors at the school level are seen as conditions for what goes on at the classroom level. However, conditions can be either clear (e.g. the curriculum) or less clear (e.g. the structure of the organisation). The latter factors can also affect the instructional process by, for example, influencing what happens between headteachers and teachers (see, for example, Rosenholz, 1989; Teddlie and Stringfield, 1993).

A distinction is also made between the educational and organisational aspects of the quality of instruction (see Figure 3.1). With respect to the educational aspects, the rules and agreements in the school concerning the instructional process at the classroom level are of the utmost importance, especially those related to curricular materials, grouping procedures, and teacher behaviours. For example, it is expected that there should be a school policy which defines educational goals that have to be achieved in classrooms. This does not imply having a wide range of goals that it may not be possible for the students to achieve, but realistic goals that can be achieved, as well as goals that are in line with the educational needs of the students and can give guidance to teacher behaviour in the classroom (Campbell and Kyriakides, 2000). Moreover, effective schools are expected to have an evaluation policy that directs activities at the classroom and the student level by means of a student monitoring system. Therefore, effective schools promote the testing of students and stimulate teachers to disseminate their assessment results to students and parents, to take corrective measures, and to act as necessary on the basis of their students' progress, providing opportunities for rehearsal, corrective materials, and remedial teaching. This implies that effective schools give more emphasis to the formative purposes of assessment than to the summative purposes (Kyriakides, 2005a).

The organisational aspects of quality at the school level are related to the interconnectedness (mutual supervision) of teachers and the professionalisation of teachers and headteachers. These aspects refer not only to the structure of the organisation but also to the collaboration among teachers and their headteacher, which contributes to the improvement both of the classroom practices and of the school as a whole. In this respect the effective headteacher is expected to act as an 'instructional leader' who takes responsibilities for the professional development of the teachers of his or her school. Creemers (1994) also argues that team consensus about the mission of the school and the way to fulfil this mission through shared values will support the activities of individual teachers, and result in continuity and consistency. This can create a school culture among headteachers, teachers, students, and parents that promotes effectiveness (Cheng, 1993).

Conditions for the use of time at the school level are connected with the time schedule and timetable. For all grade levels, this schedule spells out how much time should be devoted to different subjects. Apart from this, it is important to keep track of time utilisation. In less effective schools, a lot of scheduled time is wasted because there is no system to encourage, or compel, classrooms to use time effectively.

The time available for learning can be expanded by a homework policy. For this reason, homework policy is seen as an important school-level factor (Creemers, 1994). When homework assignments are well controlled and structured, and constructive feedback is given, such assignments can expand effective learning time outside the school. Moreover, contacts between schools and parents and agreements about school policies and activities may lead to the effective use of time spent on homework. Furthermore, when parents expect their children to achieve goals set by the school, the effectiveness of education increases.

Creemers (1994) also argues that measures taken at the school level can maintain an orderly environment that facilitates teaching and learning at the classroom level. Several studies on school effectiveness reveal that learning time is increased by an orderly classroom climate (Teddlie and Reynolds, 2000). At a school level, such a climate can be fostered; therefore, it is necessary to establish order and a quiet atmosphere and structure, and to support teachers trying to achieve an orderly climate in their classes.

According to the comprehensive model of educational effectiveness, at the school level, conditions that contribute to the opportunity to learn at the classroom level can be created. At the school level the opportunity to learn is provided by the development and the availability of documents such as a formal curriculum, a school working plan, and an activity plan on what has to be done to pursue the goals of the curriculum. In this document the school management team can explain its vision about education and make clear how effectiveness will be pursued in the school. Effective schools are expected to feel responsible for student achievement: it is their 'mission' to contribute to achievement. A school policy based on these principles can yield important effects (Creemers, 1994).

In summary, the following conditions at the school level can be described for *quality of instruction* related to its *educational* aspects:

- rules and agreements about all aspects of classroom instruction, especially curricular materials, grouping procedures and teacher behaviours, and the consistency between them;
- an evaluation policy and a system at school level to check on student achievement, to prevent learning problems, or to correct problems that might have emerged at an early stage; this includes regular testing, remedial teaching, student counselling, and homework assistance.

With respect to the *organisational aspects* at the school level, important conditions for *quality of instruction* are as follows:

- a school policy on supervision of teachers, heads of departments, and head-teachers by higher-ranking persons, and a school policy to support and further professionalise teachers who do not live up to the school/national standards;
- a school culture promoting and supporting effectiveness.

As far as the conditions for *time* at the school level are concerned, the model refers to the following school-level factors:

- the development and provision of a time schedule for subjects and topics;
- rules and agreements about time utilisation including the school's policy on homework, student absenteeism, and cancellation of lessons;
- the maintenance of an orderly and quiet atmosphere in the school.

Finally, factors that provide conditions for the *opportunity to learn* are as follows:

- the development and availability of a curriculum and a school working plan or activity plan;
- consensus about the mission of the school;

- rules and agreements about how to proceed and how to follow the curriculum, especially with respect to transition from one grade to another.

However, it is important to note that it was not the intention of Creemers (1994) to refer to all kinds of school factors mentioned in review studies of school effectiveness research (e.g. Levine and Lezotte, 1990; Sammons *et al.*, 1995) but rather to show that the school-level factors which refer to the conceptual notions of quality, time, and opportunity are the most important predictors of effectiveness. For example, the variable 'resources' is mentioned in several review studies but is not regarded as a separate category of school factors. This is attributed to the fact that Creemers (1994) does not assume that merely providing additional finance and resources to schools is likely to improve their effectiveness status. On the contrary, resources should be defined in such a way that their relationship to effectiveness is clarified. In other words, the influences of resources on the quality of curricular materials and on teacher behaviour or other factors of the model that support education should be described.

Main assumptions of the model and factors operating at different levels

The comprehensive model of educational effectiveness does not only refer to factors operating at different levels. Creemers' model also shows how the levels in the model influence student outcomes. Specifically, the model is based on four assumptions that help us identify the nature of interactions shown in the model and to identify how the student and the context levels are defined. First, time on task and opportunity used at the student level are directly related to student achievement. Second, the quality of teaching, the curriculum, and the grouping procedures influence the time on task and the opportunity to learn. For example, some teachers spend more time actually teaching than others, who spend more time on classroom management and keeping order. Therefore, teachers are seen as the central component in instruction at the classroom level. Third, teaching quality, time, and opportunity at the classroom level are also influenced by factors at the school level that may or may not promote these classroom factors. The school level is also influenced by factors at the context level. Outcomes therefore cannot be seen as an accomplishment of classroom factors only, as in many studies of effectiveness. The influences of the context and school levels are indirect, and mediated by the classroom level. Finally, it is acknowledged that although teachers are able to influence time for learning and opportunity to learn in their classrooms through the quality of their instruction, it is students who decide how much time they will spend on their school tasks and how many tasks they will complete. Thus, achievement is also determined by student factors such as aptitudes, social background, and motivation. Since the school- and classroom-level factors have already been described, the most important factors operating at the student and the context levels will now be briefly described. Moreover, the assumptions about the nature of the effects of individual factors are clarified. Finally, the next section will refer to the formal principles that are expected to operate in generating effectiveness. They are mainly concerned with the effects of clusters of factors.

Factors operating at the student level

In line with the literature on educational effectiveness, Creemers' model stipulates that achievement is influenced by aptitudes and social background, motivation, time on task, and opportunities used (Kyriakides, 2005a). 'Aptitudes' embraces general intelligence and prior learning, 'social background' the economic position of the parents and their cultural heritage, 'time on task' the time during which the student is actively engaged in learning, and 'opportunities used' the content of curricular subjects covered. However, it has been claimed that Creemers' model is rather vague about the importance of motivation (de Jong et al., 2004). Specifically, it is argued that 'It is pleasant when students like their schools and show some interest, because this can enhance their motivation and (indirectly) their achievement' (Creemers, 1994, p. 12). Moreover, referring to the studies of Knuver (1993) and Brandsma (1993), Creemers claims not only that motivation influences outcomes but also that academic outcomes themselves do have a recip-rocal effect on motivation and attitudes towards arithmetic, on attitudes towards school, and on the well-being of students (p. 113). This explains why Creemers outlines a reciprocal relationship between motivation and student outcomes. Moreover, by placing 'motivation' as an intermediate between student aptitudes and time on task, it seems that Creemers agrees with Carroll's (1963) notion of perseverance as a rather stable trait. However, several studies specify 'motivation' as something that is influenced by the teacher or the school (Scheerens and Bosker, 1997) – an assumption not made in either Carroll's or Creemers' model. Moreover, neither Carroll nor Creemers refers to other personal characteristics of students, such as personality traits and learning styles, that were found to be related to student achievement (Kyriakides, 2005a).

However, an essential difference between Creemers' and Carroll's model has to do with the fact that Creemers, but not Carroll, treated the social background of students as a variable predicting achievement, presumably because Carroll was looking only for alterable factors. Creemers added SES to his model because of the historical relationship between SES and EER. As was mentioned in the first chapter, although EER attempts to identify factors that can be changed in order to improve the effectiveness of education, the fact that SES is a powerful factor in explaining outcomes is acknowledged. Finally, as was mentioned above, in line with Carroll's model is Creemers' concept of 'time on task'. Creemers also adds the concept 'opportunities used', because 'time actively spent' on the learning task is not a sufficient explanation for learning gain. It needs to be complemented by content covered. In Creemers' more elaborate approach to educational effective-ness, the number of curriculum tasks performed is treated as a valuable student variable. Therefore, both 'time on task' and 'opportunities used' are treated as the key factors at the student level in the model, because they can be influenced by educational interventions.

Factors operating at the context level

The context level is described in much the same way as the school level, which was described in the subsection concerned with the conditional role of the school (p. 38). Thus, factors distinguished at the context or national level are again specifications of the three main factors: time, opportunity to learn, and educational quality. Examples of these variables are a policy that focuses on the effectiveness of education, a national policy on evaluation or testing, and training and support systems that promote effective schools and instruction. These factors have already been described in presenting the factors operating at the school level. However, note that context-level factors are expected to influence directly such things as time for learning and opportunity to learn at the classroom level as well as the relevant school-level factors.

Effects of individual factors

Each factor in Creemers' model is supposed to influence student achievement positively. As was mentioned above, factors were included in the model in the first place because positive effects on student achievement were found in educational effectiveness studies. However, factors may be related to each other to some extent, and when they are studied together as a group, some factors may diminish the effects of others. Therefore, individual factors that show no effects on achievement do not necessarily contradict the assumptions of the model. They may have effects on achievement when studied in isolation, whereas these effects disappear when they are studied together with other factors. So, positive effects or the absence of significant effects provide support for the validity of the model, whereas negative effects contradict the model's assumptions.

Relation between levels (cross-level interactions)

Finally, Creemers' model refers to relationships between levels (cross-level interactions). It is supported by research showing that national- and school-level factors as well as classroom- and school-level factors exert a joint influence on achievement. However, the model does not describe whether or, if so, how factors at different levels interact. It seems rational to assume that cross-level interactions will occur mostly between factors related to the same key concepts of quality, time, and opportunity (Reezigt et al., 1999), but this is an assumption that has to be tested.

The four formal principles of the model

Although focusing on the effects of various factors, the full, elaborated model of Creemers (1994) makes tentative statements about their joint impact on student outcomes by introducing the formal principles of *consistency, cohesion, constancy*, and *control*. These formal principles were considered a major improvement compared with other models, because they hold together the other factors in the model and can explain the joint cumulative impact of factors that together constitute learning environments. The formal principles concern the relationships between the factors of instruction – textbooks, grouping procedures, and teaching behaviour – the stability of factors over time, and mechanisms to bring the factors into practice. The idea behind the notion of formal principles is that the influence of the factors at a particular level, and between factors at different levels, can be enforced or can take place by virtue of the fact that these factors are pursued for a longer period of time and are in line with each other. Research on effective education at the classroom level shows that individual components of effective teaching do not result in strong effects on student achievement (Creemers and Reezigt, 1996). For example, good curricula need teachers who can make adequate use of them and who will show effective instructional behaviour. The same holds for grouping procedures. It is integration of components that is necessary to achieve substantial effects. An integrated approach for education rather than exclusive use of the direct instruction or the mastery learning approach is necessary (Creemers, 1994, p. 95). In this integrated approach the educational components of curricula, grouping procedures, and teacher behaviour are adapted to each other. To achieve time and opportunity to learn, Creemers (1994) argues that the three components in general should have the same effectiveness characteristics. This consistency of the effectiveness characteristics is based on the assumption that effectiveness characteristics that are in line with each other mutually reinforce each other and can have a synergistic effect that exceeds the effectiveness that the components have separately (e.g. Scheerens and Bosker, 1997, p. 65). As with consistency at the classroom level, there are four formal principles at the school level which, when they operate, ensure educational effectiveness (see Table 3.1).

Formal principles cannot be seen easily or immediately in schools, and for this reason it is difficult to test the validity of the model in relation to these four principles. However, we can assume that they exist, since the same factors are seen across instructional components, subjects, grades, and classes. Moreover, Table 3.1 reveals that *consistency*, which is based on the assumption that the effectiveness of classrooms, schools, and contexts is enhanced when the factors at these levels are in line with each other and support each other, is seen as an important condition for instruction. Thus, conditions for effective instruction related to curricular materials, grouping procedures, and teacher behaviour are expected to be in line with each other. When all members of a school team take care of consistency, *cohesion* is created, which means that every team member is

Table 3.1 School-level factors and formal principles operating in generating effectiveness

School-level effectiveness factors: characteristics of quality, time and opportunity		Formal principles
Quality/educational	• Rules and agreements about classroom instruction • Evaluation policy/evaluation system	Consistency
Quality/organisational	• Policy on intervision, supervision, and professionalisation • School culture inducing effectiveness	Cohesion
Time	• Time schedule • Rules and agreements about time use • Orderly and quiet atmosphere	Constancy
Opportunity	• School curriculum • Consensus about mission • Rules and agreements about how to implement the school curriculum	Control

Note: 'Intervision' refers to teachers learning by supervising each other, as distinct from supervision by the headteacher.

aware of the need for consistency and acts according to school-wide agreements in this respect. In this way, effective instruction between classes can be guaranteed. To optimise outcomes, schools should not change rules and policies every other year. For this reason, Creemers (1994) argues that there should be *constancy*, meaning that effective instruction is provided throughout the school career of the student. Thus, constancy implies that consistency and cohesion are guaranteed over long periods of time. Finally, the *control* principle refers not only to the fact that student outcomes and teacher behaviour should be evaluated, but also to the importance of evaluating school climate, since an orderly and quiet school climate is necessary to achieve good results. Moreover, control refers to teachers holding themselves and others responsible for effectiveness.

Although more emphasis is placed on the formal principles operating at the school level, the model is expanded above the school level to the context level, taking into account the same elements of quality, time, and opportunity and the formal principles that are expected to operate in order to generate effectiveness. Therefore, Creemers (1994) argues that at the context level, consistency, constancy, and control are again formal characteristics emphasising the importance of context factors (e.g. national policy on evaluation or testing, training and support systems) over time and of mechanisms to ensure effectiveness.

The importance of investigating the validity of Creemers' model

Taking into account that Creemers' model involves more than 30 variables that might enhance time spent learning and opportunity used on the part of the student, and also refers to cross-level interactions as well as formal principles that are expected to operate in generating effectiveness, a possible criticism concerns the complexity of the model and the difficulties of testing the model empirically. Moreover, it can be claimed that the model is not parsimonious and therefore cannot suggest priorities for educational improvement. In this context the next chapter refers to the main results of six national studies and one secondary analysis of an international study that were conducted in order to test parts of the model. Given that the model is intended to be a starting point for the development of a theoretical framework for EER, the importance of conducting empirical investigations to test the validity of the model is emphasised. The results of these studies, which will be presented in the next chapter, may also help us identify the extent to which empirical support for the model can be provided. The importance of treating the Creemers model as the starting point for establishing a dynamic model of educational effectiveness will also be raised in Chapter 4.

Empirical testing of the comprehensive model of educational effectiveness

Review of research

Introduction

In Chapter 3 the comprehensive model of educational effectiveness was presented. The importance of testing the validity of the model, which was developed to contribute to the establishment of the theoretical framework of EER, was also raised. In this chapter we will refer to the methods and the main findings of the six national studies that were conducted in order to test parts of the model. Moreover, we will refer to the main findings of a secondary analysis of the TIMSS 1999 study which was conducted in order to test aspects of Creemers' model (Kyriakides, 2006b). The strengths and weaknesses of these studies will also be discussed. We believe that the results of these studies help us identify the extent to which empirical support for Creemers' model has been generated. Suggestions for expanding the model which arise from these studies will also be identified. Finally, it will be argued that the Creemers model can be the starting point for the establishment of a dynamic model of educational effectiveness.

National studies testing the validity of Creemers' model

Six national studies (i.e. de Jong *et al.*, 2004; Driessen and Sleegers, 2000; Kyriakides *et al.*, 2000; Kyriakides, 2005a; Kyriakides and Tsangaridou, 2004; Reezigt *et al.*, 1999) conducted in two European countries with more and less centralised educational systems (i.e. the Netherlands and Cyprus) attempted to test the main aspects of Creemers' model. The methods used to test the model as well as the main methods used in these studies are presented in this section.

The Netherlands

Reanalysing the evaluation study of the Dutch Educational Priority Policy

The first study, conducted in the Netherlands, was an attempt to test the main assumptions of the model by reanalysing a large-scale longitudinal dataset that contained elementary school data on successive student cohorts, their teachers, and their schools (Reezigt *et al.*, 1999). Specifically, the research data emerged from the evaluation of the Dutch Educational Priority Policy (van der Werf, 1995). A subsample of 279 elementary schools which was representative of the population of the Netherlands as a whole was used. Student achievement in Dutch language and mathematics in grades 4, 6, and 8 was measured repeatedly, in 1988, 1990, and 1992. Moreover, the teachers of the students in grades 4, 6, and 8 answered written questionnaires, and so did the school principals. On the basis of the model's assumptions, Reezigt *et al.* (1999) attempted to provide answers to the following three research questions:

1 Do the individual classroom- and school-level factors in Creemers' model show the expected effects on student achievement?
2 Is it possible to cluster the classroom and school factors in the model in terms of the consistency principle, and what effects do these clusters have on student achievement?
3 Are there any cross-level interactions between classroom and school factors and between clusters of classroom and school factors?

To estimate the school and classroom effects on achievement, the concept of added value was used, so the researchers used multilevel analysis and estimated the school and classroom effects after controlling for student background factors. Specifically, the dependent variables were the achievement scores for language and mathematics, controlled for the prior achievement of students two years earlier. Scores obtained in 1992 were controlled for prior student scores of 1990, and scores of 1990 were controlled for prior scores of 1988. The only exception was the student cohort that was in grade 4 in 1988. For this cohort the researchers also studied the achievement of 1992 controlled for the prior achievement of 1988. Because of these two types of achievement variables, the researchers were able to examine whether the school and classroom factors in the model would have the same effects over two school years and over four school years. Since Creemers' model does not make any distinction between factors associated with a short-term effect of schools and those associated with a long-term effect of schools, an assumption that was tested had to do with the extent to which the factors included in the model were associated with both the short- and the long-term effects of schools.

The explanatory variables that were taken into account by Reezigt *et al.* (1999) were as follows. First, the following four covariates at the student level were measured: prior achievement (language and mathematics), intelligence, gender, and social background. Therefore, the student level as defined in Creemers' model (see Chapter 3) was not fully covered by the data of this study. Data concerning time on task, opportunities used, and student motivation were not available. Additionally, two other student background variables concerned with gender and ethnic origin are not included in the model. Thus, this study attempted to find out to what extent these two student background variables influence student achievement. Second, all items in the teacher and headteacher questionnaires were ordered according to the concepts of the model, and scales were constructed (for more details, see Reezigt *et al.*, 1999). For the classroom level, 11 latent variables that partly covered the model were constructed. Some factors in the model were not represented in the data at all (e.g. classroom management and high expectations) whereas some other factors were covered in only a rudimentary way. This was the case, for example, for time for learning and opportunity to learn, which are considered to be the most important variables of the model. For the school level, four factors in the model could not be covered by the data, but the coverage of the school-level factors in the effectiveness model was better than the coverage of the classroom-level factors.

The main results of this study were as follows. First, most variance was found to be located at the student level, as is the case for most effectiveness studies (Teddlie and Reynolds, 2000). Although the effect of classrooms and schools was found to be modest when compared to student background factors, the study shows that the influences on student achievement were multilevel. Classrooms had unique effects on student learning, independently of factors operating at the school and individual levels. Moreover, by controlling for both student factors and classroom contextual factors, variables at school level explained variation in achievement at school level. Second, most student factors had stable effects across subjects and across the different types of analyses (i.e. analyses of two school years versus analyses of four school years), with the exception of gender. Prior achievement and intelligence showed stable positive effects whereas social class and ethnic background had stable negative effects on achievement. Third, the assumptions of Creemers' model about the school- and classroom-level factors were partly supported. Specifically, eight out of 11 classroom factors were found to act as expected (quality of the curriculum, implementation of the curriculum, homework, clear goal-setting, use of curriculum tests, grouping procedures, evaluation, and corrective instruction). However, three out of 11 classroom factors were found to have negative or mixed effects (sometimes positive, sometimes negative). These three factors (namely feedback, time for learning, and opportunity to learn) did not support the assumptions of the model. With regard to the school factors, only two out of six had effects in line with the model: an orderly atmosphere was found to have positive effects, and rules about the implementation of the school curriculum had no effects. The remaining four factors turned out to have negative (professionalisation policy, rules about time use) or mixed effects (rules about classroom instruction, evaluation policy). Again, there was hardly any stability of effects across analyses. Fourth, the percentages of variance not accounted for remain rather high, especially for language achievement. This finding can partly be attributed to the methodological weaknesses of the study, since important factors in the model were not taken into account. Moreover, this finding implies that researchers could examine whether the model could be expanded in order to cover variables at student, classroom, and school level which explain most of the unexplained variance. Fifth, in relation to the second research question, cluster analysis was used in order to group the factors at the classroom and school level. To interpret the cluster groups that emerged, the concept of consistency, which refers to a balance between factors that may enhance effectiveness, was used. Although it was found that some teachers and schools are more consistent than others, consistency did not affect the achievement of their students. Finally, cross-level interaction effects were not found.

This description of the methodology of the study and its main findings reveals that the study did not lead to much evidence about the validity of the model, but important variables such as student motivation, time on task, and opportunity to learn were not available. Therefore, the main conclusion that emerged from this study was that the concepts of the model should be more adequately operationalised in future research.

Testing the consistency principle of the Creemers model

The major question of the second study conducted in the Netherlands (Driessen and Sleegers, 2000) was whether student achievement levels vary according to the consistency of the teaching approach after controlling for socio-ethnic and ethnic background at both the individual and class levels. As was mentioned in Chapter 3, Creemers (1994) introduced the notion of consistency as a theoretical concept and suggested that isolated instructional components do not show a strong effect on student achievement. It is argued that an integrated approach at the class level is needed along with the introduction of the consistency principle. The combined and coordinated elements of effective teaching behaviour, teaching materials, and group composition produce a synergetic effect, according to the Creemers model. In this context, the second study was concerned with the following three research questions:

1   To what extent can we speak of consistency in the teaching approaches of teachers from different grades within a school?
2   What aspects of teaching methods appear to play a role in the explanation of the observed differences in achievement?
3   What relation exists between the effects of teaching methods and the consistency of the teaching approach within the team on student achievement?

In order to answer these questions the researchers made use of the data collected within the framework of the national cohort study 'Primair Onderwijs' (Primary Education; PRIMA). This study was started in the 1994/1995 school year with an initial data-collection round among approximately 60,000 students attending approximately 700 elementary schools (i.e. 10 per cent of the total number of elementary schools in the Netherlands). The PRIMA data were collected using various research instruments from students and their parents, schools, school management teams, and classroom teachers. In brief, PRIMA was designed as follows. At the end of 1994 and the beginning of 1995, tests were administered to the students in grades 4, 6, and 8; at the same time, the teachers who had taught the students in the previous year (grades 3, 5, and 7) completed a questionnaire with regard to the teaching strategy they used. Such an approach was opted for because the teachers who had taught the students in the previous year were presumably more familiar with the students than the teachers currently teaching them (i.e. teachers with a full year versus six months of experience with the students). It was also assumed that any effects of teaching strategy were more likely to be a result of the teachers who had taught the students in the previous year than of the present teachers. The sample for the second study was selected from the PRIMA data and consisted of 7,410 students from 492 grade 8 classes and 447 schools. Analyses to check for selective non-response showed the analysed sample to be a good reflection of the original sample (Driessen and Sleegers, 2000).

In view of the fact that no baseline measurements were taken and it was therefore not possible to check the entry capacities of the children, individual socio-ethnic background was taken into account. The socio-ethnic variable combines information on socio-economic background and country of origin. Although this variable is actually at an ordinal measurement level, it was interpreted at the interval level because its relationship to the test results appeared to be linear.

As far as the measure of quality of teaching is concerned, the teacher questionnaire was not based on Creemers' (1994) review on the topic of effective instruction. It was based on a review of empirical Dutch studies of factors that might explain differences in elementary school performance. Thus, the research questions were not formulated from a particular theoretical point of view but rather were based on empirical relevance. Exploratory factor analysis was performed, but the various teaching aspects proved to be rather loosely correlated. However, the dimensions of teaching methods that emerged from factor analysis closely resembled the characteristics of effective instruction distinguished by Creemers (1994). Some typical elements were an emphasis on the acquisition of basic skills, high expectations of the students, regular evaluation of learning progress, opportunity to learn, and time on task.

The main results of the multilevel analysis, which was conducted in order to provide answers to the questions of this study, were as follows. First, for the multilevel analyses, three levels could be distinguished in principle: student level (background, test results), teacher/class level (class composition, teaching approach), and school level (consistency, which is an aggregated variable). However, a three-level multilevel analysis did not prove useful. This was attributed to the fact that 80 per cent of the schools of the sample in this study had only one grade 8 class. This made the calculation of a reliability estimate on the basis of the 'class within school' variance impossible (Goldstein, 2003). For this reason, a two-level analysis was decided on with student and teacher/class as the levels, and consistency as a (contextual) predictor variable at the level of the class. Second, a finding common to almost all effectiveness studies emerged from the two-level analyses, which had to do with the fact that most variance in student achievement was found to be located at the student level. Third, the most important effectiveness factor appeared to be the socio-ethnic background of the students. Ethnic minority students were found to perform less well than native Dutch working-class students, who in turn performed less well than the other students studied. In addition, students in classes with a relatively high proportion of so-called disadvantaged students performed less well regardless of their individual socio-ethnic background. Fourth, with regard to teaching approach, the effects of both the particular aspects of the teaching approach and the overall teaching approach were examined. Only one out of 15 aspects of teaching approach, namely instructional orientation, had an effect on language test score. Moreover, three out of 15 aspects of teaching approach were found to produce significant effects on mathematics achievement: instructional orientation, checking students' work to assign a grade, and special emphasis on acquisition of basic skills. Fifth, no interaction effect between teaching approach and consistency, for either the language or the maths results, was identified. Thus, Driessen and Sleegers (2000) argue that the results of multilevel analyses showed consistency of teaching approach to be unrelated to achievement levels. However, these results were not interpreted as a lack of validity of Creemers' model in relation to consistency. As in the study by Reezigt et al. (1999), the principal explanation concerns the methodology used. Data from teachers were collected via written questionnaires. The use of observations and in-depth interviews to increase the validity of the data collected was recommended for future research.

Using multiple methodologies to test the validity of the Creemers model

The third study (de Jong et al., 2004) used multiple methodologies to investigate the validity of Creemers' model and thereby took into account the methodological limitations of the previous studies. Creemers' model was tested in a field situation in the Netherlands. Teachers and students were observed, interviewed, and tested during lessons of mathematics in the first year of secondary education. Classes were equally divided among tracks (lower, middle, and upper tracks). The schools had to use one of the two most frequently used mathematics curricula in order to reduce curriculum variance, and participation in the project was voluntary. The research sample consisted of 28 schools and a total of 56 classes. The schools that participated in the study were situated all over the Netherlands.

As far as the variables of the study are concerned, the dependent variable 'mathematics achievement' was measured using a test based on the two curricula used in the schools administered by the research team. In relation to student background variables, it was taken into account that Creemers' model refers to three important background variables: 'aptitudes', 'social background', and 'motivation'. General intelligence, prior attainment in the subject to be studied, and the ability to understand instruction were considered as measures of aptitudes. Gender and ethnic background were also added to the background variables taken into account by this study.

As far as the measure of student motivation is concerned, students were asked to complete a questionnaire, and the following four homogeneous scales emerged: school motivation, maths motivation, self-confidence, and perseverance. Time factors were measured in two different ways: absence from lessons, and time on task during lessons, as estimated by teachers. Specifically, absence from lessons was registered by the teacher, who kept a logbook for the whole of the school year, whereas a proxy for the variable time on task was used since the teacher was asked to rank the students to the extent they paid attention to an average lesson. Finally, the time spent doing homework in a year was used as an opportunity factor at the student level.

At the classroom level, three main explanatory variables that account for learning on the part of the student were taken into account: quality of instruction, time, and opportunity. The quality of instruction was measured by independent observers. Time at the class level was operationalised as 'instruction time' (Anderson, 1995), and information was obtained from teachers' logbooks. Finally, opportunity factors were taken into account by investigating the number of homework assignments, which was established on the basis of a logbook that the teachers kept, in which they noted the number of exercises done during and after each lesson. The total number of homework tasks was an addition of the tasks mentioned in all allocated lessons in the logbook.

Since at each school both teachers were using the same curriculum, the curriculum in this study was considered not as a class but as a school factor. Other school factors included in Creemers' model are concerned with the rules and agreements made at the school or department level related to the quality, time, and opportunity at the class level. Thus, in-depth interviews with two teachers of each school concerned with the school rules and agreements about the quality of teaching in classrooms were conducted. Specifically, the teachers were asked to give their opinion on a five-point scale ranging from 1 (no rules in this matter; the teacher is autonomous) to 5 (clear rules which have to be followed by the teachers).

Multilevel analysis was performed to identify the extent to which variables included in the model show the expected effects. The main results of this study were as follows. First, influences on student achievement in mathematics were found to be multilevel. Second, as far as the effect of background variables is concerned, prior achievement, visualisation, arithmetical speed, and information processing ability all had effects on mathematics achievement, the strongest of which came from prior achievement. Third, maths motivation, self-confidence (motivation), attentiveness, and student absenteeism were found to have strong effects, and support the assumptions of the model concerned with the impact of student-level factors on achievement. Fourth, the following four classroom-level factors were found to have significant effects on mathematics student achievement: average prior achievement in mathematics, grouping of students, task directness (quality), and amount of homework assigned (opportunity). Fifth, as far as the effects of the school-level factors are concerned, the variables socio-economic background, curriculum, and school track did not show any statistically significant effect. On the other hand, the quality factor concerned with the departmental rules did have a significant effect. This means that this study reveals that the school level shows evidence that effective departments are those that regulate the quality of teaching by developing a commitment to rules concerning curriculum, testing, student behaviour, and staff development. Finally, cross-level interactions were not identified and the final model was not able to explain 35 per cent of the total variance, but most of that 35 per cent, namely 30 per cent, remained unexplained at the student level.

Cyprus

During the past decade, three studies have been conducted in Cyprus in order to test the validity of Creemers' model: those of Kyriakides *et al.* (2000), Kyriakides (2005a) and Kyriakides and Tsangaridou (2004). All of them used multiple methodologies and provided empirical support to the model. Moreover, different criteria were used for measuring the effectiveness of Cypriot primary schools, and thereby the extent to which the model could be considered as a generic model was tested. Thus, this subsection refers to the methods and the main results of each study.

Using data from an evaluation study in primary mathematics to investigate the validity of Creemers' model

The first study (Kyriakides *et al.*, 2000) was conducted during the school year 1997/1998 and was an evaluation study in mathematics in which 30 schools, 56 classes, and 1051 students from the final year of primary school in Cyprus participated. Specifically, stratified sampling (Cohen *et al.*, 2000) was used to select 30 out of 142 Cypriot primary schools. All the year 6 students from each class of the school sample were chosen. The chi-square test did not reveal any statistically significant difference between the research sample and the population in terms of students' sex ($\chi^2 = 1.10$, d.f. = 1, $p < 0.34$) and location of school ($\chi^2 = 0.64$, d.f. = 1, $p < 0.42$). Moreover, the *t*-test did not reveal any statistically significant difference between the research sample and the whole population in terms of the size of class ($t = 0.31$, d.f. = 17894, $p < 0.77$). It may therefore be claimed that a nationally representative sample of Cypriot year 6 students was drawn.

Over 30 variables that might enhance time spent learning and opportunity used to learn on the part of the student are represented in Creemers' model. In order to test the main assumptions of the model, a selection was made of all possible variables, and these were categorised as context, time, opportunity, and quality factors. Specifically, questionnaires were administered to students and teachers in order to collect data about explanatory variables at the student, classroom, and school level. Both the internal reliability of each scale associated with each explanatory variable and the generalisability of the data that emerged from student questionnaires in relation to the quality of their mathematics teaching were examined (see Kyriakides *et al.*, 2000). Moreover, research data on students' achievement in mathematics at the end of the final year of primary school were collected by using two forms of assessment: external assessment and teachers' assessment.

Multilevel analysis was used to examine whether the student, classroom, and school variables showed the expected effects on student achievement in mathematics. The findings provided support for the main assumptions of the model. It was shown that the influences on student achievement were multilevel. Classrooms had unique effects on student learning, independently of factors operating at the school and individual levels. Moreover, by controlling for both student factors and classroom contextual factors, variables at the school level explained some variation in achievement at school level. Furthermore, the results revealed the importance of the main factors in the model: time spent, opportunity to learn, and the quality of instruction were most important in predicting mathematics achievement. However, the analysis of the data of this study revealed that 3.0 per cent of the total variance remained unexplained at the school level, 3.6 per cent of the variance remained unexplained at the classroom level, and 26.2 per cent of the variance remained unexplained at the student level. This can be attributed not only to methodological limitations in terms of measuring the variables included in Creemers' model but also to the fact that some further variables, especially at the student level, might have needed to be included in the model. Thus, one of the aims of the second study concerning Creemers' model was to identify additional variables at the student level which could be included in the model.

Extending the comprehensive model of educational effectiveness by an empirical investigation into cognitive and affective outcomes of schooling

The main aim of the second study was to test the validity of Creemers' model in relation to different criteria of measuring effectiveness (both cognitive and affective). It was also examined whether the variables 'personality' and 'thinking style' explained variance in achievement at student level and should be included in Creemers' model. Both aims emerged from a review of studies investigating the validity of the model conducted in the 1990s in both Cyprus and the Netherlands. Specifically, a common finding in these studies is that more than 25 per cent of the variance remained unexplained at the student level. This was attributed to the fact that some further variables at the student level might have needed to be included in Creemers' model.

In line with the literature on educational effectiveness, Creemers' model specifies that student achievement is influenced by aptitudes and socio-economic background, motivation, time on task, and opportunities used. However, Reynolds *et al.* (2002) argue that the future progress of educational effectiveness may partly depend upon the extent to which researchers on educational effectiveness can broaden their remit and interact with all those disciplines that attempt to identify factors associated with student achievement. It was therefore decided to look closely at studies within psychology which examine the relationship among student achievement, types of personality, and styles of thinking. The main lessons drawn from a review of these studies will now be presented.

For nearly a century, psychologists have attempted to identify the major predictors of individual academic performance (Harris, 1940; Thorndike, 1920). Although past research has explored the relationship between personality and school performance (e.g. Cattell and Butcher, 1968; Kline and Gale, 1977), it was claimed that academic achievement was typically associated with intelligence rather than personality (e.g. Elshout and Veenman, 1992; Harris, 1940). There is, however, long-standing empirical evidence indicating that both personality and intelligence are important predictors of school performance (e.g. Busato *et al.*, 1999; Diseth, 2003; Chamorro-Premuzic and Furnham, 2003; Lounsbury *et al.*, 2003). Both intelligence and personality comprise salient individual differences that influence performance: intelligence through specific abilities that facilitate understanding and learning, personality through certain traits that enhance and/or handicap the use of these abilities.

Although there have been several models of personality traits, this study was concerned only with the factors specified by the so-called Big Five model. This decision was attributed to the fact that the Big Five model dominates current research and theory, and many scholars (e.g. Goldberg, 1993; Taylor and MacDonald, 1999) have argued that this model accounts for a large amount of the variability in personality. Moreover, most of the Big Five personality traits have been found to be associated with academic performance (e.g. Blickle, 1996; Busato *et al.*, 1999; Chamorro-Premuzic and Furnham, 2003; DeFruyt and Mervielde, 1996; Shuerger and Kuma, 1987; Wolfe and Johnson, 1995). However, it is not known whether personality traits are associated with cognitive and/or affective achievement gains, especially when students' background characteristics, intelligence, and initial achievement are taken into account. It was therefore considered important to examine whether personality characteristics could explain part of the variance at student level which remained unexplained from the studies used to test the validity of Creemers' model.

The reasons why the theory of mental self-government (Sternberg, 1988), dealing with specific types of thinking style, was also taken into account in the design of this study are provided below. It is first of all important to note that in the search for variables that contribute to school achievement, psychologists have devoted considerable attention to the so-called stylistic aspects of cognition. The idea of a style reflecting a person's typical or habitual mode of problem-solving, thinking, perceiving, and remembering was initially introduced by Allport (1937). In the past few decades the style construct has enjoyed a great deal of research interest (Morgan, 1997), and many theoretical models have been postulated (see

Grigorenko and Sternberg, 1995; Kagan and Kogan, 1970; Kogan, 1983; Riding and Cheema, 1991; Sternberg, 1988; Vernon, 1973). Grigorenko and Sternberg (1995) classified the various theories of thinking styles into three approaches: cognition centred, personality centred, and activity centred. The cognition-centred and the personality-centred approaches typically imply that styles are either–or constructs. For example, a person could be either field independent or field dependent, but not both. In these approaches, styles are consistent across various tasks and situations, and can be modified very little during the course of a person's life. Therefore, styles are seen as 'givens' in a training or educational setting (Riding and Cheema, 1991). In contrast, researchers working in the activity-centred framework view styles as processes, which can be built on and used to compensate for, or to remediate, weaknesses. In this interpretation, styles are seen as dynamic. Students are, therefore, expected to find or develop 'optimal' styles for particular situations in order to improve their achievement.

Given that EER attempts to identify factors of effective education that could be introduced or changed in education through school improvement projects (Creemers, 2002), it was decided to examine whether theories of thinking styles in the activity-centred framework could help us identify variables at the student level that could be included in Creemers' model. Moreover, there are many studies which reveal that thinking styles in the activity-centred framework, and especially styles associated with the theory of mental self-government (Sternberg, 1988), explain individual differences in performance that are not explained by abilities (e.g. Grigorenko and Sternberg, 1997; Zhang and Sternberg, 1998; Zhang, 2001a). A final reason for taking into account the theory of mental self-government in the design of this study was concerned with the fact that the few studies which attempted to examine the relationship between thinking styles and personality types (Zhang, 2001b; Zhang and Huang, 2001) revealed that overlap between thinking styles and personality is limited (Zhang, 2002). This implies that researchers in the area of EER should measure both thinking styles and personality traits in order to find out the extent to which these two constructs could explain part of the unexplained variance of achievement at the student level.

As far as the second aim of this study is concerned, the fact that all studies which provided empirical support for the validity of Creemers' model examined school effectiveness in the core subjects (mathematics and language) was the main reason why Kyriakides (2005a) attempted to investigate the generalisability of Creemers' model. Specifically, it was considered important to test the main assumptions of the model in relation to different outcome criteria of measuring effectiveness. This argument is supported by the fact that there is some evidence that schools which are among the most effective in enhancing cognitive achievement are not necessarily among the most effective in helping their students achieve non-cognitive outcomes (Opdenakker and Van Damme, 2000). This implies that there is a need to investigate the extent to which factors at both the school and the class level are associated with effectiveness in different subjects and in different broad domains (cognitive and affective).

The procedure used to test and expand the Creemers model (see Kyriakides, 2005a) was similar to the one used in the first study conducted in Cyprus. Specifically, stratified sampling was used to select 32 Cypriot primary schools, and all the year 6 students ($N = 1,721$) from each class ($N = 81$) of the school sample were chosen. Data on students' cognitive achievement in mathematics and Greek language were collected by using two forms of assessment (external assessment and teacher assessment). Affective outcomes of schooling were measured by asking students to answer a questionnaire concerning their attitudes towards peers, teachers, school, and learning. The questionnaire and the two forms of assessment in mathematics and Greek language were administered to all year 6 students of the school sample at the beginning and at the end of the school year 2001/2002. The constructions of the tests and the questionnaire were subject to controls for reliability and validity (see Kyriakides, 2005a). Questionnaires were administered to the students of year 6, teachers, and headteachers in order to collect data about the variables used to test Creemers' model. In addition, observations were conducted in order to measure teacher behaviour in the classroom. Moreover, students' personality was measured by the 'Personality Inventory', which included a total of 50 items, ten for each of the Big Five factors of personality (Costa and McCrae, 1997). The items included in this inventory were selected according to the results of a previous study so as to represent the main facets involved in each of the Big Five factors (Demetriou *et al.*, 2003). Finally, students' thinking style was measured using a short version of the 'Thinking Styles Inventory'. The items included in this inventory were selected according to the results of a previous study (Demetriou *et al.*, 1999) so as to represent the thinking styles of each of the five dimensions of mental self-government (Sternberg, 1988). On the basis of the results of five exploratory factor analyses of students' responses to the items of each of the five dimensions of mental self-government, it was possible to identify factors representing each thinking style other than the 'oligarchic' thinking style. Thus, for each student an average score was calculated for each of the 12 thinking styles, and the value of the Cronbach alpha for the scale of each thinking style was higher than 0.72.

In order to examine the extent to which the variables in Creemers' model show the expected effects upon each of the three dependent variables, multilevel analyses were performed separately for each dependent variable. The main findings of this study were as follows. The influences on student achievement in both the cognitive and the affective areas of schooling were multilevel. Moreover, most of the variables in Creemers' model showed the expected effects, irrespective of the criterion used to measure effectiveness. Therefore, it was claimed that Creemers' model could be considered a generic model. As far as the aim of the study concerning the identification of additional variables at the student level is concerned, it was found that some types of personality (e.g. conscientiousness and openness to experience) and some styles of thinking (e.g. executive and liberal) were related to either cognitive and/or affective achievement gains. Although there was no consistency in relation to the effect of most styles of thinking on achievement within the components of each outcome measure of effectiveness, the inclusion of variables concerning students' personality and styles of thinking significantly improves the explained percentage of achievement variation at the student level in each outcome measure. Thus, the unexplained variance at the student level in the last model of each outcome measure of this study is much smaller than the variance remaining unexplained in the first study conducted in Cyprus. In addition, this study seems to reveal that both personality and thinking style should be included in Creemers' model and should be considered to be predictors of both cognitive and affective outcomes of schooling (Kyriakides, 2005a). However, further research is needed in order to identify some further variables at the student level that are related to achievement gains in the cognitive and affective outcomes of schooling, since at student level more than 13 per cent of variance in each outcome measure remained unexplained.

A study on school and teacher effectiveness in physical education

In this context the third study attempted to examine whether the variable 'student self-efficacy beliefs' could be included in Creemers' model. Moreover, given that the two earlier studies examined the validity of the model in relation to the achievement of cognitive and affective outcomes of schooling, it was considered important to examine whether the model could explain variation in student achievement of psychomotor skills. Thus, the third study, which was an evaluation study in physical education (Kyriakides and Tsangaridou, 2004), was an attempt to examine the extent to which Creemers' model can explain school effectiveness in achieving not only the cognitive and affective, but also the psychomotor, outcomes of schooling. The importance of this study also arises from the fact that there is no other study investigating school effectiveness in teaching physical education (Siedentop and Tannehill, 2000). This implies that it is important to test the main assumptions of Creemers' model in relation to different outcome criteria of measuring school effectiveness. Furthermore, the literature on effective teaching has identified mostly generic variables related to teacher effectiveness. Although scholars have been concerned with the classification of context-specific data that describe how effective teachers teach particular content in particular settings, research findings in this area are very limited (Graber, 2001; Rink, 2003; Silverman and Skonie, 1997). Therefore, it was argued that if Creemers' model is tested in relation to different criteria of measuring effectiveness, the robustness of the theory might be strengthened and the extent to which the model could be used as a theoretical framework for research measuring effectiveness across the school curriculum might be identified.

This study also attempted to identify the importance of investigating the relationship between generic and differential effectiveness. Campbell *et al.* (2004) proposed a differentiated model of teacher effectiveness. The following three dimensions of differential effectiveness, presented in this model, were examined:

(1) differences in the components of subjects, (2) differences in the background characteristics of their students, and (3) differences in cultural and organizational context.

Thus, this study used a methodology similar to that used in the previous two studies conducted in Cyprus to investigate the validity of Creemers' model. Specifically, stratified sampling was used to select 23 Cypriot primary schools. All the year 4 students ($N = 1,142$) from each class ($N = 49$) of the school sample were chosen. As far as the measurement of the dependent variable is concerned, a performance test was designed to collect data on student achievement in PE. Since the curriculum for year 4 is primarily focused on the psychomotor domain of PE, only this domain was covered in the test. The test was administered to the students both when they were at the beginning of year 4 and when they were at the end of year 4. Two members of the research team recorded the responses of each student to the tasks of the test. The inter-rater reliability coefficient (ϱ^2) was 0.80. The construction of the test was also subject to control for reliability and validity (see Kyriakides and Tsangaridou, 2004). Using the same procedure as in the earlier studies, questionnaires to students and their teachers were administered in order to collect data about the variables being used to test Creemers' model. Moreover, structured interviews with teachers and headmasters were conducted in order to collect data about explanatory variables at the school level dealing with their school policy on PE. Finally, in this study, quality of teaching was measured by external observations using the revised Academic Learning Time in Physical Education (ALT-PE) system developed by Siedentop et al. (1982).

The main findings of this study were as follows. First, the factors found to be associated with student achievement in mathematics and language were also associated with achievement in the main psychomotor outcomes of physical education. This implies that it is possible for researchers to develop generic models of effectiveness. Second, the results of this study revealed the importance of the main factors in Creemers' model: time spent, opportunity to learn, and the quality of instruction were most important in predicting achievement in physical education (PE). Thus, further empirical support for Creemers' model is provided. Third, the findings of this study did not provide support for the argument that the variable 'student self-efficacy beliefs' could be included in Creemers' model. This implies that further research is needed to identify variables that can explain variation in achievement at student level and could be included in the model. Finally, there was some limited evidence to support the further exploration of a differential model of effectiveness. Specifically, different cluster groups of teachers, according to how effective they were in achieving different aims of PE, were identified. Moreover, differences in the effectiveness of teachers who were expected to teach PE in different schools were identified and can be attributed to differences in the organisational context of their schools. However, on other dimensions of differentiation, such as effectiveness with different socio-economic groups, gender, and ability, there was less evidence for differential effectiveness, at least as measured in this study, than might have been hypothesised. Therefore, further research on differential teacher and school effectiveness is required to improve theory-building in EER.

Comparative studies testing the validity of Creemers' model: a secondary analysis of the TIMSS 1999 study

Although the educational system of Cyprus, which is highly centralised, is not similar to the educational system of the Netherlands, the variables in Creemers' model showed the expected effects in studies conducted both in Cyprus and in the Netherlands. However, there is a need to conduct comparative studies in order to investigate the validity of Creemers' model. Unless the variables in the model showed the expected effects on student outcomes in various countries, the extent to which the model can be considered a generic model cannot be identified. Moreover, the model refers to factors at the national level which are again specifications of the three main effectiveness factors: time, opportunity, and quality of teaching. Only comparative studies are able to examine the effect of these factors upon student achievement. For example, comparative studies could investigate the effect of the attempt of different educational systems to provide training and support systems that promote effective instruction upon student achievement gains. At the same time, the effects of these support systems on the quality of teaching at classroom level can be examined, especially since the model assumes that there are indirect effects from higher-level factors through lower-level factors on student achievement. Although the model does not describe explicitly whether or, if so, how classroom, school- and context-level factors interact, it seems sensible to assume that indirect effects will occur mostly between factors related to the same key concepts of quality, time, and opportunity. Therefore, comparative studies on educational effectiveness could be conducted in order to test the assumptions of the model mentioned above. However, some of these assumptions could also be tested through secondary analyses of comparative evaluation studies. In this context, a secondary analysis of the TIMSS 1999 was conducted in order to test the main assumptions of Creemers' model (Kyriakides, 2006b).

Methods: identifying explanatory variables of TIMSS 1999

Based on the main assumptions of Creemers' model, a selection of relevant TIMSS 1999 variables was made. The variables were categorised as context, time, opportunity, and quality factors, and emerged from the student, teacher, and school questionnaires. These variables were organised in three levels (i.e. student, teacher, and country level) corresponding to the three-level model that best described the TIMSS 1999 data.

Only four explanatory variables at student level were measured: student background factors, expectations, time factors, and opportunity factors. Information on these variables was collected through the student questionnaire. Specifically, three student background factors were measured: age, sex, and SES. Moreover, a proxy for time on task was measured. Therefore, the student-level factors included in the model were only partly covered, and important variables such as aptitude and prior knowledge were not available.

The following explanatory variables at teacher level were taken into account. First, variables concerned with the context of each classroom, such as the average of each of the three SES indicators mentioned above, and the percentage of girls, were measured. The contextual factors were aggregated from the student-level data. Second, variables concerning the characteristics of teachers, and especially characteristics such as sex and length of teaching experience, were also taken into account. As far as teachers' subject and pedagogical knowledge is concerned, data on whether teachers held an initial degree in mathematics and/or mathematics education and whether they held relevant postgraduate qualifications were also available.

Third, quality of instruction at classroom level is considered by Creemers (1994) to be one of the main variables that account for learning. Relevant information was collected through items included in the student and teacher questionnaires. Items concerning the grouping of students during a lesson, and the frequency with which specific teaching tasks are employed (e.g. students explain the reasoning behind an idea, or practise computational skills), were also used. A five-factor model was derived from exploratory factor analysis of students' responses to the items concerning teacher behaviour in mathematics. The five factors consisted of items that refer to teachers' ability in (1) classroom management, (2) providing practice and application opportunities, (3) using assessment information for formative purposes, (4) providing opportunities for collaborative work, and (5) using different teaching means and sources. Since these factors are similar to those included in the comprehensive model of educational effectiveness, for each teacher five different scores for the quality of teaching were generated, by calculating the classroom average of each factor score.

Fourth, although the actual time spent on teaching mathematics was not measured by TIMSS 1999, it was possible to use a proxy for this variable based on students' responses to an item concerned with the extent to which their teachers were interrupted. An average of his or her students' responses was calculated for each teacher. Finally, opportunity to learn was measured through three sets of items included in the teacher questionnaire that were concerned with the amount of homework their students are usually asked to undertake, the type of homework students are assigned, and the way teachers proceed with completed homework. It can be argued that although the classroom level as defined in Creemers' model (see Chapter 3) was not fully covered by the data of the TIMSS 1999 study, coverage of the classroom-level factors in the effectiveness model was better than the coverage of the student-level factors.

All explanatory variables beyond average SES at the country level were aggregated from the headteachers' questionnaires. Specifically, the following explanatory variables were taken into account. First, contextual factors concerning average SES indicators were taken into account. These factors were all aggregated from the student-level data. Second, conditions for the quality of instruction at school and country levels can be measured by investigating the extent to which each school has developed rules and agreements about aspects of classroom instruction in mathematics (Creemers, 1994). Therefore, the measurement of quality factors emerged from two items on the school questionnaire that asked headteachers to indicate whether their school (1) has its own written statement of the curriculum content to be taught, and (2) has developed relevant instructional materials to address the curriculum. Quality factors were also measured by collecting data from ten items concerning the extent to which parents were involved in school life. Furthermore, the extent to which the school has a policy on differentiation was measured by taking information from a relevant set of items from the school questionnaire. Third, time factors at the school level were measured from an item asking headteachers to evaluate the extent to which students are absent on a typical day. Finally, consensus about the 'mission' of the school was seen as an indication of the conditions for the opportunity to learn at the school level. Thus, items asking headteachers to indicate the extent to which their teachers share ideas and materials, and discuss instructional goals, were taken into account.

Because the observations emerging from the TIMSS 1999 study are inter-dependent and because of the use of multistage sampling, multilevel analysis was conducted. The first step in the analysis was to determine which levels had to be considered in order to reflect the hierarchical structure of the data. Empty models with all possible combinations of the levels of analysis (i.e. student, class, teacher, school, and country) were established and the likelihood statistics of each model were compared (Snijders and Bosker, 1999). An empty model consisting of student, teacher, and country levels represented the best solution. This result could be attributed to the TIMSS 1999 sampling procedure, where in almost all countries one class was selected per school and therefore the school level coincided with the class level (Foy and Joncas, 2000). Moreover, the inclusion of the teacher level rather than the school level seems to be more plausible, since the TIMSS 1999 sample included some countries in which two different teachers were teaching students from the same school. This implies that the teacher rather than the class or the effect of the school can better explain variation in student achievement. The above arguments seem to provide support for the student–teacher–country-level model as the most appropriate model for investigating the factors affecting student achievement.

In subsequent steps, explanatory variables at different levels were added, starting at the student level. The following factors included in Creemers' model were found to be associated with mathematics achievement. First, the effects of all student background factors were statistically significant ($p < 0.05$). Specifically, it was found that boys achieved higher scores than girls in mathematics and that all variables related to student SES had a positive relationship to achievement.

Second, as far as the effects of the student-level factors are concerned, only the time factor indicator was found to be associated with student achievement. Third, as far as the effects of the classroom-level factors are concerned, SES indicators aggregated at the classroom level were found to be associated with student achievement in mathematics. Moreover, none of the variables concerning teacher background characteristics had a statistically significant effect. Fourth, only six of the explanatory variables at the teacher level that are included in Creemers' model were found to have a statistically significant effect on student achievement. However, these six variables reflect all three main categories of variables included in Creemers' model (i.e. time factors, quality of teaching, and opportunity to learn). Fifth, the only context factor at the country level that had a statistically significant effect was the existence of a school policy on attendance. Moreover, the only measure of quality of instruction associated with student achievement was related to the existence of policy on active parental involvement. Although no form of parental involvement other than active parental involvement was found to be associated with student achievement, this finding falls into line with the results of meta-analyses revealing that active involvement has a more noticeable effect than other dimensions of parental involvement on student academic achievement (Fan and Chen, 2001; Kyriakides, 2005b). Finally, none of the variables concerning opportunity to learn had significant effects, and only one time factor indicator was found to be associated with student achievement. It can therefore be claimed that the secondary analysis of the TIMSS 1999 study reported here provides further empirical support for the validity of Creemers' model. It was shown that the influences on student achievement are multilevel. Moreover, variables linked to the three main factors of Creemers' model (i.e. time, opportunity, and quality) were associated with student achievement.

Strengths and weaknesses of studies testing the validity of Creemers' model: implications for the development of EER

A criticism that may arise from the theoretical background and the outline of the comprehensive model of educational effectiveness presented in Chapter 3 concerns the complexity of the model and the difficulties of testing it empirically. The studies that have been conducted during the past decade in order to test the validity of Creemers' model have revealed that the model is a theoretical model that can be put to the test. However, it is not easy to test the complete model in a single research study because the model refers to more than 30 variables that are expected to enhance time spent learning and opportunity used on the part of the student. Nevertheless, the studies that have been conducted in order to test Creemers' model have been able to measure the effect of the main factors included in the model. Therefore, this section refers to the main implications of these studies for the development of research into the theoretical modelling of educational effectiveness.

First, if one looks critically at the methods of the six national studies, it can be claimed that researchers investigating the validity of the model should make use of multiple methodologies to increase the reliability and validity of the data on effectiveness factors included in the model. For example, the measure of quality of teaching cannot emerge only from teacher questionnaire data. Researchers responsible for the first two validation studies which were conducted in the Netherlands acknowledged that the use of this method of data collection is one of the most significant methodological weaknesses of their studies (Driessen and Sleegers, 2000; Reezigt et al., 1999). By contrast, the other four studies testing the validity of the model made use of external observers and student questionnaires to measure the quality of teaching, and managed both to generate valid and reliable data on quality of teaching and to provide some empirical support for Creemers' model (see de Jong et al., 2004; Kyriakides, 2005a).

Second, the three studies conducted in the Netherlands as well as the first study conducted in Cyprus investigated the effects of factors included in the model on cognitive outcomes only. This implies that it is important to test the main assumptions of Creemers' model in relation to different criteria of measuring effectiveness. The above argument is also supported by the fact that Kyriakides (2005a) has shown that the main factors included in the model are associated with not only the cognitive (i.e. achievement in mathematics and Greek language) but also the affective outcomes of schooling. Moreover, Kyriakides and Tsangaridou (2004) provided support for the validity of the model in relation to the achievement of psychomotor objectives in physical education. However, given that studies investigating the impact of factors included in the model on affective and psychomotor outcomes of schooling were conducted only in one country, it can be argued that further studies are needed to examine the extent to which the model can be considered a generic model of educational effectiveness (Campbell et al., 2004). In terms of investigating the generalisability of the model, the importance of conducting studies at different stages of education and in relation to the achievement of the new goals of learning (see Chapter 2) should also be stressed. For example, none of the studies was looking at the effect of factors included in the model on achievement of students in either early primary education or upper secondary education. Such studies are needed in order to find out whether the model can be considered a generic model of educational effectiveness.

Third, a common finding across the six national studies is concerned with the importance of student-level factors, since most of the variance on student achievement was found to be located at student level. Moreover, most of the unexplained variance was located at the student level. It can therefore be argued that studies attempting to expand the model by identifying variables at student level that could explain part of the unexplained variance are needed. In this context, Kyriakides (2005a) has shown that both personality and thinking style should be included in Creemers' model and should be considered as predictors of both cognitive and affective outcomes of schooling. However, further research is needed in order to identify some further variables at student level, since after adding these two types of variables almost 15 per cent of the total variance in each outcome measure remained unexplained at the student level. Moreover, de Jong *et al.* (2004) have shown that the concept of student motivation has to be clarified further. It was also claimed that the concept of self-regulation should be used. Furthermore, researchers found difficulties in collecting valid and reliable data on opportunity to learn at student level. Homework time was used as a proxy for opportunity. However, it should have been measured as the amount of tasks performed (within and outside the classroom with success), but such measures cannot easily be obtained. Thus, further studies could concentrate on developing better methods to measure the student-level factors included in the model.

Fourth, research is also needed to examine relationships between levels and, specifically, indirect effects from higher-level factors through to lower-level factors on student achievement. Although no empirical support was provided for the model in relation to the existence of indirect effects, the conceptualisation of indirect and direct effects between levels needs attention. Researchers should search for the existence not only of additive but also of causal effects. In this context, the use of multilevel path-analytic methods (Heck and Thomas, 2000) is needed in order to examine the nature of the cross-level relationships. At the same time, it is necessary for more teachers within departments or schools to participate in future studies in order to examine whether the four formal principles of Creemers' model can be demonstrated and whether they might contribute to achievement in cognitive and/or affective outcomes of schooling. The findings of these studies may contribute to building a strong theoretical framework for EER.

Fifth, the results of the secondary analysis of the TIMSS 1999 study revealed that comparative studies are needed in order to test the validity of the model. This argument can be attributed to two limitations of the national studies. Conducting a national study may not enable researchers to examine the effect of those factors for which no variability within a country can be observed. For example, none of the Cypriot studies could examine the effect of the curriculum, since there is only one national curriculum and a single series of textbooks that teachers are expected to use. Similarly, de Jong *et al.* (2004) treated the curriculum factor as a school-level factor since Dutch teachers within a particular school all use the same textbook. However, curriculum is seen as a class-level factor in Creemers' model. This factor is considered to have an impact on the quality of instruction because it determines the content taught, the exercises to be performed in the classroom or at home, and the testing of students. Moreover, the effect of context-level factors included in the model cannot be examined since no variation within a country can be identified. In this context, Kyriakides (2006b) conducted a secondary analysis of the TIMSS 1999 study to test the model. Although some empirical support for the model has been provided, two main limitations of conducting secondary analysis of comparative studies can be identified.

The inclusion of aptitude variables in International Association for the Evaluation of Educational Achievement (IEA) studies could lead to more coherent conclusions, since the effect of aptitude in the national effectiveness studies was found to be even stronger than the effect of student SES variables, which, according to the results of the secondary analysis of TIMSS 1999, have the most significant effects. Therefore, the fact that the secondary analysis of the TIMSS 1999 study revealed that most of the variance of student achievement was not explained even after adding a large number of variables included in the student, teacher, and school questionnaires of TIMSS can be attributed to the fact that no measure of student aptitude was taken into account.

Although a number of variables related to three of the factors identified in Creemers' model were found to be associated with student achievement, it should be stressed that these variables explained only a small percentage of the un-explained variance. It could be assumed that if the instruments of IEA studies had provided more information concerning these three factors, more variance would have been explained. This especially holds true for the country level, since variables associated with different educational policies that may affect the three main factors of Creemers' model at the school or teacher level were absent. However, it should be acknowledged that the comparative studies such as those conducted by IEA and the OECD had to achieve broad goals and did not specifically aim at detecting educational effectiveness factors. This implies that there is a need to design comparative studies drawing on theoretical frameworks that define precisely the effectiveness factors included in the model (see Reynolds, 2006; Teddlie *et al.*, 2006).

Finally, the importance of conducting longitudinal studies in order to examine the impact of factors included in the model on student achievement gains is emphasised. Kyriakides and Creemers (2006a) claim that longitudinal studies can not only help us investigate the long-term effect of schools and teachers but also help us to expand the models of educational effectiveness. For example, the extent to which effectiveness factors are associated not only with student achievement but also with changes in the effectiveness status of schools or teachers could be identified. It should, however, be emphasised that one of the main criticisms that one can direct at most studies on long-term teacher effects concerns their failure to take into account the teachers who follow the one whose long-term impact is being evaluated. Yet these effects may be carried over from the teachers the students had in the meantime. Therefore, measuring the long-term effect of teachers and schools implies that information on all the teachers that the students had during the period under consideration should be taken into account (see Kyriakides and Creemers, 2006a). It can also be argued that if researchers use the above approach in designing longitudinal studies they will be able not only to measure the long-term effect of teachers and schools but also to investigate the extent to which Creemers' model can explain changes in the effectiveness status of teachers and schools.

Main conclusions emerging from the results of studies testing Creemers' model

In this last main section of the chapter we will refer to the main conclusions that emerge from the results of studies that attempt to test the Creemers model. The extent to which the model can be considered as the starting point for establishing a dynamic model of educational effectiveness is also raised. It is first of all important to note that studies conducted in two different countries as well as the secondary analysis of the TIMSS 1999 study revealed that the influences on student achievement are multilevel, as was demonstrated in the previous section. Moreover, it was found that most of the variables in Creemers' model showed effects in the expected directions. However, the need to expand the model at the student level has also been pointed out, since most of the unexplained variance was found to be located at this level. The importance of looking at studies in the field of psychology to identify student-level factors has already been stressed (see also Kyriakides, 2005a). Nevertheless, researchers within the field of EER should be critical about the extension of the model and select only variables that have stable effects and can help us establish a model that is in line with the parsimony principle. At the same time, it should be acknowledged that looking at the student-level factors is not a critical issue for the development of the theoretical framework of EER. The main aim of EER is to identify factors of effective education that could be introduced or changed in education through school improvement projects (Creemers, 2002). Therefore, it is important to identify student-level variables that not only are related to student achievement but also interact with other effectiveness factors operating at the classroom and/or school level. For example, Kyriakides (2005a) has shown that the variable 'thinking styles' that emerged from the theory of mental self-government (Sternberg, 1988) are associated with student achievement. Given that thinking styles are seen as dynamic, it can be claimed that it is possible to design projects attempting to help students develop 'optimal' styles in order to improve their achievement. This implies that high-quality teaching is expected to help students develop optimal thinking styles. It has also been shown that there is an interaction between measures of quality of teaching and measures of the personal characteristics of students. This implies that teachers should differentiate their teaching practice in order to respond to the learning needs of their students. Obviously, further research is needed to investigate the generalisability of these findings, but it should be acknowledged that such studies not only could help us expand the model at the student level but also are in line with the main aims of EER, since the complexity of educational effectiveness is illustrated.

Second, none of the studies presented in this chapter was able to illustrate statistically significant cross-level interactions. Moreover, the two Dutch studies were unable to provide some support for one of the main principles of the model. Consistency was not found to be associated with student achievement gains. However, the difficulties the studies had in identifying cross-level interactions might be attributed to the fact that Creemers' model (like all the other models of educational effectiveness) does not explicitly refer to the measurement of each effectiveness factor. On the contrary, it is often assumed that these factors represent unidimensional constructs. For example, the comprehensive model of educational effectiveness states that there should be control at school level, meaning that goal attainment and the school climate should be evaluated (Creemers, 1994). In line with this assumption, studies investigating the validity of the model have revealed that schools with an assessment policy focused on the formative purposes of assessment are more effective (e.g. Kyriakides *et al.*, 2000; Kyriakides, 2005a). However, the examination of assessment policy at school level can be examined not only in terms of its focus on the formative purpose but also in terms of many other aspects of the functioning of assessment such as the procedures used to design assessment instruments, the forms of record-keeping, and the policy on reporting results to parents and students. This implies that there is a need to develop a dynamic model of educational effectiveness capable of identifying the dimensions upon which each factor can be measured. Considering effectiveness factors as multidimensional constructs provides a better picture of what makes teachers and schools effective and helps us develop specific strategies for improving educational practice. Moreover, the relationships between the dimensions of factors operating at different levels will be more easily identified.

Third, the findings of the studies conducted in order to test the validity of Creemers' model provide support for the argument that models of effectiveness should be multilevel in nature. However, the analyses of the results of these studies also revealed that in addition to the multilevel nature of effectiveness, the relationship between factors at different levels might be more complex than assumed in the models. This is especially true for interaction effects among factors operating at classroom and student level, which reveal the importance of investigating differential effectiveness (Campbell *et al.*, 2004; Kyriakides, 2004a). Therefore, the dynamic model should demonstrate the complexity of improving educational effectiveness by illustrating relationships not only between factors operating at different levels but also among factors operating at the same level. Walberg's (1984) model is one of the most significant educational productivity models that attempts to illustrate such relationships. Aptitude, instruction, and the psychological environment are seen as major direct causes of learning. They also influence one another and are in turn influenced by feedback on the amount of learning that takes place. This implies that there is a need to develop a dynamic model of effectiveness revealing the relationships between the effectiveness factors that operate at the same level. Such an approach to modelling educational effectiveness might reveal optimal combinations of factors that make teachers and schools effective.

At the same time, the dynamic model could incorporate in the measurement of effectiveness factors the differentiation dimension, which refers to the extent to which activities associated with a factor are implemented in the same way for all the subjects involved with it (Creemers and Kyriakides, 2006). The importance of treating differentiation as a separate dimension of measuring effectiveness factors arises from the fact that students of any age and in any culture will differ from one another in various intellectual and psychomotor skills, in both generalised and specialised prior knowledge, in interests and motives, in their socio-economic background, and in personal styles of thoughts and work during learning (Dowson and McInerney, 2003). Researchers in the area of educational effectiveness have shown that these differences are related to differences in students' learning progress (e.g. Kyriakides, 2005a; Slavin, 1987b; Teddlie and Reynolds, 2000). These relations imply individual predispositions that somehow condition student readiness to profit from the particular instructional environments provided. Despite the fact that educational practice has remained basically fixed and non-adaptive in most countries, research into differential effectiveness seems to reveal that teachers and schools may be differentially effective in promoting the learning of different groups of students (Campbell *et al.*, 2004).

Main conclusions to emerge from Part I of the book

The main arguments that emerge from the first part of the book will be presented in this final section of the chapter. It is argued that the comprehensive model of educational effectiveness (Creemers, 1994) is in line with at least two of the starting points upon which the dynamic model is based. Specifically, the comprehensive model of educational effectiveness is based on the assumption that the influences on student achievement are multilevel, and thereby it refers to factors at different levels (i.e. student, classroom, school, system) which are related to student achievement. Direct and indirect relations between the levels and the outcomes are also identified.

In this chapter it has been shown that the studies which investigated the validity of the model lent support to the importance of establishing a multilevel integrated model of educational effectiveness, such as Creemers' model. The importance of the main effectiveness factors has also been demonstrated. However, empirical support for the importance of cross-level interactions and for the main principles of the model has not been provided. Therefore, it will be claimed in the next chapter that a dynamic model could be established, having as its starting point the comprehensive model of educational effectiveness. In the next chapter the main features of the proposed dynamic model will be illustrated by taking into account the major weaknesses of the current models of educational effectiveness as these emerge from the results of studies testing the Creemers model. In the last section of the present chapter, two main characteristics of the proposed dynamic model have been identified. It is claimed that the proposed dynamic model should refer explicitly both to cross-level relationships between factors and to the relationships among factors that operate at the same level. Moreover, the dynamic model should refer to the measurement dimensions of each effectiveness factor and grouping of factors. Thus, the dynamic model of educational effectiveness, to be presented in the second part of this book, should not only be parsimonious but also be able to describe the complex nature of educational effectiveness. This implies that the model could be based on specific theory, but at the same time the factors included in the major constructs of the model which are interrelated within and/or between levels should be identified. Thus, the next chapter will be an attempt to illustrate the main characteristics of the dynamic model, which are based on the critical review of EER presented in Chapter 2, as well as on the major findings of studies investigating the validity of Creemers' model, since it is believed that this model could provide the starting points for developing a dynamic model of educational effectiveness.

Part II

The dynamic model of educational effectiveness

Chapter 5

Essential features of the dynamic model

Introduction

In this chapter we illustrate the essential characteristics of the proposed dynamic model. In the final section of Part I, we formulated the main conclusions to have emerged from the critical review of EER and the findings of empirical studies testing the validity of the comprehensive model of educational effectiveness. In this introductory section we focus on the following three issues that emerged from the first part of the book, which we will use as a guide in identifying the starting points for developing a dynamic model of educational effectiveness.

First, it has been argued that the dynamic model should take into account the new goals of education and additionally their implications for teaching and learning. This means that the outcome measures should be more broadly defined rather than being restricted to the achievement of basic skills. It also implies that new theories of teaching and learning can be used in order to specify variables associated with the quality of teaching.

Second, it was claimed that the models of educational effectiveness should be established in such a way as to help policy-makers and practitioners to improve educational practice by making rational decisions concerning the optimal fit of effectiveness factors and the present situation in the schools or educational systems. Decisions can also be made about the design of relevant interventions as well as evaluations of the implementation and the effects of these interventions.

Finally, it was claimed that the dynamic model may be more complex than the current models of effectiveness, but this can be attributed to its attempt to describe in more detail the complex nature of educational effectiveness. This implies that the model should be based on specific theory, but that at the same time the factors included in the major constructs of the model are expected to be interrelated within and between levels. The essential characteristics of the model will now be illustrated, departing from the main conclusions of the first part of the book.

The essential characteristics of the model

First of all, it is important to point out that the proposed dynamic model takes into account the fact that effectiveness studies conducted in several countries reveal that the influences on student achievement are multilevel (Teddlie and Reynolds, 2000). Therefore, the proposed model belongs to the integrated approach to educational effectiveness modelling, since it refers to multiple factors of effectiveness that operate at different levels. It is acknowledged here that initially EER made no distinction between different levels within schools, such as departments and classrooms, in order to make the following point as strongly as possible: schools matter. Different kinds of characteristics related to the input, process, and context of schools at the different levels were included without much distinction, as long as it was evident that there was a difference between effective and less effective schools. Later, this loose 'framework' of school effectiveness was criticised, and replaced by more theoretical models of educational effectiveness, together with the development of a conceptual framework that contains more levels in addition to the student level. Initially only two levels in the schools were discerned: the classroom level and the school level. However, other levels in the school organisation, for example the department level, might be important for effectiveness, as might the levels immediately above the school, such as the school governing body and the wider educational context. For this reason the proposed dynamic model is multilevel in nature and refers to four different levels, which are shown in Figure 5.1.

Figure 5.1 reveals the main structure of the dynamic model of educational effectiveness. It is shown that the teaching and learning situation is emphasised and the roles of the two main actors (i.e. teacher and student) are analysed. Thus, the next chapter refers to factors at the student and classroom level associated with student achievement gains. Above these two levels the dynamic model also refers to school-level factors. It is expected that school-level factors influence the teaching–learning situation by developing and evaluating the school policy on teaching and the policy on creating a learning environment at the school. The final level refers to the influence of the educational system via more formal channels, especially through developing and evaluating the educational policy at the national or regional level. It is also taken into account that the teaching and learning situation is influenced by the wider educational context in which students, teachers, and schools are expected to operate. Factors such as the values of the society as regards learning and the importance attached to education play an important role both in shaping teacher and student expectations and in the development of the perceptions of various stakeholders about effective teaching practice. Thus, Chapter 7 will refer to the school- and context-level factors and illustrates how these factors influence the teaching and learning situation both directly and indirectly.

Figure 5.1 refers to the four levels of the dynamic model and each level's association with student outcomes, and illustrates the interrelations between the components of the model. In this way the model assumes that factors at the school

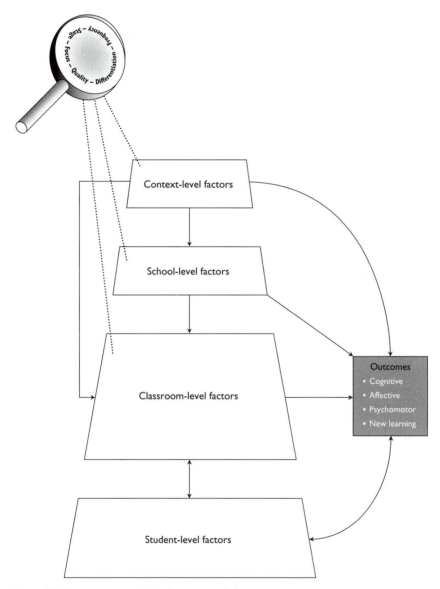

Figure 5.1 Main structure of the dynamic model.

and context level have both direct and indirect effects on student achievement since they are able not only to influence student achievement directly but also to influence the teaching and learning situations. The fact that some context-level factors may indirectly influence the teaching and learning situation by affecting the school policy for teaching while other factors, such as the values of the wider educational context, may directly affect the teaching and learning situation, is also shown.

Beyond the fact that the proposed dynamic model is multilevel in nature, the model takes as its point of departure the fact that learning, especially differences in learning outcomes, has to be explained by the primary processes at the classroom level. Therefore, teaching is emphasised, and our description of the classroom level refers mainly to the behaviour of the teacher in the classroom, and especially to his or her contribution in promoting learning at the classroom level. At the same time, other theoretical perspectives are investigated in relation to the teaching and learning situation.

Finally, it is important to acknowledge that not all the models that are cited in the literature on educational effectiveness specify school-level factors. Relatively early models (e.g. Slavin, 1987b; Walberg, 1984) are restricted to the student level and to the teacher or classroom level. During the past two decades, several models of effectiveness that do specify school-level factors have been proposed as a contribution to theory development (e.g. Creemers, 1994; Scheerens, 1992; Slater and Teddlie, 1992; Stringfield and Slavin, 1992). Although the school-level factors described in these models are partly selected on the basis of their empirical support (often postulated as direct relationships with student achievement), they are mainly included in the models because of their presumed influence on classroom processes (and therefore their indirect relationships to student achievement). In this context the proposed dynamic model is based on the assumption that school factors are able to influence classroom-level factors, and especially teaching practice. Therefore, the defining of factors at the classroom level is seen as a prerequisite for defining the school and the system level. Moreover, the dynamic model refers to factors at school and context level that are related to the same key concepts of quantity of teaching, provision of learning opportunities, and quality of teaching as were used to define classroom-level factors (Creemers and Kyriakides, 2005a).

The above three characteristics of the dynamic model seem to be in line with most of the integrated models of educational effectiveness (see Chapter 2), and especially with Creemers' model (see Chapter 3). As has been explained in Chapter 3, the comprehensive model of educational effectiveness (1) is multilevel in nature, (2) gives more emphasis to classroom-level factors and especially to the behaviour of teachers in promoting learning, and (3) is based on the assumption that higher levels are expected to provide conditions for lower levels.

However, the dynamic model also assumes that the impact of the school-level factors and the impact of the context-level factors have to be defined and measured in a different way from how the impact of classroom-level factors is measured. Policy on teaching and actions taken to improve teaching practice must be measured over time and in relation to the weaknesses that occur in a school. The assumption is that schools and educational systems which are able to identify their weaknesses and develop a policy on aspects associated with teaching and the learning environment of the school are also able to improve the functioning of classroom-level factors and their effectiveness status both directly and indirectly.

This has some significant methodological implications, especially for studies attempting to test the validity of the dynamic model at the school level. First, longitudinal studies should be conducted in order to measure how changes in the functioning of the factors are associated with changes in the effectiveness status of schools (see Kyriakides and Creemers, 2006a). Second, evaluation processes are seen as very crucial, since only changes in those factors for which schools face significant problems are expected to be associated with the improvement of school effectiveness. For example, at schools where teacher and/or student absenteeism rarely occurs, a change in their policy on absenteeism is not expected to be associated with the improvement of the effectiveness status of the school. This implies that the impact of school- and context-level factors depends on the current situation of the objects under investigation. This is seen as an essential characteristic of the proposed dynamic model, which reveals an essential difference in the nature of this model with all the current models of educational effectiveness.

Therefore, the dynamic model incorporates results of research into differential effectiveness and also is in line with contingency theories which support the proposition that the optimal organisation/leadership style is contingent upon various internal and external constraints (e.g. Carew *et al.*, 1986; Goodson *et al.*, 1989; Hersey and Blanchard, 1993; Ralph, 2004). No single contingency theory has been postulated, but three of them, all of which have been extensively researched, are Fiedler's contingency theory, Hersey and Blanchard's situational theory, and Vroom and Yetton's decision participation contingency theory or the normative decision theory. In the next section we shall refer to three further characteristics of the dynamic which raise methodological implications for the development of EER.

Elements of the model that raise some methodological implications for educational effectiveness research

Searching for non-linear relations

Meta-analyses of the effect of some effectiveness factors upon student achievement have revealed that although they have been perceived as factors affecting teacher or school effectiveness, the research evidence is problematic. For example, teacher subject knowledge is widely perceived as a factor affecting teacher effectiveness (Scriven, 1994), but teachers' subject knowledge, regardless of how it is measured, has rarely correlated strongly with student achievement (Borich, 1992; Darling-Hammond, 2000). The explanation may be, as Monk (1994) reported, that the relationship is curvilinear: a minimal level of knowledge is necessary for teachers to be effective, but beyond a certain point, a negative relation occurs. Similar findings have been reported for the association of self-efficacy beliefs with teacher effectiveness (Schunk 1991; Stevenson *et al.* 1993) and for the impact of classroom emotional climate and teacher management upon effectiveness. A negative emotional climate usually shows negative correlations, but a neutral climate is at least as supportive as a warm climate. Beyond an optimal level of teacher direction, drill or recitation becomes dysfunctional (Soar and Soar, 1979). Rosenshine (1971) suggests inverted-U curvilinear relationships with student learning for verbal praise, difficulty level of instruction, teacher questions, and amount of student talk. The possibility of interaction with students' individual differences is also supported. Therefore, the dynamic model of educational effectiveness is based on the assumption that the relation of some effectiveness factors with achievement may not be linear.

This assumption has implications for both the design and the analysis of effectiveness studies, since the investigation of non-linear relations implies not only that more complex statistical techniques should be used in analysing the data but also that more emphasis should be given to the quality of the measures.

As far as the analysis of data is concerned, two issues need attention. Since the dynamic model belongs to the category of integrated models, it is important to use multilevel modelling techniques which are able to identify variables at student, teacher, school, and system levels that are associated with student achievement. However, an issue that has to be taken into account is that the dynamic model also assumes that some variables are not related in a linear way with student achievement. In the case of education we give emphasis to the existence of inverted-U curvilinear relations, since such relations reveal that there is an optimal point for the function of a specific factor. After the optimal point there is a negative relation with achievement, and hence the identification of the optimal point has important implications for improving educational practice. If researchers search for inverted-U relations, both the effect of the various explanatory variables (X_i) and the effect of the second power of these variables (i.e. X_i^2 values) upon student achievement have to be identified. This approach may allow us to discover the optimal value of this factor (i.e. the values of X for which Y has a maximum value). Obviously, other non-linear relations might exist. In the event that there is more than one optimal point, the efficiency of application of a certain factor after the first optimal point can be questioned.

The second issue that needs further consideration is concerned with the fact that the measurement errors of the variables under consideration act as significant obstacles in establishing non-linear relations. This implies that researchers should give more emphasis to measurement issues in order to increase the quality of the data collected. This is due to the fact that the investigation of non-linear relations is based on seeking to determine whether the second or even a higher power of a factor is able to explain variation of student achievement. In this case, instead of dealing with the measurement error of a factor you have to deal with the relevant power of this error. As a consequence, it is much more difficult to identify statistically significant relations. This implies that researchers should give more emphasis to measurement issues in order to increase both the quality of the data collected and their statistical power (i.e. reduce the type II error), since whenever a study does not reveal any non-linear relation one may claim that this does not necessarily imply that the relation is linear but rather that the finding is an artefact of the relatively high measurement error of the effectiveness factor.

Finally, a possible failure to demonstrate non-linear relations may be attributed to the difficulties of establishing enough variation in the functioning of the factors, especially since almost all the effectiveness studies have been conducted in a single country. There are two alternative approaches to searching for non-linear relations. First, experimental studies can be conducted that aim to create enough variance in the functioning of each factor and then search for optimal values. However, attention should be given to the ecological validity of experimental studies as well as to the ethical issues associated with the experimentation (Miller, 1984; Robson, 1993). On the other hand, comparative studies can be conducted to test the validity of the model, and especially the existence of non-linear relations. International longitudinal studies can tap the full range of variation in school and classroom quality, and therefore in potential school and classroom effects. Thus, international studies could help us identify non-linear relations since in national studies the lack of a significant effect might be due to the difficulties we have in identifying variation in either the student outcomes or, more likely, in the explanatory variables.

Investigating relations among factors operating at the same level

The second essential characteristic of the dynamic model that has methodological implications for the development of EER refers to our argument that there is a need to carefully examine the relationships between the various effectiveness factors that operate at the same level. The results of a study testing the validity of Walberg's (1984) model, which attempts to illustrate such relationships, provide support for this argument, as was mentioned in Part I of the book. It is argued here that such an approach to modelling educational effectiveness might reveal a grouping of factors that make teachers and schools effective. Therefore, specific strategies for improving effectiveness that are more comprehensive in nature may emerge.

This suggestion has significant implications for the analysis of data that have emerged from effectiveness studies. To search for relations between factors operating at the same level, different statistical methods for analysing data can be used, such as structural equation modelling procedures. It is also possible to use multilevel path-analytic methods (Heck and Thomas, 2000) in order not only to examine relationships between factors operating at the same level but also to identify relevant cross-level relationships. Cross-level relationships can also be identified through multivariate multilevel modelling techniques which allow us to have more than one dependent variable. For example, the relationship between two factors associated with a teacher's role in promoting learning (e.g. structuring and orientation) and with student achievement gains can be tested by treating one of them (e.g. orientation) as an explanatory variable and treating both the second factor (i.e. structuring) and student achievement as dependent variables.

A generic model that incorporates findings of differential educational effectiveness research

Although the dynamic model is expected to be a generic model, it takes into account the findings of research into differential educational effectiveness (e.g. Campbell *et al.*, 2004; Kyriakides and Tsangaridou, 2004). Specifically, effectiveness factors are seen as generic in nature, but it is acknowledged that their impact on different groups of students or teachers or schools may vary (Kyriakides and Creemers, 2006b). For example, structuring is considered to be an important classroom-level factor since achievement is maximised when teachers not only actively present materials but structure the lesson by (1) beginning with overviews and/or a review of objectives; (2) outlining the content to be covered and signalling transitions between lesson parts; (3) calling attention to the main ideas; and (4) reviewing the main ideas at the end (Rosenshine and Stevens, 1986). At the same time, studies investigating teacher differential effectiveness in relation to student socio-economic status have revealed that low-SES students need more structure and more positive reinforcement from the teacher (Brophy, 1992). Therefore, effective teachers are expected not only to structure their lessons but also to respond to the different learning and affective needs of their students by providing more structuring tasks to those groups of students who need them most (e.g. low-ability students). The identification of interactions between teacher behaviours in the classroom and student characteristics reveals that it is primarily the teacher's adaptive instructional behaviour which makes teachers able to provide equal opportunities to students with different background and personal characteristics. Similar arguments can be made in relation to the functioning of the school and context-level factors. Therefore, from the point of view of theory-building, it is argued here that we should not overestimate the differential nature of teacher and school effectiveness. Kyriakides and Creemers (2006b) have shown that most variables measuring teaching skills (e.g. practical application opportunities, giving information) have a general effect on student achievement gains but also operate differentially in relation to the student background characteristics. This suggests that the concept of differential teacher effectiveness ought not to be polarised against a generic concept. Rather, the former should be incorporated as a refinement into the latter. In this context the dynamic model is based on the assumption that different dimensions for measuring the functioning of effectiveness factors are used. The use of different measurement dimensions reveals that looking at just the frequency of an effectiveness factor (e.g. the quantity that an activity associated with an effectiveness factor is present in a system or school or classroom) does not help us identify those aspects of the functioning of a factor that are associated with student achievement. It is considered important to see whether teachers, or schools, or systems respond to the learning needs of different groups of students, or teachers, or schools. This can be attributed to the fact that adaptation to the specific needs of each subject or group of subjects will increase the successful implementation of a factor and ultimately maximise its effect on student learning outcomes.

Dimensions of measuring effectiveness factors

One of the major criticisms of the current models of educational effectiveness is that they do not explicitly refer to the measurement of each effectiveness factor. On the contrary, it is often assumed that these factors represent unidimensional constructs. For example, the comprehensive model of educational effectiveness states that there should be control at school level, meaning that goal attainment and the school climate should be evaluated (Creemers, 1994). In line with this assumption, studies investigating the validity of the model have revealed that schools with an assessment policy focused on the formative purpose of assessment are more effective (e.g. Kyriakides *et al.*, 2000; Kyriakides, 2005a). However, the examination of assessment policy at school level can be examined not only in terms of its focus on the formative purpose but also in terms of many other aspects of the functioning of assessment, such as the procedures used to design assessment instruments, the forms of record-keeping, and the policy on reporting results to parents and students. This implies that researchers who attempt to establish a dynamic model should not only refer to the various factors of effectiveness but also explain the various dimensions upon which each factor can be measured. Considering effectiveness factors as multidimensional constructs not only provides a better picture of what makes teachers and schools effective but also helps us develop more specific strategies for improving educational practice. In this context the idea is supported here that, in principle, each factor – which refers to the classroom, the school, and the system – can be measured by taking into account the following five dimensions: frequency, focus, stage, quality, and differentiation. Table 5.1 illustrates the operational definition of these five dimensions, which reveal the importance of collecting both quantity and quality information about the functioning of each factor. The importance of taking each dimension into account will be discussed in what follows, but it should be acknowledged that studies investigating the validity of the proposed measurement framework of effectiveness factors are needed.

Frequency

The *frequency* dimension refers to the extent to which an activity associated with an effectiveness factor occurs in a system, school, or classroom. This is probably the easiest way to measure the effect of a factor on student achievement, and most effectiveness studies have used this dimension to define effectiveness factors. For example, personal monitoring at school level can be measured by taking into account how often the principals use a monitoring system to supervise their teachers. EER could attempt to identify whether this dimension of measuring

Table 5.1 Operational definitions of the five dimensions of measuring each effectiveness factor and ways of measuring each dimension

Dimension	Operational definition	Ways of measuring
Frequency	Refers to the *quantity* that an activity associated with an effectiveness factor is present in a system, school or classroom.	Two indicators are used: • How many tasks are used? • How long does each task take?
Focus	Reveals the function of the factor at classroom, school and system level. The following two aspects of focus of each factor are measured: • specificity; • the number of purposes for which an activity takes place.	• Specificity is measured by investigating the extent to which activities are too specific or too general. • How many purposes are expected to be achieved?
Stage	Refers to the *period* at which they take place. It is assumed that the factors need to take place over a long period of time to ensure that they have a continuous direct or indirect effect on student learning.	• When does the task take place? (Based on the data that emerge from this question, data about the continuity of the existence of a factor are collected.)
Quality	Refers to the properties of the specific factor itself, as these are discussed in the literature.	• What are the properties of tasks associated with a factor which reveal the functioning of each factor? • To what extent is the function of each task in line with the literature?
Differentiation	Refers to the extent to which activities associated with a factor are implemented in the same way for all the subjects involved with it.	To what extent are different tasks associated with each factor provided to different groups of subjects involved with this factor?

personal monitoring is related not only directly to student achievement but also indirectly, through teacher behaviour in the classroom. Further, it is questionable whether there is a linear relation between frequency of personal monitoring and both types of outcomes. It may be assumed that after a monitoring system has been used optimally, the result may not be an additional effect on outcomes. Indeed, there may even be negative effects on teacher behaviour and ultimately on student outcomes.

Focus

The effectiveness factors are measured by taking into account the *focus* of the activities that reveal the function of the factors at the classroom, school, and system level. Two aspects of focus for each factor can be measured. The first refers to the *specificity* of the activities, which can range from specific to general. For example, in the case of school policy on parental involvement, the policy could either be more specific in terms of concrete activities that are expected to take place (e.g. the school policy may refer to specific hours when parents can visit the school) or more general (e.g. it informs parents that they are welcome to visit the school but without giving them specific information about what, how, and when). The second addresses the *purpose* for which an activity takes place. An activity may be expected to achieve single or multiple purposes. In the case of policy on parental involvement, the activities might be restricted to a single purpose (e.g. parents visit schools to get information about student progress) or might address more than one purpose (e.g. parents visit the school to exchange information about children's progress and to assist teachers in and outside the classroom).

The measurement of the focus of an activity, either in terms of its specificity, or in terms of the number of purposes that it is expected to achieve, may be related in a non-linear way to student outcomes. For example, guidelines on parental involvement which are very general may not be at all helpful in establishing positive relations between parents and teachers, which, when good, can result in the supporting of student learning. On the other hand, a school policy that is very specific in defining activities may restrict teachers and parents from being productively involved and creating their own ways of implementing the school policy. Similarly, if all the activities are expected to achieve a single purpose, then the chances of achieving that purpose are high, but the effect of the factor might be small, owing to the fact that other purposes are not achieved and/or synergy may not exist since the activities are isolated. On the other hand, if all the activities are expected to achieve multiple purposes, there is a danger that specific purposes will not be addressed in such a way that they can be implemented successfully. This example also reveals the importance of investigating whether for some effectiveness factors there may be an interaction between these two aspects of their focus dimension.

Stage

The activities associated with a factor can be measured by taking into account the *stage* at which they take place. It is assumed that the factors are needed to take place over a long period of time to ensure that they have a continuous direct or indirect effect on student learning. This assumption is partly based on the fact that evaluations of programmes aiming to improve educational practice reveal that the extent to which these intervention programmes have any impact on educational practice is partly based on the length of time for which the programmes are implemented in a school. Moreover, the importance of using the stage dimension to measure each effectiveness factor arises from the fact that it has been shown that the impact of a factor on student achievement depends partly on the extent to which activities associated with this factor are provided throughout the school career of the student (e.g. Creemers, 1994; Slater and Teddlie, 1992). Finally, the use of the stage dimension to measure effectiveness factors is in line with one of the principles of the comprehensive model of educational effectiveness, namely constancy. As was mentioned in Chapter 3, Creemers (1994) argues that there should be constancy, meaning that effective instruction is provided throughout the school career of the student. This implies that the duration of the effect of a factor should be taken into account. For example, school policy on quantity of teaching, which refers to policy on cancellation of lessons and absenteeism, is expected to be implemented throughout the year and not only through specific regulations announced at a specific point of time (e.g. at the beginning of the school year). It is also expected that the continuity will be achieved when the school is flexible in redefining its own policy and adapting the activities related to the factor by taking into account the results of its own self-evaluation mechanism (Creemers and Kyriakides, 2005b). Although the measurement of the stage dimension gives information about the continuity of the existence of a factor, it is pointed out here that the activities associated with the factor may not necessarily be the same. Therefore, using the stage dimension to measure the functioning of a factor can help us identify the extent to which there is constancy at each level and flexibility in using the factor during the period when the investigation is taking place. As a consequence, linear relations of the stage dimension of each factor with student achievement gains are expected to exist.

Quality

The *quality* dimension refers to the properties of the specific factor itself, as these are discussed in the literature. The importance of using this dimension arises from the fact that looking at the quantity element of a factor ignores the fact that the functioning of the factor may vary. Moreover, the literature has shown that using only certain activities associated with a factor has positive effects on student outcomes. It is also important to point out that only a linear relation of the quality dimension of each effectiveness factor with student achievement gains is expected to exist, since activities associated with a factor that are not in line with the literature are not expected to influence achievement. For instance, school policy on assessment can be measured by looking at the mechanisms that have been developed in order to establish instruments meeting psychometric standards (i.e. valid, reliable, representative of the content taught, making use of different techniques). At the same time, it can be examined whether this policy makes clear and guarantees that teachers are expected to make use of assessment information for formative rather than summative reasons (Black and Wiliam, 1998; Harlen and James, 1997; Kyriakides *et al.*, 2000). It is assumed that only schools with a policy on assessment that is in line with the above requirements are effective. Having a policy on assessment that promotes the summative purpose may not have any effect and is very likely to be even less effective than having no policy at all on assessment.

Differentiation

Finally, the dimension *differentiation* refers to the extent to which activities associated with a factor are implemented in the same way for all the subjects involved with it (e.g. all the students, teachers, schools). It is expected that adaptation to the specific needs of each subject or group of subjects will increase the successful implementation of a factor and ultimately maximise its effect on student learning outcomes. Although differentiation could be considered a property of an effectiveness factor, it was decided to treat differentiation as a separate dimension of measuring each effectiveness factor rather than to incorporate it into the quality dimension. In this way, the importance of taking into account the special needs of each subject or group of subjects is recognised. Therefore, the dynamic model is based on the assumption that it is difficult to deny that persons of all ages learn, think, and process information differently.

One way to differentiate instruction is for teachers to teach according to individual student learning needs, as these are defined by their background and personal characteristics such as gender, socio-economic status, ability, thinking style, and personality type (Kyriakides and Creemers, 2006b). For example, effective teachers provide more active instruction and feedback, more redundancy, and smaller steps with a higher success rate to their low-SES or low-achieving students. On the other hand, they are aware of the fact that high-SES students thrive in an atmosphere that is academically stimulating and somewhat demanding, and create such a learning environment for them. Warmth and support, in addition to good instruction, are provided to low-SES students, who are more frequently encouraged for their efforts. A similar argument can be made in relation to the way teachers should be treated by their school leaders. For example, instructional leadership should not be seen as equally important for all the teachers in a school. Therefore, effective principals are expected to adapt their leadership to the specific needs of the teachers by taking into account the extent to which they are ready to implement a task (Hersey and Blanchard, 1993). Similarly, policy-makers are expected to adapt their general policy to the specific needs of groups of schools and encourage teachers to differentiate their instruction. Research into differential educational effectiveness reveals that teachers' objectives as well as organisational and cultural factors should be taken into account when the dimension of differentiation is measured (Dowson and McInerney, 2003; Hayes and Deyhle, 2001; Kyriakides and Tsangaridou, 2004).

However, the differentiation dimension does not imply that the subjects are not expected to achieve the same purposes. On the contrary, adapting the policy to the special needs of each group of schools, or teachers, or students may ensure that all of them will become able to achieve the same purposes. This argument is partly supported by research into adaptive teaching and the evaluation projects of innovations concerned with the use of adaptive teaching in classrooms (e.g. Houtveen *et al.*, 2004; Noble, 2004; Reusser, 2000). Therefore, policy-makers should make explicit to teachers what they are expected to achieve through differentiating their instruction and through responding to the different needs of their students.

This is particularly crucial for establishing an effective policy on equal opportunities, since research has shown that some existing educational practices are maladaptive (e.g. Kyriakides, 2004a; Peterson *et al.*, 1984). The classic example is ability grouping. In secondary education and even sometimes in primary schools, abilities reflected in test data, prior grades, teacher observations, or some combination of these are used to classify students into homogeneous ability groups or tracks. Policy-makers should evaluate teaching practice to find out whether teaching practice in some schools is maladaptive. Moreover, schools should be encouraged to develop a policy on quality of teaching such that the way students are classified into groups receiving different instructional treatments acts to improve all students' chances of reaching the common goals of education. Although the intent may be to adapt instruction to different ability levels, such grouping in some schools may impose a slower pace and lower goals on lower-ability students. Research suggests that being a member of a lower-ability group may diminish a student's achievement by reducing his or her opportunities to learn. In such groups, more time may be spent on administration and discipline, less time may be spent on teaching, and the quality of teaching and instructional materials may often be lower (e.g. Kyriakides, 2004a; Peterson *et al.*, 1984). Therefore, policy-makers should provide support to those schools where teaching practice is maladaptive and help them to act in such a way that differentiation of instruction does not result in lower achievers being held back and individual differences being increased.

Concluding comments

Based on the critical review of EER and the findings of studies testing the validity of Creemers' model presented in Part I of the book, the essential characteristics of the proposed dynamic model have been presented in this chapter. It has been shown here that the proposed dynamic model (1) is multilevel in nature and thereby refers to the most important effectiveness factors that operate at the student, classroom, school, and context levels; (2) gives more emphasis to the teaching and learning situation, and hence the roles of the two main actors (i.e. teacher and students) are analysed; and (3) refers to school- and context-level factors that have not only direct effects on student achievement but also indirect effects through their influence on the teaching–learning situation. These three characteristics of the dynamic model are in line with most of the integrated models of educational effectiveness, and especially with Creemers' model. They can be seen as starting points for the development of the dynamic model. However, the next four characteristics of the dynamic model reveal its essential difference from the current models of educational effectiveness and help us identify its dynamic nature. First, the model assumes that the impact of the school- and context-level factors has to be defined and measured in a different way from the classroom-level factors. Effectiveness factors, irrespective of whether they operate at the classroom or higher levels, are seen as essential components of effective education. According to the dynamic model, the impact of school and context factors depends on the current situation of the school or system and especially on the types of problems or difficulties that the school or system is facing. Therefore, longitudinal studies are needed to measure the impact of these factors by looking at the problems or difficulties that schools or systems are facing and how changes in the relevant factors or actions taken towards solving these problems are associated with improvement in effectiveness.

Second, the dynamic character of the model is also reflected in the fact that we assume that the relation of some effectiveness factors to student achievement may not necessarily be linear. This implies that the effect of the improvement of these factors on student outcomes depends on the situation each individual teacher or school or context is in at the moment. This means that a teacher who attempts to improve, for example, his or her orientation skills may succeed in improving student outcomes more than if the teacher has attempted to improve his or her skills in teaching-modelling. A completely different interpretation can be drawn for another teacher by looking at the situation that teacher is in at the moment. Therefore, specific suggestions for improving the effectiveness of teachers or schools or contexts can be provided. It can also be claimed that the dynamic model may contribute to the establishment of stronger links between EER and improvement of practice (Creemers and Kyriakides, 2005a).

Third, the establishment of stronger links with the improvement of practice is also supported by the fact that the dynamic model assumes that there is a need to carefully examine the relationships between the various effectiveness factors operating at the same level. It is therefore possible to identify groups of factors that are associated with student achievement gains. As a consequence, comprehensive strategies for improving practice might emerge, especially since the existence of curvilinear relations may reveal not only the optimal points of specific factors but also optimal combinations of effectiveness factors.

Finally, effectiveness factors are not considered to be unidimensional constructs; rather, five dimensions are used to define them. Table 5.1 illustrates the operational definition of these five dimensions, which reveals the importance of collecting both quantity and quality information about the functioning of each factor. Moreover, treating differentiation as a separate dimension of measuring each effectiveness factor reveals the importance of differentiation in teaching and helps us incorporate research on differential effectiveness into the theoretical framework of EER.

In this chapter we have described in general the five dimensions that can be used to measure each effectiveness factor. In order to explain more thoroughly how these five dimensions can be used to establish the dynamic model of educational effectiveness, the following chapter will refer to the specific measurement of the classroom factors that are expected to be related to student achievement gains. Factors at the student level will also be presented, but it is once more to be noted that the measurement framework of the effectiveness factors refers to the classroom, school, and context systems. Moreover, the decision to present the classroom level first rather than the upper levels is based on the fact that EER studies show that this level is more significant than the school and the system levels (e.g. Hextall and Mahony, 1998; Kyriakides *et al.*, 2000; Yair, 1997). In addition, the defining of factors at the classroom level is seen as a prerequisite for defining the school and the system level. Therefore, the description of the dynamic model at the school and context level will be given in Chapter 7, and this will help readers understand how the factors in the upper levels are related to the classroom-level factors presented in Chapter 6.

The dynamic model

Factors operating at student and classroom levels

Introduction

This chapter provides a description of the student- and classroom-level factors of the proposed dynamic model. The reader can see that the way these two levels are defined is in line with the main principles of the model presented in Chapter 5. Although the dynamic model is multilevel in nature, more emphasis is given to factors operating at the teacher and the school level, since the main aim of EER is to identify factors in education that promote learning. For that reason, this chapter gives an overview of the factors operating at student level included in the dynamic model. Student background characteristics are taken into account because they explain to a large extent the variance between students in learning and achievement. At the classroom level the teacher is an important actor. Teacher background characteristics such as gender, age, education, beliefs, and motivation are an important topic in theory and research because these characteristics can explain the differences between teachers in the way they behave in classrooms. However, these characteristics are not included in the dynamic model, which concentrates on the teaching activities teachers perform in order to initiate, promote, and evaluate student learning.

Factors operating at the student level

In line with the literature on educational effectiveness, Creemers' model specifies that student achievement is influenced by aptitudes, socio-economic background, motivation, time on task, and opportunities used. However, the dynamic model includes not only student-level factors referring to background variables but also the personal characteristics of students that were found to affect learning. Therefore, the following two main categories of background factors operating at student level that can influence the effectiveness of education are included in the dynamic model: (1) socio-cultural and economic background variables that emerged from the sociological perspective of EER, and (2) background variables that emerged from the psychological perspective of EER. In addition, variables related to specific learning tasks that emerged from the psychological perspective are also treated as significant student-level factors. Some evidence showing that these variables affect learning will be provided in this chapter.

Moreover, a distinction is made among the student-level factors by referring to factors that are unlikely to change (e.g. gender, SES, ethnicity, personality) and factors that may change over time (e.g. subject motivation, thinking styles). Factors that are likely to change over time are more closely related to the aims of EER, since they could be treated both as explanatory and as outcome variables. For example, subject motivation may be related to student achievement gains, but it is also likely to change as a result of teacher behaviour. Helping children to increase their motivation could therefore be considered an affective outcome of schooling. However, in Chapter 2 the debate on the criteria for measuring effectiveness was discussed, and it was made clear that EER is concerned with the intended outcomes of schooling, as these are defined by the policy-makers and/or other stakeholders. Therefore, in the dynamic model, although we treat student-level factors that are likely to change as predictors of student achievement gains, it is also acknowledged that since these factors are not stable, longitudinal studies are needed to investigate their impact on student achievement (see also Chapter 10).

Finally, it is argued that research into differential educational effectiveness in relation to factors that are not very likely to change, as well as in relation to factors that are likely to change, could help teachers identify how to adapt their teaching practice to the specific learning needs of groups of students and thereby become more effective (Kyriakides and Creemers, 2006b). In this context, relations between factors operating at the student level and factors operating at higher levels, such as the teacher level, are expected to exist, and research into differential effectiveness could help us identify these relations. As a consequence, the dynamic model can be seen as a generic model which incorporates findings of research into differential effectiveness by revealing relations between student-level factors and factors operating at higher levels.

Socio-cultural and economical background variables that emerged from the sociological perspective of EER

The first group of student-level factors of the proposed dynamic model refers to socio-cultural and economical background variables that emerge from the sociological perspective of EER, such as SES, ethnic background, and gender. The treatment of these variables as student-level factors is strongly related to the history of EER, and especially to the sociological perspective of educational effectiveness (see Chapter 2). As has been mentioned, many studies have shown that the greater part of the variance in student outcomes can be explained by student background characteristics such as SES, ethnicity, and gender (Sirin, 2005). In this context, the integrated models of educational effectiveness treated background variables as student-level factors. Moreover, coming from the history of research in inequality in education, it was evident that EER would look at the educational outcomes of disadvantaged children in particular and search for equity in schools (see also Chapter 2). Therefore, we not only treat these variables as student-level factors but also raise the importance of using these variables as criteria for measuring effectiveness in terms of the equity dimension. It is also argued that the evaluation of any policy promoting equality of opportunities should be based on investigating its impact on promoting the educational progress of socially disadvantaged students and on reducing unjustifiable gender differences at the school level (see also Chapter 11).

For example, Kyriakides (2004a) has shown that there are marked differences in mathematics attainment between groups of Cypriot students differentiated by sex and socio-economic status at a very early stage of their education (i.e. when they entered primary school) as well as two years later (i.e. when they were at the end of year 2). More importantly, differences in *rate of progress* between students tend to increase rather than decrease between the ages of 5 and 7 years. Students from the working class start behind their peers and fall even further behind during the first two years of primary school. This finding is in line with findings of early school effectiveness research (e.g. Douglas, 1964). Moreover, like studies on differential effectiveness conducted in the United Kingdom (e.g. Jesson and Gray, 1991; Thomas *et al.*, 1997), this study has shown that the schools were not differentially effective, in the sense that the most effective schools overall were not more effective with girls or with working-class students than other schools. Thus, even in the most effective schools, boys' progress rate in mathematics was greater than girls'. This finding reveals that research into differential effectiveness may help us evaluate the effectiveness of micro-level policies on equality of opportunities in education. It has been shown, for example, that gender differences in mathematics were reduced substantially in schools that introduced more liberal curriculum policies (Lamb, 1996).

Beyond indicating the importance of treating background variables as student-level factors and providing suggestions on how research into differential effectiveness could help teachers, or schools, or systems to become more effective, the dynamic model also refers to the importance of looking at relations between these variables. Our attempt to search for relations among factors operating at the same level can be seen as one of the most essential differences between the dynamic model and the current models of educational effectiveness (see Chapter 5). Specifically, it is argued here that the majority of school effectiveness studies have focused on the effects of either sex or socio-economic circumstances on educational attainment (Grant and Sleeter, 1986). However, even in the few studies where these two factors are evaluated simultaneously, interactions between them are rarely made explicit (Mortimore *et al.*, 1988; Sammons *et al.*, 1993). Thus, the dynamic model is defined at the student level in such a way as to raise the importance of a systematic investigation on differential school and teacher effectiveness in relation to student background characteristics. For example, the extent to which there are significant interactions between social groups and sex, indicating that the gender effect is not consistent across all social classes, has been investigated in a study on differential school effectiveness conducted in Cyprus

(Kyriakides, 2004a). The results of this study revealed that gender differences are bigger in lower-SES groups. A similar finding emerged from a study on gender differences conducted in England (Gray *et al.*, 2004). In practice, this means that researchers could include interaction terms in their multilevel models and examine whether their use significantly improved the models' fit to the data relative to models testing main effects alone. In the event that an interaction model between gender and SES fits better, we could claim that the main effect model provides a less accurate picture of the data because it assumes that the effect of sex is consistent across all social class groups. It can also be argued that researchers could consider combinations of individual student background factors (e.g. working-class girls) as groups whose educational progress it is important to examine.

Finally, it is important to acknowledge that at the level of the classroom, students should be treated as individuals rather than as representing stereotypical groupings, so that the promotion of learning for all students is encouraged. However, at the level of the school or the system, if groups of students are systematically being disadvantaged in their rate of learning by comparison with other groups, as some effectiveness studies in different countries have shown (e.g. Gorard *et al.*, 2001; Gray *et al.*, 2004; Beaton *et al.*, 1996; Harskamp, 1988; Kyriakides, 2004a), issues for educational policy at both the school and the system level could be raised.

Background variables that emerged from the psychological perspective of EER

The dynamic model also refers to five background variables that emerged from the psychological perspective of EER and were found to be related with student achievement: aptitude, motivation, expectations, personality, and thinking style. A brief review of the literature revealing the impact of each variable upon student achievement follows.

Aptitude

Aptitude is seen as one of the most critical background variables associated with student achievement. Aptitude embraces general intelligence and prior learning. This variable was included in the early educational productivity models, and was treated by Carroll (1963) as a factor that defines the actual time spent on teaching. Specifically, aptitude is considered as the amount of time students require in order to learn under optimal instructional conditions (Creemers, 1994). Walberg (1986b) points out that although all theories of learning yield some good ideas, the theories have not been sufficiently supported empirically. However, this applies to a lesser extent to Carroll's (1963) model, which embodied a learning theory that could be of use for educational practice. Moreover, as was mentioned in Chapter 3, aptitude is included in the comprehensive model and is seen as a significant variable at student level (Creemers, 1994). Furthermore, studies investigating the validity of Creemers' model, presented in Chapter 4, reveal the importance of this variable. It is important to note that these studies also reveal that the effect of aptitude on student achievement is even higher than the effect of socio-economic status (e.g. de Jong *et al*., 2004; Kyriakides, 2005a). In this context, aptitude is included in the dynamic model and is considered to be one of the most important factors operating at student level.

Motivation

As was mentioned in Chapter 3, Creemers' model stipulates that achievement is influenced not only by aptitudes and social background but also by motivation. Specifically, it is argued not only that motivation influences outcomes, but also that academic outcomes do have an effect on motivation (Creemers, 1994, p. 113). This explains why Creemers draws a reciprocal relationship between motivation and student outcomes (see Figure 3.1 in Chapter 3). In line with the comprehensive model, the dynamic model also treats motivation as an important student-level factor. Moreover, the importance of considering motivation as a student-level factor is justified by the studies conducted in order to test the validity of the comprehensive model of educational effectiveness (see Chapter 4). However, it should be acknowledged that Creemers did not make explicit what the 'motivation' factor is expected to cover. As a consequence, student motivation was measured in different ways by researchers investigating the validity of the model. Scales measuring general school motivation, subject motivation, self-efficacy, and perseverance have been developed (see de Jong *et al*., 2004; Kyriakides, 2005a; Kyriakides and Tsangaridou, 2004). Nevertheless, not all dimensions of motivation were found to be related to achievement gains. Some conceptions of motivation, such as perseverance, were found to have a good place in the comprehensive model of educational effectiveness (de Jong *et al*., 2004; Kyriakides, 2005a). It is also important to note that 'perseverance' is the main motivation concept included in Carroll's (1963) model, and several studies in the area of educational psychology revealed that this variable is associated with the achievement of students of any age (i.e. students at the school and the university level). Therefore, it was decided to treat perseverance as a factor operating at the student level. Moreover, this conception of motivation is placed between student aptitude and time on task in order to explain that we treat perseverance as a rather stable trait (see Figure 6.1).

On the other hand, other conceptions, such as self-confidence and self-efficacy beliefs, were not found to be related to achievement gains (e.g. de Jong *et al*. 2004; Kyriakides and Tsangaridou, 2004). Taking into account that there are hardly any studies demonstrating a relationship between efficacy beliefs and efficacy (not only at student but also at teacher level), we decided not to treat this conception of motivation as a student-level factor. Drawing on the literature on efficacy beliefs (e.g. Bandura, 1996, 1997; Marsh and Parker, 1984; Muijs, 1997; Pajares and Schunk, 2001), one may claim that this association could also be negative. As Bandura (1997) argued, one could be quite competent in a certain domain, but still harbour low-efficacy beliefs.

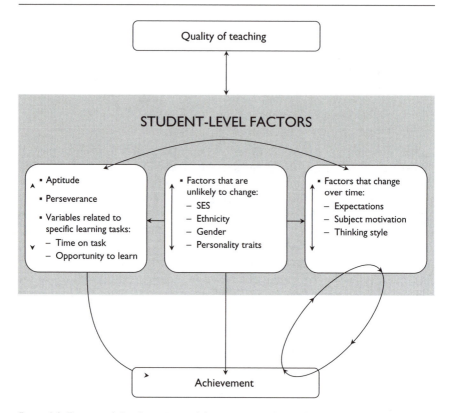

Figure 6.1 Factors of the dynamic model operating at the student level.

Finally, subject motivation is included in the dynamic model, and it is argued that a scale measuring the extent to which students like each subject is likely to be associated with their achievement gains in the particular subject (Wentzel and Wigfield, 1998). At the same time, it is taken into account that subject motivation may also be related to students' perceptions about the teacher who is offering the subject. Moreover, teacher behaviour in the classroom is likely to influence (positively or negatively) subject motivation (Baumert and Demmrich, 2001). As was mentioned above, some of the student factors, especially those that are likely to change, can be treated as outcomes of schooling (e.g. helping children to develop optimal thinking styles and to increase their motivation). However, it was made clear that EER is expected to be concerned with the intended outcomes. Therefore, according to the dynamic model, subject motivation is considered a predictor of student achievement (see Figure 6.1). In addition, longitudinal studies are needed to investigate the impact of this factor on student achievement.

Expectations

Studies conducted in Cyprus investigating the validity of Creemers' model (e.g. Kyriakides *et al.*, 2000; Kyriakides, 2005a; Kyriakides and Tsangaridou, 2004), as well as secondary analyses of international comparative studies such as the TIMSS study and the PISA study, revealed that 'expectations' is a significant student-level factor (Kyriakides and Charalambous, 2005; Valverde and Schmidt, 2000). Expectations can be measured by asking students to indicate the extent to which they believe that it is important to do well in the subject under consideration. The expectations that students believe that significant others (e.g. parents and friends) have of them could also be taken into account. This could be seen as a kind of external pressure that significant others may impose on students in their perceptions. A critical question is whether a linear or a non-linear relation with student achievement may exist, since after a certain point a negative relation with achievement might occur.

Given that there are individual differences in respect to prior achievement, teachers should be aware that this factor implies that they should hold different types of expectations of each student. Moreover, the concept of expectations should be seen as dynamic in nature. For example, as soon as a student makes progress, his or her expectations may become higher. At the same time, the demands of a series of lessons may induce different types of expectations in different students. It is therefore important to make sure that realistic expectations for and by each student are generated. This student-level factor is therefore strongly related to the classroom-level factors, and especially to self-regulation theories of learning, as is explained below.

Our decision to consider expectation as a student-level factor is also in line with the new theories about learning which refer to the idea of self-regulation and contain information about learning processes and the content of learning processes. Specifically, the basic idea behind self-regulation is that the initiation of learning and the learning processes itself and their subsequent evaluation are the responsibilities of the learner (Flavell, 1979). Therefore, the expectation is that if the self-regulation of learning is increased, outcomes will be better (Bamburg, 1994). This implies that students having high expectations are likely to initiate learning and evaluate the learning process, and, through that, develop their self-regulation (Ferrari and Mahalingam, 1988). Thus, self-regulation can be seen as a final outcome of learning, which is, however, achieved by gradually moving from external regulation towards self-regulation (Boekaerts, 1997). Moreover, the treatment of expectations as a student-level factor is partly justified by theories considering learning as goal oriented; these theories argue that initially goals and objectives are set externally, but later on, learners are focused in their learning processes and set their goals and objectives themselves (Entwistle and Smith, 2002). Therefore, both expectations of others and their own expectations are seen as predictors of students' achievement (see Figure 6.1).

Personal characteristics of students: personality traits and thinking styles

Finally, in our attempt to develop the dynamic model at the student level, we took into account the findings of the study conducted in Cyprus in order to expand the comprehensive model of educational effectiveness (Kyriakides, 2005a). It has been shown that both personality measures and thinking-style measures can be treated as predictors of student achievement gains. Since taking these two variables into account significantly reduced the unexplained variance of achievement at the student level, it was argued that personality measures and measures of thinking style should be treated as student-level factors. This argument is also supported by the fact that studies within the field of psychology reveal that types of personality and styles of thinking are associated with student achievement (see also Chapter 4).

Personality traits may be taken as the different modes of relating with the environment. There have been several models of these traits. Here we focus only on the so-called Big Five model, because it seems to dominate current research and theory. Indeed, many scholars (e.g. Goldberg, 1993; Taylor and MacDonald, 1999) have argued that the Big Five personality traits model accounts for a large amount of the variability in personality. According to this model, the factors of personality are as follows: *extraversion, agreeableness, conscientiousness, neuroticism,* and *openness to experience*. Extraverts are sociable, active, and uninhibited, as contrasted to introverts, who are withdrawn, shy, and inhibited. Agreeable individuals are soft-hearted, generous, forgiving, and warm, as contrasted to individuals low in agreeableness, who are suspicious, headstrong, argumentative, and aggressive. Conscientious individuals are organised, energetic, and reliable, as contrasted to individuals low in conscientiousness, who are lazy, careless, and immature. Neurotic individuals are nervous, anxious, tense, and self-centred, as contrasted to individuals low in neuroticism, who are emotionally stable, alert, and content. Finally, individuals who are open to experience are curious, original, imaginative, and non-traditional, and have wide interests, whereas individuals who are not open to experience are conservative and cautious (Costa and McCrae, 1997; Kohnstamn and Mervielde, 1998).

It has been shown that most of the Big Five personality traits are associated with academic performance. For example, *openness to experience* was found to be related to academic success in school (e.g. Shuerger and Kuma, 1987) and university (e.g. DeFruyt and Mervielde, 1996). The more traditional orthogonal trait variables of *extraversion* and *neuroticism* have also been associated with academic performance (Child, 1964). Recent studies revealed that extraverts underperform in academic settings because of their distractibility, sociability, and impulsiveness. The negative relation between academic achievement and *neuroticism* has usually been explained in terms of anxiety and stress under test conditions (Chamorro-Premuzic and Furnham, 2003). However, the personality factor more consistently associated with academic performance is *conscientious-*

ness (e.g. Blickle, 1996; Busato *et al.*, 1999; Chamorro-Premuzic and Furnham, 2003; Wolfe and Johnson, 1995). Thus, both intelligence and personality comprise salient individual differences that influence performance – intelligence through specific abilities that facilitate understanding and learning, and personality through certain traits that enhance and/or handicap the use of these abilities. This argument is in line with the way student-level factors are defined by the proposed dynamic model, since both aptitude and personality are treated as predictors of student achievement.

As far as the importance of treating measures of thinking style as a predictor of student achievement is concerned, it is important to note that in the search for variables that contribute to school achievement, psychologists have devoted considerable attention to the so-called stylistic aspects of cognition. The idea of a style reflecting a person's typical or habitual mode of problem-solving, thinking, perceiving, and remembering was initially introduced by Allport (1937). As was argued in Chapter 4, in the past few decades the style construct has been the subject of a great deal of research interest, and many theoretical models have been postulated. There are at least three reasons why we treat not only personality traits but also styles associated with the theory of mental self-government (Sternberg, 1988) as student-level factors. First, there are many studies which reveal that measures of thinking styles associated with this theory explain individual differences in performance not attributable to abilities (e.g. Grigorenko and Sternberg, 1997; Zhang and Sternberg, 1998; Zhang, 2001a). Second, it has been shown that the thinking styles and personality overlap is limited (see also Chapter 4). Messick (1996) suggested that style should be the construct that can be used to build a bridge between intelligence and personality in education. Similarly, Sternberg (1994) claimed that thinking styles are at the interface between intelligence and personality. This implies that not only intelligence and personality traits but also thinking styles should be taken into account in order to explain variation in student achievement. Finally, there is some evidence to support the existence of differential effectiveness in relation to student personality traits and styles of thinking (Kyriakides, 2005a).

We finally point out that there is an essential difference between these two student-level factors. Personality traits can be modified very little during one's life. Thus, personality traits are seen as 'givens' in a training or educational setting. Teachers are expected to differentiate their teaching practice in order to respond to the needs of different groups of students. On the other hand, according to the theory of mental self-government, thinking styles are seen as processes, processes that can be built on and used to compensate for or to remediate weaknesses. In this interpretation, styles are seen as dynamic. Therefore, teachers are expected to help students find or develop 'optimal' styles for particular situations in order to improve their achievement. Thus, the student-level factor concerned with the thinking style of students belongs to the category of the factors that change over time, and an important aim of education is to help students develop 'optimal' styles for particular situations. Nevertheless, as mentioned above, we do not treat the factors in this category as indicators of criteria for measuring effectiveness but as explanatory variables which teachers should take into account. For instance, teachers could attempt to teach according to individual thinking styles and personality traits. It is also supported that generic teaching skills found to be consistently correlated with student achievement (e.g. Brophy and Good, 1986; Doyle, 1986; Walberg, 1986a) do not have the same effect upon students of different thinking style and personality type (Kyriakides, 2005a). However, further research is needed not only to indicate how big the effect sizes of these two background factors are but also to find out in which way a generic teaching style can deal with different personality types and thinking styles of students. Such research may also reveal the importance of using the differentiation dimension to measure teacher-level factors.

Variables related to specific learning tasks that have emerged from the psychological perspective of EER

Our third category of variables included in the dynamic model refers to the two main student-level factors of the comprehensive model of educational effectiveness which are related to specific learning tasks (Creemers, 1994). As was mentioned in Chapter 3, Creemers (1994) developed Carroll's (1963) model of learning by adding to the general concept of opportunity (i.e. time allowed for learning) the more specific opportunity to learn. Moreover, Creemers made a distinction between available time and opportunity and actually used time and opportunity. Thus, time on task and opportunity used are seen as directly related to student achievement (see Creemers, 1994, p. 118). Since studies investigating the validity of Creemers' model provided empirical support for this assumption of the model (see Chapter 4), both variables are included in the dynamic model, and their impact on achievement will now be discussed.

Time on task (time students are really involved in learning tasks)

We have argued that achievement is determined by the background and personal characteristics of students, aptitude, and motivation. In this section, the impact of time on task on student achievement is discussed. The variable *time on task* refers to the time students are willing to spend on learning and on educational tasks, and is determined not only by motivation and expectations but also by the time provided by the school or teacher and by processes at the school and classroom levels. It is also important to note that time on task refers to the time during which students are really involved in learning, provided that this time is filled with opportunities to learn. Therefore, there are several reasons why, in our model, the variables *time on task* and *opportunity to learn* belong in the same category. An obvious reason is concerned with the fact that both variables refer to specific learning tasks that define the criteria for measuring effectiveness. In addition, these variables belong to the same category because they are not only determined by student background factors but also influence learning directly. Thus, time on task and opportunity to learn are seen as the first steps in the search for intermediary processes such as the cognitive processes of students and mediating teacher activities. In our dynamic model, time on task and opportunity to learn are put in such an intermediary position, since elements of education at classroom level, such as the ability of teachers to manage the classroom time, can contribute to an increase in time on task when they are effective (Kumar, 1991).

Our special attention to time on task stems directly from the models that have emerged from the psychological perspective of EER (see Chapter 2) and from the comprehensive model of educational effectiveness (see Chapter 3), which relate time spent on learning to achievement. It has been argued that greater quantities of allocated time and time on task and a high level of task relevance enhance achievement (see Fond Lam, 1996). In a teaching strategy for effective reading instruction developed by Marzano *et al.* (1987), the various aspects of academic learning time were converted into teacher interventions. Several studies then related teacher actions to learning time. As a consequence, positive correlations between several aspects of learning time and achievement were identified. It was shown that allocated time, especially the proportion of allocated time students spend on learning (i.e. time on task), was essential in the relationship between learning time and student achievement. This holds not only for the 'regular/typical' classroom situation but also for students at risk (e.g. Brophy, 1992; Gettinger, 1991; Greenwood, 1991). However, Gage, among others, criticised the concept of effective teaching time because of its psychologically empty and quantitative nature. According to Gage (1977, p. 75), it is necessary to investigate what kinds of activities are offered during this learning time, and what learning processes take place. Nevertheless, this argument cannot necessarily be seen as a criticism of the concept of time on task, but it basically implies that beyond the time on task factor, factors concerned with the quality of teaching and the quality of the content of teaching offered during the learning time should be examined. As we shall see, this criticism is taken on board, and variables concerned with the quality of teaching as well as the variable *opportunity to learn* are treated as effectiveness factors at the teacher, school, and context levels.

Opportunity to learn

The variable *opportunity to learn* refers to the fact that in order to achieve educational outcomes, students should at least have some opportunity to acquire knowledge and skills. Actually, in international comparative studies, the presentation of subjects in curricula and/or by teachers has been called 'opportunity to learn'. This variable was initially measured by checking whether subjects reflected in test items were present in education. Large-scale studies often measure 'opportunity to learn' in a simple but unreliable manner, for example, by measuring years spent in education and/or by looking at the policies in the school curriculum on the topics to be covered in the attended grades. A less easy but more reliable measurement technique is to ask teachers to keep a logbook in which they write down the subject areas that are covered in their classroom and are related to the test items. Teachers may also indicate how they taught each of these curriculum areas. Classroom observation is an even more valid technique, since teachers do not always stick to intended curricular contents; sometimes additional subjects are offered more or less extensively (Creemers, 1994).

Despite the difficulties of measuring opportunity to learn at classroom or even at higher level, this variable has been included in international studies conducted by the IEA, which show that variations between countries in the opportunity to learn are very large (Campbell and Kyriakides, 2000). These are related to the age of selection and to the degree of tracking in the educational system. Moreover, the opportunity to learn and student achievement have been found to be more closely related in countries with a tracked educational system. This variation is one of the reasons why, among others, Oakes and Lipton (1990) criticise tracking in American education, where depending on their class levels, students get different opportunities to learn. Lugthart et al. (1989) present an overview of studies looking at the relationship between opportunity to learn and student achievement. These studies reveal the importance of the variable *opportunity to learn* in accounting for variations between schools and teachers. Variation increases when students are the unit of analysis, since differences in curricula are not the only source that creates variation in opportunity to learn. Other overview studies confirm the importance of opportunity to learn, and in educational policy the research findings are used in the formulation of standards for education (Guiton and Oakes 1995; McDonnell 1995). In recent debates, opportunity to learn as an indicator for the content of education is mixed with process characteristics relating to the quality of education, which might confuse the concept (Schwartz, 1995).

Studies investigating the validity of Creemers' model (e.g. de Jong et al., 2004; Kyriakides, 2005a; Kyriakides et al., 2000) have revealed that time spent doing homework and time spent on private tuition could also be seen as measures of the opportunity to learn factor. These measures of the opportunity factor were also found to be closely related to student achievement (e.g. Brookhart, 1997; Trautwein et al., 2002). However, it has to be acknowledged that the amount of time students spend voluntarily on specific learning tasks (e.g. tasks in mathematics, music, physical education) may be seen not only as a measure of opportunity to learn but also as an indicator of students' interests and motivation concerning the subject associated with these tasks. Moreover, spending additional time on private tuition or on homework does not necessarily mean that the students make use of this extra time for learning purposes (Kyriakides and Tsangaridou, in press). Therefore, a distinction is made between learning opportunities offered in the instructional process during and/or after the school time and the actual use of these opportunities that each student makes (see also Creemers, 1994). In this context the students' use of opportunities to learn is treated as a student-level factor whereas the findings of studies investigating the impact of opportunity to learn on student achievement are taken into account in defining factors at teacher, school, and context levels.

At the same time, we acknowledge the difficulty of measuring the variable opportunities used and stress the need to conduct studies exploring the impact of this variable on student achievement. Such studies may also reveal the importance of making a distinction between the variable *opportunities used* and the more general variable *opportunity to learn*.

Factors operating at the classroom or teacher level

In Chapter 5 the essential characteristics of the dynamic model were described. It was mentioned that a framework for measuring effectiveness factors has been adopted. Thus, the five measurement dimensions of the dynamic model have been described. In order to better explain how these five dimensions can be used to establish such a model, this section refers to the specific measurement of the eight factors concerning teacher behaviour in the classroom (see Figure 6.2) which, according to the dynamic model, are related to student achievement gains. As was mentioned in the introduction to this chapter, teacher background characteristics that might explain variance in teacher behaviour in the classroom are not included in the model because the model concentrates on the learning of students and student achievement gains. Specifically, on the basis of the main findings of teacher effectiveness research (e.g. Brophy and Good, 1986; Darling-Hammond, 2000; Doyle, 1990; Dunne and Wragg, 1994; Kyriakides et al., 2002; Muijs and Reynolds, 2000; Rosenshine and Stevens, 1986; Wang et al., 1993), our dynamic model refers to eight effectiveness factors that describe teachers' instructional role: orientation, structuring, questioning, teaching-modelling, applications, teacher role in making classroom a learning environment, management of time, and classroom assessment. These eight factors do not refer only to one approach of teaching such as the direct teaching model or the constructivist approach. In Chapter 2 it was mentioned that an integrated approach in defining quality of teaching should be adopted. Therefore, we refer not only to skills associated with direct teaching and mastery learning such as structuring and questioning but also to orientation and teaching-modelling, which are in line with new theories of teaching. In recent years, constructivists and others who support the 'new learning' approach (e.g. Choi and Hannafin, 1995; Collins et al., 1989; Savery and Duffy, 1995; Simons et al., 2000; Vermunt and Vershaffel, 2000) have developed a set of instructional techniques that are supposed to enhance the learning disposition of students such as modelling, coaching, scaffolding and fading, articulating, reflection, exploration, generalisation, collaborative learning, provision of anchors, goal orientation, and self-regulated learning. Creemers (2007) has demonstrated that the eight factors of the dynamic model at least partly cover all these approaches. For example, the collaboration technique is included under the overarching factor *contribution of teacher to the classroom learning environment*. Most of these approaches are subsumed in the factors *teaching-modelling* and *orientation*. Thus, the eight factors of the dynamic model will now be described

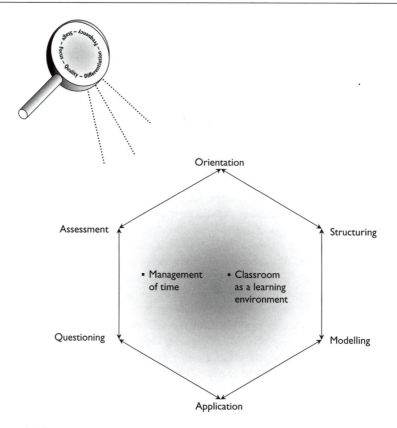

Figure 6.2 Factors of the dynamic model operating at the classroom level.

and will help us identify the importance of using the model to improve teaching practice and provide learning opportunities to students of different socio-cultural groups.

Orientation

Orientation refers to the teacher behaviour of providing the objectives for which a specific task, lesson, or series of lessons takes place and/or challenging students to identify during the lesson the reason why a particular activity takes place. It is expected that the engagement of students with orientation tasks might encourage them to participate actively in the classroom, since it makes the tasks that take place meaningful for them (e.g. De Corte, 2000; Paris and Paris, 2001). In this context the measurement of this factor using the five proposed measurement dimensions will now be described.

FREQUENCY

The measurement of frequency is based on an examination of the number of orientation tasks that take place in a typical lesson as well as how long each orientation task takes place. These two indicators may help us identify the importance attached to this factor.

FOCUS

As far as the focus dimension is concerned, it is possible that an orientation task may refer to a part of a lesson, to the whole lesson, or even to a series of lessons (e.g. a lesson unit). This classification refers to the specificity of the orientation task. The second aspect of focus, which refers to the purpose of the activity, can be measured by examining the extent to which an orientation task is restricted to finding one single reason for doing a task or to finding multiple reasons for doing it. The measurement of this dimension of orientation reveals the extent to which teachers help their students understand the importance of finding the meanings of each task in which they are expected to be involved.

STAGE

Stage, the third dimension of measuring orientation, refers to the stage at which an activity takes place. It is expected that orientation tasks will take place in different parts of a lesson or series of lessons (e.g. introduction, core, ending of the lesson) and in lessons that are expected to achieve different objectives. Further, it is expected that the teacher will be able to take other perspectives into account during these orientation tasks. For example, students may come with suggestions for the reasons for carrying out a specific task, which an effective teacher is expected to take into account (Gijbels *et al.*, 2006).

QUALITY

The measurement of the dimension quality refers to the properties of the orientation task, especially to whether it is clear for the students and whether it has any impact on their learning. For example, teachers may present the reasons for carrying out a task simply because they have to do it as part of their teaching routine, without having much effect on student participation. In contrast, others may encourage students to identify the purposes that can be achieved by carrying out a task and therefore increase their students' motivation towards a specific task, or lesson, or series of lessons (Kyriakides 2006a).

DIFFERENTIATION

Finally, differentiation is measured in a similar way for each of the eight factors. In the case of orientation it is assumed that effective teachers are those who provide different types of orientation tasks to students by taking into account differences in (1) the personal and background characteristics of their students, (2) the teaching objectives, and (3) the organisational and cultural context of their school or classroom. Research into differential teacher effectiveness reveals the importance of adapting teaching by taking into account these three dimensions of differences (Kyriakides and Tsangaridou, in press).

Structuring

Rosenshine and Stevens (1986) point out that achievement is maximised when teachers not only actively present materials but structure it by (1) beginning with overviews and/or review of objectives, (2) outlining the content to be covered and signalling transitions between lesson parts, (3) calling attention to main ideas, and (4) reviewing main ideas at the end of the lesson. Summary reviews are also important, since they integrate and reinforce the learning of major points (Brophy and Good, 1986). It can be claimed that these structuring elements not only facilitate memorising of the information but allow for its apprehension as an integrated whole, with recognition of the relationships between parts (Case, 1993). Moreover, achievement is higher when information is presented with a degree of redundancy, particularly in the form of repeating and reviewing general views and key concepts (e.g. Leinhardt et al., 1987). Therefore, structuring is measured as follows.

FREQUENCY

The dimension frequency is measured by taking into account the number of structuring tasks that take place in a typical lesson as well as how long each task takes place (e.g. the percentage of teaching time spent on structuring).

FOCUS

The focus dimension is measured by investigating whether a structuring task refers to a part of a lesson, to the whole lesson, or even to a series of lessons (e.g. a lesson unit). As far as the second aspect of focus is concerned, a structuring task may refer to the achievement of a single objective or to the relation of the elements of the lesson in relation to multiple objectives. It is expected that the structuring tasks which have a strong impact on student behaviour are those that refer to the achievement of multiple objectives, since the tasks that refer to a single objective may increase the fragmentation of the learning process.

STAGE

The stage dimension of structuring is measured in the same way as in the case of orientation. It is, therefore, taken into account that structuring tasks may take place in different parts of a lesson or series of lessons (e.g. introduction, core, ending of the lesson).

QUALITY

The dimension of quality is measured by examining the impact that the task has on student learning. It is expected that structuring tasks not only are clear for the students but also help them understand the structure of the lesson. For this reason, clarity is not seen as a property of structuring or as an independent factor of teacher effectiveness. Clarity is seen as a condition for helping students to understand the structure and the content of a lesson or series of lessons. Moreover, the properties of a structuring task are examined. Specifically, we investigate the extent to which teachers organise their lessons or series of lessons in such a way as to move from easier tasks to more complicated ones. This assumption is based on the fact that research on teacher effectiveness reveals that students learn more when the information is not only well structured but also sufficiently redundant and well sequenced (Armento, 1977; Nuthall and Church, 1973; Smith and Sanders, 1981).

DIFFERENTIATION

Finally, in the case of structuring, differentiation is measured by investigating the extent to which teachers provide different types of structuring tasks to students according to their learning needs. Teachers are also expected to take into account the objectives of their lessons in providing structuring tasks.

Questioning techniques

Muijs and Reynolds (2000) indicate that effective teachers ask numerous questions and attempt to involve students in class discussion. Although the data on the cognitive level of question yield inconsistent results (Redfield and Rousseau, 1981), the developmental level of students defines, to a large extent, optimal question difficulty. It seems clear that most questions (almost 75 per cent) should elicit correct answers (Anderson et al., 1979; Brophy and Evertson, 1976) and that most of the rest should elicit overt, substantive responses (incorrect or incomplete answers) rather than failures to respond at all (Anderson et al., 1979; Brophy and Good, 1986). Optimal question difficulty should also vary with context. For example, basic skills instruction requires a great deal of drill and practice, and thus requires frequent fast-paced review in which most questions are answered rapidly and correctly. However, when teaching complex cognitive content or trying to get students to generalise, evaluate, or apply their learning, effective teachers usually raise questions that few students can answer correctly or that have no single correct answer at all.

Brophy (1986) argues that issues surrounding the cognitive level of questions cannot be reduced to frequency norms. Researchers should take into account the teacher's objectives, the quality of the questions, and their timing appropriateness. As far as their timing appropriateness is concerned, Bennett et al. (1981) pointed out that not only the frequency of errors is important but also their timing and quality. Early in a unit, when new learning is occurring, relatively frequent errors may be expected. Later, when mastery levels should have been achieved, errors should be minimal. It has been shown that there should be a mix of product questions (i.e. expecting a single response from students) and process questions (i.e. expecting students to provide explanations). Effective teachers are also expected to ask more process questions (Askew and William, 1995; Evertson et al., 1980).

FREQUENCY

Therefore, the frequency dimension has to be measured by taking into account not only the total number of questions but also the ratio between process and product questions. Another way of measuring the frequency dimension of this factor has to do with the length of pause following questions, which is expected to vary according to the difficulty level of questions. Brophy and Good (1986) point out that a question calling for application of abstract principles should require a longer pause than a factual question.

FOCUS

The focus dimension of this factor is measured by looking at the type of each question and especially at its relation to the tasks that take place during a lesson (i.e. specificity), as well as to the objectives that are expected to be achieved through asking the question.

STAGE

As far as the measurement of stage is concerned, it is taken into account that teachers may raise questions at different parts of the lesson and for different reasons. For example, teachers may ask questions during the introduction of the lesson in order to link the new lesson with previous lessons, and during the core of the lesson in order to discover problem(s) that students have with the content of the lesson or identify need(s) for further clarification. Questions may also be raised at the end of the lesson as part of an attempt by the teacher to assess students for formative reasons. Thus, the measurement of this dimension needs to be shifted from the individual question to the question sequences as the unit of analysis (Brophy, 1992).

QUALITY

Quality is measured by taking into account the clarity of a question, especially the extent to which students understand what they are expected to find out. Sometimes questions are vague, or the teacher asks two or more questions without stopping to get an answer. Another property that is also measured is the appropriateness of the difficulty level of the question; it is possible that students may understand the question but still do not answer because it is too difficult for them. Furthermore, quality is measured by looking at the way in which the teacher deals with student responses. Correct responses should be acknowledged as such, because even if the respondent may know that the answer is correct, some other students may not. Responses that are partly correct require affirmation of the correct part and rephrasing of the question (Brophy and Good, 1986; Rosenshine and Stevens, 1986). Following incorrect answers, teachers should begin by indicating that the response is not correct but avoid personal criticism and show why the answer is incorrect (Rosenshine, 1971). In responding to students' partly correct or incorrect answers, effective teachers not only acknowledge whatever part may be correct, but if there is a good prospect for success, they try to elicit an improved response. Therefore, effective teachers are more likely than other teachers to sustain the interaction with the original respondent by rephrasing the question or giving clues rather than to terminate it by giving the answer or calling on someone else (Anderson *et al.*, 1979; Clark *et al.*, 1979).

DIFFERENTIATION

Finally, differentiation is measured by looking at the extent to which teachers direct questions to specific students or take answers from specific students. It is also expected that the pauses following questions will vary in their complexity or cognitive level (Tobin, 1987). Moreover, the feedback that teachers give to student answers varies according to the learning needs of students and their personal characteristics (i.e. personality type and thinking styles). Furthermore, it is expected that the types of questions used by the teacher will depend on his or her teaching objectives and the characteristics of his or her students (Altiere and Duell, 1991). Effective teachers are expected to take into account the goals of each lesson when asking questions. For example, sometimes they may begin with a higher-level question and then proceed with several lower-level follow-up questions, since this has been found to be an appropriate approach for some objectives (e.g. asking students to suggest an application of an idea and then probing for details). A different objective (e.g. stimulating students to integrate certain facts and draw a conclusion from them) may require a series of lower-level questions (to call attention to the relevant facts) followed by higher-level questions.

Teaching-modelling

Although there is a long tradition in research on teaching higher-order thinking skills and especially problem-solving, these teaching and learning activities have been given more attention during the past decade, owing to the emphasis in policy on the achievement of the new goals of education (Aparicio and Moneo, 2005; Boekaerts, 1997; Creemers, 1994). Thus, EER has shown that effective teachers help students to use strategies and/or develop their own strategies which can help them solve different types of problems (Creemers and Kyriakides, 2005a). As a result of this, it is more likely that students will develop skills that help them organise their own learning (e.g. self-regulation, active learning) (Kraiger *et al.*, 1993). The measurement of the teaching-modelling factor using the five proposed measurement dimensions will therefore now be described.

FREQUENCY

The frequency dimension of teaching-modelling can be measured by looking at the number of teaching-modelling tasks that take place in a lesson and the teaching time devoted to them.

FOCUS

As far as the focus is concerned, teaching-modelling tasks can be examined in relation to the extent to which they refer to strategies that can be used to solve problems under various conditions (e.g. problems of different subjects). This measure refers to the specificity aspect of the focus dimension. Moreover, focus can be seen in relation to the extent to which teachers provide opportunities for students to use or develop more than one strategy to solve specific problems, or types of problems (Kyriakides *et al.*, 2006a; Marshall, 1995).

STAGE

The stage dimension is concerned with the sequence under which a teaching-modelling task is offered. It is possible that initially students are faced with a problem and then are expected to use, or develop, a particular strategy to solve it. On the other hand, teachers may teach a strategy or different strategies to students, and then students are asked to use these strategies in order to solve a problem.

QUALITY

The measure of the quality deals with the properties of teaching-modelling tasks, and especially with the role that the teacher is expected to play in order to help students to use a strategy to solve their problems. Effective teachers may either present a strategy with clarity or invite students to explain how they solve a problem and subsequently use that information for promoting the idea of modelling. The latter approach may encourage students not only to use but also to develop their own strategies for solving problems.

DIFFERENTIATION

Differentiation can be seen in terms of adapting teaching-modelling to the specific needs of a group of students. These might result in (1) more emphasis on applying a single strategy for a group of students to solve problems, (2) more emphasis on using multiple strategies for a group of students, and (3) the development of different strategies for different groups of students. Effective teachers are also expected to take into account the different thinking styles of their students when presenting strategies for problem-solving (Kyriakides, 2005a; Sternberg, 1988).

Application

Effective teachers also use seatwork or small-group tasks since they provide needed practice and application opportunities (Borich, 1992). This factor is linked to the direct teaching model (Rosenshine, 1983), which emphasises the immediate exercise of topics taught during the lesson and direct feedback provided by the teacher at either an individual or a group level. Thus, the measurement of this factor will now be illustrated.

FREQUENCY

First, the frequency dimension can be measured by looking at the total time devoted to application tasks (e.g. percentage of teaching time). This measure reveals the emphasis given by teachers to this classroom-level factor.

FOCUS

Focus is measured by investigating the specificity of the application tasks that students are expected to perform. Specifically, we can examine the extent to which the application tasks refer to some parts of the lesson, to the whole lesson, or even to a series of lessons. This way of measurement is also related to the second aspect of focus, since it enables us to examine the number of purposes that are expected to be achieved by each application task.

STAGE

The stage dimension is measured in the same way as for all other classroom-level factors. Specifically, it is considered important to look at the phase of the lesson in which each application task takes place. The extent to which application tasks are offered at only some phases of a lesson and/or a series of lessons is identified.

QUALITY

To measure the quality of the application tasks, the appropriateness of each task is measured by looking at the extent to which the students are asked simply to repeat what they had already covered with their teacher or whether the application task is more complex than the content covered in the lesson, perhaps even being used as a starting point for the next step in teaching and learning. The extent to which application tasks are used as starting points of learning can also be seen as an indication of the impact that application tasks have on students.

DIFFERENTIATION

Finally, differentiation refers to the extent to which teachers give more opportunities for application to students who need them (e.g. low-achieving students). It also refers to teacher behaviour in monitoring, supervising, and giving corrective feedback during application activities. Brophy and Good (1986) argue that once the students are released to work independently, effective teachers circulate to monitor progress and provide help and feedback. However, effective teachers are expected to provide encouragement for their efforts more frequently to low-SES and low-achieving students and to praise their success (Kyriakides and Creemers, 2006b).

The classroom as a learning environment: the contribution of the teacher

Classroom climate is a factor that teacher effectiveness research has found to be significant (e.g. Creemers and Reezigt, 1996; Kyriakides et al., 2002; Muijs and Reynolds, 2000). The climate is usually seen as associated with the behaviour of the stakeholders, whereas culture is seen as measuring the values and norms of the organisation (Heck and Marcoulides, 1996; Hoy et al., 1990). A healthy organisation deals effectively with outside forces while directing its energies towards its goals. Classroom climate research is described as the stepchild of psychological and classroom research (Creemers and Reezigt, 1996). The classroom effects research tradition initially focused on climate factors defined as managerial techniques (e.g. Doyle, 1986). Management is necessary to create conditions for learning and instruction, but management itself is not sufficient to achieve good student results (Creemers, 1994). On the other hand, the psychological tradition of classroom environment research paid a great deal of attention to instruments for the measuring of students' perceptions of climate. Many studies report on their psychometric characteristics (Fraser, 1991), but climate factors (such as the way a teacher behaves towards the students) and effectiveness factors (e.g. quality of teaching) have been studied as isolated constructs (Johnson and Johnson, 1993; Wubbels et al., 1991). In this context the definition of the classroom learning environment adopted here is an attempt to integrate elements of different research traditions. Thus, the dynamic model refers to the teacher's contribution in creating a learning environment in his or her classroom, and five elements of the classroom as a learning environment are taken into account: teacher–student interaction, student–student interaction, students' treatment by the teacher, competition between students, and classroom disorder. The first two elements are important components of measuring classroom climate, as classroom environment research has shown (Cazden, 1986; den Brok et al., 2004; Fraser, 1991). However, the dynamic model refers to the type of interactions that exist in a classroom rather than to how students perceive teacher interpersonal behaviour. The other three elements refer to the attempt of teachers to create a businesslike and supportive environment for learning (Walberg, 1986a). The ways used to measure these five elements are briefly described in what follows. Specifically, interactions are measured by taking into account the role of the teacher in establishing interaction between students (e.g. Rohrbeck *et al.*, 2003; Slavin, 1983; Slavin and Cooper, 1999) and between students and the teacher him- or herself (Emmer and Stough, 2001; Košir, 2005).

FREQUENCY

The dimension frequency refers to the number of interactions taking place between students and between students and the teacher.

FOCUS

Focus is measured by classifying each interaction according to the purpose(s) that it is expected to serve (e.g. managerial reasons, learning, social encounter).

STAGE

As far as the stage is concerned, interactions are seen in relation to the phase of the lesson in which they take place.

QUALITY

Quality is measured by investigating the immediate impact that teacher initiatives have on the establishing of relevant interactions. We are mainly interested in identifying the extent to which the teacher is able to establish on-task behaviour through the interactions she or he promotes, since several studies (e.g. de Jong *et al.*, 2004; Kyriakides, 2005a; Teddlie and Reynolds, 2000), as well as the comprehensive model of effectiveness (Creemers, 1994), emphasise the importance of keeping students on task.

DIFFERENTIATION

Finally, differentiation is measured by looking at the different strategies the teacher uses in order to keep different groups of students involved in the classroom interactions, which promotes student learning.

As far as the other three elements of this classroom-level factor are concerned, they are measured by taking into account the teacher's ability to establish rules, persuade students to respect and use the rules, and maintain them in order to create a learning environment in his or her classroom (Evertson and Harris, 1992; Marzano and Marzano, 2003). The first element refers to more general problems that can arise when students do not believe that they are treated fairly and respected as individual persons by their teacher, whereas the other two deal with specific situations in the classroom that might create difficulties in promoting learning (i.e. competition between students, classroom disorder). Therefore, the measurement of these three elements of the overarching factor concerned with the classroom as a learning environment will now be described.

FREQUENCY

Frequency is measured by looking at the number of problems that arise in the classroom (e.g. classroom disorder, fights between two students) and the various ways that teachers deal with them.

FOCUS

Focus is measured by looking at the specificity of the problem that is observed (e.g. an incidental one or a continuous one that takes the classroom back to problems that were not solved successfully), as well as at the reaction of the teacher in terms of the purpose(s) that he or she is attempting to achieve (e.g. solving only the specific problem or creating an atmosphere that avoids the further existence of similar problems). For example, if the way teachers deal with negative effects of competition is being investigated, the teacher can either deal with the specific problem that arises or put the problem in a more general perspective to help students see the positive aspects of competition and avoid the negative ones.

STAGE

The stage dimension is measured by looking at the phase of the lesson at which the problem arises.

QUALITY

Quality is seen in relation to the impact that the teacher's behaviour has on solving the problem(s) that arise, as measured through students' behaviour. For example, a teacher may not use any strategy at all to deal with a classroom disorder problem, may use a strategy that solves the problem only temporarily, or may use a strategy that has a long-lasting effect.

DIFFERENTIATION

Differentiation is measured by looking at the extent to which teachers use different strategies to deal with problems caused by different groups of students. For example, individual student(s) might cause a problem in order to attract attention from classmates and/or the teacher. It is probably a better strategy not to pay attention when the problem is small, since any reaction from the teacher may lead to problems continuing. Similarly, effective teachers attempt to change the classroom participation rules if they find out that classroom disorder problems are caused by a group of students owing to the fact that the existing rules are not sensitive to the difference between participation rules common in some cultural groups and those typical of conventional schools.

Management of time

The comprehensive model of educational effectiveness (Creemers, 1994) considers opportunity to learn and time on task as two of the most significant effectiveness factors, and they operate at different levels. Moreover, opportunity to learn is related to student engagement and time on task (Emmer and Evertson, 1981). Therefore, effective teachers are expected to organise and manage the classroom environment as an efficient learning environment and thereby to maximise engagement rates (e.g. Creemers and Reezigt, 1996; Emmer et al., 1980; Wilks, 1996). In this context, the dynamic model supports the argument that management of time is one of the most important indicators of a teacher's ability to manage the classroom in an effective way.

FREQUENCY

Thus, frequency is measured by taking into account how much time is used for teaching per lesson and how much time is covered within the time framework.

FOCUS

The focus dimension is not measured separately, since the main interest of this factor is whether students are on task or off task.

STAGE

Stage is measured by taking into account the time allocated to different phases of the lesson.

QUALITY

As far as the quality dimension is concerned, this is measured through the data collected in relation to the factor concerning the role of the teacher in creating a learning environment in his or her classroom. Specifically, we are looking at the actions taken by the teacher to maximise the learning time during the lesson by dealing with disturbing factors, as these are described in the factor concerning the classroom as a learning environment.

DIFFERENTIATION

Finally, differentiation is measured by looking at the allocation of time for different groups of students.

Assessment

Assessment is seen as an integral part of teaching (Delandshere, 2002; Stenmark, 1992; Willis, 1993); formative assessment, especially, is one of the most important factors associated with effectiveness at all levels, especially at the classroom level (de Jong *et al.*, 2004; Kyriakides, 2005a; Shepard, 1989). Information gathered from student assessment should enable teachers to identify their students' needs as well as to evaluate their own teaching practice (Krasne *et al.*, 2006; Kyriakides, 2004b). As a consequence, the measurement of this factor according to the proposed measurement framework is provided below.

FREQUENCY

Frequency is measured in terms of the number of assessment tasks and the time they take. It is expected that there will be a curvilinear relation between the frequency of teacher evaluation and student outcomes, since an overemphasis on evaluation might reduce the actual time spent on teaching and learning. On the other hand, teachers who do not collect any information are not able to adapt their teaching to student needs.

FOCUS

Focus is measured by looking at the ability of a teacher to use a range of different ways of measuring student skills (Rao *et al.*, 2002). It is also important to examine whether the teacher makes more than one use of the information she or he collects (e.g. identifying needs of students, conducting self-evaluation, adopting her or his long-term planning, using evaluation tasks as a starting point for teaching) (Black and Wiliam, 1998).

STAGE

Stage is measured by investigating the period at which the evaluation tasks take place (e.g. at the beginning of, during, and at the end of a lesson or unit of lessons) and the time lapse between collecting information, recording the results, reporting the results to students and parents, and using them for planning lessons.

QUALITY

Quality is measured by looking at the properties of the evaluation instruments used by the teacher, such as the different forms of validity, the internal and external reliability, the practicality, and the extent to which the instruments cover the teaching content (AERA, APA, and NCME, 1999; Cronbach, 1990; Kyriakides, 2004b; Popham, 1997). We also examine the type of feedback the teacher gives to his or her students and the way students use the teacher feedback. Effective teachers are expected to provide constructive feedback that has positive implications for teaching and learning (Bennetts, 2005; Brookhart, 2004; Muijs and Reynolds, 2001).

DIFFERENTIATION

Finally, differentiation is examined in relation to the extent to which teachers use different techniques for measuring student needs and/or different ways to provide feedback to different groups of students by taking into account their background and personal characteristics, such as their thinking style (Kyriakides, 2005a). It is also considered important for teachers to take into account the fact that students' perceptions of the importance of testing may vary because of differences in their background characteristics, and this variation in perceptions may explain variation in achievement. For example, some Native American cultures value cooperation rather than independent achievement. Therefore, teaching and assessment that relies on or encourages a high need for achievement may be maladaptive for some Native American children. In addition, ability and achievement tests that assume a high need for achievement may result in underestimates for such groups of students.

Factors at the classroom level not included in the model

In the second section of this chapter we referred to the eight factors operating at the classroom level of the dynamic model which are concerned with teacher behaviour in the classroom. This last section is an attempt to acknowledge the fact that other classroom-level factors may have an indirect impact on achievement. For example, some teacher background factors, such as subject knowledge, pedagogical knowledge, and teacher expectations, may influence different dimensions of teacher behaviour such as those described above. Although we acknowledge the importance of these factors, we restrict our model to the classroom factors that may have a direct impact on student learning through the actions of the teacher that can be observed in classroom.

It should also be acknowledged that curriculum is not treated as a factor operating at classroom level. Creemers (1994) distinguishes three components of the quality of classroom instruction (i.e. curriculum, grouping procedures, and teacher behaviour). As far as the grouping procedures are concerned, Creemers (1994) pointed out that there are conflicting research findings. Moreover, the implementation of grouping procedures is examined by looking at the factors concerned with teacher behaviour and through the use of different dimensions to measure teacher behaviour (e.g. differentiation).

As far as the treatment of the curriculum component is concerned, our decision to treat it not as a classroom-level but as a school-level factor can be attributed to the way curriculum is conceptualised here. According to both the dynamic model and the comprehensive model, teachers are considered to be the central component in instruction. It is teachers who make use of curricular materials, and carry out grouping procedures (such as mastery learning, ability grouping, and cooperative learning). This implies that both models hold that the most important classroom factor is teacher behaviour. However, it could be claimed that curriculum should be considered as a classroom-level factor of the dynamic model, since it affects opportunity to learn. Nevertheless, the fact that we do not treat the official curriculum as a classroom-level factor has to do with the way the term 'curriculum' is conceptualised.

It is taken into account that the literature refers to three different forms of curriculum: the intended curriculum, which refers to the expected standards (i.e. the standards set through educational policy in official curricula); the implemented curriculum, which refers to the way teachers plan and deliver the official curricula for their particular class; and the achieved curriculum, which reveals the standards attained by students on a given set of test items (Campbell and Kyriakides, 2000; Schmidt *et al.*, 1997). All three forms of curriculum are taken into account by the proposed dynamic model. Since our model refers to criteria of measuring effectiveness which emerge from the official curriculum, the measurement of the outcomes of schooling is expected to help us identify the achieved curriculum. The eight factors operating at the classroom level of the dynamic model help us measure the implemented curriculum. Finally, the intended curriculum is considered to be a factor affecting opportunity to learn at either the school and/or the context level (see Chapter 7). This can be attributed to the fact that in most countries, teachers at the same school use the same curriculum, and that is the reason why the curriculum in this study cannot be treated as a classroom factor. It is also important to note that policy-makers assume that setting standards at the national level feeds directly into both teachers' planning and student attainment – and thereby that raising standards helps. However, this assumption is problematic, as the meta-analysis by Wang *et al.* (1990) and secondary analyses of international comparative studies (e.g. Campbell and Kyriakides, 2000; Kyriakides and Charalambous, 2005) have revealed. These studies concluded that educational policy variables had little association with learning outcomes, whereas classroom or psychological variables which are associated with teacher behaviour in the classroom (e.g. classroom management, quantity of instruction, classroom climate, peer group influence) were more important. The above conceptualisation of the curriculum and the findings of studies investigating the impact of national policy variables on school effectiveness provide support for our argument that all factors operating at the classroom level should refer to teacher behaviour in the classroom, which defines quality of teaching.

Chapter 7

The dynamic model

Factors operating at school and context levels

Introduction

Factors of the dynamic model operating at the student and classroom levels were presented in the previous chapter. This chapter will describe the dynamic model at the school and context levels. We shall show how our measurement framework is used to define each school- and context-level factor of the proposed dynamic model. Some evidence supporting the importance of each factor will also be provided. More information regarding the importance of effectiveness factors will be provided in Part III of the book. Specifically, Chapter 9 will refer to the results of a meta-analysis of studies searching for school-level factors that have been conducted during the past two decades. The results of this analysis provide further justification for the importance to be accorded to the factors in the dynamic model that operate at the school level. Finally, the importance of searching for interactions among factors operating at the same level will be discussed.

Effectiveness factors at the school level

The definition of the school level is based on the assumption that factors at the school level are expected to have not only direct effects on student achievement but also effects that are mainly indirect (see Chapter 5). School factors are expected to influence classroom-level factors, especially the teaching practice. This assumption is based on the fact that EER studies show that the classroom level is more significant than the school and the system levels (e.g. Kyriakides *et al.*, 2000; Yair, 1997; Teddlie and Reynolds, 2000) and that defining factors at the class-room level is seen as a prerequisite for defining the school and the system levels (Creemers, 1994). Therefore, the dynamic model refers to factors at the school level that are related to the same key concepts of quantity of teaching, provision of learning opportunities, and quality of teaching as were used to define classroom-level factors (see Chapter 6). Specifically, emphasis is given to the following two main aspects of the school policy which affect learning at the levels both of teachers and of students: (1) school policy regarding teaching, and (2) school policy regarding creating a learning environment at school. Guidelines are seen as one of the main indications of school policy, and this is reflected in the way each school-level factor is presented in this chapter. However, in using the term 'guidelines' we refer to a range of documents, such as minutes of staff meetings, announcements, and action plans, that make the policy of the school more concrete to the teachers and other stakeholders. It should also be acknowledged that this factor does not imply that each school should simply develop formal documents to install the policy. The factors concerned with the school policy mainly refer to the actions taken by the school to help teachers and other stakeholders have a clear understanding of what they are expected to do. Support offered to teachers and other stakeholders to implement the school policy is also an aspect of these two overarching factors. The term 'policy' is also used in a similar way to describe a relevant overarching factor at the context level concerned with national educational policy (see the second section of this chapter).

On the assumption that the essence of a successful organisation in the modern world is the search for improvement (Barber, 1986; Kyriakides and Campbell, 2004), we also examine the processes and the activities that take place in the school for the purpose of improving the teaching practice and the learning environment. For this reason, the processes that are used to evaluate the school policy for teaching and the learning environment of the school are investigated. Thus, the following four overarching factors at the school level are included in the model:

- school policy regarding teaching, and actions taken to improve teaching in practice;
- evaluation of school policy regarding teaching, and actions taken to improve teaching;
- policy towards creating a school learning environment and actions taken towards improving the school learning environment;
- evaluation of the learning environment.

Note that leadership is not considered as a school-level factor. This can be attributed to the fact that a current meta-analysis of studies investigating the possible impact of the principal's leadership on student achievement confirms earlier research findings on the limitations of the direct effects approach to linking leadership with student achievement (Witziers et al., 2003). Similar results have been obtained from the few studies conducted in order to measure indirect effects of leadership on student achievement (Leithwood and Jantzi, 2006). Therefore, the model is concerned not with who is in charge of designing and/or implementing the school policy but with the content of the school policy and the types of activities that take place in school. This reveals one of the major assumptions of the model, which is focused not on individuals as such but on the effects of the actions that take place at classroom, and school, and context levels. This holds for the students, teachers, principals, and policy-makers. Our decision is also consistent with the way classroom-level factors are measured, since instead of measuring the teaching style of the teacher, we are focused on the actual behaviour of the teacher in the classroom. Similarly, instead of measuring the leadership style of a principal we look at the impact of the end result of leadership (e.g. the development of school policy on teaching or the evaluation of school policy). As far as the context-level factors are concerned, we examine not the leadership style of policy-makers (e.g. the use of specific approaches in administering the system) but the content of the national policy, which reveals the end result of the activities that policy-makers undertake. A description of each overarching factor operating at the school level will now follow.

School policy for teaching and actions taken for improving teaching

Since the definition of the dynamic model at the classroom level refers to factors related to the key concepts of quality, time on task, and opportunity to learn, the model attempts to investigate aspects of school policy for teaching associated with quantity of teaching, provision of learning opportunities, and quality of teaching (Creemers and Kyriakides, 2005b). Actions taken to improve these three aspects of the practice of teaching, such as the provision of support to teachers for improving their generic teaching skills, are also taken into account. More specifically, the following aspects of school policy on quantity of teaching are taken into account:

- school policy on the management of teaching time (e.g. lessons starting and finishing on time; lack of interruptions of lessons for staff meetings and/or for preparation of school festivals and other events);
- policy on student and teacher absenteeism;
- policy on homework;
- policy on lesson schedule and timetable.

School policy on provision of learning opportunities is measured by looking at the extent to which the school has a mission concerning the provision of learning opportunities which is reflected in its policy on curriculum. We also examine school policy on long-term and short-term planning and school policy on providing support to students with special needs. Furthermore, the extent to which the school attempts to make good use of school trips and other extra-curricular activities for teaching–learning purposes is investigated. Finally, school policy on the quality of teaching is seen as closely related to the eight classroom-level factors of the dynamic model, which refer to the instructional role of teachers (see Chapter 6).

Therefore, the way school policy for teaching is examined reveals that effective schools are expected to make decisions on maximising the use of teaching time and the learning opportunities offered to their students. In addition, effective schools are expected to support their teachers in their attempt to help students learn by using effective teaching practices, as these are defined by the classroom-level factors of the model. In this context, the definition of the first overarching school-level factor is such that we can identify the extent to which (1) the school makes sure that teaching time is offered to students, (2) learning opportunities beyond those offered by the official curricula are offered to the students, and (3) the school attempts to improve the quality of teaching practice. Therefore, we measure the impact of the school on the three major constructs of effectiveness research concerned with *time on task*, *opportunity to learn*, and *quality of teaching*. The importance of each of these factors has been discussed in the previous chapters, and Chapter 9 will present the main findings of a review of effectiveness studies exploring the impact of school factors on student achievement conducted during the past two decades. The findings of this review justify the importance of two overarching school factors of the dynamic model concerned with policy on teaching and policy on the school learning environment. A brief summary of the measurement of each of the three aspects of school policy for teaching is provided below.

Quantity of teaching

As far as the policy on quantity of teaching and the actions taken to increase opportunity to learn is concerned, this overarching factor refers to the following aspects of school policy: management of time, absenteeism of teachers and students, homework, and lesson schedule and timetable. This factor is measured using the five proposed dimensions as follows.

FREQUENCY

The frequency dimension is measured by identifying how many of the above aspects of policy on quantity of teaching are covered by the school policy. Actions taken to improve these aspects of policy on quantity of teaching are also taken into account. For example, we could examine the type of activities undertaken by the school to provide support to teachers in relation to the quantity of teaching aspect of their teaching practice. More specifically, a school may ask that teachers attend courses concerned with quantity of teaching, or encourage peer-teaching with the aim of helping teachers develop their management of time skills. It is possible to use supervision techniques to help teachers develop their management of teaching time skills. Support could also be provided to students, since at least two aspects of this policy (i.e. student absenteeism and homework) are directly related to their role as learners.

FOCUS

As far as the measurement of the focus dimension is concerned, we examine whether the guidelines given and/or the actions taken for improving teaching practice are too specific in terms of what the teacher is expected to do. Another indicator of the specificity of the school policy factor has to do with whether the policy refers to specific curriculum areas or subjects and/or grade levels. For example, a high score in specificity is obtained by a school policy that refers to homework in a single subject, done by a specific age group of students (e.g. policy on homework for reading at grade 1). In contrast, a very low score in specificity on policy on homework could be given to a school which considers that anything associated with homework (e.g. quantity, ways of correcting the homework, ways of giving feedback) should be more or less left up to the teachers. The second aspect of focus, which refers to the purpose(s) of the school policy, can be measured by examining the number of purposes that are expected to be achieved. For example, in the case of policy on homework, high scores on specificity are given to schools that try to develop guidelines in order to simply solve one specific problem concerning the way homework is done by a group of students. On the other hand, a lower score on specificity is given to a school that develops guidelines and/or takes actions with a view not merely to solving a specific problem concerned with the homework but also to establishing better relations with parents.

STAGE

The stage dimension of school policy on quantity of teaching refers to the school period at which the policy is established. According to the dynamic model, effective schools are those which develop a policy that is flexible. This is reflected in the fact that, from time to time, changes in the policy regarding teaching take place. This argument is supported by studies investigating the impact of school factors on student achievement (e.g. Cousins and Leithwood, 1986; Thomas, 2001). A review of the literature also reveals that continuity in school policy is a critical element of an effective school (e.g. Johnson, 1998; Preskill et al., 2003). Specifically, changes in school policy are expected to emerge from the results of a systematic evaluation of policy for teaching (Creemers, 1994; Kyriakides, 2005a; Teddlie and Reynolds, 2000), which is also treated as a school-level factor (see 'Evaluation of school policy for teaching . . .', p. 129). Therefore, a close relation between the two factors operating at the school level and dealing with teaching practice is expected to exist (see Figure 7.1).

QUALITY

The dimension quality is measured by investigating the properties of the policy guidelines, especially whether these are clear, concrete, and in line with the literature, and provide support to teachers and administrators to implement the policy. Specifically, concrete guidelines may include the kinds of measures that should be taken when it is realised that a problem is about to be created. For example, concrete guidelines in policy on absenteeism refer to the kinds of measures that should be taken if a teacher and/or students are sick and have to be away from school for a long period.

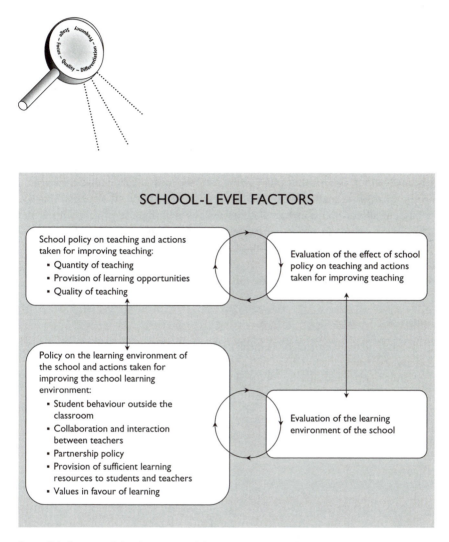

Figure 7.1 Factors of the dynamic model operating at the school level.

DIFFERENTIATION

Finally, differentiation is measured by investigating the extent to which school policy is designed in such a way that further support is given to teachers and students who have difficulties in implementing the school policy on teaching. For example, a school's policy on absenteeism might give further support to teachers or students who are in danger of losing time (e.g. students who are out of school for a long period, teachers who drop out regularly or before vacation periods).

Provision of learning opportunities

The factor 'provision of learning opportunities' refers to the policy on provision of learning opportunities and the actions taken to provide extra opportunities to learn beyond those offered by the official curriculum. Aspects of school policy associated with the provision of learning opportunities are those concerned with the mission of the school, as this is reflected in its policy on curriculum, addressing issues such as the content of the curriculum, the teaching aims, the textbooks, other resources that can be used, and the learning arrangements that the school can take. Policy on long-term and short-term planning could also address issues associated with the provision of learning opportunities to students. Furthermore, schools could develop policy on providing support to students with extra learning needs, such as students who are at risk, or gifted and talented students. Finally, policy guidelines may address issues associated with the use of school trips and other extra-curricular activities for teaching–learning purposes. Although the way this factor is measured is similar to the way school policy on quantity of teaching is measured, we shall now illustrate very briefly how the five measurement dimensions can be used to examine this school-level factor.

FREQUENCY

First, the frequency dimension is measured by identifying how many of the above aspects concerning the provision of learning opportunities are covered by the policy of each school, especially by its mission. The types of activities that the school personnel undertake in order to provide learning opportunities beyond those offered by the official curricula are also examined. For example, support could be provided to teachers in order to help them provide learning opportunities to students with special educational needs (e.g. students at risk or gifted students).

FOCUS

As far as the measurement of the focus dimension is concerned, we examine whether the guidelines given and/or the actions taken for improving teaching practice are too specific in terms of what each teacher is expected to do. For example, a high score on specificity of a policy on short-term planning could be given to a school where teachers are asked to use a specific form to plan their lessons or where teachers are told exactly how often they are expected to do their short-term planning (e.g. every day, or twice a week). Similarly, a high score on specificity is given to a school policy that indicates exactly where and when children can go on a school trip. As was mentioned earlier, we also examine the purpose(s) that are expected to be achieved. We especially examine whether school policy on a specific aspect of provision of learning opportunities attempts to achieve a single purpose (e.g. only on dealing with the specific problem) or attempts not only to solve a problem but also to increase provision of learning opportunities in a more general way (e.g. the policy on curriculum may be related to the policy on extra-curricular activities).

STAGE

The stage dimension of the school policy on provision of learning opportunities is measured in a similar way to the policy on quantity of teaching. According to the proposed dynamic model, effective schools are expected to develop a policy that is flexible, as reflected in the fact that, from time to time, changes in the policy on provision of learning opportunities take place. Continuity of school policy on provision of learning opportunities is also examined. Therefore, we measure the extent to which changes in school policy on provision of learning opportunities emerged from the results of a systematic evaluation of policy for teaching.

QUALITY

Quality is measured by investigating the properties of the policy guidelines on provision of learning opportunities, especially whether these are clear, concrete, and in line with the literature, and provide support to teachers, students, and administrators to implement the policy. As it has been mentioned above, concrete guidelines include the kinds of measures in place to deal with an impending problem. For example, policy guidelines on provision of learning opportunities may explain what could be done when it is found that there is discrepancy between long-term and short-term planning in terms of curriculum coverage. Moreover, the measures to be taken might be related to other aspects of this factor (e.g. policy on extra-curricular activities) or to aspects of other factors (e.g. homework, partnership). As far as the second aspect of this factor dealing with the actions taken for increasing opportunity to learn is concerned, the quality dimension investigates the extent to which support is provided to teachers to improve their teaching practice.

DIFFERENTIATION

Finally, differentiation is measured by investigating the extent to which school policy is designed in such a way that more support is given to teachers and students who have difficulties in implementing the policy on provision of learning opportunities. For example, novice teachers could be asked to produce different type(s) of short-term planning, or to do their planning more often than more experienced teachers. It might also be pointed out that students who need more learning opportunities should receive them.

Teacher instructional behaviour

Policy on teacher instructional behaviour is about a teacher's attempt to make use of time and learning opportunities in order to help students learn. Therefore, this aspect of policy on teaching is concerned with the quality of teaching practice, as measured by the eight classroom-level factors of the dynamic model presented in Chapter 6. In this context, the measurement of this factor is provided below.

FREQUENCY

The dimension of frequency identifies how many of the eight classroom-level factors concerning teacher instructional behaviour are covered by the school policy guidelines on teaching. We also measure the extent to which the school takes actions to improve teaching practice in relation to any of the eight classroom-level factors.

FOCUS

Focus is concerned with the extent to which policy guidelines on quality of teaching are too specific in terms of what the teacher is expected to do or are more general. We also examine the purpose(s) that are expected to be achieved, especially whether the policy refers to a single factor only, to a single subject, or to one age group of students only. For example, a high score on specificity is given to policy guidelines that refer specifically to orientation for year 4 in reading. On the other hand, a low score is given to a school that has established guidelines which refer to the relation of classroom-level factors, such as the relation of teacher assessment to questioning techniques, across subjects and grade levels.

STAGE

The stage dimension of policy on teacher instructional behaviour is measured in the same way as the other two aspects of policy on teaching and actions taken to improve teaching. Therefore, we examine the school period at which the policy was established. Effective schools are expected to develop a policy that is flexible, so that changes in the policy on teacher instructional behaviour take place. As it has already been mentioned, the continuity of school policy on teacher instructional behaviour is also examined.

QUALITY

As far as the measurement of the quality dimension of policy on teacher instructional behaviour is concerned, we examine whether the policy guidelines are clear, concrete, and in line with the literature. We also investigate the extent to which the school provides support to teachers to implement policy on quality of teaching and/or improve their teaching practice. Specifically, concrete guidelines may include specific forms for lesson preparation, or suggestions concerning the material that can be used in order to help teachers to implement policy on quality of teaching. Access to the literature and other sources in relation to the use of the eight classroom-level factors could also be given. We also examine the extent to which teacher practice is influenced by the guidelines and to which teachers' instructional behaviour is improved.

DIFFERENTIATION

Finally, the differentiation dimension of policy on teacher instructional behaviour is examined by investigating whether teachers who are less effective in a specific aspect of their instructional behaviour (e.g. teaching-modelling) are provided with appropriate, or more, guidelines and support. At the same time, we investigate whether the importance of the differentiation dimension of the eight effectiveness factors at the classroom level is emphasised.

Evaluation of school policy for teaching and of actions taken to improve teaching

Creemers (1994) claims that control is one of the major principles operating in generating educational effectiveness. This implies that goal attainment and the school climate should be evaluated. Since studies investigating the validity of the model have provided empirical support for the importance of this principle (e.g. de Jong *et al.*, 2004; Kyriakides *et al.*, 2000; Kyriakides, 2005a), it was decided to treat evaluation of policy for teaching and of other actions taken to improve teaching practice as an overarching factor operating at school level. The measurement of the stage dimension of the first factor concerned with policy on teaching and actions taken to improve teaching is also associated with the importance of evaluating policy on teaching and actions taken to improve teaching. Thus, we will now briefly describe the measurement dimensions of this factor.

FREQUENCY

First, frequency is measured by investigating how many times during the school year the school collects evaluation data concerning its own policy on teaching and the actions taken to improve teaching. Emphasis is also given to the sources of evaluation data which are used. This is attributed to the fact that studies on school evaluation seem to reveal that evaluators should employ a multidimensional approach in collecting data on school and teacher effectiveness (e.g. Danielson and McGreal, 2000; Johnson, 1997; Kyriakides and Campbell, 2004; Nevo, 1995), as comparisons of various sources (e.g. external observation, student ratings, colleagues' views) might increase the internal validity of the evaluation system (Cronbach, 1990; Kyriakides, 2004b). Moreover, the involvement of all con-stituencies in the evaluation process may foster participatory policies that result in less stakeholder criticism of the evaluation system (Patton, 1991; van den Berg and Ros, 1999). This argument is in line with the fact that EER has revealed that multi-source assessments that tap the collective wisdom of supervisors, peers, students, parents, and others provide the opportunity to improve teaching more effectively, and document its quality (Kyriakides and Pashiardis, 2005; Wilkerson *et al.*, 2000). Thus, the two indicators of the frequency dimension can be used to identify the extent to which a systematic evaluation of school policy for teaching and of actions taken to improve teaching takes place.

FOCUS

The focus dimension refers to the aspects of the school policy for teaching which are evaluated. Evaluation of school policy for teaching could refer to the properties of the school policy (e.g. clear, concrete, in line with the literature), its relevance to the problems which teachers and students have to face, and its impact on school practice and student outcomes (Kyriakides *et al.*, 2006a). Also examined is whether each school evaluates not only the content of the policy for teaching and of the actions taken to improve teaching practice but also the abilities of people who are expected to implement the policy (Creemers and Kyriakides, 2006). Moreover, the specificity aspect of the *focus* dimension is measured by looking at the extent to which information gathered from the evaluation is too specific (e.g. teacher X cannot do this) or too general (teachers are not able to teach effectively). The relation between student outcomes and specificity of evaluation is expected to be curvilinear. Research on school self-evaluation reveals that data collected should not be too specific and should not apportion blame to any individual for the fact that the school is not particularly effective; such an approach serves the summative purpose of evaluation and does not help the schools to take decisions on how to improve their policy (e.g. Fitz-Gibbon, 1996; Hopkins, 1989; Patton, 1991; Visscher and Coe, 2002). At the same time, information gathered from evaluation should not be too general but should be focused on how to influence decision-making, especially the process of allocating responsibilities to school partners in order to introduce a plan for improving the effectiveness of their school (Kyriakides and Campbell, 2004; MacBeath, 1999; Meuret and Morlaix, 2003). Finally, focus is examined by investigating the purposes for which the evaluation data are collected, especially whether evaluation is conducted for formative or summative reasons (Black and Wiliam, 1998). Studies on EER reveal that effective schools are those that use evaluation data for formative reasons (e.g. Harlen and James, 1997; Kyriakides, 2005a; Scheerens and Bosker, 1997; Teddlie and Reynolds, 2000; Worthen *et al.*, 1997).

STAGE

The stage dimension of this factor is examined by looking at the period when evaluation data are collected. Schools could either conduct evaluation at the end of certain periods (e.g. end of semester) or establish evaluation mechanisms that operate on a continuous basis throughout the school year. The dynamic model is based on the assumption that a continuous model of school evaluation is needed in order to allow schools to adopt their policy decisions on the needs of different groups of school stakeholders (Hopkins, 2001; Jordan, 1977; Kyriakides, 2004b). This assumption is also in line with the main principles upon which the comprehensive model of educational effectiveness is based (Creemers, 1994). We also expect the schools to review their own evaluation mechanisms and adapt them in order to collect appropriate and useful data (see also Cousins and Earl, 1992; Torres and Preskill, 2001; Preskill et al., 2003; Thomas, 2001).

QUALITY

Quality is measured by looking at the psychometric properties of the instruments (i.e. whether they are reliable, valid, useful) used to collect data on school policy towards teaching and actions taken to improve teaching (Cronbach, 1990; Kane, 2001). We emphasise here that validity is a critically important issue, and for that reason, in this section we discuss how schools could deal with this important element of their evaluation policy in order to increase their effectiveness.

The term 'validity' denotes the scientific utility of a measuring instrument, broadly statable in terms of how well it measures what it purports to measure (Nunnally and Bernstein, 1994). Therefore, the quality of the evaluation factor is measured by specifying how well each evaluation instrument meets the standards by which it is judged. However, contemporary discussion of validity emphasises two important precepts that are relatively recent in the evolution of validity theory. First, Madaus and Pullin (1991) argue that evaluation instruments do not have universal validity; they are valid only for specific purposes. Moreover, Sax (1997) claims that validity should be defined as the extent to which measurements are useful in making decisions and providing explanations relevant to a given purpose. To the extent that measurements fail to improve effective decision-making by providing misleading or irrelevant information, they are invalid. No matter how reliable they are, measurements lack utility if they are not valid for some desired purpose.

In this context, we argue that more emphasis should be given to the interpretive validity of the instruments rather than to their traditional forms of validity, such as the construct and content validity of the instruments. The validity of inferences derived from test scores is not a direct consequence of the test development process (Hambleton and Sireci, 1998). School stakeholders (i.e. teachers, students, and parents), as end users of the school evaluation instruments, contribute a distinctive perspective on validity, one that is concerned with the clarification and justification of the intended interpretations and uses of observed scores – that is, with inferential validity (see Kyriakides, 2004b). Our decision is also in line with the consideration of validity adopted by the 1999 *Standards for Educational and Psychological Testing* (AERA, APA, and NCME, 1999). Note that it is the interpretation that should be validated, and not the test or the test score. Thus, the measurement of the quality of this factor is expected to include an evaluation of the consequences of test uses, and proposed uses should be justified by illustrating that the positive consequences outweigh the anticipated negative consequences (AERA, APA, and NCME, 1999, 1.19–1.25). This implies that the measure of the quality of the evaluation of school policy on teaching is seen as an integrated evaluation of the interpretation of the school evaluation mechanisms rather than as a collection of techniques.

DIFFERENTIATION

Finally, the differentiation dimension is measured by looking at the extent to which the school gives more emphasis to conducting evaluation of specific aspects of or reasons for policy regarding teaching which refer to the major weaknesses of the school. For example, if policy on homework is considered problematic, the school may decide to collect data on homework more often and in greater depth than for any other aspect of school policy on teaching.

School policy for creating a school learning environment (SLE) and actions taken for improving the SLE

School climate factors have been incorporated in effectiveness models in different ways. Stringfield (1994) defines the school climate very broadly as the total environment of the school. This makes it difficult to study specific factors of the school climate and examine their impact on student achievement gains (Creemers and Reezigt, 1999b). In contrast, Creemers (1994) defines climate factors more narrowly and expects them to exert influence on student outcomes in the same way as the effectiveness factors do. The proposed dynamic model refers to the extent to which a learning environment has been created in the school. This element of school climate is seen as the most important predictor of school effectiveness, since learning is the key function of a school. Moreover, EER has shown that effective schools are able to respond to the learning needs of both teachers and students and to be involved in systematic changes in the school's internal processes in order to achieve educational goals more effectively in conditions of uncertainty (Harris, 2001). In this context, the following five aspects which define the school learning environment are taken into account:

- student behaviour outside the classroom;
- collaboration and interaction between teachers;
- partnership policy (i.e. the relations of school with community, parents, and advisers);
- provision of sufficient learning resources to students and teachers;
- values in favour of learning.

The first three of these aspects refer to the rules that the school has developed for establishing a learning environment inside and outside the classrooms. Here the term 'learning' does not refer exclusively to the student learning. For example, collaboration and interaction between teachers may contribute to their professional development (i.e. learning of teachers) but may also have an effect on teaching practice and thereby improve student learning.

The fourth aspect refers to the policy on providing resources for learning, and thereby helping the teachers and the school to provide more learning opportunities to students. The availability of learning resources in schools may also have an effect on the learning of teachers. For example, the availability of computers and software for teaching geometry may contribute to teachers' professional development since it encourages teachers to find ways to make good use of the software in their teaching practice and thereby to become more effective.

The fifth aspect is concerned with the strategies the school has developed in order to encourage teachers and students to develop positive attitudes towards learning. The fact that the importance of the school climate is seen only in relation to the extent to which there is a learning environment within the school implies that values of the people not related to learning are not seen as effectiveness factors but may be related to the outcomes of schooling (see Chapter 2). Following an approach similar to that concerned with school policy on teaching, the proposed dynamic model attempts to measure the school policy for creating a school learning environment. Actions taken for improving the SLE beyond the establishment of policy guidelines are also taken into account. More specifically, actions taken to improve the SLE can be directed at either (1) changing the rules in relation to the first three aspects of the SLE factor mentioned above, (2) providing educational resources (e.g. teaching aids, educational assistance, new posts), or (3) helping students or teachers to develop positive attitudes towards learning. For example, a school may have a policy that seeks to promote teacher professional development, but this might not be enough, especially if some teachers do not consider professional development to be an important issue. In this case, actions should be taken to help teachers develop positive attitudes towards learning, which may help them to become more effective. Given that the definition of this overarching factor is similar to that of the first overarching factor concerned with teaching, we use a very similar approach in measuring these two factors.

FREQUENCY

The dimension frequency of the factor concerned with the SLE is measured by identifying the number of aspects covered by the school policy which are concerned with the establishment of the SLE and with the actions taken for improving the SLE. Specifically, school policy for creating an SLE is expected to raise issues associated with all five aspects that define the SLE. As far as the types of actions that the school takes in order to improve the SLE is concerned, we can examine whether the school attempts to create a safe environment for the students outside the classroom; facilitates collaboration between teachers (e.g. through giving them time to work together); establishes close relations with the school community, the parents, and other professional bodies (e.g. advisers, school inspectors, curriculum development units); improves educational resources; and attempts to develop positive attitudes towards learning on the part of school stakeholders.

FOCUS

The focus dimension of this factor is measured by investigating the specificity of the policy guidelines and the specificity of the types of actions taken towards improving the SLE. For example, schools may develop a policy on teacher collaboration that is either too specific, by indicating what each group of teachers are expected to do (e.g. teachers of the same grade are expected to do common long-term planning and develop common tests), or more general (e.g. teachers are encouraged to collaborate/go along with each other). The same approach is used for measuring the specificity of actions taken to improve the SLE. In terms of specificity, we also look at the relevant literature and identify how many of the types of strategies that could be used in order to establish a school learning environment either are being used by the school or are referred to in the policy guidelines. For example, we can identify the extent to which policy guidelines on partnership and/or the actions taken to improve partnership are in line with any of the five types of partnership proposed by Epstein (1992).

The second aspect of the focus dimension is concerned with the purpose(s) that are expected to be achieved. Therefore, we should try to find out whether the policy refers to a single purpose (e.g. only dealing with a specific problem, such as disorder outside the classroom) or to multiple purposes (e.g. trying also to create positive attitudes towards learning).

STAGE

The stage dimension is measured by identifying the period in which the policy is established and whether the policy is flexible. The flexibility of the policy is measured by investigating whether the school alters its policy from time to time. Moreover, changes in the school policy on the SLE should emerge from the results of evaluation of the school environment (i.e. the fourth school-level factor). This implies that there is continuity in the attempt of the school to develop its own policy regarding the SLE. A similar approach is used for measuring the stage dimension of the actions taken for improving the SLE.

QUALITY

As far as the quality of this factor is concerned, we examine the properties of the policy guidelines, and especially whether they are clear, concrete, and in line with the literature, and provide support to teachers and students to implement the policy on SLE. Moreover, the extent to which the school practice is influenced by the announcement and implementation of the school policy is examined. This means that the adoption of the school policy is able to improve the learning environment of the school. As far as the actions taken to improve SLE are concerned, it is examined whether they are directly related to the information that emerged from the formative evaluation of school policy (i.e. using an evidence-based approach) or are based on more subjective views of stakeholders (internal or external).

DIFFERENTIATION

Finally, differentiation is measured by investigating the extent to which further support is given to teachers and/or students who are more in danger of creating problems in the SLE or are not able to contribute to the attempt of the school to establish a learning environment. For example, extra support is given to teachers who either do not want to collaborate with their colleagues and/or believe that they are not in need of further professional development. Moreover, different improvement strategies are used for students and teachers with different personalities, and different values concerning learning. For example, a school may exert pressure on some teachers in order to engage them in improvement processes, whereas another group of teachers may be persuaded by seeing examples of colleagues who succeeded in improving professionally and have become more effective (Campbell *et al.*, 2004).

Evaluation of the school learning environment

Since school climate is expected to be evaluated (Creemers, 1994), the dynamic model also refers to the extent to which a school attempts to evaluate its learning environment. A similar approach to the one used to measure the school-level factor concerning the evaluation of school policy of teaching is used to measure the factor focused on the evaluation of the school learning environment.

FREQUENCY

The frequency dimension is measured by identifying how often the school collects evaluation data which refer to the school learning environment. We also examine how many sources of evaluation data are used. The importance of these two indicators of the frequency dimension of the school evaluation mechanisms was raised in the section concerned with the evaluation of school policy for teaching. It can be argued that these two indicators help us identify whether the school has established systematic evaluation mechanisms which measure its learning environment.

FOCUS

The focus dimension refers to the aspects of the learning environment which are evaluated (e.g. partnership policy, teacher collaboration). The specificity of this factor is also examined by investigating whether the evaluation is not only concerned with various aspects of the school environment but also focused on the abilities of people to implement the school policy for improving the school learning environment. Moreover, the specificity is measured by looking at the extent to which information gathered from the evaluation is too specific (e.g. teacher X cannot collaborate with other colleagues in writing a common test) or too general (teachers are not committed to continuous learning). Finally, focus is examined by investigating the purposes for which the evaluation data are collected, especially whether the evaluation of the SLE is conducted for formative or for summative reasons. As was mentioned earlier, effective schools are expected to conduct evaluation of their SLE for formative reasons.

STAGE

The stage dimension of this factor is examined by looking at the period in which evaluation data are collected. Both schools that conduct evaluation only at the end of certain periods (e.g. the end of each semester) and schools that treat evaluation as a continuous process may be identified. Effective schools are expected to treat evaluation as a continuous process. Moreover, they are expected to review their own evaluation mechanisms and adapt them in order to collect relevant and appropriate data at each stage.

QUALITY

Quality is measured by looking at the psychometric properties of the data collected (i.e. whether they are reliable, valid, useful). As was mentioned in the section concerned with the evaluation of policy on teaching, more emphasis is placed on the inferential validity of the evaluation mechanisms than on any other type of validity. Thus, the extent to which information gathered from evaluation is used in making decisions that aim to improve the school learning environment is identified.

DIFFERENTIATION

Finally, the differentiation dimension refers to the extent to which the school leaders place more emphasis on conducting evaluation for specific aspects of the learning environment. For example, if bullying behaviour is common among students at a school, the school may decide to collect data more often and in greater depth on bullying than on any other aspect of the SLE. Such an approach may help a school to make decisions on how to solve this problem and make the school more effective (Ma, 2002).

Final remarks about the school-level factors

We would like to finish this first section of the chapter, which is concerned with effectiveness factors operating at the school level, by raising some general issues associated with the way the school-level factors are operationalised in the dynamic model. First, the way we measure the school level reveals that effectiveness factors have an effect on student outcomes through their impact on improving either teaching practice or the learning environment of the whole school. This can be attributed to the fact that the main function of a school is learning. Learning can take place either in the classroom, and is therefore expected to be associated with the achievement of the outcomes of schooling; or outside the classroom. In the latter case, effectiveness factors refer to the learning of all the other members of the school community and not only to student learning. Professional development of teachers and other school stakeholders is seen as a way to improve not only the quality of teaching inside the classroom but also the quality of learning opportunities offered outside the classroom. Thus, ultimately student achievement is expected to increase.

Second, the establishment of school policy and the various actions taken to improve the teaching and learning environment are seen as central components of an effective school. Actually, evaluation is treated as one major action that schools are expected to take in order to improve either teaching and/or the SLE. In this context, school evaluation mechanisms concerned with the school policy on teaching and with the SLE are seen as school-level factors.

Third, using the stage dimension to measure school-level factors helps us identify the extent to which changes in the school policy and actions taken to improve teaching and learning practice take place. At the same time, it has to be acknowledged that change is not only the mission of the school, since innovations could also arise from the centre. This implies that information for improving school policy on teaching and on SLE could arise either from internal or from external evaluation procedures. The model refers only to the internal evaluation procedures and treats them as school-level factors. This is attributed to the fact that in most educational systems the external evaluation refers to the adoption of national reform policies and helps policy-makers to improve their national policy. Therefore, external evaluation mechanisms are treated as factors operating at the national, or context level (see the next section).

Finally, owing to the emphasis of EER on the achievement of school outcomes, culture and climate are defined within the school as a learning environment. Therefore, people's values not related to learning are not taken into account. Our emphasis on the school stakeholders' values concerning learning can be attributed not only to the fact that the main mission of the school is learning but also to the fact that although the pressure for achievement can come from outside, it may also emanate from the mission of the school. School effectiveness studies have shown that the school's mission is an important school factor, especially the emphasis that the school gives to helping students develop positive values for learning (e.g. Kyriakides and Campbell, 2004; Kyriakides and Demetriou, 2005a; Levine and Lezotte, 1990; Teddlie and Reynolds, 2000). This implies that according to the dynamic model, effective schools are expected to help students consider 'achievement pressure' (coming from outside the school or even from within the school) as motivation for learning, which leads to performance, since an attitude that encourages all students to want to learn (i.e. succeed) is developed.

Effectiveness factors at the system/context level

In this section we refer to the most important factors operating at the system level (see Figure 7.2) that may affect achievement gains. We do not refer to all of the characteristics of an educational system which reveal variations in the operation of the educational systems around the world. As a consequence, the dynamic model does not refer to the structure of the system but to aspects of the national policy that affect learning inside and outside the classroom. Our assumption is supported by the fact that international studies and meta-analyses of comparative studies reveal that the effectiveness of an educational system is not determined by whether it is a centralised or a decentralised system, since neither a centralised nor a decentralised system can promote curriculum changes that may improve the effectiveness of the system (Fullan, 1991; Kyriakides and Charalambous, 2005; Schmidt et al., 1998; Schmidt and Valverde, 1995). Moreover, the fact that the few effectiveness studies that have investigated the impact of middle-level factors (such as the effect of the LEAs) have revealed that the impact of this level is very small (e.g. Tymms et al., 2006) can be attributed to the fact that in the countries where these studies were conducted, these levels are not in a position to directly influence school policy on teaching or the learning environment of the schools. For example, the curriculum is defined at the national level, and schools belonging to different authorities are expected to use the same curriculum. Therefore, we argue that those authorities that are only responsible for solving administrative problems that are faced at the school and/or the system level may not have any significant effect on student achievement gains.

Given that not many studies have been conducted in order to identify factors operating at the context level, in our attempt to define context-level factors we take into account the two major overarching factors operating at the school level which may directly affect (1) student learning through improving teaching practice (i.e. school policy for teaching), and (2) learning that takes place outside the classroom and is addressed to all the school stakeholders (i.e. policy in relation to the school learning environment). As a consequence, a similar overarching factor at the national level is included in the dynamic model. This factor refers to the national educational policy in relation to the teaching practice and the learning environment of the school, and is expected to directly affect teaching practice and the SLE, or even have an indirect effect by providing support to the schools to develop their own policies on teaching and their SLE. As in the case of the school level, actions taken to improve national policy in relation to teaching and the learning environment of the schools are also taken into account. Moreover, the term 'guidelines' is used in a broader sense to indicate all kinds of documents sent to schools by the context level which try to clarify the national or regional policy for teachers and other stakeholders and ensure they know what they are expected to do.

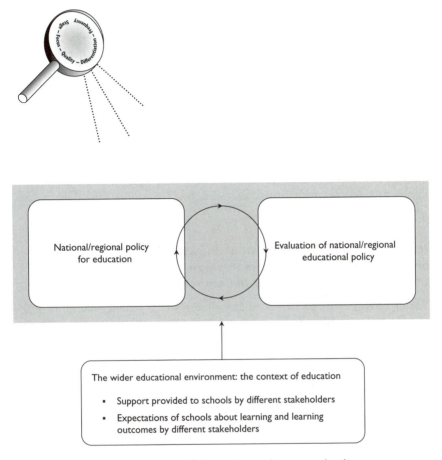

Figure 7.2 Factors of the dynamic model operating at the context level.

However, it is acknowledged that the model mainly refers to policies at the national level rather than to the specific actions. This is due to the fact that there is a variety of actions that can be taken in different countries, owing to the different structures of the national system and the societal context. On the other hand, in the case of the classroom level, and maybe to a lesser extent the school level, the range of actions taken in different countries is more restricted, owing to the more generic nature of learning and teaching. Related to this reason, the dynamic model is focused on presenting more precisely the classroom- and school-level factors and gives more general guidelines for how the context level may affect student achievement. International comparative studies may gradually help us to further develop the model by collecting data not only on the policy level but also about the different ways of implementing policy in relation to school policy, teacher behaviour, and, ultimately, student achievement.

Finally, the evaluation mechanism of the national educational policy, which may contribute to the improvement of the national policy and, through that, to the improvement of educational effectiveness, is also treated as an overarching factor operating at the system level. However, an essential difference between the factors operating at the system and those operating at the school level is concerned with the fact that not only policy on the teaching and learning environment is taken into account in the case of the context level but also the wider environment of education. Specifically, the wider educational environment of a country, and its ability to increase opportunities for learning and develop positive values for learning, is considered an important context-level factor. This is due to the fact that it is acknowledged that student learning is expected to take place not just in the schools but also in the wider school community. In this last section of the chapter, we illustrate the way in which these three overarching factors operating at the national level are measured.

National policy for education with consequences for, or actions taken towards, the improving of teaching and the learning environment of the school

The first overarching context-level factor refers to the national education policy in relation to teaching and in relation to aspects associated with the learning environment of the school. As far as the national policy on teaching is concerned, the factor refers to the same three aspects as are included in the relevant school-level factors (i.e. quantity of teaching, provision of learning opportunities, and quality of teaching). Specifically, in the case of quantity of teaching, we search for national policy or regulations concerned with the school timetable, the long-term and short-term planning, and the policy on absenteeism and drop-out. In an effective educational system these regulations may ensure that the quantity of teaching is kept to a maximum level, or may even provide support to the schools to keep it at a maximum level. As far as the quality of teaching is concerned, educational systems may develop standards for teaching to ensure that teaching practice is in line with each of the eight classroom-level factors or build teacher evaluation policy in such a way that criteria for teacher evaluation refer to the quality of teaching in relation to the eight classroom-level factors of the dynamic model. Finally, national policy on provision of learning opportunities is associated with the policy on the national curriculum. This aspect of the first overarching factor is also concerned with policy-makers' attempt to support or encourage students, teachers, or schools to undertake extra-curricular activities that contribute to the achievement of the aims of the curriculum (e.g. encourage students or schools to participate in maths Olympiads or other competitions; or encourage participation in action research projects attempting to help students to achieve curricular aims). The measurement of the national policy with consequences for improving teaching using the five proposed dimensions will now be described.

FREQUENCY

As far as the frequency dimension is concerned, we identify the extent to which aspects associated with teaching practice, such as those presented above, are covered by the national policy. Since this factor refers not only to the national policy but also to the actions taken for improving teaching, we also examine the types of activities that the policy-makers undertake in order to provide support to schools or teachers or students in relation to quantity of teaching, quality of teaching, and provision of learning opportunities.

FOCUS

The focus dimension is measured by identifying whether the policy guidelines and the actions taken to improve teaching are too specific in terms of what the teachers or schools are expected to do, or too general. We also examine the purpose(s) that are expected to be achieved, especially whether the policy refers to a single purpose (e.g. only on dealing with drop-out) or to more than one purpose (e.g. providing opportunities to learn beyond those of the typical curriculum).

STAGE

The stage dimension of this factor is measured in a similar way to the relevant school-level factors. Specifically, we just examine when the policy is established and when the policy-makers take specific actions to improve teaching. As mentioned above, data concerning the stage dimensions are expected to help us identify whether there is continuity in the functioning of this factor. We also examine whether there is flexibility in the national policy, as this is reflected in the fact that changes are made from time to time and are based on data emerging from formative evaluation of the national policy on teaching. This implies that a close relationship between the stage dimension of this factor with the factor concerning the evaluation of national policy (see p. 144) is expected to exist in effective educational systems.

QUALITY

The quality too is measured similarly to other school-level factors concerned with the school policy. Specifically, the properties of national policy guidelines on issues associated with teaching and the properties of the actions taken to improve teaching are examined. We measure the extent to which they are clear, concrete, and in line with the literature. Moreover, we identify the extent to which support is provided to teachers and/or schools to implement the policy.

DIFFERENTIATION

Finally, differentiation is measured by investigating the extent to which further support is given to teachers or schools that need it more. A typical example is the introduction and implementation of educational priority programmes.

As has been mentioned, the second aspect of this factor is concerned with (1) the national education policy, with consequences for improving the learning environment of the schools; and (2) actions taken by policy-makers to improve the learning environment of the schools. Specifically, the second aspect of this factor may refer to the provision of guidelines or rules and the establishment of strategies that may:

- support collaboration of teachers within a school (e.g. by giving teachers free time to use for coordination);
- help schools establish networks to support each other;
- encourage schools to use specific partnership types in order to improve their effectiveness;
- provide suggestions on how schools can treat student misbehaviour outside and inside the classroom (e.g. how to deal with bullying).

The educational system is also expected to provide resources to schools for improving their learning environment (Spencer *et al.*, 2000). These could refer to the financial support that is provided to the schools and/or to other types of support associated with learning such as the provision of:

- in-service training for school staff, which not only is expected to help teachers improve their teaching practice but also may refer to strategies that can be used to improve the learning environment of the school;
- school advisory systems that may provide support to schools in improving teaching practice and/or their learning environment;
- textbooks, teaching aids, and other learning resources.

The national policy in relation to teacher/student ratio is also an indication of the support that is provided to schools to enable them to improve teaching practice and maximise learning. However, evaluation studies of initiatives in some countries to reduce class size have revealed that this type of reform did not lead to any improvement of educational effectiveness (Bosker, 2006). The improvement of effectiveness can arise only if policy-makers not only reduce the teacher/student ratio but also help teachers identify ways to make good use of their smaller class sizes. This implies that in effective educational systems there will be a close relation between the functioning of this factor and factors concerning teachers' professional development.

Comparing the way this aspect of the first national factor is defined with the way the school-level factor concerning the school learning environment is defined, we can see that there is only one major difference in the way these two factors are measured. This difference refers to the fact that one of the aspects of the school-level factor concerning the SLE refers to the students' and teachers' values with respect to learning. In our attempt to define the factors at the national level, we assume that this aspect of the learning environment of the schools is affected by the third overarching national-level factor, which refers to the wider educational context. This factor will be presented in more detail in the last part of this section. Thus, the next part of this section refers to the measurement of the second aspect of the overarching factor at the context level which is able to influence the learning environment of each school.

FREQUENCY

The frequency dimension refers to the extent to which the aspects associated with the school learning environment mentioned earlier are covered by the national policy guidelines and/or by the actions that policy-makers take to improve the school learning environment. For example, we examine the types of actions that policy-makers take in order to encourage collaboration within each school.

FOCUS

As far as the measurement of the focus is concerned, we examine whether the guidelines given by the policy-makers to the schools and/or the actions taken by the policy-makers to improve the school learning environment are too specific or too general in terms of what the teachers or schools are expected to do. We also examine the number of purposes that are expected to be achieved, especially whether the policy guidelines and/or the actions taken by the policy-makers refer to a single purpose (e.g. only to how teachers or schools can deal with bullying) or to the achievement of more than one purpose (e.g. the actions attempt not only to help them deal with bullying but also to promote collaboration between students and teachers).

STAGE

The stage dimension is measured by taking into account the period when the policy is established and/or the actions to improve the SLE are taken. This dimension investigates whether the policy guidelines are flexible (as reflected in the fact that changes in the policy guidelines take place from time to time) and whether there is continuity in the development of policy guidelines and in the actions taken for improving the SLE. A typical example of a high score in continuity is an educational system that develops its policy guidelines by taking into account the results of the relevant evaluation mechanisms that exist in the system. Thus, our assumption is that effective systems are those which make good use of the empirical evidence in order to develop their policy (Fitz-Gibbon, 1996).

QUALITY

The approach used to measure the quality dimension of this factor is the same as the one used to measure two relevant school-level factors. The properties of the policy guidelines and the properties of actions taken to improve the SLE are examined. Specifically, we focus our attention on the extent to which these guidelines and/or actions are clear, concrete, in line with the relevant literature, and able to provide support to teachers or schools to implement the national policy.

DIFFERENTIATION

Finally, differentiation is measured by investigating whether further support is given to schools that have major problems with their learning environment. For example, more financial support is provided to underperforming schools, or in these schools, policy-makers keep the teacher/student ratio to a lower level than in other schools.

Evaluation of national educational policy with consequences for, or actions taken towards, the improving of teaching and the learning environment of the schools

The second overarching national-level factor is concerned with the evaluation mechanisms that each educational system may establish in order to collect data about the appropriateness of its national policy with consequences for improving teaching practice and the learning environment of the schools. Evaluation data concerning other actions taken by policy-makers to improve teaching and the school learning environment could also be collected. This factor is measured in a very similar way to the two relevant school-level factors concerning the evaluation of the school policy.

FREQUENCY

More specifically, frequency is measured by looking at the aspects of educational policy associated with the first school level that are evaluated. We also measure how frequently evaluation projects are undertaken; how many sources of data (i.e. views of different stakeholders) are used in evaluating the national policy; and the types of actions taken by policy-makers to improve teaching and the learning environment of the schools. Finally, it is important to find out whether internal and/or external evaluation mechanisms are used. The latter indicator of frequency is probably the main difference from the two school-level evaluation factors, which are concerned only with the internal (i.e. school) evaluation mechanisms.

FOCUS

The focus dimension is measured by investigating whether each attempt of the system to evaluate its national policy with consequences for improving teaching and the SLE refers to one or more aspects of the policy. It is also important to find out whether each evaluation mechanism investigates only the appropriateness of the policy or whether data on the abilities of the school stakeholders to implement the policy are also collected. Further, we examine whether the information collected is too specific (e.g. teacher or school X cannot implement this aspect of the national policy) or too general (e.g. the evaluation simply reveals that textbooks should be more relevant to the experiences of students) in terms of helping the policy-makers to make decisions. As with the school-level factors, a curvilinear relation with the focus dimension of this factor is expected to exist. Finally, we examine the purposes for which the evaluation data are collected, and especially whether evaluation is conducted for formative and/or for summative reasons.

STAGE

As far as the measurement of the stage dimensions is concerned, we look at the period when evaluation data are collected. This helps us discover whether there is a continuous evaluation system or the evaluation is undertaken only at the end of certain periods (e.g. after the completion of a reform policy). We also expect the policy-makers to review their evaluation mechanisms and adapt them in order to improve the quality of the evaluation data.

QUALITY

Quality is examined by investigating the quality of the data collected (i.e. whether they are reliable, valid, useful). As was mentioned above, the dynamic model places more emphasis on the interpretive validity of the data than on any other property of the evaluation data. This implies that the quality dimension of this factor is mainly concerned with the extent to which evaluation affects policy-making, and especially with the extent to which evaluation data help policy-makers and other stakeholders to make decisions that may improve national policy.

DIFFERENTIATION

Finally, identifying differentiation in the national evaluation system means that, depending on the situation of the system, more emphasis is given to conducting evaluation for a specific reason. For example, if policy on drop-out is considered problematic, policy-makers may decide to ask for more in-depth analysis of data on the appropriateness of the national policy on drop-out, or for further collection of data, such as the collection of data not only through surveys but also through relevant case studies. Case studies of schools that are more successful in keeping drop-out rates at low levels may be found to be useful in developing better policy guidelines and in providing further support to those schools that may need it.

The wider educational environment: the context of education

The final overarching factor refers to the wider educational environment of schools. However, instead of referring in a very general way to the context of education, the dynamic model concentrates on two aspects of the wider educational environment that are expected to influence learning. First, we examine the support provided to schools from different stakeholders (e.g. church, companies, universities, educational researchers, institutions responsible for providing support or advice or in-service training to schools). However, we are not only concerned with the financial support that different stakeholders provide to schools. Support provided to schools may refer to strategies or advice offered to schools which may help them improve their teaching practice or establish better learning environments (e.g. help them establish better relations among teachers and/or between teachers and students; help them identify ways to treat student misbehaviour outside and inside the classroom; or support their attempts to undertake extra-curricular activities that are related to the official aims of the curriculum). The measurement of the first aspect of this overarching factor will now be briefly described.

FREQUENCY

First, frequency is measured by investigating how many (if any) of the afore-mentioned stakeholders provide support to schools. We also examine the quantity of the support which is provided by each stakeholder. For example, in the case where one stakeholder provides fiancial support to schools, the amount of money offered is taken into account.

FOCUS

Second, focus is measured by identifying whether the support given is too specific in terms of how the teachers or students can use it (e.g. a church gives materials, money, or gifts to schools but asks them to use them only for a specific reason) or more general (e.g. a church gives money to schools and the schools can use it as they want). We also examine the purpose(s) that are expected to be achieved, especially whether the support provided is such that only a single purpose can be achieved (e.g. teaching materials given by the church can only be used for teaching religious education) or more than one purpose can be achieved (e.g. the teaching materials provided to schools can be used for teaching several subjects).

STAGE

The stage dimension is concerned with whether support to schools is given just once by the stakeholders or whether they provide support on a regular basis to schools (i.e. whether there is continuity).

QUALITY

As far as the quality dimension is concerned, the properties of the support provided to schools are examined. Specifically, we identify whether the support is clear, concrete, and in line with the literature. Moreover, we identify the extent to which teachers and students make use of the support provided to them. For example, we examine whether innovations that are sponsored by stakeholders (e.g. an action research project sponsored by a research foundation) are in line with the relevant literature and whether teachers or students are involved in this project.

DIFFERENTIATION

Finally, differentiation is examined by investigating whether further support is provided by the stakeholders to those schools or teachers who need it more (e.g. more financial support is provided to schools where the majority of students are working class).

The second aspect of the third overarching factor refers to the expectations of different stakeholders (e.g. employers, policy-makers, parents, and the public) from schools about learning and learning outcomes. These expectations may result in achievement press and, through that, in student achievement gains (Valverde and Schmidt, 2000). The importance of the second aspect of this overarching factor is justified by the results of a secondary analysis of PISA 2000 data (from 32 countries, 4,159 schools, and 97,384 students). This analysis was conducted in order to identify school and teacher effectiveness factors that are present in different educational contexts (Kyriakides and Demetriou, 2005a). It was found that the PISA index of 'achievement press' aggregated at the country level is associated with student achievement. This implies that the schools of most effective countries are driven by a quest for academic excellence. It can therefore be claimed that the construct 'achievement press' is an effectiveness-enhancing factor associated with student achievement in different societies. Although further empirical evidence to support the generalisability of this finding is needed, the fact that this factor, and not any other contextual factor measured by the PISA study (e.g. the average SES of students), was found to be associated with student achievement has to be emphasised. Thus, the measurement of the second aspect of this overarching factor will be briefly given.

FREQUENCY

First, frequency is measured by identifying how many of the stakeholders have high, or low, or no expectations from schools as regards learning and learning outcomes. As far as the focus is concerned, we examine whether the expectations are too specific or too general. A typical example of a very specific expectation is to expect students to do well in mathematics in order to pass the university entrance exams (i.e. holding an instrumental view of education). On the other hand, a typical example of excessively general expectations refers to the idea that students should develop their capacities.

FOCUS

The second aspect of the focus dimension is concerned with the number of purposes that stakeholders believe schools should achieve. Their expectations could either refer to only one type of purpose, such as the development of positive attitudes towards the school (e.g. be happy in the school), or to more than one type of purpose. For example, Summerhill School concentrated on only one purpose, namely that its students should be happy (see Vaughan *et al.*, 2006). On the other hand, research on the criterion *consistency of effectiveness* reveals that effective schools expect to achieve multiple purposes (i.e. both cognitive and affective). A relation between the two aspects of the *focus* dimension is expected to exist, and it is even possible to find an interaction between them.

STAGE

The stage dimension investigates whether the expectations of stakeholders from schools have to do only with specific age groups of students or whether they refer to the whole student population irrespective of age. For example, in some countries stakeholders and policy-makers may have high expectations only for those students who are going to take university entrance exams.

QUALITY

The quality dimension refers to the extent to which the expectations of stakeholders are realistic (i.e. neither too high nor too low). This implies that their expectations arise from evaluation data that reveal what the students, teachers, or schools are able to achieve.

DIFFERENTIATION

Finally, the differentiation dimension is measured by looking at the extent to which expectations of stakeholders are different for different groups of students, since their abilities are taken into account. For example, a talented or a gifted student is expected to achieve much more highly than the national standards.

Final remarks about the context-level factors

We would like to finish this chapter by raising the importance of testing the validity of the dynamic model. This is especially true for the context level, owing to the fact that very few international studies on educational effectiveness have been conducted (Reynolds, 2000). Although EER has expanded rapidly during the past three decades in many countries, there has clearly been no science of educational effectiveness studies across countries (Creemers, 2006). In this context, the creation of the Methodology of Research and Effectiveness (MORE) network and its first symposium at the annual ICSEI 2005 conference were intended to initiate a network of researchers with an explicit international and comparative focus. A special issue on 'international studies in educational effectiveness', which provides a record of the contributions made at this event, has been published in the journal *Education Research and Evaluation* (volume 12 (6)). The papers in this special issue reveal the importance of conducting international studies on educational effectiveness. Moreover, implications for the design of international studies on educational effectiveness are requested. It is also claimed that the involvement of researchers in comparative studies, which will be designed by giving more attention to the theoretical framework upon which they are based, will help us gain a better understanding of what works in education, and why (Kyriakides, 2006b). Such studies are needed to test the validity of the dynamic model, especially at the context level. Given that such studies do not exist at the moment, the next two chapters (i.e. Part III of the book) will provide some empirical evidence supporting the validity of the model at the classroom and school levels, respectively. This helps us examine the importance of conducting international comparative studies in order to identify the extent to which factors at the classroom and school levels are able to explain achievement gains in different educational systems. Moreover, international effectiveness studies will help us identify the effect of context-level factors on achievement gains in different educational systems.

Main conclusions to emerge from Part II of the book

The main arguments that have emerged from the second part of the book will now be presented in this final section. It is argued that the dynamic model not only should be multilevel in structure and parsimonious but also:

- takes into account the new goals of education and their implications for teaching;
- searches for interactions among factors operating at the same level;
- investigates the extent to which non-linear relations among some factors and student achievement may exist;
- uses different measurement dimensions to define the functioning of each effectiveness factor;
- describes the complex nature of educational effectiveness.

In this way the proposed dynamic model will be able to provide suggestions on how the knowledge base of EER can be used for improving practice. On the basis of the essential characteristics of the dynamic model as listed above, effectiveness factors included at the student, classroom, school, and context levels were described. It has been explained that the model places more emphasis on the classroom and

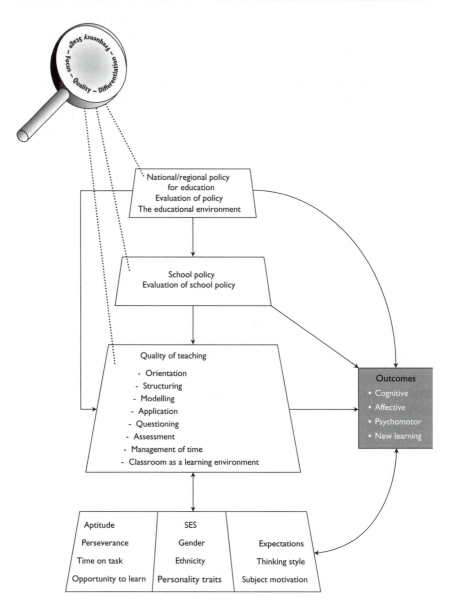

Figure 7.3 The dynamic model of educational effectiveness.

school level, since EER is focused on identifying factors that can not only explain variation in student achievement but also explain how changes in their functioning are likely to induce changes in student achievement. Figure 7.3 illustrates the dynamic model by not only referring to the structure of the model presented in Chapter 5 but also including the factors described in Chapters 6 and 7.

Researchers who develop such models are often challenged to show whether a theoretical model can be the subject of empirical research, or to provide arguments for the model. As a consequence, in Part III of the book, evidence supporting the validity of the model will be provided. It is also shown that the testing of the validity of the model can be done through both empirical studies and quantitative meta-analysis of existing effectiveness studies. Specifically, Chapter 8 will refer to the findings of the first phase of a longitudinal study testing the validity of the model at the classroom level. It is shown that although the model is complex in nature, it is possible to test it empirically. Suggestions for further development of the model at the classroom level will also be made. Chapter 9 will present the main results of a meta-analysis of effectiveness studies searching for school-level factors conducted during the past 20 years. Empirical support for the importance of the two main overarching school-level factors will be provided, and implications for the development of research on school effectiveness given. The third part of the book will illustrate in detail the way research on testing the validity of the model has been conducted.

Readers who are interested in conducting their own studies may find suggestions in relation to how their studies could be designed in order to collect and analyse their data. It is also pointed out that we need empirical studies to test the validity of the model at the school level, as well as meta-analyses for testing it at the classroom level by synthesising research on the impact of teacher behaviour on student achievement. Further implications of the dynamic model for research and evaluation as well as for policy and practice will be provided in Part IV of the book.

Empirical support for the dynamic model of educational effectiveness

Testing the dynamic model

A study investigating the impact of classroom-level factors on student achievement

Introduction

Part III of the book will provide some supportive material for the validity of the proposed dynamic model. Our attempt to do this is due to the fact that many theories die not because of any demonstrated lack of merit but because even their creators fail to provide any evidence at all that supports even some of the ideas forming part of their theory (see also Snow, 1973). Thus, Chapter 8 will illustrate the results of the first phase of a study conducted in Cyprus in order to test the validity of the dynamic model at the classroom level. This study aims to find out whether the dynamic model can be tested empirically. Specifically, we examine the validity of the proposed measurement framework. In the previous chapters it was made explicit that one of the main differences of the dynamic model from all the existing theoretical models is concerned with its attempt to show that effectiveness factors are multidimensional constructs and can be measured in relation to specific dimensions. Therefore, it is important to identify whether the proposed factors are multidimensional constructs and if the five dimensions can be used to measure each one. But beyond examining whether the factors can be measured in relation to the five dimensions, the added value of using these five dimensions of the effectiveness factors to explain variation in student achievement should be identified. Not only should the construct validity of the measurement framework be demonstrated, but also its significance for, and relevance to, the field of EER should be investigated. This study can be considered to be the first attempt to show that each dimension of the factors included in the model is associated with student achievement. Moreover, the extent to which it is possible to identify non-linear relations between factors of the model and student achievement is investigated. The importance of searching for non-linear relations is attributed to the fact that the model places emphasis on the identification of such relations, and this was seen as one of the significant features of the dynamic model. Finally, in the first two parts of the book a distinction was made between generic and differentiated models. It was claimed that the dynamic model can be considered a generic model of educational effectiveness. This assumption is tested through the study reported in this chapter, since the effects of effectiveness factors upon four different outcomes of schooling (both cognitive and affective) are examined.

The methods used to test the validity of the dynamic model and the main results of the study will be illustrated in the first two sections of the chapter. In the last section, implications of findings for the development of the model will be drawn. It is emphasised that although this study is only a first attempt to test the model, and the generalisability of its findings can be questioned, a methodology for testing the model is offered. Moreover, arguments for the main features of the dynamic model are provided and may help in the design of further studies seeking to test, expand, and use the model. Some further evidence that supports the model will be presented in Chapter 9. This chapter will show how quantitative syntheses of effectiveness studies can be used to test the validity of the model. Since this chapter is concerned with the classroom-level factors, the importance of the school-level factors will be examined through the meta-analysis reported in Chapter 9.

Research aims

The studies that have sought to test the validity of Creemers' model (i.e. de Jong *et al.*, 2004; Kyriakides, 2005a; Kyriakides *et al.*, 2000; Kyriakides and Tsangaridou, 2004) reveal the importance of using multiple measures of effectiveness factors and of conducting longitudinal studies rather than case studies in order to be able to identify the relations that exist between the various measures of each factor and student achievement gains (see also Chapter 4). For this reason, we decided to conduct a longitudinal study in order to develop and test the dynamic model and to measure teacher and school effectiveness in relation to more than one outcome of schooling. Specifically, the study does not merely attempt to investigate educational effectiveness in mathematics and language; measures concerning the main aims of religious education are also taken into account. In this respect – as well as student knowledge on mathematics, language, and religious education presented in the national curriculum of Cyprus – student achievement in the affective aims of religious education is measured. This implies that this study helps us identify the extent to which the dynamic model can be considered a generic model. In this chapter the results of the first phase of the study, which is concerned with the importance of classroom-level factors included in the dynamic model, are presented. Specifically, the first phase of the study attempts to identify:

- the extent to which each of the eight factors that refer to teacher behaviour in the classroom are multidimensional constructs and can be defined by reference to the five dimensions of the model;
- the type(s) of relations that each factor and its dimensions have with student learning outcomes in mathematics, Greek language, and religious education.

Methods

Participants

Stratified sampling (Cohen *et al*., 2000) was used to select 52 Cypriot primary schools, but only 50 schools participated in the study. All the year 5 students (n = 2,503) from each class (n = 108) of the school sample were chosen. The chi-square test did not reveal any statistically significant difference between the research sample and the population in terms of students' sex (χ^2 = 0.84, d.f. = 1, p = 0.42). Moreover, the t-test did not reveal any statistically significant difference between the research sample and the population in terms of class size (t = 1.21, d.f. = 107, p = 0.22). It may be claimed that a nationally representative sample of Cypriot year 5 students was taken.

Dependent variables: student achievement in mathematics, Greek language, and religious education

As far as the dependent variables of this study are concerned, data on student achievement in mathematics, Greek language, and religious education were collected by using external forms of assessment designed to assess knowledge and skills in mathematics, Greek language, and religious education identified in the Cyprus Curriculum (Ministry of Education, 1994). Student achievement in relation to the affective aims included in the Cyprus curriculum for religious education was also measured. The three written tests, in mathematics, Greek language, and religious education, were administered to all year 5 students of the school sample at the beginning and at the end of the school year 2004/2005. The construction of the tests was subject to controls for reliability and validity. Specifically, the Extended Logistic Model of Rasch (Andrich, 1988) was used to analyse the emerging data in each subject separately, and four scales referring respectively to student knowledge in mathematics, Greek language, and religious education, and to student attitudes towards religious education, were created and analysed for reliability, fit to the model, meaning, and validity. Analysis of the data revealed that each scale had satisfactory psychometric properties. Thus, for each student, four different scores for his or her achievement at the beginning of the school year were generated by calculating the relevant Rasch person estimate in each scale. The same approach was used to estimate student achievement at the end of the school year in relation to these four outcomes of schooling.

By estimating the correlations between the baseline Rasch score of students in each outcome and their Rasch score in the final assessment, it was found that each of them was statistically significant (p < 0.001). It was also found that the values of these four correlation coefficients were higher than 0.62. This finding provides a satisfactory starting point for conducting analysis of value added in each outcome and for searching for factors that explain student progress at the classroom level. Although there is a statistically significant correlation between the student estimates in the two Rasch scales of religious education which emerged both at the beginning ($r = 0.29$, $n = 2,503$, $p < 0.001$) and at the end ($r = 0.27$, $n = 2,503$, $p < 0.001$) of the school year 2004/2005, the relatively small values of these two correlation coefficients reveal that the two scales that emerged from the two measurement periods refer to two different constructs (Cronbach, 1990). Therefore, two separate value added analyses of student progress in religious education were conducted, which were concerned with the achievement of the cognitive aims and the affective aims, respectively, of the religious education curriculum.

Explanatory variables at student level

Aptitude

Aptitude refers to the degree to which a student is able to perform the next learning task. As mentioned above, for the purpose of this study it consists of prior knowledge of each subject (i.e. mathematics, Greek language, and religious education) and prior attitudes towards religious education as emerging from student responses to the external forms of assessment administered to students at the beginning of the school year (i.e. the baseline assessment).

Student background factors

Information was collected on two student background factors: sex (0 = boys, 1 = girls) and SES. Five SES variables were available: father's and mother's education level (i.e. graduate of primary school, graduate of secondary school, or graduate of a college or university), the social status of father's job, the social status of mother's job, and the economic situation of the family. Following the classification of occupations used by the Ministry of Finance, it was possible to classify parents' occupation into three groups of roughly similar sizes: occupations held by the working class (34 per cent), occupations held by the middle class (36 per cent), and occupations held by the upper-middle class (30 per cent). Relevant information for each child was taken from the school records. Then, standardised values of the above five variables were calculated, resulting in the SES indicator.

Explanatory variables at classroom level: quality of teaching

While there has been substantive development of teacher effectiveness research with regard to content, the issue of measurement has been largely neglected. In the literature there is a debate about whether quality of teaching is best evaluated by independent observers or by students (Aleamoni, 1981; Fraser, 1995). Both methods have their advantages and disadvantages (Ellett, 1997; Rosenshine and Furst, 1973). Thus, the explanatory variables of the study, which refer to the eight factors dealing with teacher behaviour in the classroom, were measured by both independent observers and students. Specifically, taking into account the way the five dimensions of each effectiveness factor are defined (see Chapter 6), one high-inference and two low-inference observation instruments were developed. One of the low-inference observation instruments is based on Flanders' (1970) system of interaction analysis. However, we developed a classification system of teacher behaviour that is based on the way each factor of the proposed dynamic model is measured. Moreover, the observer is expected to identify the students who are involved in classroom interaction. As a consequence, the use of this instrument enables us to generate data about teacher–student and student–student interaction. The second low-inference observation instrument refers to the following five factors of the model: orientation, structuring, teaching-modelling, questioning techniques, and application. This instrument is designed in a way that enables us to collect more information in relation to the quality dimension of these five factors. Thus, the two instruments helped us to generate data for all eight factors and their dimensions. The high-inference observation instrument covers the five dimensions of all eight factors of the model, and observers are expected to complete a Likert scale (part A) to indicate how often each teacher behaviour was observed (e.g. the teacher spent time explaining the objectives of the lesson). Moreover, a second scale (part B) was used to allow us to search for curvilinear relations between some factors and student outcomes, as predicted by the dynamic model. Specifically, some of the items from part A were also included in part B. This time the observers were asked to judge the amount of the observed behaviour by indicating whether it was observed 'not at all', 'scarcely', 'satisfactorily', or 'more than enough'. However, the reliability of the scale of part B was not satisfactory, and therefore only the data from the Likert scale (i.e. part A) were used. Finally, it is important to note that the use of different types of observation instruments allows us to cover all the factors and dimensions mentioned in the dynamic model.

Observations were carried out by six members of the research team who attended a series of seminars on how to use the three observation instruments. During the school year, the external observers visited each class nine times and observed three lessons per subject by using both types of low-inference observation instruments. On each occasion the observers completed the rating scale of the high-inference observation instrument. For each scale of the three observation instruments, the alpha reliability coefficient was higher than 0.83, and the inter-rater reliability coefficient ϱ^2 was higher than 0.81.

The eight factors and their dimensions were also measured by administering a questionnaire to students. Specifically, students were asked to indicate the extent to which their teacher behaves in a certain way in their classroom (e.g. at the beginning of the lesson the teacher explains how the new lesson is related to previous ones). A Likert scale was used to collect data. A generalisability study (Cronbach et al., 1972; Shavelson et al., 1989) on the use of students' ratings was conducted. Given that most of the teachers were classroom teachers and thereby were responsible for teaching all three subjects in their classroom, two models of G-theory were tested concerning the extent to which (1) the teacher could be treated as the object of the measurements emerging from the student questionnaires, and/or (2) the instructional event (i.e. teacher X teaching subject Y) could be seen as the object of measurements. It was found that the data collected from almost all the questionnaire items could be used for measuring the quality of teaching of each teacher in each subject separately (i.e. the instructional event). However, three items of the questionnaire concerned with assessment in religious education and one item concerned with the differentiation dimension of learning strategies in both Greek language and religious education had to be removed. Thus, the score for each teacher in each of the questionnaire items found to be generalisable was the mean score of the year 5 students of the class she or he taught.

Results

The two parts of this section will provide answers to the research questions concerned with the main characteristics of the dynamic model. The purpose of the first part of this section, as was indicated in the introduction, is to provide empirical support for the measurement framework of effectiveness factors proposed in the dynamic model. The extent to which the classroom-level factors can be considered to be multidimensional constructs is examined. Therefore, the first part of the results section investigates whether the five dimensions can be used to measure each classroom-level factor. More specifically, for each subject a specialised type of confirmatory factor analysis (CFA) model was used to examine the extent to which each of the eight factors at classroom level can be measured by taking into account the five dimensions of the model and the instruments from which the data emerged. The second part of this section is an attempt to identify the added value of using these five dimensions to measure the classroom effectiveness factors in relation to explaining student achievement gains in different outcomes of schooling. In this way we examine the importance of the five measurement dimensions of the classroom effectiveness factors and the extent to which the model can be considered generic. Thus, we present the results of the four multilevel analyses which have been conducted in order to examine whether the five dimensions of each classroom-level factor show the expected effects upon four dependent variables (i.e. achievement in mathematics, achievement in Greek language, achievement of the cognitive aims of religious education, and achievement of the affective aims of religious education). We also identify the extent to which there are curvilinear relations between the factors and student achievement.

Testing the validity of the framework used to measure each effectiveness factor

Since its inception in 1959 (Campbell and Fiske, 1959), the multi-trait multi-method (MTMM) matrix has provided researchers with an invaluable tool for the assessment of construct validity. In essence, this matrix involves factorially combining a set of traits with a set of measurement methods. This factorial combination of traits and methods allows an examination of variance that is due to traits, variance that is due to methods, and unique or error variance. Campbell and Fiske (1959) proposed a set of rules of thumb to evaluate the degree of convergent and discriminant validity present in an MTMM matrix. Although the criteria proposed by Campbell and Fiske contributed substantially to the understanding and assessment of convergent and discriminant validity, they were widely criticised for several reasons, including ambiguity of what constitute satisfactory results and the use of correlations that are based on observed variables to draw conclusions about underlying trait and method factors. In this context a range of formal statistical techniques that could be used to estimate MTMM models were proposed. Two general traditions have been developed. The first has often been referred to as the analysis of variance approach (Kavanaugh *et al.*, 1971; Kenny and Kashy, 1992; Schmitt and Stults, 1986). The second tradition is the factor analysis approach. Within the factor analysis approach, initial efforts were focused on applying exploratory factor analysis to MTMM data (Jackson, 1969). Over time, this strategy has been replaced by CFA techniques. In recent years, CFA has become the method of choice in analysing the MTMM matrix. With CFA, the researchers can define alternative models that posit a priori trait and method effects and test the ability of such models to fit the data (Marsh and Byrne, 1993).

In this study, for each subject separate CFA analyses for each effectiveness factor were conducted in order to identify the extent to which each factor can be measured in relation to the five dimensions proposed by the dynamic model. The results of the analysis concerned with the classroom-level factor that refers to the structuring skills of teachers will now be presented. Figure 8.1 represents the CFA model that was tested in order to provide empirical support for the measurement framework of effectiveness factors proposed by the dynamic model. Specifically, each measured variable was related to one of the five trait factors representing a specific dimension of measuring structuring skills of teachers and one method factor representing one of the four methods used to collect data (i.e. student questionnaire, high-inference observation, low-inference observation instrument 1, low-inference observation instrument 2). The uniqueness associated with each measured variable was posited to be uncorrelated with that of the other measured variables.

The measured variables in our MTMM analyses which emerged from the two low-inference observation instruments were based on scale scores, whereas those that emerged from the student questionnaire and the high-inference observation instrument were factor scores. Specifically, for each subject we identified a large number of statistically significant correlations ($p < 0.001$) among students' responses to items of the student questionnaire concerned with the same classroom effectiveness factor. These correlations were further analysed by using exploratory factor analysis to identify underlying 'factors' that explain these correlations. Specifically, for each subject, separate exploratory factor analyses based on the data that emerged from the student questionnaire in relation to each effectiveness factor were conducted. Based on the results of these eight factor analyses, factor

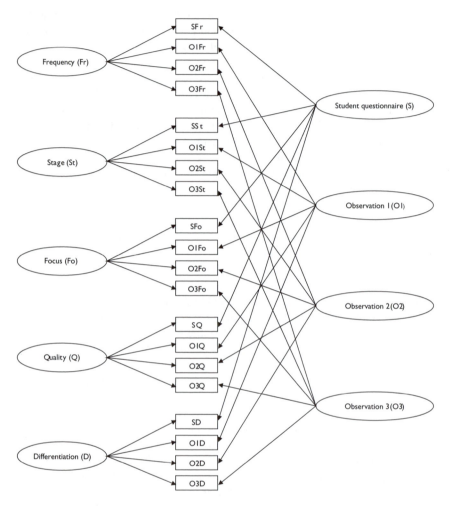

Figure 8.1 The five correlated traits, four correlated methods model used to test the measurement framework of structuring.

Note: Each box is determined by a combination of the instrument (i.e. the method factor) from which data emerged and the dimension that is measured (i.e. the trade factor). For example, the first box (SFr) refers to the data that emerged from the student questionnaire (S) in relation to the *frequency* dimension (Fr). Ellipses are latent constructs and rectangles are measured variables. Owing to limitations of space, intercorrelations among the traits and among the methods are not depicted.

scores concerned with the five dimensions of each classroom-level factor in each subject were produced. Since the next part of this section will illustrate in detail the results concerned with the validation of the proposed measurement framework of structuring skills of teachers, it is pointed out here that each of the three factor analyses concerned with the structuring skills of teachers in each subject revealed that five eigenvalues were greater than 1 and that more than 65 per cent of the total variance is attributable to the first five factors in each analysis. This means that for each subject, a model with five factors could be considered as adequate to represent the data. A varimax rotation procedure was subsequently used to analyse students' responses, since it transforms the initial factor matrix into one that is easier to interpret (Kline, 1994). Following this procedure, it was found that for each subject the 19 questionnaire items concerned with the structuring skills of teachers could be classified into five broader categories that refer to the five measurement dimensions proposed by the dynamic model. High inter-item reliability was also identified, with all item-total correlations within each factor being highly significant ($p < 0.001$). Moreover, acceptable levels of internal consistency were indicated by Cronbach's alpha coefficients ranging from 0.67 to 0.75 for all the factors. Similar results emerged from exploratory factor analyses of student questionnaire items concerned with each of the other seven classroom effectiveness factors. The approach described above was also used in analysing data emerging from the high-inference observation instrument. Using the exploratory factor analysis, factor scores for each dimension of the structuring factor in each subject were estimated. The results that emerged from analysing data collected in relation to each of the three different subjects were comparable. However, limitations associated with the use of factor scores and/or scale scores instead of raw variables in our CFA analyses of the MTMM matrices have to be acknowledged (see Byrne and Goffin, 1993; Marsh and Byrne, 1993).

Analytical procedure

The scalings for the measures were vastly different from one another, and considered arbitrary. Constraining method indicators to be equal, a standard procedure in MTMM models, presented interpretive problems (Stacy *et al.*, 1985). Therefore, the data were standardised across the entire sample, and covariance matrices used in the analyses. The CFA procedures were conducted using the EQS program (Bentler, 1989) with maximum-likelihood (ML) estimation. The ML estimation procedure was chosen because it does not require an excessively large sample size. More than one fit index was used to evaluate the extent to which the data fit the models tested. More specifically, the scaled chi-square, Bentler's (1990) comparative fit index (CFI), the root mean square error of approximation (RMSEA) (Brown and Mels, 1990), and the chi-square to degrees of freedom ratio were examined. Furthermore, the factor parameter estimates for the models with acceptable fit were examined to help interpret the models. Finally, procedures for testing hierarchically nested models suggested by Marsh and Hocevar (1985), Stacy *et al.* (1985), and Widaman (1985) for comparing first- and second-order structures and MTMM models were taken into account. Specifically, comparisons were made between the most restrictive and the least restrictive nested models. The null model (most restricted) hypothesised no correlations among the scores concerned with structuring skills of the teacher sample in relation to each of the five dimensions of measuring structuring skills. Less restrictive hypothesised models were then tested in a hierarchical manner and compared to the null model as well as to each other. The goodness of fit for each of the models was evaluated using the indices mentioned above. The chi-square difference test was also used to evaluate the improvement of fit among hierarchically nested models.

Once the best-fitting model was determined, including traits and methods, the method effects on each measure were assessed. By squaring the loadings on each of the trait and method factors, the amount of variance attributable to each method was calculated. Comparisons of these effects on each of the measures were made. Often, method effects are assumed to be unidimensional and therefore uncorrelated. It was hypothesised that there would be no significant correlations among the method factors (i.e. the methods would be unidimensional). This was tested by setting the correlations among these factors to be free or fixed at zero and evaluating a difference of chi-square between the two models as well as the parameter estimates.

Results concerned with the structuring skills in each subject

This subsection presents results concerned with the testing of various types of CFA models that can be used to analyse MTMM data which refer to the structuring skills of teachers in teaching Greek language, mathematics, and religious education. Specifically, for each subject the null model and the five nested models are presented in Table 8.1. The null model (model 1) represents the most restrictive model, with 20 uncorrelated variables measuring the structuring skills of teachers in each subject. Models 1–4 are first-order models, and comparisons between the chi-squares of these models helped us evaluate the construct validity of the framework used to measure structuring skills, including determination of the convergent and discriminant validity and the number and type of method factors present in the measures. Models 5 and 6 were higher-order models tested and compared to account for the lower-order baseline model. Following selection of a best-fitting or baseline model, further examination of the validity and reliability of each of the measures, and the method's effects on each, was made.

The following observations arise from Table 8.1. First, comparing the null model with model 2, we can observe that although the overall fit of model 2 was not acceptable, it was a significant improvement in chi-square compared to the null model. In addition, the standardised factor loadings were all positive and moderately high (i.e. their standardised values ranged from 0.68 to 0.79, and 12 of them were higher than 0.70). This result can be seen as an indication of convergent validity for the traits. Moreover, the correlations among the five traits were positive but relatively low, an indication of discriminant validity.

Second, model 2 can be compared with models 3 and 4 to determine the best structure for explaining method variance present in these five traits. Model 3 represents the five correlated traits of measuring the dimensions of the structuring factor and the addition of the four method instruments used to collect data (see Figure 8.1). On the other hand, model 4 hypothesised a structure of five correlated

Table 8.1 Goodness-of-fit indices for structural equation models used to test the validity of the proposed framework for measuring structuring skills in each subject

SEM models	Greek language					Mathematics					Religious education				
	χ^2	d.f.	CFI	RMSEA	χ^2/d.f.	χ^2	d.f.	CFI	RMSEA	χ^2/d.f.	χ^2	d.f.	CFI	RMSEA	χ^2/d.f.
1 Null model	4,199.1	190	—	—	22.10	4,069.8	190	—	—	21.42	3,819.0	190	—	—	20.10
2 Five correlated traits, no method	628.8	160	0.878	0.13	3.93	555.2	160	0.891	0.11	3.47	596.8	160	0.884	0.12	3.73
3 Five correlated traits, four correlated methods	296.1	134	0.901	0.09	2.21	347.1	134	0.896	0.10	2.59	322.9	134	0.891	0.09	2.41
4 Five correlated traits, three correlated methods	248.0	137	0.947	0.03	1.81	253.4	137	0.942	0.03	1.85	261.7	137	0.935	0.04	1.91
5 One second-order general, three correlated methods	614.9	142	0.921	0.08	4.33	671.7	142	0.913	0.09	4.73	472.9	142	0.921	0.06	3.33
6 Two correlated second-order general, three correlated methods	351.1	141	0.936	0.05	2.49	410.3	141	0.930	0.06	2.91	308.8	141	0.939	0.05	2.19

Note: CFI = comparative fit index; RMSEA = root mean square error of approximation.

traits of the structuring factor and three correlated method factors, since the student questionnaire from model 3 was retained, whereas the factor scores of the high-inference observation instrument and the scale scores of the second low-observation instrument which refer to the focus and quality of structuring were considered to belong to the second method factor. The other three scale scores of this instrument (i.e. frequency, stage, and differentiation), and the scale scores of the first observation instrument were considered to belong to the third method factor. The chi-square difference between models 2 and 3 showed a significant decrease in chi-square and a significant improvement over the trait-only model. Clearly, method variance was present, and the addition of method factors to the model increased the amount of covariation explained. Moreover, model 4, which fitted reasonably well, was a significant improvement over model 2 and explained more method variance than model 3. This implies that the three method factors described above are able to explain better the data than the four method factors of model 3. Model 3 was based on the assumption that each instrument should be treated separately, since the quality of each instrument is different (e.g. each one is associated with different measurement errors). On the other hand, model 4 assumes that data emerging from the four instruments refer to three factors. Looking at the description of these three factors, one may claim that this model is concen-trated on the different advantages and limitations of using three different methods to measure quality of teaching (i.e. student questionnaires, low-inference observations, and high-inference observations).

Third, models 5 and 6 were examined to determine whether a second-order structure would explain the lower-order trait factors more parsimoniously. Specifically, model 5 hypothesised that scores concerned with the structuring skills of teachers in each subject could be explained by five first-order factors (representing the five dimensions of measuring the factor) and one second-order factor (i.e. structuring skills in general). On the other hand, model 6 was a model with two correlated second-order traits. Figure 8.2 illustrates the structure of this model. Specifically, it is examined whether covariation between the frequency and stage dimensions of structuring skills can be explained by their regression on one second-order factor, whereas covariation among the focus, quality, and differentiation dimensions can be explained by their regression on the other second-order factors. We also tested three additional second-order models with varying factor structures, but none of them was significantly better than either model 5 or model 6. In comparing first- and second-order models, a second-order model rarely fits better than a lower-order model. Because there are fewer parameters estimated in higher-order models compared to lower-order models of the same measures, the degrees of freedom increase, as does the chi-square. In this study, for each subject the fit indices of models 5 and 6 as well as a chi-square difference test between the two models reveal that model 6 fits better than model 5 ($p < 0.001$). Moreover, the fit values of model 5 do not meet the criteria for acceptable level of fit. This finding provides support for arguing the importance of measuring each of the five dimensions of effectiveness factors separately rather

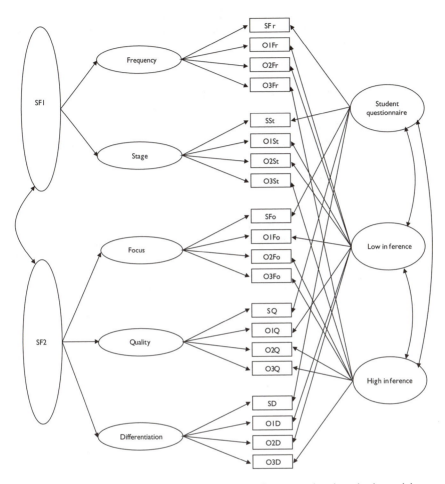

Figure 8.2 The two correlated second-order traits, three correlated methods model
measuring structuring skills.

than treating them as unidimensional. Finally, the fit of the data that emerged from
measuring the structuring skills of teachers of religious education to model 6 could
be treated as adequate. But although model 6 could be considered more parsimonious in explaining the interrelations among the five factors rather than model
4, the latter model fits the data better.

*Validity of the measures concerning structuring skills of teachers in
each subject*

The results of hierarchical model comparisons demonstrated convergent and
discriminant validity for the traits. Individual standardised loadings on trait

and method factors also provided an indication of the convergent validity of the observed variables. High loadings on trait factors (i.e. higher than 0.60) and low loadings on method factors (i.e. lower than 0.40) demonstrated good convergent validity. The standardised loadings on traits can be considered validity coefficients for each measure. The two exceptions were the student questionnaire factor score on differentiation in teaching religious education (0.552) and the factor score of high-inference observation instrument on quality in teaching Greek language (0.514). Moreover, there did not appear to be any strong general method effects, but method effects were exceptionally high for high-inference observation.

Trait and method effects concerning structuring skills of teachers in each subject

The variances for traits, methods, and error for each of the observed measures were calculated by squaring the loading of each respective factor in model 4. Moreover, the reliability for each measure was calculated by adding the trait and method variance. In each subject it was found that the trait variance for at least 16 of the 20 measures was moderate to high (i.e. higher than 0.60), with method variance substantially lower than trait and random error variance. Exceptions to these findings were not specific to one method, but most of them were concerned with the use of high-inference observation.

The CFA models of the remaining classroom-level factors: a condensed presentation

This subsection is an attempt to present the main results that emerged from analysing the MTMM data concerned with each of the other seven classroom-level factors of the dynamic model in relation to each subject. Results from hierarchical confirmatory factor analyses indicated that both the convergent and the discriminant validity of the measures associated with the five dimensions for each classroom-level factor were high and method effects were low. Specifically, for each subject the first-order factor model, which was found to be the most appropriate for describing each classroom-level factor, is shown in Table 8.2. Moreover, Table 8.2 illustrates the second-order factors that were found to fit reasonably well with MTMM data in relation to some classroom-level factors. The following observations arise from this table.

First, the two models found to fit reasonably well with data concerning the orientation skills of teachers have the same structure as those that emerged from analysing the MTMM data on the structuring skills of teachers. Moreover, the models found to fit reasonably well with the questioning skills of teachers are similar to those of the structuring skills of teachers, but six instead of five correlated first-order factors were found to exist. This is due to the fact that each method generated three different scores in relation to the quality of questioning skills which

Table 8.2 Goodness-of-fit indices for the best-fitting structural equation models used to test the validity of the proposed framework for measuring each classroom-level effectiveness factor in each subject

SEM models	Greek language					Mathematics					Religious education				
	χ^2	d.f.	CFI	RMSEA	χ^2/d.f.	χ^2	d.f.	CFI	RMSEA	χ^2/d.f.	χ^2	d.f.	CFI	RMSEA	χ^2/d.f.
Orientation															
1 Five correlated traits, three correlated methods	253.4	137	0.941	0.03	1.85	246.6	137	0.940	0.04	1.80	260.3	137	0.935	0.04	1.90
2 Two correlated second-order general, three correlated methods	322.9	141	0.938	0.05	2.29	396.2	141	0.930	0.06	2.81	301.7	141	0.939	0.05	2.14
Questioning															
1 Six correlated traits, four correlated methods	553.7	301	0.947	0.03	1.84	562.9	301	0.946	0.03	1.87	574.9	301	0.943	0.04	1.91
2 Two correlated second-order general, four correlated methods	584.0	309	0.942	0.04	1.89	614.9	309	0.940	0.05	1.99	689.1	309	0.935	0.06	2.23
Application															
1 Five correlated traits, three correlated methods	231.5	137	0.965	0.02	1.69	226.1	137	0.969	0.02	1.65	261.7	137	0.938	0.04	1.91

continued

Table 8.2 continued

SEM models	Greek language					Mathematics					Religious education				
	χ^2	d.f.	CFI	RMSEA	χ^2/d.f.	χ^2	d.f.	CFI	RMSEA	χ^2/d.f.	χ^2	d.f.	CFI	RMSEA	χ^2/d.f.
Teaching-modelling															
1 Four correlated traits, three correlated methods	251.0	141	0.953	0.03	1.78	245.3	141	0.952	0.03	1.74	262.3	141	0.942	0.04	1.86
Management of time															
1 Four correlated traits, three correlated methods	63.1	33	0.942	0.05	1.91	61.1	33	0.948	0.03	1.85	56.1	33	0.953	0.03	1.70
Teacher evaluation															
1 Five correlated traits, two correlated methods	28.1	14	0.936	0.05	2.01	30.9	14	0.930	0.06	2.21	28.7	14	0.945	0.05	2.05
Classroom as a learning environment															
1 Two correlated second-order, two correlated methods	795.0	363	0.930	0.06	2.19	722.4	363	0.932	0.05	1.99	729.6	363	0.935	0.04	2.01

Note: Abbreviations as in Table 8.1.

refer to (1) the clarity of the questions, (2) the difficulty level of the questions, and (3) the feedback that teachers provide to student answers. The SEM analyses revealed that the measures of the quality of feedback that teachers give to students belong to a separate factor rather than the factor scores concerned with the other two elements of the quality dimension of questioning skills.

Second, there is no second-order factor model that was found to fit reasonably well with the MTMM data which refer to four classroom-level factors of the dynamic model (i.e. application, teaching-modelling, management of time, teacher evaluation). More specifically, all four of these models seem to provide strong support for the use of five dimensions for measuring effectiveness factors and for taking into account the methods used to collect data about teacher behaviour in the classroom. Let us repeat here that according to the dynamic model, the focus dimension of the management of time is not measured separately, and thereby four factors were expected to emerge from the SEM analysis. However, in the case of teaching-modelling, four rather than five factors were identified, and this is due to the fact that the variables associated with quality and differentiation were found to belong to the same factor.

Third, the 30 scores that emerged from the two methods (i.e. student questionnaire and high-inference observation) used to measure the dimensions of the five elements of the factor concerned with the role of the teacher in creating a learning environment in his or her classroom (i.e. teacher–student interaction, student–student interaction, students' treatment by the teacher, competition between students, and classroom disorder) were found to be explained by ten first-order factor traits and two second-order factors. Specifically, the factor scores that refer to the same dimension of three elements of the classroom environment (i.e. teacher–student interaction, students' treatment by the teacher, and classroom disorder) were found to belong to the same first-order factor, whereas those that emerged from the other two elements (i.e. student–student interaction and cooperation) were found to belong to the other five factors. Then, the five first-order factors that refer to the five dimensions of the three elements of the classroom learning environment concerned with teacher–student relations were found to belong to the same second-order general factor whereas the other five were found to belong to another second-order general factor that can be called student relations. These two general factors were also found to be correlated. It is finally important to note that the 30 factor scores were also found to belong to two method factors representing the two methods used to collect data (i.e. student questionnaire and high-inference observation instrument). It can be claimed that the findings that emerged from the structural equation modelling (SEM) analysis of classroom learning environment in each subject provides support for the way this factor is measured by the dynamic model. However, our findings suggest that the classroom learning environment could be described in a more parsimonious way, and instead of treating it as an overarching factor consisting of five factors (elements), we could claim that this overarching factor consists of only two factors (elements) which are concerned with the relations of the teacher with his or her students and the contribution of the teacher in creating relations among students in relation to learning.

Summary of the SEM results of the classroom-level factors

The results of this study seem to provide support for the construct validity of the five measurement dimensions of most effectiveness factors at the classroom level. The few exceptions that were identified reveal the difficulty of defining the quality dimension. In the case of questioning, aspects of quality were found to belong to two separate factors. Similarly, in the case of teaching-modelling, the differentiation and the quality dimensions were found to belong to the same factor. Moreover, the results of this study seem to reveal that the overarching factor 'classroom as a learning environment' cannot be treated as a single overarching factor; rather, it should be treated as two interrelated overarching factors that refer to relations among students in the classroom and relations between the teacher and his or her students. Second, the comparison of CFA models used to test each factor confirmed convergent and discriminant validity for the five dimensions. Convergent validity for most measures was demonstrated by the relatively high (i.e. higher than 0.59) standardised trait loadings, in comparison to the relatively low (i.e. lower than 0.42) standardised method loadings. These findings support the use of multi-method techniques for increasing measurement validity and construct validity. Stronger support for the validity of subsequent results is also provided. Third, the three-method-factor model was determined to be the best fitting rather than the four-method-factor for most factors, and this implies that the method factors were concerned with the advantage of the three methods typically used to collect data about teacher behaviour rather than with the four instruments used to collect data. This argument is supported by the fact that the measures of quality and focus of an activity emerging from using the second low-inference observation instrument were found to belong to the same factor as the data that emerged from the high-inference observation instrument. This result could be attributed to the fact that these two measures are not so easily interpretable as the measures of frequency, stage, and differentiation taken by this instrument. Thus, the other three dimensions of the second low-inference observation instrument were found to belong to the same factor as the measures of the first low-inference observation instrument (i.e. the one based on Flanders' system of interaction analysis), which can all be collected in a relatively straightforward way. Moreover, all the method factors were unidimensional factors as determined by their zero correlations with each other. Furthermore, examination of the proportion of variance accounted for by trait, method, and error (squared loadings) proved useful in assessing their specific influence on each measure. It was clear that the proportion of trait variance was generally high and method variance quite low. This implies that method effects did not strongly influence the measures. Finally, there did not appear to be any consistent method bias across traits or within traits for student questionnaires, high-inference observations, and low-inference observations, which provides additional support for the convergent validity of the measures. The absence of problems due to method bias in the present study indicates that the use of both types of observations and student questionnaires strengthens the reliability and validity of the constructs of classroom-level effectiveness factors and lends further support to the validity of the dynamic model.

The effects of classroom-level factors on achievement in four outcomes of schooling

Having established the construct validity of the framework used to measure the dimensions of the eight effectiveness factors of the dynamic model, we decided to examine the extent to which the first-order factors which were established through SEM analyses show the expected effects upon each of the four dependent variables, and therefore the analyses were performed separately for each variable. Specifically, the dynamic model was tested using 'MLwiN' (Goldstein *et al.*, 1998), because the observations are interdependent and because of multi-stage sampling, since students are nested within classes and classes within schools. The first step in the analysis was to determine the variance at individual, class, and school level without explanatory variables (empty model). In subsequent steps, explanatory variables at different levels were added. Explanatory variables, except grouping variables, were centred as Z-scores with a mean of 0 and a standard deviation of 1. This is a way of centring around the grand mean (Bryk and Raudenbush, 1992), and yields effects that are comparable. Thus, each effect expresses how much the dependent variable increases (or decreases, in the case of a negative sign) by each additional deviation on the independent variable (Snijders and Bosker, 1999). Grouping variables were entered as dummies with one of the groups as baseline (e.g. boys = 0). The models presented in Tables 8.3a and b and 8.4a and b were estimated without the variables that did not have a statistically significant effect at 0.05 level.

A comparison of the empty models of the four outcome measures reveals that the effect of the school and classroom was more pronounced on achievement in mathematics and Greek language than in religious education. Moreover, the teacher (classroom) effect was found to be higher on achievement of cognitive rather than affective aims of religious education. This finding is not in line with results of a study conducted in Cyprus which revealed that the effect of the school was more pronounced on achievement in affective outcome measures than on achievement in cognitive measures (Kyriakides, 2005a), but it is in line with studies investigating the effect of school on both cognitive and affective outcomes conducted in other countries (e.g. Konu *et al.*, 2002; Opdenakker and Van Damme, 2000). Finally, in each analysis the variance at each level reaches statistical significance ($p < 0.05$), and this implies that MLwiN can be used to identify the explanatory variables that are associated with achievement in each outcome of schooling (Goldstein, 2003).

In model 1 the context variables at student, classroom, and school levels were added to the empty model. The following observations arise from the figures of

Table 8.3a Parameter estimates and (standard errors) for the analyses of mathematics achievement

Factors	Model 0	Model 1	Model 2a Frequency	Model 2b Stage	Model 2c Focus	Model 2d Quality	Model 2e Differentiation
Fixed part/intercept	0.36 (0.05)	0.30 (0.05)	0.13 (0.02)	0.11 (0.02)	0.10 (0.02)	0.10 (0.02)	0.10 (0.02)
Student Level							
Prior knowledge		0.71 (0.12)	0.70 (0.12)	0.70 (0.12)	0.69 (0.12)	0.70 (0.12)	0.68 (0.12)
Sex (boys = 0, girls = 1)		−0.18 (0.07)	−0.15 (0.07)	−0.14 (0.07)	−0.16 (0.07)	−0.14 (0.07)	−0.13 (0.07)
SES		0.60 (0.25)	0.55 (0.24)	0.50 (0.24)	0.51 (0.24)	0.53 (0.24)	0.52 (0.24)
Classroom level							
Context							
Average knowledge		0.31 (0.11)	0.28 (0.10)	0.26 (0.11)	0.25 (0.11)	0.23 (0.11)	0.24 (0.11)
Average SES		0.15 (0.04)	0.13 (0.04)	0.10 (0.04)	0.09 (0.04)	0.09 (0.04)	0.10 (0.04)
Percentage of girls		−0.05 (0.02)	−0.05 (0.02)	−0.05 (0.02)	−0.04 (0.02)	−0.05 (0.02)	−0.05 (0.02)
Quality of teaching							
Structuring			0.07 (0.02)	0.04 (0.02)	0.03 (0.01)	0.05 (0.02)	N.S.S.
Orientation			0.11 (0.02)	0.02 (0.01)	0.05 (0.02)	0.02 (0.01)	N.S.S.
Questioning			0.08 (0.02)	N.S.S.	N.S.S.	NA	0.05 (0.02)
Application			0.08 (0.03)	0.07 (0.02)	0.04 (0.02)	N.S.S.	0.08 (0.02)
Teaching-modelling			N.S.S.*	N.S.S.	0.11	(0.03)NA	NA
Assessment			N.S.S.	N.S.S.	0.03 (0.01)	0.06 (0.02)	N.S.S.
Time management			0.10 (0.03)	N.S.S.	NA**	N.S.S.	N.S.S.
Teacher–student relations			0.03 (0.01)	0.03 (0.01)	N.S.S.	0.03 (0.01)	0.04 (0.02)
Student relations			0.10 (0.02)	N.S.S.	N.S.S.	N.S.S.	0.03 (0.01)
Quality of questions						0.04	(0.02)
Quality of feedback						0.05	(0.02)
Quality of modelling and differentiation						0.05 (0.02)	

School level

Context							
Average SES		N.S.S.	N.S.S.	N.S.S.	N.S.S.	N.S.S.	N.S.S.
Average knowledge		0.11 (0.05)	0.08 (0.04)	0.07 (0.04)	0.08 (0.04)	0.06 (0.03)	0.08 (0.04)
Percentage of girls		N.S.S.	N.S.S.	N.S.S.	N.S.S.	N.S.S.	N.S.S.
Variance components							
School	11.5%	8.1%	7.5%	7.5%	7.9%	7.5%	7.4%
Class	15.4%	9.3%	7.3%	6.9%	6.7%	6.0%	6.2%
Student	73.1%	30.9%	29.7%	30.0%	30.3%	29.5%	30.0%
Explained		51.7%	55.5%	55.6%	55.1%	57.0%	56.4%
Significance test							
X^2	1224.3	984.9	795.9	885.7	883.6	821.4	861.4
Reduction		239.4	189.0	99.2	101.3	163.5	123.5
Degrees of freedom		7	7	4	5	6	5
p-value		0.001	0.001	0.001	0.001	0.001	0.001

Notes

Each alternative model 2 investigates the effect of each measurement dimension (i.e. model 2a is concerned with frequency, model 2b is concerned with stage, model 2c is concerned with focus, model 2d is concerned with quality and model 2e is concerned with differentiation) of the classroom factors. The reduction of each model is estimated in relation to the deviance of model 1. * N.S.S. = No statistically significant effect at 0.05 level; ** NA: This factor is not measured in relation to this dimension.

Table 8.3b Parameter estimates and (standard errors) for the analyses of Greek language achievement

Factors	Model 0	Model 1	Model 2a Frequency	Model 2b Stage	Model 2c Focus	Model 2d Quality	Model 2e Differentiation
Fixed part/intercept	−0.39(0.08)	−0.33 (0.08)	−0.29 (0.08)	−0.30 (0.08)	−0.31 (0.08)	−0.27(0.08)	−0.30 (0.08)
Student level							
Prior knowledge		0.49 (0.05)	0.47 (0.05)	0.46 (0.05)	0.45 (0.05)	0.48 (0.05)	0.48 (0.05)
Sex(boys = 0, girls = 1)		0.23 (0.10)	0.21 (0.09)	0.20 (0.09)	0.22 (0.09)	0.21 (0.09)	0.19 (0.09)
SES		0.32 (0.06)	0.28 (0.05)	0.29 (0.05)	0.25 (0.05)	0.26 (0.05)	0.27 (0.05)
Classroom level							
Context							
Average knowledge		0.15 (0.05)	0.11 (0.04)	0.12 (0.05)	0.13 (0.04)	0.12 (0.04)	0.10 (0.04)
Average SES		0.09 (0.04)	0.08 (0.04)	0.09 (0.04)	0.08 (0.04)	0.07 (0.03)	0.06 (0.03)
Percentage of girls		NSS	NSS	NSS	NSS	NSS	NSS
Quality of teaching							
Structuring			0.09 (0.02)	0.04 (0.02)	NSS	0.05 (0.02)	NSS
Orientation			0.07 (0.02)	0.02 (0.01)	0.07 (0.02)	NSS	NSS
Questioning			0.08 (0.02)	NSS	NSS	NA	0.04 (0.02)
(Questioning)^2			−0.02 (0.01)	NSS	NSS	NA	NSS
Application			0.06 (0.03)	0.07 (0.02)	NSS	NSS	0.06 (0.02)
Teaching-modelling			NSS	NSS	0.09 (0.03)	NA	NA
Assessment			0.06 (0.02)	NSS	0.03 (0.01)	0.06 (0.03)	NSS
(Assessment)^2			−0.02 (0.01)	NSS	NSS	NSS	NSS
Time management			0.10 (0.03)	NSS	NA	NSS	NSS
Teacher–student relations			NSS	NSS	NSS	0.03 (0.01)	NSS
Quality of questions			0.10 (0.02)	0.03 (0.01)	0.03 (0.01)	0.04 (0.02)	0.03 (0.01)
Quality of feedback						0.04 (0.02)	
Quality of modelling and differentiation						0.06 (0.02)	0.03 (0.01)

School level

Context							
Average SES		NSS	NSS	NSS	NSS	NSS	NSS
Average knowledge		0.13 (0.05)	0.12 (0.05)	0.11 (0.05)	0.10 (0.05)	0.12 (0.05)	0.11 (0.05)
Percentage of girls		NSS	NSS	NSS	NSS	NSS	NSS
Variance components							
School	9.5%	7.7%	7.6%	7.6%	7.7%	7.5%	7.6%
Class	15.2%	11.1%	8.8%	9.2%	9.3%	8.7%	8.9%
Student	75.3%	31.5%	28.3%	28.6%	28.5%	28.2%	28.5%
Explained		49.7%	55.3%	54.6%	54.5%	55.6%	55.0%
Significance test							
X^2	1015.6	686.7	428.8	558.8	579.2	497.4	581.5
Reduction		328.9	257.9	127.9	107.5	189.3	105.2
Degrees of freedom		6	9	4	4	6	4
p-value		0.001	0.001	0.001	0.001	0.001	0.001

Note: Abbreviations as in Table 8.3a.

Table 8.4a Parameter estimates and (standard errors) for the analyses of achievement in religious education (cognitive outcomes)

Factors	Model 0	Model 1	Model 2a Frequency	Model 2b Stage	Model 2c Focus	Model 2d Quality	Model 2e Differentiation
Fixed part/intercept	-0.79 (0.11)	-0.63 (0.09)	-0.61 (0.08)	-0.60 (0.08)	-0.62 (0.08)	-0.64 (0.08)	-0.60 (0.08)
Student level							
Prior knowledge		0.51 (0.05)	0.49 (0.05)	0.48 (0.05)	0.50 (0.05)	0.46 (0.05)	0.50 (0.05)
Sex (boys = 0, girls = 1)		0.23 (0.09)	0.19 (0.09)	0.20 (0.09)	0.21 (0.09)	0.21 (0.09)	0.20 (0.09)
SES		0.12 (0.05)	0.10 (0.05)	0.09 (0.04)	0.11 (0.05)	0.10 (0.05)	0.08 (0.04)
Classroom level							
Context							
Average knowledge		0.25 (0.07)	0.21 (0.07)	0.22 (0.07)	0.23 (0.07)	0.22 (0.07)	0.20 (0.07)
Average SES		0.09 (0.04)	0.08 (0.04)	0.09 (0.04)	0.08 (0.04)	0.07 (0.03)	0.06 (0.03)
Percentage of girls		NSS	NSS	NSS	NSS	NSS	NSS
Quality of teaching							
Structuring			0.11 (0.02)	0.05 (0.02)	0.07 (0.02)	0.05 (0.02)	NSS
Orientation			NSS	0.02 (0.01)	NSS	NSS	NSS
Questioning			0.10 (0.02)	NSS	0.03 (0.01)	NA	0.07 (0.02)
Application			0.06 (0.03)	0.08 (0.02)	0.05 (0.02)	0.04 (0.02)	0.08 (0.02)
Teaching-modelling			NSS	NSS	NSS	NA	NA
Assessment			NSS	NSS	NSS	NSS	NSS
Time management			0.10 (0.03)	NSS	NA	NSS	NSS
Teacher–student relations			NSS	0.05 (0.02)	NSS	0.03 (0.01)	0.02 (0.01)
Student relations			0.05 (0.02)	0.03 (0.01)	0.04 (0.02)	0.04 (0.02)	0.03 (0.01)
Quality of questions						0.09 (0.02)	
Quality of feedback						0.08 (0.02)	
Quality of modelling and differentiation							0.03 (0.01)

School level

Context							
Average SES		NSS	NSS	NSS	NSS	NSS	NSS
Average knowledge		0.13 (0.05)	0.12 (0.05)	0.11 (0.05)	0.10 (0.05)	0.12 (0.05)	0.11 (0.05)
Percentage of girls		NSS	NSS	NSS	NSS	NSS	NSS
Variance components							
School	8.0%	7.7%	7.6%	7.6%	7.7%	7.5%	7.6%
Class	13.2%	11.1%	8.8%	8.2%	8.3%	7.7%	8.9%
Student	78.8%	34.5%	30.3%	29.6%	30.5%	29.2%	29.5%
Explained		46.7%	53.3%	54.6%	53.5%	55.6%	54.0%
Significance test							
X^2	1823.6	1457.1	1337.6	1309.2	1359.6	1277.6	1331.9
Reduction		366.5	119.5	147.9	97.5	179.5	125.2
Degrees of freedom		6	5	5	4	6	5
p-value		0.001	0.001	0.001	0.001	0.001	0.001

Note: Abbreviations as in Table 8.3a.

Table 8.4b Parameter estimates and (standard errors) for the analyses of achievement in religious education (affective outcomes)

Factors	Model 0	Model I	Model 2a Frequency	Model 2b Stage	Model 2c Focus	Model 2d Quality	Model 2e Differentiation
Fixed part/intercept	0.61 (0.08)	0.50 (0.07)	0.43 (0.07)	0.41 (0.07)	0.42 (0.07)	0.40 (0.07)	0.44 (0.07)
Student level							
Prior knowledge		0.41 (0.10)	0.40 (0.10)	0.40 (0.10)	0.39 (0.10)	0.40 (0.10)	0.38 (0.10)
Sex(boys = 0, girls = 1)		0.18 (0.07)	0.15 (0.07)	0.15 (0.07)	0.16 (0.07)	0.14 (0.07)	0.15 (0.07)
SES		NSS	NSS	NSS	NSS	NSS	NSS
Classroom level							
Context							
Average knowledge		0.21 (0.08)	0.18 (0.07)	0.16 (0.07)	0.15 (0.07)	0.19 (0.07)	0.20 (0.18)
Average SES		NSS	NSS	NSS	NSS	NSS	NSS
Percentage of girls		0.05 (0.02)	0.04 (0.02)	0.04 (0.02)	0.04 (0.02)	0.04 (0.02)	0.03 (0.01)
Quality of teaching							
Structuring			0.09 (0.02)	0.06 (0.03)	0.03 (0.01)	0.05 (0.02)	NSS
Orientation			NSS	NSS	0.05 (0.02)	0.02 (0.01)	NSS
Questioning			0.09 (0.02)	NSS	0.04 (0.02)	NA	0.05 (0.02)
Application			NSS	0.07 (0.02)	0.11 (0.03)	NSS	0.08 (0.02)
Teaching-modelling			NSS	NSS	NSS	NA	NA
Assessment			NSS	NSS	NSS	0.06 (0.02)	NSS
Time management			0.10 (0.02)	NSS	NA	NSS	NSS
Teacher–student relations			0.03 (0.01)	0.03 (0.01)	0.03 (0.01)	0.03 (0.01)	0.04 (0.02)
Student relations			0.07 (0.02)	NSS	NSS	NSS	0.03 (0.01)
Quality of questions						0.04 (0.02)	
Quality of feedback						0.05 (0.02)	
Quality of modelling and differentiation							0.05 (0.02)

School level

Context						
Average SES		NSS	NSS	NSS	NSS	NSS	NSS
Average knowledge		0.08 (0.02)	0.06 (0.02)	0.05 (0.02)	0.07 (0.02)	0.06 (0.02)	0.07 (0.02)
Percentage of girls		NSS	NSS	NSS	NSS	NSS	NSS
Variance components							
School	7.5%	7.0%	6.7%	6.6%	6.7%	6.4%	6.5%
Class	10.4%	9.3%	6.3%	7.2%	6.7%	6.4%	6.5%
Student	82.1%	32.6%	31.7%	31.4%	31.3%	31.1%	31.0%
Explained		51.1%	55.3%	54.8%	55.3%	56.1%	56.0%
Significance test							
X^2	1024.5	835.1	705.2	758.9	719.8	700.6	711.6
Reduction		189.4	129.9	76.2	115.3	134.5	123.5
Degrees of freedom		5	5	3	5	6	5
p-value		0.001	0.001	0.001	0.001	0.001	0.001

Note: Abbreviations as in Table 8.3a.

the four columns illustrating the results of model 1 for each analysis. First, model 1 explains approximately 50 per cent of the total variance of student achievement in each outcome, and most of the explained variance is at the student level. However, more than 30 per cent of the total variance remained unexplained at the student level. Second, the likelihood statistic (χ^2) shows a significant change between the empty model and model 1 ($p < 0.001$), which justifies the selection of model 1. Second, the effects of all contextual factors at student level (i.e. SES, prior knowledge, sex) are significant, but SES was not found to be associated with achievement of affective aims in religious education. Moreover, gender was not found to be consistently associated with student achievement in each outcome. Girls were found to have better results in relation to every outcome except mathematics. The results concerning gender differences in Greek language and mathematics are in line with findings of effectiveness studies conducted in Cyprus (Kyriakides *et al.*, 2000; Kyriakides, 2005a; Kyriakides and Creemers, 2006a). Third, prior knowledge (i.e. aptitude) has the strongest effect in predicting student achievement at the end of the school year. Moreover, aptitude is the only contextual variable that had a consistent effect on student achievement when aggregated at either the classroom or the school level. Finally, the standard errors show that the effect sizes of the context variables are significant and stable.

At the next step of the analysis, for each dependent variable five different versions of model 2 were established. In each version of model 2 the factor scores of SEM models which refer to the same dimension of measuring the classroom-level effectiveness factors of the dynamic model were added to model 1. Thus, the fitting of these five models was tested against model 1, and the likelihood statistic (χ^2) shows a significant change between model 1 and each version of model 2 ($p < 0.001$). This implies that variables measuring the five dimensions of the classroom effectiveness factors have significant effects on student achievement gains in the four outcomes of schooling taken into account for this study. This approach was deliberately chosen, since the dimensions of the same factor are interrelated, as shown in the SEM analyses, and thereby adding all dimensions into a single model makes it difficult to identify which variables have effects on student achievement. For example, some variables may correlate with achievement when they are studied in isolation, but, because of multicollinearity, their effects may disappear when they are studied together. This implies that factors that do not show the expected effects in a multilevel analysis do not necessarily contradict the assumptions of the model. Therefore, it was considered appropriate to study the effect of each dimension of the classroom-level factors in isolation.

The following observations arise from the figures of model 2a which refer to the impact of the frequency dimension of the effectiveness factors on each of the four dependent variables. First, the only factor which did not have a statistically significant effect on any student outcome is concerned with the frequency of teaching-modelling. On the other hand, the structuring and the management of time were found to be associated with student achievement gains in each of the four dependent variables. Second, although curvilinear relations were assumed to exist between most of the frequency factors and student achievement, only two such relations were identified, and both of them refer to student achievement in Greek language. Specifically, a curvilinear relation between achievement in Greek language and the frequency dimension of the factor concerned with asking questions was identified. Moreover, the frequency dimension of the factor concerned with teacher assessment was found to be related in a non-linear way to achievement in Greek language.

As far as the figures of the models which refer to the impact of the stage dimension of the classroom-level factors are concerned, we can observe that the stage dimension of two factors (i.e. structuring and application) is associated with each outcome measure, whereas the stage dimension of three other factors (i.e. questioning, assessment, and management of time) does not have a statistically significant effect on any outcome. Moreover, the effect of the stage dimension of the application factor was found to be the strongest. The figures of model 2c reveal that the focus dimension of at least four factors is associated with student achievement gains in each dependent variable. However, there is no factor that has a statistically significant effect across the four outcomes or any factor that is not associated with at least one dependent variable. The figures of model 2d refer to the impact of the quality dimension of each effectiveness factor upon student achievement. We can observe that for each outcome measure, the quality dimension of six factors is associated with student achievement. Moreover, for each outcome measure, model 2d explains more variance than any alternative model 2, and this reveals the importance of using this dimension to measure the impact of effectiveness factors on student achievement gains. Finally, for each outcome the figures of model 2e reveal that the differentiation dimension of three factors (i.e. questioning, application, and classroom learning environment) is consistently related to student achievement gains whereas the differentiation dimension of all the other factors is not associated with student achievement gains on any outcome measure.

At the next stage of the analysis we attempted to identify the amount of variance that can be explained when researchers take into account the effects of the frequency dimensions of the classroom-level factors and the effects of at least one other dimension. For this reason, four alternative models were created which took into account combination of frequency dimension with another dimension of the eight factors. Each model was compared with model 2a, which takes into account only the frequency dimension. The likelihood statistics for each model justify the inclusion of more than one dimension of factors in the model. Table 8.5 illustrates the total explained variance of model 2a and of the five alternative models, taking into account combinations of frequency with other dimensions of measurement. We can observe that for each outcome, each alternative model explains more than the variance explained only by considering the frequency dimension. Moreover, the model with a combination of frequency and quality dimensions of the classroom-level factors explains more total variance than any other combination of frequency with each of the other three dimensions. Finally, the model combining

Table 8.5 Percentage of explained variance of student achievement for each student outcome provided by each alternative model testing the effect of the frequency dimension of the classroom-level factors and the effect of combinations of frequency dimensions with each of the other dimensions

Alternative model	Greek language	Mathematics	Cognitive religious education	Affective religious education
Model 2a (frequency dimension of classroom-level factors)	55.3%	55.5%	53.3%	55.3%
Model 2f (frequency and stage dimensions)	59.2%	57.8%	56.7%	58.7%
Model 2g (frequency and focus dimensions)	58.7%	56.8%	55.9%	57.9%
Model 2h (frequency and quality dimensions)	59.7%	59.1%	57.1%	59.1%
Model 2i (frequency and differentiation dimensions)	58.9%	58.1%	56.2%	58.9%
Model 3 (all five dimensions of classroom-level factors)	60.9%	60.1%	59.0%	59.8%

all five dimensions explains most of the variance and was found to fit better than any alternative model. This model is able to explain more than 70 per cent of the variance at the classroom level of student achievement in each outcome. This implies that all five dimensions should be taken into account in order to explain as much variance as possible at the classroom level. However, none of these models explains more than about 60 per cent of the total variance. Nevertheless, this can be attributed to the fact that we did not take into account the impact of any school-level factor. Moreover, only some factors at the student level were taken into account (see Chapter 6). Therefore, it is important to examine whether including the five dimensions of the school-level factors could help us explain most of the unexplained variance of model 3 for each outcome.

Implication of findings for the development of the dynamic model

Our findings have implications for the development of the dynamic model. First, a criticism that may arise from the theoretical background and the outline of the dynamic model concerns the complexity of the model and the difficulties of testing it empirically. For example, it can be claimed that the model is not parsimonious, since it contains more factors and more dimensions than previous models and it is therefore not possible to illustrate priorities for educational improvement. More-over, the inclusion of different dimensions for measuring each factor complicates the data collection and the analysis. However, this study seems to reveal that the dynamic model is a theoretical model that can be put to the test. It can also be treated as a framework for future studies investigating the validity of the theoretical background of the dynamic model and the essential characteristics of the factors included in the model, such as the existence of curvilinear relations between dimensions of effectiveness factors and student achievement. Specifically, the results of the study provide support for the construct validity of the five measure-ment dimensions of most effectiveness factors at the classroom level. It has been shown that the classroom-level effectiveness factors cannot be considered to be unidimensional constructs, since the one second-order factor model was not considered psychometrically appropriate for measuring any of the eight effec-tiveness factors. This might reveal a weakness of previous effectiveness studies focused on the classroom level, which have usually treated frequency as the only measurement dimension of effectiveness factors.

Moreover, the comparison of CFA models used to test each factor confirmed convergent and discriminant validity for the five dimensions. These findings also support the use of multi-method techniques for increasing measurement and construct validity. Specifically, the three-method-factor model, considered the most appropriate, was concerned with the advantage of the three methods typically used to collect data about teacher behaviour. This study seems to reveal that it is inefficient to concentrate on the debate regarding the advantages and limitations of external observations versus student ratings of teacher behaviour. It might be more beneficial to make use of multiple methods and instruments and use SEM approaches to test the convergent and discriminant validity of data collected on teacher behaviour. Moreover, both low- and high-inference observation instruments are needed in order to collect valid data about the five dimensions of the model, especially since two dimensions are focused on quantitative aspects of teacher behaviour whereas the other three examine issues concerned with the quality of teacher behaviour. In summary, the SEM results reveal that it is psychometrically appropriate to measure each effectiveness factor at the classroom level by taking into account the five proposed dimensions and that it is necessary to make use of all three methods of measuring teacher behaviour. Studies further investigating the validity of the model at the classroom level, especially considering that this study took place in a single country and its generalisability has still to be proved, could consider the possibility of using this methodological approach to collect data on the five dimensions of the eight classroom-level factors and testing the construct validity of the dynamic model.

Second, this study reveals the added value of using five dimensions to measure the classroom-level factors for explaining variation of student achievement gains in different outcomes. Specifically, it has been shown that the five alternative models used to examine the impact of each of the five measurement dimensions fit the data better than model 1, which was concerned with the impact of contextual factors on student achievement. This implies that all five dimensions can be used to identify factors associated with student achievement gains in both cognitive and affective aspects of education. Moreover, taking into account the combination of frequency dimension with other dimensions of classroom-level factors increases the explained variance on student achievement gains. Furthermore, there are factors that were found to have no statistically significant effect on student achievement when the impact of their frequency dimension was measured but did have a significant impact on student achievement when other dimensions were taken into account (see Tables 8.3 and 8.4). This implies that previous studies concerned only with the frequency dimension might have drawn incorrect conclusions about the impact of a factor and have failed to explain as much variance as possible at the classroom level. For example, in this study the frequency dimension of teaching-modelling was not associated with student achievement on any outcome, but the quality dimension of this factor had an impact on achievement. This finding reveals that emphasis should be given to other dimensions of effectiveness factors and not only to frequency, which has been used predominantly in all studies in the past. When this finding is supported and expanded upon by other studies, it can give directions to link effectiveness research with educational practice, and especially improvement efforts, by indicating ways of improving education other than just increasing the presence of effective factors in the classroom (see Chapter 12). Moreover, such results might help us develop the model and make it less complicated by focusing on the dimensions of factors that matter most. This holds for the case of management of time, which is measured in a valid way in relation to the dimensions of the model, but only the frequency dimension was found to be associated with student achievement. This finding implies that in the case of management of time, the frequency dimension alone might be sufficient to explain variation in student achievement gains.

Third, in order to facilitate the understanding of the results of the four multilevel analyses, Table 8.6 was constructed. This table illustrates the identified effects of the dimensions of each factor on student achievement in the four outcomes of schooling. Looking at the impact that each of the proposed factors has on student achievement, we can claim that generally the importance of the eight classroom-level factors is confirmed. The factors of the dynamic model were found to be associated with student achievement on different outcomes of schooling which refer not only to the two core subjects of the Cyprus curriculum but also to one of the subsidiary subjects. Moreover, they were found to be related to the achievement of both cognitive and affective aims of schooling. It could, therefore, be claimed that these eight factors can be considered to belong to a generic model of educational effectiveness. However, comparing the impact of each factor on the four outcomes of schooling, the eight factors can be classified into three groups.

First, the great majority of the measurement dimensions of four factors (i.e. structuring, application, questioning, and classroom as a learning environment) were found to be consistently associated with student achievement on each of the four outcomes of schooling. This implies that, in general, strong evidence supporting the validity of the dynamic model for these four factors is provided by this study. These factors could be considered as generic factors. Second, there were two factors (i.e. teaching-modelling and management of time) that were associated with student achievement when only some measurement dimensions were taken into account. Teaching-modelling was found to be associated with student achievement on each outcome when aspects of its quality were taken into account. Similarly, only the frequency dimension of the management of time factor had an impact on student outcomes. This finding reveals possibilities for creating a more parsimonious model. Finally, the impact of the last two factors (i.e. assessment and orientation) on student outcomes, at least as measured in this study, seems to be subject-specific. Specifically, most dimensions of both factors are related to achievement in the two core subjects, but almost none of them is related to achievement in any type of aims of religious education. The above classification of factors reveals that, in general, the model could become more parsimonious by indicating factors that should be measured across the five dimensions and factors for which it is not necessary to measure across all dimensions. Moreover, the existence of subject-specific factors in this study might imply that aspects of the dynamic model have to be specified in relation to the criteria used to measure effectiveness. On the other hand, the lack of impact of the two 'subject-specific' factors on student achievement in religious education might be considered a context-specific result, especially since variance in relation to these two factors was much smaller than in the case of the two core subjects.

Fourth, the study provided some support for the existence of curvilinear relations, but in both cases such relations were found to exist in relation to the

Table 8.6 Overview of the impact of the five dimensions (i.e. frequency (Freq), stage (Stag), focus (Foc), quality (Qual), and differentiation (Diff)) of the classroom-level factors of the dynamic model on student outcomes (i.e. achievement in Greek language, achievement in mathematics, achievement of cognitive aims of religious education, and achievement of affective aims of religious education)

Factor	Greek language					Mathematics					Religious education cognitive					Religious education affective				
	Freq	Stag	Foc	Qual	Diff	Freq	Stag	Foc	Qual	Diff	Freq	Stag	Foc	Qual	Diff	Freq	Stag	Foc	Qual	Diff
Structuring	+	+		+		+	+	+	+	+	+	+	+	+	+	+	+	+	+	
Orientation	+	+	+			+	+	+	+			+						+	+	
Questioning	Curv			++	+	+			++	+	+		+	++	+	+		+	++	+
Application	+	+			+	+	+	+		+	+	+	+	+	+		+	+		+
Teaching-modelling			+		+			+		+					+				+	+
Assessment	Curv		+	+		Curv		+	+										+	
Management of time	+		N/A			+		N/A			+		N/A			+		N/A		
Classroom-level environment																				
1 Teacher-student relations				+	+	+	+		+	+	+	+		+	+	+	+	+	+	+
2 Student relations	+	+	+	+	+	+			+	+	+	+	+	+	+	+				+

Note: The trait factors, which emerged from the CFA used to measure the validity of the proposed measurement frameworks, are presented here. For this reason, in the box concerned with the quality dimension of questioning skills, the relations between the two quality factors and student achievement are examined. Moreover, the quality and differentiation dimensions of teaching-modelling were found to belong to only one factor. Finally, two overarching factors concerned with the classroom as a learning environment were identified (i.e. teacher–student relations, student–student relations).

+: A statistically significant effect ($p < 0.05$) upon student achievement was identified.

Curv: A curvilinear relationship was identified.

++: Both factors concerned with quality of questioning skills were found to be related to achievement.

teaching of Greek language. However, it can be claimed that the difficulty of demonstrating curvilinear relations may be due to the difficulty of establishing enough variation in the functioning of the factors, especially since this study was conducted in a single country. To further demonstrate our argument, we can refer to the fact that the variance of frequency of questioning in Greek language was much higher than in the case of mathematics, and a curvilinear relation only with teaching Greek language was identified. There are two alternative approaches to searching for curvilinear relations. First, experimental studies could be conducted with a view to creating enough variance in the functioning of each factor by using the factorial design (see Shadish *et al.*, 2002). It might then be possible to identify curvilinear relations, and thereby the optimal values for the frequency and focus dimensions of the classroom-level factors could be identified. However, attention should be paid not only to threats to the internal validity of each experimental study but also to its ecological validity and the ethical issues associated with the experimentation (Miller, 1984; Robson, 1993). On the other hand, comparative studies can be conducted to test the validity of the model. International longitudinal studies can tap the full range of variation in school and classroom quality, and therefore in potential school and classroom effects. It is also likely that the existing estimates of the size of educational influences (i.e. schools and classrooms/teachers together) upon student outcomes are potentially merely artefacts of the studies' lack of school and classroom variation. Thus, international studies could help us identify curvilinear relations, since in national studies the lack of a significant effect might be due to the difficulties we have in identifying variation either in the student outcomes or, more likely, in the explanatory variables. In addition, international studies on EER could show that the model travels across countries and can be considered a generic model. Suggestions on how these two approaches can be used for investigating the existence of curvilinear relations as well as the extent to which the model can travel across countries will be given in Chapter 10.

Chapter 9

Testing the dynamic model

A synthesis of studies investigating the impact of school factors on student achievement

Introduction

The previous chapter was an attempt to illustrate how readers could conduct an empirical study that may help us test the validity of the model. The findings of this study provided support both for the validity of the model at the classroom level and for the proposed framework for measuring the functioning of each effectiveness factor. It is acknowledged that the generalisability of this study can be questioned. However, it can be seen as a starting point for research on the model, especially in relation to the impact of classroom-level factors. As far as the investigation of school-level factors is concerned, the results of the meta-analysis reported here provide some support for the model and some directions for further research. Specifically, the meta-analysis reported here is an attempt to synthesise the results of effectiveness studies exploring the impact of school factors on student achievement conducted during the past 20 years. The extent to which the results of this meta-analysis provide support for the validity of the dynamic model at the school level is therefore discussed. Thus, Part III of the book reveals that the dynamic model could be tested both through empirical studies specifically designed to test the model and through systematic meta-analyses of effectiveness studies. For instance, a meta-analysis similar to the one presented here could also be conducted to investigate the validity of the model at the classroom level.

Scientists have known for centuries that a single study will not resolve a major issue. Indeed, a small sample study will not even resolve a minor issue. The foundation of science is the cumulation of knowledge from the results of many studies. There are two steps to the cumulation of knowledge: (1) the cumulation of results across studies to establish facts, and (2) the formation of theories to organise the facts into a coherent and useful form. Meta-analysis is concerned with the first step – that is, with the resolution of the basic facts from a set of studies that all bear on the same relationship. Meta-analysis is rapidly increasing in importance in the behavioural and social sciences, as will be discussed in the next section. It is not merely the use of meta-analysis that has increased; the number of different techniques and methods in meta-analyses has also increased dramatically during the past decade. Thus, the importance of conducting meta-analyses to test and expand the dynamic model will be discussed. In this context the aims of our meta-analysis will be pointed out in the third section of this chapter. The next two sections refer to the methods and the main findings of the meta-analysis, whereas implications for the development of the dynamic model are considered in the last section.

The importance of using meta-analyses to test the validity of the dynamic model

The goal in any science is the production of cumulative knowledge. Ultimately, this means the development of theories that explain the phenomena that are the focus of the scientific area. One example is theories that identify the school factors associated with student achievement. Unless we can precisely calibrate relationships among variables (e.g. leadership style and student achievement), we do not have the raw materials out of which to construct theories; there is nothing for a theory to explain. For example, if the relationship between instructional leadership and student achievement varies capriciously across different studies from a strong positive to a strong negative correlation and everything in between, we cannot begin to construct a theory of how leadership might affect achievement. This implies that there is a need for researchers in any field to conduct meta-analyses that integrate the findings across studies and reveal the simpler patterns of relationships that underlie research literatures, thus providing a basis for theory development. Moreover, meta-analysis can correct for the distorting effects of sampling error, measurement error, and other artefacts that produce the illusion of conflicting findings (Hunter and Schmidt, 2004).

Before meta-analysis, the usual way in which scientists made sense of research literature was by use of the narrative subjective review of literature. In many research literatures there were not only conflicting findings, but also a large number of studies. This combination made the standard narrative subjective review a nearly impossible task. The answer, as developed in many narrative reviews, was what came to be called 'the myth of the perfect study'. Reviewers convinced themselves that most of the available studies were methodologically deficient and should not be considered in the review. These judgements of methodological deficiency were often based on idiosyncratic ideas. For example, textbook authors would often pick out what they considered to be the two or three 'best' studies and then base textbook conclusions on just those studies, discarding the vast bulk of the information in the literature. In this context the myth of the perfect study emerged. However, there are no perfect studies. All studies contain measurement errors in all measures used. For example, measurement errors associated with our attempt to examine the dimensions of all of the classroom effectiveness factors have been reported in the previous chapter. Independent of measurement error, no study's measures have perfect construct validity (Cronbach, 1990). Furthermore, there are typically other artefacts that distort study findings. Even if a hypothetical study suffered from none of these distortions, it would still contain sampling error.

Therefore, it can be claimed that no single study or even a small number of studies can provide an optimal basis for scientific conclusions about cumulative knowledge.

However, this does not mean that since there is no perfect study, all studies should be included in a meta-analysis. Only those studies that meet some basic quality criteria, such as the provision of information regarding the validity of the study, should be taken into account for a meta-analysis. Nevertheless, we do not adopt the idea that only studies using true experimental approaches should be selected or given more emphasis than survey studies, as proposed by the best evidence approach (Slavin, 1986, 1987c), since reliance on 'perfect studies' does not provide a solution to researchers when they are confronted with the problem of conflicting research findings. On the contrary, characteristics of the studies used to conduct the meta-analysis (e.g. research design employed, country context, statistical techniques employed) can be taken into account, and researchers may try to find out the extent to which these characteristics can predict variation in observed effect sizes.

Looking at the history of the use of meta-analysis in social sciences, one could infer that starting in the late 1970s, new methods of combining findings across studies on the same subject were developed. These methods were referred to collectively as meta-analysis, a term coined by Glass (1976). Applications of meta-analysis to accumulated research literatures (e.g. Schmidt and Hunter, 1977) showed that research findings were not nearly as conflicting as had been thought (e.g. Cronbach, 1975; Meehl, 1978) and that useful and sound general conclusions could in fact be drawn from existing research. In fact, meta-analysis has even produced evidence that the cumulativeness of research findings in the behavioural sciences is as great as that in the physical sciences (see Hedges, 1987). The major lesson drawn during the past two decades from the attempts of researchers to conduct meta-analysis in different subject areas of social sciences is that many discoveries and advances in cumulative knowledge are being made not by those who do primary research studies but by those who use meta-analysis to discover the latent meaning of existing research literatures (Hunter and Schmidt, 2004). It was also found that the meta-analytic process of cleaning up and making sense of research literatures not only reveals the cumulative knowledge that is there but also provides clearer directions about what the remaining research needs are.

Usually, meta-analyses are conducted for two main reasons. First, researchers are interested in finding out at what stage the cumulative knowledge in a field is, and the main aim is to provide the state of the art, which can be used by both researchers and practitioners. Second, researchers may also be interested in using the findings of a meta-analysis as an argument or starting point for building a theory or for designing further studies. In the case of EER, a large number of reviews were conducted in the 1990s, but most of them did not follow the quantitative approach to estimate the average effect sizes of school factors on student achievement. Their main purpose was to provide the research community and policy-makers with the state of the art of the field (e.g. Creemers and Reezigt, 1996; Levine and Lezotte,

1990; Sammons *et al.*, 1995). On the other hand, Scheerens and Bosker (1997) conducted a quantitative synthesis of effectiveness studies in order to determine the estimated effect size of variables mentioned in the school effectiveness literature upon student outcomes. This approach to the field of EER enabled a significant contribution to the knowledge base to be made. The meta-analysis reported here uses the same statistical approach as the one used by Scheerens and Bosker (1997) but departs from an attempt to test a proposed dynamic model. The main questions that guide this meta-analysis are concerned with the importance of the proposed effectiveness factors as well as with the extent to which other factors that gain empirical support are not included in the model. In this way the meta-analysis is used as a step for validation of the model and not as a starting point for building, as is the case of meta-analysis in most fields of social sciences. More information regarding the aims of this meta-analysis is given in the next section, whereas the rest of this chapter refers to the methods and the main findings of our meta-analysis.

Aims of the quantitative synthesis of studies investigating the impact of school factors on student achievement

The meta-analysis reported here used a quantitative approach to synthesise the findings of multinational research studies conducted during the past 20 years in order to estimate the effect size of school effectiveness factors on student achievement. The focus is on the substantive findings that emerged from the meta-analysis. Specifically, the extent to which the findings of the review justify the importance of the school factors presented in the dynamic model is examined. We shall also attempt to identify the factors (or moderators) that account for the variation in effect sizes. As mentioned above, the effect sizes of studies involved in a meta-analysis are very likely to vary, owing to differences in procedures, instrumentation, study contexts, and treatments. Identifying the impact that these factors have on effect sizes gives an even clearer insight into the potential impact of school factors because it might clarify the conditions under which each of them is able to influence effectiveness. For this reason, the extent to which the impact of factors depends on the criteria used for measuring effectiveness will be identified. This analysis may reveal that the model can be considered a generic one. Some further conceptual and methodological issues will also be identified. Specifically, the way each school factor is measured by the school effectiveness studies will be compared with the five measurement dimensions of the dynamic model. The importance of grouping factors will also be investigated. Finally, suggestions for research on testing the validity of the dynamic model will be drawn.

Methods

Selection of studies

Our research team conducted a search of documentary databases containing abstracts of empirical studies. Specifically, the following databases were taken into account: the Educational Resources Information Centre (ERIC), the Social Sciences Citation Index, Educational Administration Abstracts, SCOPUS, Pro Quest 5000, and PsycArticles. We also paged through volumes of educational peer-reviewed journals with an interest in EER such as the journals *School Effectiveness and School Improvement*, the *British Educational Research Journal*, the *Oxford Review of Education*, and *Learning Environment Research*. Finally, relevant reviews of school effectiveness studies (e.g. Creemers and Reezigt, 1996; Fan and Chen, 2001; Fraser *et al.*, 1987; Hallinger and Heck, 1998; Levine and Lezotte, 1990; Sammons *et al.*, 1995; Scheerens and Bosker, 1997) and handbooks focused on effectiveness (e.g. Teddlie and Reynolds, 2000; Townsend *et al.*, 1999) were examined for references to empirical studies.

Criteria for including studies

The next step consisted of selecting studies from those collected in the first stage. The following three criteria for including studies were used. First, we selected only studies conducted during the past 20 years which had been purposely designed to investigate the effect of school factors on student outcomes. Second, the studies had to include explicit and valid measures of student achievement in relation to cognitive, affective, or even to psychomotor outcomes of schooling. In addition, studies that use more global criteria for academic outcomes, such as drop-out rates, grade retention, and enrolment in top universities, were also selected. Finally, the meta-analysis reported here focuses on studies investigating the direct effects of school effectiveness factors upon student achievement. This is due to the fact that only a few studies ($n = 5$) were found which attempted to examine the indirect effect of school effectiveness factors on achievement, and the number of reported effect sizes ($n = 15$) in these studies is insufficient to give a clear indication of variation of indirect effect sizes of school-level factors within and across studies. The studies included in the meta-analysis are listed in the Appendix.

Computation of effect sizes

To indicate the effect of each school-level factor, we follow the same approach as Scheerens and Bosker (1997). Specifically, the Fisher's Z transformation of the correlation coefficient was used. Moreover, since not all studies presented their results in terms of correlations, all other effect-size measures were transformed into correlations using the formulae presented by Rosenthal (1994). For small values of the correlation coefficient, Z_r and r do not differ much (see also Hunter and Schmidt, 2004). Furthermore, the Cohen's d (Cohen, 1988) is approximately twice the size of the correlation coefficient when the latter is small (i.e. $-0.20 < r < 0.20$). Specifically, the three statistics d, t, and r are all algebraically transformable from one to the other. It is finally important to note that the meta-analysis was conducted using MLwiN (Goldstein et al., 1998). Specifically, we adopted the procedure suggested by Lamberts and Abrams (1995), which was also used in a number of meta-analyses conducted in the area of effectiveness (e.g. Scheerens and Bosker, 1997; Witziers et al., 2003). More specific information on the procedure used to conduct the meta-analysis is given below.

The multilevel model was applied to analyse the observed effects of each study, and the sources of variances among the findings emerged from different studies investigating the effect of the same school-level factor on student achievement (Raudenbush and Bryk, 1985). Specifically, the studies that were found to investigate the effect of the same factor on student achievement, such as the school policy on quantity of teaching, are considered to be a sample from the population of studies investigating the relationship between this factor of the dynamic model and student achievement. Nested under each study are the schools. Each study can then be viewed as an independent replication. This concept could be used but does not solve the problem of multiple results from one study, such as when effects are reported for more than one outcome of schooling (e.g. mathematics and language achievement, or mathematics and development of positive attitudes towards the school) in one study while using the same sample of schools and students. To deal with this problem, the two-level model for meta-analysis was expanded to a three-level model. As a consequence, the highest level of the studies is referred to as the across-replication level and the multiple results within a study as the within-replication level. The main advantage of the statistical meta-analysis employed here is that the information from each study is weighted by the reliability of the information, in this case the sample size. Moreover, the multilevel model helps us identify factors that are responsible for the variation in observed effect sizes of each of the main school-level factors affecting student achievement that emerged from this synthesis of school effectiveness studies. Therefore, differences in reported effect sizes are modelled as a function of study characteristics, such as differences in the types of outcomes used to measure student achievement, the level of education at which the study was conducted, and the nature of the study. Some further information on the statistical modelling technique follows.

It is first of all important to indicate that the multilevel model for the meta-analysis (Raudenbush and Bryk, 1985; Raudenbush, 1994), starting with the 'within-replications model', is given by the following equation:

$$d_{rs} = \delta_{rs} + e_{rs}$$

This equation implies that the effect size d in replication r in study s (d_{rs}) is an estimate of the population parameter (δ_{rs}) and the associated sampling error (e_{rs}). The sampling error is attributed to the fact that in each replication, only a sample of schools is studied. As far as the between-replications model is concerned, the following equation is used:

$$\delta_{rs} = \delta_s + u_{rs}$$

In the above model it is acknowledged that the true replication effect size is a function of the effect size in study s and sampling error u_{rs}. Finally, the between-studies model is formulated as follows:

$$\delta_s = \delta_0 + v_s$$

The above formula basically implies that the true unknown effect size as estimated in study s (δ_s) is a function of the effect size across studies (δ_0) with random sampling error v_s, which is attributed to the fact that the studies are sampled from a population of studies.

To assess the effects of study characteristics, we extended the between-replication model to one that took into account the effect of explanatory variables which are presented below. Since all explanatory variables were grouping variables, they were entered as dummies, with one of the groups as baseline. Specifically, the following explanatory variables which refer to the characteristics of the studies included in the meta-analysis were entered in the model.

Outcomes of schooling

A grouping variable was available to examine the impact of the types of outcomes of schooling employed in each study. Specifically, it was possible to identify four types of outcomes that were taken into account by a relatively large number of studies: (1) mathematics achievement, (2) language achievement, (3) general measures of academic outcomes (e.g. drop-out rates, rates of grade retention), and (4) measures of psychomotor and affective outcomes of schooling (e.g. self-concept, attitudes towards mathematics, attitudes to teachers, attitudes to peers). Therefore, three dummy variables were entered, and mathematics achievement was treated as the baseline variable. It is important to note that neither outcomes of schooling associated with new learning, nor the achievement of psychomotor aims could be entered as separate groups of outcomes of schooling, since very few studies treated them as criteria for measuring school effectiveness. This seems to be in line with one of our major criticisms of EER (see Chapter 2). However, we decided to treat the few studies that took these types of outcomes into account in the same group as those looking at affective outcomes of schooling. Thus, our fourth group was concerned with studies that did not consider the achievement of cognitive aims as criteria for measuring effectiveness.

Level of education

It was possible to classify the studies into groups according to the sector in which each of them took place. Unfortunately, only three studies were concerned with school effectiveness factors in higher education. Therefore, only one dummy variable could be entered in the equation, and the group of studies that were conducted only in the primary education sector were treated as the baseline group.

Country in which the study was conducted

Apart from assessing the impact of the types of outcomes employed and the sector in which the study took place, we also assessed the effects of study characteristics in relation to the country in which the study was conducted. Specifically, the studies were classified into the following five groups according to the country where the study took place: the United States, the Netherlands, the United Kingdom, Asian countries, and other countries. Studies conducted in the United States were treated as the baseline group.

The study design employed

We also examined the study design employed, and found it possible to classify the studies into the following four groups: cross-sectional studies, longitudinal studies, experimental studies, and outlier studies. The group of cross-sectional studies was treated as the baseline group. Our initial intention was to classify the longitudinal studies into two groups: studies that lasted for up to two years, and longitudinal studies that took place over a period longer than two years. However, the latter were very small in number. For this reason, all longitudinal studies were treated as a single group.

Statistical techniques employed

Another characteristic of the studies that was taken into account for conducting our meta-analysis was concerned with the extent to which researchers used multilevel or unilevel analysis in order to investigate the effect of each factor on student achievement. For this reason, a relevant dummy variable was entered into the model in order to see whether the statistical technique employed could predict variation on the effect sizes.

The measurement dimensions used to examine the functioning of each factor

Since the dynamic model is based on the assumption that not only frequency but also four other dimensions should be taken into account for measuring the impact of each factor on student achievement, the measurement dimensions of each factor were one of the study characteristics that we took into account. However, almost all studies used the frequency dimension. Therefore, it was not possible to search for the impact of this explanatory variable.

Grouping of variables

Finally, we assessed the effect of a characteristic of studies that refers to the extent to which each effectiveness factor was treated as functioning independently of other effectiveness factors or as part of a group of variables that emerged from a theoretical approach to modelling educational effectiveness (see Chapter 2). This classification of studies allows us to identify the extent to which researchers simply attempted to search for factors that are associated with achievement or whether they attempted to test the validity of a theory and were therefore in a position not only to search for effects but also to explain how factors operating at the same level are related to each other and how these combinations of factors influence learning.

In order to assess the impact of the above explanatory variables, we extend the between-replication model into the model shown below:

$$\delta_{rs} = \delta_0 + \gamma_1 \text{ outcome-language}_{rs} + \gamma_2 \text{ general-measures}_{rs} + \gamma_3 \text{ outcome-affective}_{rs}$$
$$+ \gamma_4 \text{ secondary}_{rs} + \gamma_5 \text{ netherlands}_{rs} + \gamma_6 \text{ uk}_{rs} + \gamma_7 \text{ asiancountries}_{rs} + \gamma_8 \text{ othercountries}_{rs}$$
$$+ \gamma_9 \text{ longitudinal}_{rs} + \gamma_{10} \text{ experimental}_{rs} + \gamma_{11} \text{ outlier}_{rs} + \gamma_{12} \text{ multilevel}_{rs}$$
$$+ \gamma_{13} \text{ grouping}_{rs} + v_s$$

where:

outcome-language	0 = else, and 1 = language achievement
general-measures	0 = else, and 1 = general measures of academic outcomes
outcome-affective	0 = else, and 1 = measure of non-cognitive outcomes of schooling (i.e. achievement of affective or psychomotor aims)
secondary	0 = primary, and 1 = secondary
netherlands	0 = else, and 1 = conducted in the Netherlands
UK	0 = else, and 1 = conducted in the United Kingdom
asiancountries	0 = else, and 1 = conducted in Asian countries
othercountries	0 = else, and 1 = conducted in countries other than the United States, the Netherlands, the United Kingdom, or any of the Asian countries
longitudinal	0 = else, and 1 = longitudinal study

experimental	0 = else, and 1 = experimental study
outlier	0 = else, and 1 = outlier study
multilevel	0 = unilevel analysis, and 1 = multilevel analysis.
grouping	0 = no search of grouping of factors, and 1 = search for the existence of grouping of variables

It is important to note that the use of the above statistical model in which the effects of study characteristics are estimated is problematic when the sample size is small. This means that in some cases, only the bivariate relationships between moderators and effect sizes are presented. The results of these analyses were only used to check the robustness of the findings focusing on the bivariate relationships. Finally, the multilevel analyses were conducted twice. The first time, we included all studies; in the second analysis, the so-called sensitivity analysis, the outliers were removed from the samples to check the robustness of the findings.

Findings

Table 9.1 provides information about the characteristics of studies investigating the effect of different school effectiveness factors upon student achievement. The average effect size of each factor is also provided. The following observations arise from this table. First, the values of the average effect sizes of the school effectiveness factors seem to provide support for the argument that effective schools should develop a policy on teaching and a policy on how to establish a learning environment at the school. All six of these factors which belong to the two overarching school-level factors of the dynamic model were found to have an effect larger than 0.15. On the other hand, not enough data are available to provide support for the importance of investigating the evaluation mechanisms that the schools develop in order to examine the appropriateness of their policies on teaching and on their learning environment. The lack of studies investigating the evaluation mechanisms of schools and the improvement decisions that arise from these mechanisms may be attributed to the fact that only eight out of 67 studies are longitudinal studies that took place over a period of more than two school years. Moreover, the majority of the effectiveness studies (i.e. 55.2 per cent) are focused on investigating differences between schools in their effectiveness at a certain point in time, the so-called cross-sectional approach, or collected data at two time points only. Therefore, there was no attempt to examine the effect of school-level factors on changes in the effectiveness status of the schools (see also Kyriakides and Creemers, 2006a).

Second, we can also observe that the great majority of school effectiveness studies used the frequency dimension to measure the effect of each school-level factor. It is important to note here that the stage dimension was used by only two studies but provided support for the importance of this measurement dimension. Moreover, a dimension not proposed in the dynamic model, namely consistency, was used by one study which attempted to measure the impact of the school policy on quality of teaching upon student achievement (Reezigt *et al.*, 1999). This dimension was, however, taken into account, owing to the fact that this study was conducted in order to test the validity of the comprehensive model of effectiveness (Creemers, 1994). Nevertheless, the fact that this study did not provide support for the importance of this principle seems to justify our decision not to use this dimension as a way to measure the impact of school-level factors.

Third, the figures in the 'Grouping' columns of Table 9.1 reveal that very few effectiveness studies have attempted to search for relations among school-level factors (i.e. to identify grouping of factors). Moreover, the majority of them (i.e. four out of seven) were conducted in order to test the validity of Creemers' model.

Fourth, almost all the studies that have been reviewed here collected data from either the primary and/or the secondary school level, and only four of them refer to effectiveness factors at the higher education level. However, almost twice as many studies were concerned with the primary school level, in comparison to studies of the secondary school level.

Fifth, the last part of Table 9.1 refers to the average effect of those factors that are not included in the dynamic model. We can see that a relatively high percentage of studies (i.e. 42.0 per cent) were conducted in order to measure the effect of leadership upon student achievement. However, the average effect size of this factor on student achievement that emerged from this review, as well as the results of a recent quantitative analysis of the effect of leadership on student achievement (i.e. Witziers *et al.*, 2003), reveal that leadership has a very weak effect on student achievement. On the other hand, it could be claimed that the dynamic model should refer to two other school-level factors that were found to have an effect larger than 0.15. These factors refer to the school admittance policy and teacher empowerment. However, only two studies were conducted in order to test the effect of teacher empowerment. Therefore, further studies investigating the generalisability of the observed effects of this factor on student achievement are needed. As far as the effect of admittance policy is concerned, it should be kept in mind not only that very few studies have been conducted to assess its impact on student achievement ($n = 5$) but also that this factor refers mainly to the input of the school, since the existence of an admittance policy has a direct and strong effect on the prior knowledge of students entering the school. Therefore, the school admittance policy cannot be treated as a school effectiveness factor, since it does not reveal how the functioning of schools can contribute to student achievement gains.

It is finally important to acknowledge that the review reported here does not provide support for one basic assumption of the dynamic model, namely that emphasising the importance of identifying curvilinear relations. This can be attributed to the fact that only one study revealed a curvilinear relation, which was concerned with the relation of an input school-level factor (i.e. resources) and student achievement. This finding cannot be attributed to the fact that most of the studies did not use appropriate statistical techniques to identify such relations, since a relatively high percentage of studies employed multilevel modelling techniques. However, the fact that no curvilinear relationship was identified could be attributed

Table 9.1 Characteristics of studies investigating the effect of school-level factors on student achievement and types of effects identified

School-level factor	Average effect	Number of studies[a]	Outcome[b]			Studies per sector				Grouping		Measurement	
			Cogn	Affect	Psych	Primary	Sec'ry	Both	Other	Yes	No	Freq.	Other
1 Policy on teaching													
• Quantity of teaching	0.16	18	14	6	2	9	6	2	1	4	14	16	2
• Opportunity to learn	0.15	13	11	3	2	7	4	1	1	3	10	12	1
• Quality of teaching	0.17	26	22	4	1	13	7	5	1	4	22	24	2
– Student assessment	0.18	12	10	4	0	8	3	1	0	3	9	10	2
2 Evaluation of policy on teaching	0.13	6	8	1	0	4	1	1	0	2	4	5	1
3 Policy on the school learning environment													
• Collaboration	0.16	31	27	5	1	11	14	6	0	4	27	28	3
• Partnership policy	0.17	21	14	9	0	8	10	3	0	4	17	19	2
4 Evaluation of policy on the learning school environment	–	0	0	0	0	0	0	0	0	0	0	0	0

continued

Table 9.1 continued

School-level factor	Average effect	Number of studies[a]	Outcome[b]			Studies per sector				Grouping		Measurement	
			Cogn	Affect	Psych	Primary	Sec'ry	Both	Other	Yes	No	Freq.	Other
5 Other factors													
• Leadership	0.07	29	22	10	0	16	8	4	1	2	27	29	0
• School climate	0.12	24	22	5	0	9	8	6	1	4	20	24	0
• Autonomy	0.06	3	3	0	0	1	1	1	0	1	2	3	0
• Teacher empowerment	0.17	2	2	0	0	0	2	0	0	0	2	2	0
• Resources and working conditions (e.g. salary)	0.14	13	10	3	1	7	4	1	1	3	10	13	0
• Admittance policy, selection tracking	0.18	5	4	1	0	0	4	1	0	0	5	5	0
• Staff experience (teachers and headteachers)	0.08	4	4	0	0	1	0	3	0	0	4	4	0
• Job satisfaction	0.09	3	3	0	0	1	1	0	1	0	3	3	0

a Some studies reported more than one observed effect.
b Some studies searched for effects on more than one type of outcome of schooling.

to the use of mainly cross-sectional and longitudinal studies in the field of educational effectiveness. It is therefore important to identify the extent to which similar results could emerge from using other methodological approaches, such as experimental studies, that help us to establish enough variation at the functioning of school effectiveness factors and search for curvilinear relations.

The next step in the meta-analysis was to use the multilevel approach to estimate the mean effect size of the following five factors: (1) policy on school teaching; (2) policy on the school learning environment: partnership; (3) policy on the school learning environment: collaboration; (4) leadership; and (5) school climate and culture. The multilevel analysis allows us to estimate the mean effect size of the overarching factors of the dynamic model as well as the effect size of two factors which are not included in the dynamic model but which a large number of researchers paid a lot of attention to, in order to assess their impact on achievement. In this way we could justify our decision to include the first three factors in the model and exclude the other two. Another important question is whether effect sizes vary across and within studies. Table 9.2 illustrates the estimated effect sizes for each of the above five school effectiveness factors and their standard deviations across and within replication. This table gives information on whether the standard deviation in effect sizes across and within replications differs significantly from zero. Low p values indicate that the amount of variation within and between replications differs significantly from zero, whereas the reverse is true, of course, for high p values. Because the p values in Table 9.2 are generally low, the conclusion is that there is a large variation in effect sizes within and across studies. However, this variation seems to be smaller in the case of the partnership policy and the school policy of teaching, and much larger in the case of leadership.

The third step in our analysis was concerned with the question of which moderators can be held responsible for the variation in the effect sizes of the five

Table 9.2 Estimated effect size for each school effectiveness factor and standard deviation across and within replication and their p values (in parentheses)

School-level factor	Mean effect size across replications	Standard deviation within replications	Standard deviation
1 *Policy on teaching*	0.179 (0.001)	0.033 (0.037)	0.036 (0.032)
2 *Policy on the school learning environment*			
• Collaboration	0.158 (0.001)	0.043 (0.005)	0.040 (0.005)
• Partnership policy	0.172 (.001)	0.032 (0.040)	0.031 (0.043)
3 *Other factors*			
• Leadership	0.068 (0.042)	0.060 (0.001)	0.057 (0.001)
• School climate	0.116 (0.005)	0.049 (0.005)	0.042 (0.005)

school effectiveness factors. Table 9.3 shows the results of the analyses in which an attempt is made to predict differences between effect sizes with such study characteristics as criteria for measuring effectiveness (i.e. the use of different outcomes of schooling for measuring effectiveness), sector of education, country, study design employed, use of multilevel rather than unilevel statistical techniques, and the grouping of factors into overarching factors that emerge from a model of educational effectiveness. The following observations arise from Table 9.3.

First, the results show that only in a few cases moderators had a significant relationship with the effect size. Moreover, there is no moderator that was found to have a significant relationship with the effect size of all five overarching factors. However, looking at country differences, it appears that there are large discrepancies between several educational contexts. Specifically, the results for the two overarching factors that are not included in the dynamic model are true only for studies conducted outside the Netherlands. In the Netherlands the effect size of leadership is about zero, whereas the effect of school climate is very small (i.e. smaller than 0.06). Moreover, in the Asian countries the effects of the two main indicators of the overarching factor concerned with the policy of the school for establishing a learning environment are higher. However, country differences were not identified in the case of the first overarching factor of the dynamic model concerned with school policy on teaching.

Second, the use of different criteria for measuring school effectiveness concerned with different types of outcomes of schooling is not associated with the effect size of three overarching factors. However, the effect of two overarching factors of the dynamic model (i.e. policy on teaching and partnership policy) upon achievement in non-cognitive outcomes is smaller than in the achievement of cognitive outcomes. The only other significant effect pertains to the study design employed, since it was found that longitudinal studies help us to identify a larger effect of the first overarching factor of the dynamic model (i.e. school policy for teaching), whereas experimental studies help us to identify a larger effect of the overarching factor concerned with partnership policy. Finally, on average, school leadership effects are almost absent in secondary education, whereas they are related to student achievement in primary schools but at a very small size.

As has already been mentioned, our last attempt to analyse the results emerging from the studies investigating the effect of school factors on student achievement was concerned with our attempt to repeat the statistical procedure described earlier but with the outliers removed from the samples to check the robustness of the findings (i.e. a sensitivity study). The results of our sensitivity analysis show that the effect size of leadership style is reduced considerably when the outliers are removed from the sample. Although this implies that there is still a positive and significant relationship between leadership style and student outcomes, the indicator loses much of its relevance. On the other hand, the sensitivity study of those studies that measure the effect of the other four overarching factors did not reveal that these factors will lose much of their relevance. On the contrary, in the case of school policy of teaching, the estimated reduction of the effect size was very small.

Table 9.3 Predicting difference in effect sizes of each of the five overarching school factors

	Policy on teaching	Policy on SLE: partnership policy	Policy on SLE: collaboration	Leadership	School climate and school culture
	Estimate (p value)	Estimate (p value)	Estimate (p value)	Estimate (p value)	Estimate (p value)
Intercept	0.18 (0.001)	0.17 (0.001)	0.16 (0.001)	0.07 (0.001)	0.12 (0.001)
Language	−0.02 (0.778)	−0.02 (0.710)	0.01 (0.834)	−0.01 (0.812)	−0.02 (0.792)
Drop-out	0.01 (0.482)	0.02 (0.549)	0.01 (0.793)	0.00 (0.962)	0.02 (0.781)
Non-cognitive	−0.05 (0.005)[a]	−0.06 (0.041)[a]	0.00 (0.951)	0.04 (0.082)	−0.02 (0.542)
Secondary	−0.03 (0.117)	−0.04 (0.058)	0.01 (0.741)	−0.05 (0.038)[a]	0.03 (0.41)
The Netherlands	−0.04 (0.141)	0.01 (0.812)	0.03 (0.179)	−0.03 (0.042)[a]	−0.07 (029)[a]
UK	0.02 (0.791)	0.00 (0.955)	0.01 (0.817)	0.01 (0.816)	0.00 (0.971)
Asian countries	0.02 (0.548)	0.05 (0.041)[a]	0.04 (0.042)[a]	0.04 (0.102)	0.03 (0.041)[a]
All other countries	0.02 (0.729)	0.01 (0.805)	NA	0.04 (0.115)	0.00 (0.958)
Longitudinal	0.02 (0.005)[a]	0.00 (0.901)	0.01 (0.829)	0.02 (0.812)	0.01 (0.712)
Experimental	NA	0.03 (0.011)[a]	0.00 (0.919)	NA	NA
Outlier	NA	0.01 (0.887)	NA	−0.03 (0.048)[a]	0.04 (0.050)[a]
Unilevel v. multilevel	−0.05 (0.103)	0.02 (0.656)	0.01 (0.804)	0.01 (0.789)	0.02 (0.612)
Grouping v. no grouping	0.00 (0.842)	NA	NA	NA	0.00 (0.608)

NA: It was not possible to test the effect of this explanatory variable, since almost all the studies that assessed the impact of this factor belong to only one of the two groups that are compared.

a A statistically significant effect at level 0.05 was identified.

Implications of our findings for the development of EER

This last main section of the chapter is an attempt to draw out implications of the findings of this meta-analysis for the development of the dynamic model and for research on educational effectiveness. We also make suggestions as to how the methodology of EER can be improved.

To what extent is the dynamic model supported by this and early reviews?

The first part of this section attempts to provide answers to the question concerned with the extent to which the dynamic model is supported by this and early reviews (e.g. Creemers and Reezigt, 1996; Fan and Chen, 2001; Fraser *et al.*, 1987; Hallinger and Heck, 1998; Levine and Lezotte, 1990; Sammons *et al.*, 1995; Scheerens and Bosker, 1997). In relation to this question, we would like first of all to point out that the studies on school effectiveness are concerned with various school factors of effectiveness. As a consequence, the quantitative synthesis of the studies concerned with some of these factors cannot be based on a relatively large number of studies, and thereby its statistical power could be considered problematic (see Table 9.1). It is argued here that the lack of a strong theoretical basis for EER explains the wide conceptual variety of school factors. However, looking at the factors which have been examined, we can see that there are factors referring to the behaviour of persons in the organisation (mainly the principal), to the behaviour of persons related to the school (mainly parents), to material conditions (e.g. the quality of the school curriculum), to organisational elements (e.g. admittance policy), and to school culture (e.g. the presence of an orderly school climate). Although all these dimensions may be important for school effectiveness, it is necessary to arrange them according to theoretical notions to make their importance for student achievement easier to understand. The dynamic model attempts to provide such a framework by giving a clear answer about the relationships between school factors and classroom-level factors. It is emphasised that school factors are expected to influence classroom-level factors, especially the teaching practice, and thereby they are expected to influence learning that takes place either in the classroom and/or in the school. As a consequence, the proposed model does not refer to a wide variety of factors as such identified through this and early reviews. Moreover, the figures concerning the effects of the eight school-level factors, which are not included in the model but are taken into account for measuring their association with student achievement, are not strong enough for us to argue that the dynamic model should incorporate them. Specifically, four factors have an average effect that is smaller than 0.10, compared to only two of them that have relatively large effect size (i.e. teacher empowerment and admittance policy). Nevertheless, the estimation of the average effect size of one of these factors concerned with teacher empowerment is based on only two studies. This implies that there is a need for further studies investigating the impact of teacher empowerment on student achievement in order to estimate the effect size of this factor. As far as the impact of the second factor is concerned, it is important to note that although this factor refers to organisational elements of the school, its functioning has a direct impact on the prior knowledge and skills of student achievement and thereby can be considered to be an input rather than a process variable (Glasman and Binianimov, 1981).

This review provides empirical support for the importance of two overarching school-level factors included in the model which are concerned with the school policy on teaching and the school policy on creating a school learning environment. Specifically, the estimated effect size of each of these two overarching components was larger than 0.15. Moreover, the four components of the overarching factor on policy for teaching as well as the two components of the factor concerned with the school policy on learning environment were significantly associated with student achievement, and their effect sizes were larger than 0.15. Furthermore, it was found that although a large variation in effect sizes within and across studies was identified, this variation was much smaller in the case of the factors included in the dynamic model than for factors not included in the model (see Table 9.2). In addition, the results of the multilevel analysis attempting to identify the extent to which the explanatory variables could predict variation in the estimated effect sizes of each factor reveal that the two overarching factors of the dynamic model could be generic in nature, since the size of their effects does not vary in different countries. In addition, although the effect of the factor concerned with school policy on teaching is larger when cognitive rather than non-cognitive outcomes are used to measure school effectiveness, its effect is at least larger than 0.10, even when non-cognitive outcomes are used to measure effectiveness.

What are the new elements of the dynamic model?

This second part of the section is concerned with the following three elements or assumptions of the dynamic model that have not been tested empirically by the effectiveness studies conducted during the past 20 years: (1) dimensions of measuring effectiveness factors, (2) factors concerned with the evaluation mechanisms of the school, and (3) grouping of factors. Therefore, suggestions for the development of research methods on educational effectiveness will be made in the last part of this section.

Dimensions of measuring effectiveness factors

It is first of all important to note that this review reveals that most EER studies do not explicitly refer to the measurement of each effectiveness factor. Almost all of them (i.e. 94.2 per cent) seem to take for granted that each factor is a unidimensional construct and measure it in relation to the frequency dimension of the proposed dynamic model. Therefore, empirical studies should be conducted in order to examine whether the proposed five different dimensions of measuring each effectiveness factor may provide clear results concerning the effect size of each factor. Moreover, in using this measurement framework, the methodology of effectiveness studies may be improved, since researchers will be encouraged to treat effectiveness factors as multidimensional rather than unidimensional constructs and may reveal the complexity of the process of improving practice. As was mentioned in Chapter 8, studies investigating the validity of the proposed measurement framework of effectiveness factors should also be undertaken, especially since the results of the empirical study testing the validity of this framework provided support for the importance of using all five dimensions to measure factors of effectiveness (see Chapter 8).

Factors concerned with the evaluation of school policy and their improvement mechanisms

Although among the main categories of school factors mentioned by several reviewers (e.g. Creemers and Reezigt, 1996; Hallinger and Heck, 1998; Levine and Lezotte, 1990; Sammons *et al.*, 1995; Scheerens and Bosker, 1997) is the monitoring of student progress, a significant number of studies were concerned with student evaluation, but almost no study investigated the impact of the evaluation mechanisms for any other aspect of school policy. Moreover, no study attempted to examine systematically the processes that are used by the schools in order to improve their teaching practice and their learning environment. It can therefore be claimed that the dynamic model refers to two relatively new school-level factors, and the operational definition attached to them has significant implications for the design of effectiveness studies. Specifically, our emphasis on actions taken to evaluate and change school policy implies that longitudinal studies should be conducted to measure the impact of these factors on the effectiveness status of schools rather than investigating the relation between the existing practice and student achievement. This is in line with the dynamic character of the model and reveals the importance of using the stage as a measurement dimension of each effectiveness factor.

Grouping of factors

Most of the studies (i.e. 60 out of 67) did not investigate relationships between school-level factors. This can be attributed to the fact that most studies are not associated with the development and testing of theoretical models of educational effectiveness. However, both this and early reviews reveal that some school-level factors, especially those not included in the dynamic model, are partly overlapping, whereas some other factors are caused by, or at least influenced by, other factors (for example, the orderly school learning environment is likely to be influenced by educational leadership). It can be claimed that these relationships need the most clarity to interpret effects of school factors correctly. In this context, the dynamic model can be seen as a response to this need, especially since the relationships between the proposed school effectiveness factors are made explicit, and suggestions for searching for grouping of factors at both the classroom and school level are made (see Creemers and Kyriakides, 2006).

Main conclusions to emerge from Part III of the book

In Part III the results of two kinds of studies testing the validity of the model have been reported. The results of these studies provided some support for the validity of the dynamic model. The empirical study reported in Chapter 8 was specifically designed to test the main assumptions of the model at the classroom level. Support for the importance of using the five dimensions of measuring the classroom-level factors was provided. The meta-analysis reported in the present chapter provides some support for the validity of the model at the school level. It is claimed here that both approaches are needed in order to test and expand the model. As far as the limitations of using only empirical studies to test the validity of the model are concerned, the second section of this chapter raised doubts about the myth of a perfect study. It is argued that synthesis of studies can provide the best approach to develop a theory. On the other hand, the results of a meta-analysis depend on the primary studies. This was clear in the case of the meta-analysis reported here, since some of the main features of the dynamic model could not be tested, owing to the fact that no attention has been given so far to the individual studies. This reveals the importance of conducting a sufficient number of primary studies specifically designed to test the validity of the model. For this reason, we shall elaborate on the implications of the model for research in Chapter 10. Implications for policy and improvement will also be considered in Part IV of the book, since the results of the empirical study and the meta-analysis reported here at least provide some support for the model and do not reveal any contradictory arguments. Furthermore, the use of the model in policy and practice may provide further evidence about the interpretive validity of the model, which is considered to be one of the most important criteria for judging a theory.

Part IV

Implications for research, policy and practice

Chapter 10

Implications for research and evaluation

Introduction

This chapter examines implications for research and evaluation. In respect to research, suggestions for further research to test the validity of the model are provided. We shall consider the possibility of using four different types of studies to test the validity of the model: (1) longitudinal studies on effectiveness, (2) quantitative syntheses of effectiveness studies, (3) international studies on effectiveness, and (4) experimental studies. Specifically, we shall present suggestions for the design of longitudinal studies which emerge from the findings of the study presented in Chapter 8 concerned with the validity of the model at the classroom level. Moreover, the extent to which quantitative syntheses of national studies can generate empirical support for the model will be investigated. Thus, we shall provide suggestions for conducting meta-analyses which arise from our attempt to conduct a quantitative synthesis of school effectiveness studies in order to test the validity of the model at the school level (see Chapter 9). Finally, we shall raise the possibility of using experimental and international studies that can help us create enough variation in the functioning of each effectiveness factor and thereby to search for non-linear relations between effectiveness factors and outcomes. A programme for international studies will be outlined and is expected to help us identify the generic character of the dynamic model.

In respect to evaluation, we attempt to link the main characteristics of the model presented in Chapter 5 with the design of evaluation studies that attempt to examine the impact of reform efforts. The importance of taking the multilevel nature of education into account, the effectiveness factors included in the model, and the proposed measurement framework of the model will be emphasised. It is expected that in this way, the dynamic model can be used both to detect the strengths and weaknesses of a reform plan and to design formative evaluations of the implementation of a reform policy. Finally, we propose a framework upon which a theory-driven evaluation of educational policy can be built. To establish this approach, we draw from both the literature on evaluation of reform policies and the main assumptions and characteristics of the dynamic model. Moreover, the importance of investigating both the direct and indirect impact of reform policy on student outcomes is raised. It is also argued that formative evaluation should search for factors associated with the effective implementation of a reform.

Testing the validity of the model

One of the major conclusions that arises from Part III of the book is that the dynamic model is a theoretical model that can be tested. The study reported in Chapter 8 also reveals that this study can be treated as a framework for future studies investigating the validity of the dynamic model and the essential characteristics of the factors included in the model, such as the existence of curvilinear relations and the measurement dimensions of the functioning of each factor. In Chapter 9 the results of the meta-analysis of studies investigating the impact of school factors on achievement were presented. This meta-analysis not only provides some empirical support for the school effectiveness factors included in the dynamic model but also reveals that quantitative syntheses of studies conducted in different countries could also be undertaken in order to develop the dynamic model. In this section, the importance of using different types of studies to test the validity of the dynamic model will be acknowledged. Suggestions for testing and expanding the dynamic model through four types of studies are provided.

Using longitudinal studies to test the validity of the dynamic model

Although the study reported in Chapter 8 provided some support for the validity of the model, some further studies investigating its validity at the classroom level should be conducted, especially since the study reported took place in a single country and its generalisability needs to be proved. However, researchers could consider the possibility of using similar methodological approaches to collect data on the five dimensions of the eight classroom-level factors and identify their impact on student achievement in different outcomes of schooling. It is pointed out that using more than one type of outcome does not create practical problems by increasing significantly the cost of research (and evaluation), but does help us to understand much better the impact of effectiveness factors upon different outcomes (see Chapter 2). Such studies could also help us to identify the extent to which the model can be considered a generic model of effectiveness, able to explain variation in achievement in both cognitive and affective outcomes of schooling in different educational contexts.

Four issues associated with the methodology of these studies can also be raised. First, given that the dynamic model refers to more than 40 variables that are expected to affect student achievement, it is to be expected that researchers, in their attempt to test the validity of the model, will focus their attention on measuring the impact of some of these factors on student achievement. However, various EER studies in different countries (e.g. Kyriakides, 2002; Teddlie and Reynolds, 2000; Townsend et al., 1999) reveal that variables such as prior knowledge or intelligence have the most significant effect upon student achievement. This implies that studies testing the validity of the dynamic model should at least collect data measuring prior knowledge and thereby use value-added techniques to measure effectiveness (see also Chapter 2). The inclusion of aptitude variables in effectiveness studies could lead to more coherent conclusions.

Second, since one of the major assumptions of the dynamic model is concerned with the importance of using a multidimensional approach to measure the effect of each factor on student achievement, researchers should consider the possibility of testing this assumption. The study reported in Chapter 8 provided some support for this assumption in relation to the classroom-level factors. Specifically, using structural equation modelling approaches, the construct validity of the proposed theoretical framework was examined. Moreover, the extent to which each measurement dimension of the eight classroom factors explains variation in student achievement was identified. This implies that researchers should develop instruments able to measure the five dimensions of each factor under consideration. In this way it will be possible to identify the extent to which each measurement dimension is associated with student achievement. Moreover, different techniques testing the construct validity of the proposed measurement framework, such as structural equation modelling approaches (e.g. multitrait multimethod confirmatory factor approaches) or item response theory approaches (e.g. the use of the Rasch model or the use of tree-based IRT approaches), could be employed.

Third, since the dynamic model belongs to the category of integrated models, researchers testing the validity of the model should use multilevel modelling techniques, which are able to identify variables at student, teacher, school, and system level that are associated with student achievement. However, an issue that has to be taken into account is that the dynamic model also assumes that some variables are not related in a linear way to student achievement. This assumption cannot be tested unless both the effect of the various explanatory variables (X_i) and the effect of powers of these variables (e.g. X_i^2, X_i^3 values) upon student achievement are identified. This approach may allow us to find out whether some variables have inverted-U curvilinear relationships with student outcomes, and thereby be able to define their optimal values (i.e. the values of X for which Y has a maximum value). The identification of optimal values may help us to establish specific strategies for improving practice in line with the knowledge base of EER.

Finally, the dynamic model assumes that factors operating at different levels may be interrelated. To examine this assumption, different statistical methods for analysing data on classroom and school-level factors can be used. One possibility is to use multilevel path-analytic methods (Heck and Thomas, 2000) which help us identify not only cross-level relationships but also relationships between factors operating at the same level. Another approach is to use multivariate multilevel modelling techniques which allow us to have more than one dependent variable. For example, the testing of the relationship between two classroom-level factors, such as structuring and orientation, with student achievement gains can be done by treating orientation as an explanatory variable and both structuring and student achievement gains as dependent variables.

Beyond providing suggestions as to how effectiveness studies conducted in different countries could help us test the validity of the model, we would like to raise three of the most significant limitations of relying only on national longitudinal studies to test the validity of the model. First, in national studies the lack of a significant effect of a factor included in the dynamic model might be due to the difficulties that we have in identifying variation in either the student outcomes or, more likely, in the explanatory variables. For example, most of the teachers in a country may not use orientation activities at all, or very few of them may behave in a differentiated way in relation to this aspect of teacher behaviour in the classroom. In the event that these results emerge from a national study, it will not be possible to demonstrate any effect of this factor. This implies that national longitudinal studies are not in a position to help us claim that a proposed factor or a specific measurement dimension of a factor should be definitely excluded from the model because we did not find any statistically significant association of this factor with student achievement.

Second, researchers who conduct national effectiveness studies to test the assumption of the model that there are non-linear relations between some factors and student achievement will have to face the same difficulties as those mentioned above. Specifically, the fact that a researcher cannot identify a non-linear relation between a factor and student achievement may be attributed to the existence of a relatively large measurement error, which reduces significantly the statistical power of the researcher's attempt to identify non-linear relations between a factor and student achievement. The statistical power is reduced much less when one is searching for linear relations. Therefore, in a case where a researcher is not in a position to demonstrate a statistically significant relation between the second power of a factor and student achievement, this may be attributed to the existence of a relatively large type II error. Another problem that can also arise is that researchers searching for non-linear relations should be able to establish a lot of variation in the functioning of a factor or a dimension of a factor. Therefore, in a case where the functioning of a factor in a country is restricted to values that are significantly lower than the optimal value of the factor, one can only see a positive linear relation between the factor and student achievement (see Figure 10.1, section A). On the other hand, if the range of values in the functioning of a factor in a country is around the optimal value, then the researcher will only show that there is no relation between the factor and student achievement (see Figure 10.1, section B). Finally, if the range in the functioning of the factor is situated on the right-hand side of the graph (i.e. much higher than the optimal value), one may identify a negative relation between the functioning of a factor and student achievement (see Figure 10.1, section C). This implies that unless researchers use reliable and valid instruments and their studies are conducted in countries where it is possible to demonstrate enough variation in the functioning of a factor, they will not be able to search for non-linear relations.

Finally, national studies are not in a position to help us test the validity of the dynamic model at the context level. In centralised systems the functioning of some

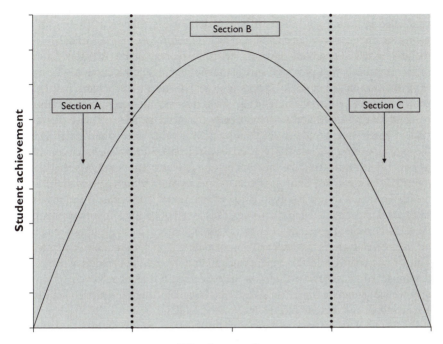

Section B

Section A

Section C

Student achievement

Effectiveness factor

Figure 10.1 An inverted-U relation between a measurement dimension of an effectiveness factor and student achievement.

of these factors may not vary at all (e.g. national policy on teaching, evaluation of policy on teaching). In these cases it is not possible to search for relations between these factors and achievement unless a reform programme is introduced and data before and after the implementation of the reform are available. Even in decentralised systems the researchers may find significant difficulties in establishing enough variation in the functioning of these factors and searching for their impact on achievement. This implies that approaches other than national studies should be used in order to help us test the validity of the model at the context level.

Testing the validity of the model through quantitative syntheses of effectiveness studies

Meta-analysis is rapidly increasing in importance in the behavioural and social sciences. In Chapter 9 we illustrated how a quantitative synthesis of school effectiveness studies helps us generate some empirical support for the validity of the dynamic model. It can be claimed that during the past decade, not only has the number of meta-analyses increased but so has the number of different techniques and methods that can be employed in meta-analyses. In this section we refer to different types of quantitative syntheses of effectiveness studies that can be conducted in testing the validity of the model. First, syntheses of studies investigating the impact of factors operating at any of the three main levels of the dynamic model (i.e. teacher, school, and context) could be conducted. A typical example of this approach was provided in Chapter 9, where studies explicitly designed to identify the impact of school factors upon achievement were included in the meta-analysis. Second, researchers could also focus their attention on specific factors (e.g. parental involvement) and search not only for the effect size of these factors on student achievement but also for their relation to other factors operating either at the same or even at other levels (e.g. the teacher level). Such an approach could help us not only to understand the functioning of this factor in a better way, but also to identify both direct and indirect effects of effectiveness factors on student achievement. We may also test the assumption of the model that factors operating at the same level may be related to each other. This assumption is an important one, since the identification of grouping of factors is seen as crucial in establishing strong links between effectiveness research and improvement of practice (see also Chapter 12). Third, researchers could also conduct quantitative syntheses of studies investigating the impact of factors not included in the model upon student achievement. In this way we can compare the effect sizes of factors included in the model and factors not included, and thereby further develop the model.

In Chapter 9 we referred to the main advantages of using quantitative syntheses of effectiveness factors relating to achievement. It was argued that meta-analyses integrate the findings across studies and reveal the simpler patterns of relationships that underlie research literatures, thus providing a basis for either theory development or the empirical testing of a theory. Moreover, meta-analysis can correct for the distorting effects of sampling error, measurement error, and other artefacts that produce the illusion of conflicting findings (Hunter and Schmidt, 2004). Furthermore, in the case of using meta-analyses to test the validity of the dynamic model, researchers could examine whether the model could be considered generic or differential. The extent to which variables such as the country where the study was conducted or the age range of the students involved in the study explain variation in the effect sizes of factors included in the model helps us to see the importance of establishing a differential rather than a generic model.

However, some limitations of using meta-analyses to test the dynamic model can also be pointed out. First, researchers may not be able to conduct quantitative syntheses of studies unless relevant statistical figures are reported in published papers. For example, in order to conduct the meta-analyses reported in Chapter 9, we managed to find more than 130 papers investigating effects of school factors upon student achievement, but only 67 of these papers were included in the quantitative syntheses, since only these papers provided enough data to estimate the effect sizes that emerged from these studies. This reveals that the quality of the published papers defines to some extent the results of the quantitative syntheses.

Second, meta-analyses are usually conducted in order to provide a synthesis of the review of the literature or to use its results in order to develop a theory. In this book we argue that meta-analyses can also be used in order to test the validity of theoretical models, such as the dynamic model. However, meta-analyses may not help us to test some aspects of the model, because the results of a quantitative synthesis are strongly dependent on the characteristics of the available studies. For instance, researchers may not be able to identify the importance of using the proposed framework for measuring effectiveness factors, since almost all the studies use only the frequency dimension to measure the functioning of effectiveness factors. The fact that only the frequency dimension was used reveals that there are no available data upon which the measurement of the effect sizes of the other four measurement dimensions can be based.

Finally, meta-analyses cannot help us identify the impact of factors operating at the context level unless comparative studies are available. This limitation is quite significant in the case of effectiveness studies, since only one comparative study on effectiveness has been conducted. Although we may solve the other two limitations of quantitative syntheses of effectiveness studies when national studies specifically designed to test the model are conducted, this problem cannot be solved unless international studies on effectiveness are conducted.

Comparative studies testing the validity of the model: the international dimension of EER

In Chapter 7 the importance of conducting international studies to test the validity of the dynamic model at the context level was raised. In this section we refer to methodological issues associated with the design of comparative studies in order to test the validity of the dynamic model. However, it is acknowledged that EER has shown heavily ethnocentric tendencies (Reynolds, 2000). Although there has been acknowledgement of the seminal American studies of Coleman *et al.* (1966), Edmonds (1979), and Brookover *et al.* (1979) and of the British studies of Rutter *et al.* (1979) and Mortimore *et al.* (1988) in virtually all school effectiveness publications in all countries, there has clearly been no science of school effectiveness studies across countries in the way that there has been an international reach in most branches of psychology and in all the 'applied' and 'pure' sciences. The absence of comparative studies on educational effectiveness must be seen as increasingly proving to be intellectually costly (Creemers, 2006; Kyriakides, 2006a; Reynolds, 2006). Comparative studies could help us identify effectiveness factors that are present in different educational contexts. Moreover, factors that are unique to specific countries as well as factors that operate differently in different educational settings should be highlighted.

Although aspects of the model can be tested through meta-analysis of national studies, which could help us identify the generic nature of factors operating at the school and classroom level, the importance of conducting comparative studies to develop the dynamic model can at least be attributed to the fact that the proposed model refers to factors at the national or context level. Only comparative studies are able to examine the effect of these factors upon student achievement. For example, comparative studies could investigate the effect of national or regional policy on quality of teaching upon student achievement gains. At the same time, the effect of this policy on the quality of teaching at classroom level can be examined, especially since the model assumes that there are indirect effects from higher-level factors through lower-level factors on student achievement.

Teddlie *et al.* (2006) argue that the most important methodological lesson from the first international effectiveness study, namely ISERP, was that the success of international studies depends on having internationally valid instruments, particularly teacher effectiveness protocols, because of the importance of the measurement of classroom processes. While others had already called for the development of such instruments (e.g. Schaffer *et al.*, 1994), ISERP provided a practical demonstration of how important they actually are. This implies that researchers attempting to conduct international studies in order to test the validity of the dynamic model will have to face not only practical difficulties in collecting data from various countries but also some important methodological difficulties concerned with the establishment of internationally valid instruments. In this section we not only discuss the constraints of comparative studies but also raise the possibility of conducting a secondary analysis of comparative evaluation studies in order to test the validity of the dynamic model.

Using secondary analysis of comparative studies to test aspects of the dynamic model

In Chapter 4 a secondary analysis of the TIMSS study, conducted in order to test the validity of Creemers' model, was presented. It has been argued that international comparative studies could help us test at least some aspects of the dynamic model and contribute to the development of the model. Specifically, the assumptions of the models can be tested by using multilevel modelling techniques, which are able to identify variables at student, teacher, school, and country level that are associated with student achievement. It is important to remind readers that the ultimate goal of comparative evaluation studies, such as the TIMSS and the PISA studies, has been to isolate those factors related to student learning which could be manipulated through policy changes in curriculum, resource allocation, or instructional practice. It has been expected that information that arises from such investigations could help policy-makers, curriculum specialists, and researchers better understand the performance of their educational systems (Mullis *et al.*, 2000). Thus, the weaknesses and strengths of educational systems at the micro or macro level could be identified, and intervention programmes attempting to improve educational effectiveness could be developed. When it is taken into account that identifying factors at different educational levels that have an effect on student achievement is among the ultimate goals of EER, it can be claimed that researchers in the area of effectiveness could make use of comparative evaluation studies in order to test those aspects of the dynamic model which are under investigation through each study. For example, given that the PISA study has focused its interest on variables at school level that define the school climate, it is possible for researchers to test the importance of factors included in the dynamic model associated with the learning environment of the school. Therefore, multilevel analyses of student achievement across countries as well as within each country that participated in each study could aid in developing a better understanding of the extent to which the dynamic model can be considered a generic or a differential model. However, limitations of using this approach in testing the dynamic model should also be outlined.

First, usually no measure of student aptitude is taken into account by most comparative studies, such as the TIMSS and PISA studies. As was mentioned above, national studies show that aptitude variables, such as prior knowledge and intelligence, have significant and relatively strong effects on student achievement. This implies that secondary analyses of comparative studies should not be used to compare the effect sizes of effectiveness factor and make decisions on the relative importance of each factor included or not included in the model. Unless the comparative studies take measures of student aptitude into account, we will not be able to investigate how the dynamic model can be developed in order to become either more parsimonious or able to explain most of the variance in student achievement.

Second, the comparative studies, such as those conducted by the IEA and OECD, had various purposes and did not aim specifically at detecting educational effectiveness factors. Therefore, researchers cannot test some aspects of the dynamic model, such as the proposed measurement framework or the importance of specific factors, unless the design of comparative studies and their instruments is based on the theoretical framework of the dynamic model. The need for the redesign of comparative studies drawing on theoretical frameworks that define precisely the significant variables in the process of education has already been identified (Bos and Kuiper, 1999; Kyriakides and Charalambous, 2005; Lassibille and Gomez, 2000). This especially holds true for the country level, since no measure of any context-level factor has been taken into account. Therefore, the effect of any context-level factor cannot be identified unless researchers collect their own data through specifically designed international studies looking at the national policy of different educational systems and their evaluation mechanisms.

An international study testing the validity of the model: a project under development

For this reason, an international study is designed in order to collect data on teacher, school, and context factors included in the dynamic model from different educational systems. The lessons drawn from the study on testing the classroom-level factors reported in Chapter 8 have been taken into account. Specifically, the instruments used to collect data on teacher behaviour were taken into account. However, having in mind the lessons drawn from the ISERP, we do not suggest the use of these instruments in each country; rather, we attempt to adopt these instruments and develop them so that they are in line with the perceptions of country panels of experts on effectiveness. Therefore, following a similar approach to those used for the development of ISTOF (see Teddlie *et al.*, 2006), we intend to further develop the observation instruments and test the construct validity of each instrument in each country before moving to the main phase of the study (i.e. the collection of the data associated with student achievement). In addition, the translation procedure of the instruments is taken into account, since this might affect the face validity of our instruments. Similarly, the importance of providing training for each local research team, particularly the observers, is taken into account, since the absence of any emphasis on training might cause significant problems with the reliability of the study. As far as the statistical analysis of the data is concerned, the testing of the validity of the model is based on analyses of data both within each country and across the countries that participated in the proposed international study. Within-country analysis will help us identify the extent to which each classroom- and school-level factor is associated with achievement, irrespective of the country in which the analysis is conducted. On the other hand, across-country analysis may help us not only identify the importance of the context-level factors but also establish the generic character of the dynamic model. A manual for the proposed international study raising the issues mentioned above is under development. It is expected that it will help us to generate an international research team and conduct a longitudinal study that will be able to test the validity of the dynamic model.

Implications of the dynamic model for the design of experimental studies

Almost no experimental approaches were used to identify cause-and-effect relations between school factors and improvement of the effectiveness status of schools. In the first part of this section, we consider the use of intervention studies in order to test the dynamic model, but the reader is reminded that attention should be paid to the ecological validity of the experiment as well as to the ethical issues associated with the experimentation (Miller, 1984; Robson, 1993). In the second part it is argued that using such approaches may not only provide strong arguments for cause-and-effect relations but also help us to establish stronger links between EER and improvement practices.

Using experimental studies to test the validity of the model

The existence of non-linear relations between effectiveness factors and student achievement can only be tested if enough variation in the functioning of each factor is established. Our suggestion for conducting international studies to test the validity of the model is partly based on the assumption that collecting data from different countries may help researchers to establish enough variation in the functioning of each factor. However, it is still possible that such variation might not be established, especially in international studies in which only a small number of countries participate. An alternative approach is to use experimental approaches to establish enough variation in the functioning of some factors and thereby not only test the model but also search for non-linear relations. For example, experimental studies might search for association between the evaluation of school policy for teaching, and student achievement. Therefore, methodological suggestions on designing experimental studies to test the validity of the dynamic model will now be provided.

Our first suggestion is concerned with the importance of using *group randomisation* to study the effects of teacher- and school-level factors on student achievement. Readers are reminded that many important social interventions aim to change whole communities or organisations. Examples of such place-based initiatives include community improvement programmes, school reforms, and employer-based efforts to retain workers. Because such programmes are designed to affect the behaviour of groups of interrelated people rather than disparate individuals, it is generally not feasible to measure their effectiveness in an experiment – that is, by randomly assigning each individual to either the experimental or the control group. By randomising at the level of groups, such as neighbourhoods, schools, or companies, however, researchers can still reap most of the methodological benefits afforded by random assignment. The use of group randomisation to study the effects of social policies is now spreading in many fields. Over the past decade it has been used to evaluate various interventions in education, as well as in other fields within the social sciences, such as 'whole-school' reforms (Cook *et al.*, 2000), community health promotion campaigns (Murray *et al.*, 2000), school-based drinking prevention programmes (Flay, 2000), and community employment initiatives (Bloom and Riccio, 2005).

There are several main reasons why a research team might choose to study the impact of an intervention programme in a place-based design using group randomisation. Each of them is related to our attempt to evaluate the impact of effectiveness factors on student achievement through building interventions associated with the functioning of specific factor(s). The first three reasons depend on features of the intervention programme to be evaluated. Specifically, it is first of all pointed out that the effects of the programme have the potential to 'spill over' to a substantial degree among participants or from participants to non-participants. Second, the programme's services are delivered most efficiently when targeted at specific locations. Finally, it is important to acknowledge that the programme is designed to address a spatially concentrated problem or situation. Because such interventions are place-based in nature, it makes sense to evaluate them in a place-based research design. This means conducting random assignment at the level of groups of people who live, work, or receive services in the places being examined.

The other two reasons for place-based evaluation relate to the difficulties of implementing random assignment experiments in real-world settings, especially in education. First, using a place-based design will reduce political opposition to randomisation, which one often has to face in the field of education, since different stakeholders may not like, or even will not allow, one to randomly locate students into different groups. Second, maintaining the integrity of the experiment requires the physical separation of programme group members from control group members. These situations involve programmes that, though not inherently place-based, are studied more readily when random assignment is conducted in a place-based way.

These five reasons explaining why a research team might choose to study the impact of an intervention programme in a place-based design using group randomisation rather than individual randomisation also explain why a research team should choose to study the impact of teacher- and school-level factors on student achievement using group randomisation. Given that the factors of the dynamic model at the teacher and school level reveal that different interventions could be introduced in order to improve achievement of a group of students by changing the behaviour of their teachers and/or their schools (see also Chapter 12), studies investigating the impact of any of these factors are expected to follow approaches similar to those used to evaluate, for summative reasons, place-based initiatives. Let us clarify this argument further.

The reader is reminded that the primary theoretical reason for place-based evaluation is spillover effects, which occur when the outcomes for some programme participants influence those for other participants or for people who are not participating in the programme. Spillover effects can reflect interdependencies among different actors for a single outcome, independencies among different outcomes for a single actor, or both. For example, improving the teaching skills of a teacher through establishing a policy on quality of teaching at school or context level might spill over in a variety of ways. The establishment of a school policy not only might help one teacher to improve his or her teaching skills but also might encourage him or her to help colleagues improve their skills too, or it might help the school to improve its learning environment (i.e. another factor of the model). Given that the above example refers to factors included in the dynamic model and since spillover effects are expected to be an important product or by-product of the functioning of the factors of the model operating at least at the school and the context levels, an evaluation of the impact of these factors should account for their spillover effects. Obviously, spillover effects are difficult to accommodate in a causal model of individual behaviour. Thus, when programme impacts on individuals are estimated, spillover effects are usually ignored or assumed not to exist. Because producing these spillover effects is an explicit reason for treating some characteristics of schools and educational systems as factors of the dynamic model (see Chapter 7, concerned with the indirect impact of school- and context-level factors), experimental studies investigating the impact of these factors should be planned to account for them by randomly assigning the whole population of a group of schools to the intervention group and the whole population of some other schools to the control group.

Another reason for conducting experimental studies that focus on groups of people defined by their location (e.g. schools) instead of a dispersed set of individuals (e.g. students or teachers) is that place can be an effective platform for service delivery. Two major ways that place-based initiatives can achieve economies of spatial concentration are by benefiting from physical proximity to target group members and by leveraging existing channels of communication. Locating a programme near its target group may (1) enhance recruitment efforts by raising its profile, (2) reduce psychological barriers to participation by enabling people to participate in familiar territory, (3) reduce the costs of transportation, and (4) enable staff to operate the programme more effectively by exposing them directly to problems and possibilities in their clients' day-to-day lives. In addition, it is easier to make direct personal contact with target group members when they are located in a small area.

Finally, some of the factors included in the dynamic model are concerned with the attempt of schools and educational systems to change the practices of existing organisations (see Chapter 7). It can be claimed that it is much easier to evaluate the impact of these factors by randomly assigning schools rather than individual students within a school and looking at the impact of the school or context factor(s) to improve the effectiveness status of schools. Our suggestion for testing the dynamic model through place-based evaluation approaches is also in line with the way two whole-school reforms have been evaluated, namely the evaluation of the School Development Program (Cook et al., 2000) and the ongoing evaluation of Success for All (Slavin, 2002).

A very different type of reason for testing the dynamic model through a place-based experimental approach refers to the fact that this approach may facilitate political acceptance of randomisation by offsetting ethical concerns about 'equal treatment of equals'. Place-based randomisation is generally easier to 'sell' than individual randomisation, in at least three ways. It takes into account the political concerns of policy-makers and programme managers, who often cannot accept random assignment of individuals within their organisations but might be open to randomisation across organisations. It can circumvent legal restrictions that prohibit programmes from treating individuals in the same political jurisdiction differently but that do not prohibit them from treating different jurisdictions differently. And it can capitalise on the fact that much programme funding is allocated at the level of political jurisdictions, which opens the door to assigning new funding to jurisdictions on a random basis – at least when funds are so limited that not all jurisdictions will receive them.

Having explored some of the most important reasons for using group randomisation to test the validity of the dynamic model, we would like to raise issues associated with the statistical properties of this approach which have implications for the design of such studies. First of all, impact estimates based on group random assignment, like those based on individual random assignment, are unbiased. But estimates based on group randomisation have less statistical power than those based on individual randomisation. Studies investigating the statistical power of group randomisation approaches reveal that the number of groups randomised is usually a more important determinant of precision than group size. Increasing the number of groups by a given proportion usually improves precision by a much greater amount than does increasing the number of individuals per group by the same proportion. Second, it is argued here that covariates can improve the precision of programme impact estimates. In the case of testing, the validity of the dynamic model, regression adjustments for a baseline covariate, especially student aptitude measures, can substantially increase the precision of the estimates of the impact of effectiveness factors on student achievement (see Chapter 6).

Our final suggestion is concerned with the importance of blocking, which can also increase statistical power. Blocking entails stratifying the groups to be randomised into blocks defined by specific combinations of baseline characteristics. After blocking, each of the groups in each block is randomly assigned to the programme or to the control group. Ordinarily, the sample allocation is held constant across blocks. In a blocking design a balanced allocation ensures that the programme and control groups each represent each block in the same proportion, which in turn guarantees that the programme and control groups are identical with respect to the factors that define the blocks.

There are two main criteria for defining blocks within which to randomise: face validity and predictive validity. Face validity is the degree to which characteristics that define blocks appear on their face to be important determinants of the outcome measure being used. Thus, when assessing the face validity provided by blocking on a set of characteristics, it is important to ask to what extent ensuring that the programme and control groups have the same distributions of these characteristics would lend credibility to the evaluation findings. Blocking with respect to individual demographic characteristics, such as age, gender, race, and ethnicity, or with respect to aggregate group characteristics, such as type of organisation and location, can boost face validity. On the other hand, predictive validity is the degree to which characteristics that define blocks predict and can be used to control for random variations in the outcome measure. Given that studies investigating the impact of different factors on student achievement revealed that aptitude measures have the strongest impact on student achievement, blocking with respect to a baseline measure of student achievement is considered the best approach to increase the statistical power of the experimental studies that will be used to help us generate empirical support for the dynamic model of educational effectiveness. An example of an experimental study that is used not only for testing the validity of the model but also for investigating whether the model can be used to improve practice is provided below. Such studies can help us to expand the methodology of EER, and reveal the importance of using this design in developing theories of school effectiveness and improvement.

Research into the use of the model to improve practice

One of our major expectations in developing the dynamic model is to establish better links between EER and improvement of practice. Currently, the emphasis is on developing and testing the model, and for that reason this chapter is mainly concerned with implications for the development of research for testing the validity of the model. But given that the ultimate goal of the development of a dynamic model is to reveal the complexity of educational effectiveness and help us establish links between EER and improvement practices, experimental studies and/or case studies should also be conducted to identify the extent to which the use of the dynamic model for building school policy contributes to the improvement of the effectiveness status of schools.

In this context an experimental study has been designed in Cyprus to provide answers to this question (Demetriou, forthcoming). Using group randomisation, three different groups of schools have been created, and the impact of different treatments on student achievement has been examined (that is, it is a multiple-treatment experimental study). Specifically, support is provided to these three groups of schools to establish self-evaluation mechanisms in order to make decisions on how to improve their policy and practice. However, only support to help them establish such mechanisms is provided to the first group of schools (i.e. treatment X_1), and thereby the decision-making process is entirely left to the schools. Beyond this support, the dynamic model and its value assumptions are presented to the second group of schools. Schools in this group are encouraged not only to collect evaluation data from different sources but also to make decisions concerning the establishment of their policy that are in line with the assumptions of the dynamic model (i.e. treatments X_1 and X_2 are provided to this group). Finally, the research team is expected not only to provide treatments X_1 and X_2 to the third group but also to support these schools in their attempt to establish a climate of trust and openness (i.e. treatment X_3) before introducing any policy on improving their policy and practice based on evaluation data and the knowledge base of the dynamic model. Comparison of the impact of these types of treatments can help us identify the extent to which the establishment of self-evaluation mechanisms cannot in itself help us improve the effectiveness status of the schools, but the schools should either make use of the knowledge base of EER or first improve their climate and then build effective improvement mechanisms. Obviously, different types of studies, both experimental studies and case studies, are needed not only to identify the extent to which schools can make use of the dynamic model but also to identify the difficulties that schools face in their attempt to make use of the knowledge base of EER to improve their practice. In the final chapter of this book, some further implications of the dynamic model for the improvement of practice will be raised.

Evaluation studies: lessons drawn from the dynamic model

This second section of the chapter is an attempt to identify implications of the dynamic model for the design of evaluation studies. It is argued that those attempting to see how the proposed dynamic model can be used in evaluation studies are expected to adopt the main assumptions and methodological suggestions of the theory-driven approach to evaluation. For this reason, we first of all briefly refer to the importance and main assumptions of the theory-driven evaluation. Then, four major implications of the dynamic model for the development of evaluation studies are elicited. These refer not only to the criteria that can be used to evaluate a reform but also to the content of the evaluation (i.e. the aspects that can be covered). Moreover, we raise methodological issues associated with the measurement of factors that define the effective implementation of the reform and the quantitative analysis of data. Finally, a framework that can be used by evaluators to build a theory-driven evaluation in line with the dynamic model is presented.

Using a theory-driven approach to evaluate reform policies

Theory-driven evaluation is a category of different methodological approaches that can be used by evaluators in order to understand the impact of a reform policy such as programme theory evaluation, theories-of-change evaluation, and realist evaluation (Bledsoe and Graham, 2005; Rosas, 2005). In all these perspectives, social programmes are regarded as products of the human imagination: they are hypotheses about social betterment (Bickman, 1985). Programmes chart out a perceived course whereby wrongs might be put to right, deficiencies of behaviour corrected, and inequalities of condition alleviated. Programmes are thus shaped by a vision of change, and they succeed or fail according to the veracity of that vision. Evaluation, in this light, has the task of testing out the underlying programme theories (Chen and Rossi, 1987). When one evaluates, one always returns to the core theories about how a programme is supposed to work and then interrogates it: is that basic plan sound, plausible, durable, practical, and, above all, valid?

Evaluation projects that are theory driven take into account the needs and issues raised by the various stakeholders associated with an innovation, such as practitioners and policy-makers. However, their evaluation agenda is not entirely defined by the stakeholders. The agenda is expanded in such a way as not only to allow evaluators to provide answers to the questions raised by stakeholders but also to help them understand the reasons why a reform is more or less effective (Weiss, 1997). In this chapter it is argued that in order to provide such answers, evaluators in education should make use of the knowledge base of EER which is concerned with effective practice. Educational effectiveness can be seen as a theoretical foundation upon which we can build evaluation studies in education.

It is taken into account here that as they are delivered, programmes are embedded in social systems (Shaw and Replogle, 1996). It is through the workings of entire systems of social relationships in and outside the classroom and/or the school that any changes in behaviours, events, and social conditions in education are effected. For evaluators to understand the variation in effective implementation of a reform, theories of educational effectiveness can help them identify factors associated with the effective implementation of a reform policy. Making use of these theories, evaluators may also contribute to the development of the knowledge base of EER.

A typical example of a theory-driven evaluation is the evaluation of a reform introduced in Cyprus in 1998 concerned with the use of schema theory in teaching mathematics (Kyriakides *et al.*, 2006a). Five years after the introduction of the reform, an evaluation study was conducted to portray the current state of the reform implementation. The study aimed to examine the main stakeholders' (i.e. teachers' and students') reaction to the reform and the factors influencing the effectiveness of the reform. The study not only provided answers for the policy-makers but also revealed that student achievement was determined by a number of factors related to teachers' and students' personal characteristics and to teachers' reaction towards the reform. The research verified the decisive role of teachers in implementing a reform. Based on the findings of this study and drawing on the theoretical assumptions of the 'emergent design' research model, a conceptual framework for conducting programme evaluations, which attributes a central role to teachers' classroom behaviour, was proposed. It was claimed that teacher effectiveness research could be a foundation upon which the design of studies evaluating reforms should be based. It can be claimed that this study reveals that EER can be seen as a foundation upon which theory-driven evaluation projects can be designed. Such projects will not only contribute to the development of the knowledge base of EER but also provide more elaborate and better answers to the questions of the various stakeholders of education. Thus, this section is an attempt to show how participatory models of evaluation can be combined with theory-driven approaches that are oriented towards the knowledge base of EER, and particularly towards the assumptions and main characteristics of the dynamic model.

Criteria of evaluation studies based on the assumptions of the dynamic model: measuring the impact of the reform on student achievement

Evaluation projects that take into account the main principles of the dynamic model are expected to recognise the importance of measuring the impact of any reform on student achievement. In Chapter 2 we refer to the debate about the different criteria that can be used to measure school and teacher effectiveness. It has been argued that effective organisations (schools or educational systems) are those which help students to achieve the aims of education. Irrespective of the nature of the reform, it is considered essential that evaluators adopting the dynamic model should search for the impact of the reform on student achievement. Given that the use of value-added assessment for measuring effectiveness is recommended, it is expected that evaluation studies should identify the extent to which the organisation units (e.g. schools or educational systems) that implement a reform improve their effectiveness status by looking at the progress that their students made during the implementation of the reform.

To achieve this purpose, both direct and indirect effects of the reform on student achievement can be measured. In the case of indirect effects, those evaluators who make use of the knowledge base of the dynamic model should try to find out whether the reform has any positive impact on the functioning of any effectiveness factors of the dynamic model. For example, evaluators searching for the impact of a national reform in using IT in teaching mathematics not only are expected to search for a direct impact of the reform on student achievement in mathematics but should also investigate whether the reform has any effect on teacher behaviour in the classroom in respect of any of the eight classroom-level factors included in the dynamic model. If the reform helps teachers to improve their generic teaching skills, we could consider the reform effective, since such a positive impact on teaching practice is expected to improve student learning.

Building an evaluation study that takes into account the multilevel nature of education

Evaluators, in their attempt to identify the impact of reform on student achievement, should take into account the multilevel structure of education. This not only means that multilevel statistical modelling approaches should be used to measure the impact of a reform on student achievement but also implies that evaluators should search for factors operating at the different levels, specifically at the school, teacher, and student levels, that are likely to influence the effective implementation of a reform. It is also acknowledged that an effective reform policy may not necessarily have direct effects on student achievement, but is more likely to have indirect effects. Therefore, in our attempt not only to design reforms but also to evaluate them for formative reasons, we should examine the extent to which the reform takes into account the skills of those associated with the reform to implement it. For example, a curriculum reform is expected to take into account not only the skills of teachers in teaching the new teaching content or in using the proposed teaching approaches but also their generic teaching skills as these are defined by the dynamic model. The extent to which the reform helps teachers to improve these skills is seen as crucial for the effectiveness of the reform. Therefore, evaluators who conduct formative evaluation should search for ways that help policy-makers improve the effective implementation of the reform associated with improving its impact on quality of teaching. In this way the formative evaluation could be directed in the implementation of the reform in a rather specific way, since the extent to which the implementation of the reform contributes to the improvement of factors operating at the different levels of education can be examined.

If we turn back to the mathematics teaching example, a significant aspect of a formative evaluation of a reform policy on using IT to teach mathematics is concerned with the impact of the reform on improving the learning environment of the school. Improvement of this school-level factor may allow teachers to cooperate and solve together the difficulties they may have to face in introducing IT into their teaching practice. This example reveals that data on formative evaluation can be used by those who are responsible for designing the reform in order to make decisions on how to improve the impact of the reform on effectiveness factors associated with the nature of the reform. This assumption is one of the major lessons drawn from the evaluation of the curriculum reform in mathematics concerned with the schema theory mentioned earlier. Specifically, the need to incorporate teacher effectiveness research in reform evaluation studies has been stressed (Kyriakides *et al.*, 2006a). Until recently, much emphasis was placed on the role of effective schools, in an attempt to specify the criteria that made a school able to introduce a reform and improve its effectiveness. However, during the past few years there has been a remarkable change: attempts at policy and practice level have been made to focus upon teacher effects and generally on issues related to the effectiveness of teachers' work. This implies that those responsible for designing reform should bear in mind how the reform can help teachers improve their behaviour in the classroom.

Implications of the dynamic model for the aspects of the reform covered by the evaluation: going beyond stakeholders' reactions towards the reform

Evaluators should take for granted that EER reveals that, irrespective of the nature of the reform, there will be variation in the ability of teachers and schools to implement the reform effectively. This is attributed to the fact that teachers and schools have significant effects on student achievement. This implies that evaluators should search for characteristics of teachers and schools that make them more or less effective in implementing the reform. In this context, evaluation studies that are able to explain most of the variance in implementing the reform are, undoubtedly, essential in any reform movement, since they provide a wealth of information that is helpful at any stage of reform implementation (Worthen *et al.*, 1997) and thereby achieve the formative purpose of evaluation (Kyriakides, 2004b).

Yet when evaluating an educational reform, researchers often face difficulties in reducing their scope of examination, since reforms constitute complex phenomena, and thus numerous aspects of them are worth examining. Elaborating on the impact that different education actors (i.e. district administrators, inspectors, consultants, principals, parents, teachers, and students) have on the implementation of reform has been considered a *sine qua non* element of any reform evaluation (Amit and Fried, 2002; Atkin, 1998; Fullan, 1991; Kelly, 1989). Acknowledging the difficulties in studying the whole spectrum of factors operating in the school environment during the introduction and subsequent implementation of the reform, we argue that evaluators should at least focus their attention on how teachers' and students' reactions towards the reform affected its effective implementation.

Teachers' and students' reactions towards the reform

Having told teachers how to teach, what texts to use, and what theory of learning to believe in and follow, reform designers have usually taken the success of a reform for granted (Campbell, 1985). However, repeated unsuccessful attempts to implement reforms in such a way have suggested that this approach is nothing but a prescription for failure. Indeed, research findings during the past two decades have underlined that teachers can play a decisive role in the implementation and future success of an innovation (e.g. Kyriakides, 1997; Polettini, 2000; Ponte et al., 1994; Sztajn, 2003; van den Berg et al., 2000). As the picture constantly changes, teachers are increasingly considered by most policy-makers and school change experts to be the centrepiece of educational change (Datnow et al., 2002). Therefore, examining teachers' attitudes, thoughts, and criticism regarding a reform is judged imperative. Yet the same emphasis does not seem to be placed on the students' role, since students' impact on the implementation of the reform continues to be considered marginal, as is evident from the scarcity of research in this domain. Acknowledging the significant role of both constituents of the teaching and learning process in affecting the implementation and success of a reform, the importance of investigating how teachers' and students' reactions may have influenced the effectiveness of a reform is pointed out.

To date, it is accepted that teachers do not passively respond to the directives mandated from higher levels of organisations; rather, they respond in a variety of ways to such directives: through advancing reform efforts, symbolically displaying reforms, or resisting them overtly or covertly (Datnow et al., 2002; Tyack and Cuban, 1995). This diversity of reactions can be attributed to the impact of characteristics related to the reform *per se* (or the way teachers conceive the reform) and/or to teachers' individual characteristics. Namely, research has so far illustrated that the magnitude of changes that teachers need to introduce into their traditional way of working, the estimation of the extra effort needed to address new requirements, the extent to which the reform addresses important needs, the way the reform is diffused, teachers' involvement in the initiation of the innovation, and their pedagogical content knowledge regarding the reform are among the factors that exert great influence on teachers' reactions towards the reform (Fullan, 1991; Ghaith and Yaghi, 1997; Kelly, 1989; Levenberg and Sfard, 1996; Lloyd and Wilson, 1998; Polettini, 2000; Ponte et al., 1994). It has also been demonstrated that when teachers are not committed to the reform, they see the additional demands associated with them as increasing the stress and pressure of their already difficult jobs (Datnow et al., 2002; Duke, 2004). Though we do not underestimate the effect of these factors, we believe that emphasis should also be given to teachers' beliefs with respect to the reform, since there is evidence suggesting that these beliefs serve as inhibitors or promoters of reform efforts (Datnow *et al.*, 2003; Fullan, 1991).

Recently, research has suggested that teachers' perspectives on, and responses to, a reform should not be considered independently of the context in which they operate. Therefore, it was stressed that rather than examining teachers' reactions uniformly, emphasis should also be given to the culture of schools, since some schools seem to implement reforms in supportive ways while others seem more resistant to the introduction of the reform (Datnow *et al.*, 2003). For example, knowing that colleagues in a school are implementing the reform successfully creates a productive atmosphere for teachers to experiment with it (Datnow *et al.*, 2000). This suggestion seems to be in line with the way the school level has been described in the dynamic model, especially since the model refers to the learning environment of the school. It is important to note, though, that educators' responses to a reform are never homogeneous, even within a school (Datnow *et al.*, 2002). For instance, a recent survey research study by Berends (2000) suggests that the variation that exists within schools can be greater than the variation across schools.

As far as the importance of investigating students' reactions towards the reform is concerned, attempts to implement an educational reform are often linked to the following paradox: even though students are regarded as potential beneficiaries of change, their attitude towards the reform is rarely taken into account (Fullan, 1991). However, during the past decade the importance of investigating students' beliefs regarding the reform has been underlined (Ponte *et al.*, 1994); emphasis has also been placed on students' self-efficacy beliefs (Pajares, 1999). Research is replete with evidence that students' efficacy beliefs are related to the goals they set; the activities they choose to engage in; their effort, energy expenditure, and persistence when pursuing certain outcomes; their use of cognitive strategies and self-regulated learning approaches; and their motivation and interest in certain domains. Moreover, there is evidence that students whose approach is highly efficacious have fewer adverse emotional reactions when they encounter difficulties; display lower levels of anxiety, stress, and depression than students who doubt their capabilities; and possess intrinsic rather than extrinsic motives (Pajares and Miller, 1994; Pajares, 1999; Pintrich, 1999). Some of these factors affecting students' beliefs are also included in the dynamic model, such as their motivation and expectations.

Looking at the impact of the reform on the behaviour of stakeholders: the importance of looking at changes in teacher behaviour in the classroom

Yet we acknowledge a number of limitations related to the idea that formative evaluation should be based on teachers' and students' reactions towards the reform. The findings of evaluation studies looking at the perceptions of stakeholders usually cannot help us explain the differences in the effective implementation of the reform from classroom to classroom and from school to school (Kyriakides *et al.*, 2006a). This implies that instead of putting the blame for the ineffectiveness of a reform on the process followed for its design and diffusion, evaluators should try to explain the differences in the way teachers react to a reform and to the different impact that the reform exerts on their existing teaching practices.

Looking at the way the factors included in the dynamic model have been defined, one could argue that the overemphasis witnessed in previous years on teachers' attitudes towards the reform should be replaced by a balanced emphasis on attitudes and behaviour in the classroom. Evaluation studies reveal that a reform is seldom implemented as planned; teachers often make adaptations to the proposed reforms either to fit with their professional judgement and ideologies or to match the realities of their experiences and meet their students' needs (e.g. Campbell, 1985; Datnow *et al.*, 2002, 2003; Kyriakides, 1997; Pollard *et al.*, 1994; Tyack and Cuban, 1995; Woods, 1994). For instance, spending more time than is prescribed in the reform manuals was the main adaptation witnessed in a series of researches conducted by Datnow and her colleagues (Datnow *et al.*, 2002). It may therefore be concluded that teachers make a predominant contribution to the effectiveness of a reform. As MacDonald (1991) stressed, what matters in an educational reform is not the availability of supporting resources but the *quality* of teachers themselves and their generative role in the curriculum change, which determines the *quality of teaching* and, consequently, the effectiveness of any curriculum change. This argument is reflected in the fact that the dynamic model is based on the assumption that the classroom level is more significant than either the school or the context level. In addition, the classroom level is entirely defined in relation to the behaviour of the teacher in the classroom.

With all this said, it seems pertinent to claim that EER should comprise another theoretical strand upon which reform evaluation studies could be based. The question is, though, in what ways could the description of teacher effectiveness in the dynamic model be helpful in evaluating a reform? We assume that the dynamic model could be informative in at least two ways. First, it could provide a list of criteria that can help researchers elaborate on and study teachers' practices during the reform implementation. Second, it could facilitate the investigation of teachers' professional development, if there is any, during the implementation of the reform. We shall discuss each theme in turn.

Educational effectiveness research could aid in focusing on *teachers' practice* and on the *quality of teaching* rather than solely elaborating on teachers' beliefs (as a lot of evaluation studies did in the past) and their knowledge (as some recent studies have done). This suggestion is in accord with current research findings showing that teacher practices exert a stronger effect on students' outcomes than their beliefs and knowledge (see Chapter 6). Therefore, rather than perceiving teachers as a unified body of people who respond similarly when receiving the same stimulus (i.e. a reform), the dynamic model could provide criteria upon which teacher practices and effectiveness could be studied. For instance, we could focus on the *structure* of their lessons (for example, do teachers call attention to the main ideas underlying the theoretical background of the reform? Do they outline the content to be covered and signal transitions between lesson parts?) or on their *questioning techniques* (for example, if the implementation of the reform requires the use of specific types of questions, do teachers use them successfully? What type of feedback do they provide regarding students' answers?).

Were the dynamic model suggesting only a number of criteria for studying teachers' practice in implementing a reform, it would offer nothing apart from a blueprint for conducting observations. Fortunately, the contribution of the dynamic model is not so limited, since it has the potential to help with studying teachers' development as regards the reform, especially since, at both the school and the context level, factors associated with the learning environment of the schools are included. This implies that empirical evidence is also needed to examine whether the introduction of a reform encourages teachers to modify their existing practice. Beyond portraying teachers' practices at a specific time, the dynamic model implies that we should also collect longitudinal data concerning teachers' classroom behaviour. Hence, we argue that the dynamic model may also help in providing a historical perspective of teachers' practice as regards the reform rather than a motionless picture of teachers' implementation of the reform at a specific time. This argument is partly based on the fact that a measurement framework is proposed by the dynamic model, which, among other things, refers to the stage of the functioning of a factor. Some further implications of the measurement framework of the dynamic model for the development of evaluation studies are drawn below.

Using the measurement framework of the dynamic model to design evaluation studies and build a meta-evaluation system

The dynamic model is based on the assumption that each effectiveness factor operating at the classroom, school, and context level can be measured in relation to five dimensions. Therefore, evaluators who follow a theory-driven approach in building their studies could also use this measurement framework in their attempt to measure each factor that may be associated with the effective implementation of a reform. It is also important to note that this framework can be used in analysing the characteristics of the reform. For this reason, we illustrate how we could measure the characteristics of the reform focused on the use of IT in teaching mathematics, mentioned earlier. As far as the frequency dimension is concerned, we may raise questions such as how many types of software are recommended or how many lesson plans are offered to teachers in order to support them in using IT in teaching mathematics. Second, the focus dimension is measured by investigating whether the guidelines given and/or the actions taken for improving teaching practice are too specific in terms of what each teacher is expected to do. We also examine the purpose(s) that are expected to be achieved by the reform policy, especially whether it attempts to achieve a single purpose (e.g. improving teaching practice) or not only to solve a problem but also to improve effectiveness of education in a more general way (for example, the reform might be related not only to quality of teaching but also to the establishment of a learning environment in each region through the establishment of networks). Third, the stage dimension is seen as a very important measurement dimension, since according to the dynamic model the reform policy should be flexible, as this is reflected in the fact that, from time to time, changes in the reform policy take place. Continuity of the reform policy is also examined. Therefore, we measure the extent to which changes in the reform policy emerge from the results of a systematic evaluation of the reform.

Fourth, quality is measured by investigating the properties of the guidelines on using IT in teaching mathematics, especially whether these are clear, concrete, and in line with the literature, and provide support to teachers, students, and administrators to implement the reform policy. As mentioned above, concrete guidelines include the kinds of measures that should be taken in instances where teachers find that a problem with the implementation of the reform is about to be created. Finally, differentiation is measured by investigating the extent to which school policy is designed in such a way that more support is given to teachers and students who have difficulties in implementing the policy on provision of learning opportunities. For example, novice teachers could be asked to produce different type(s) of short-term planning or to produce it more often than other teachers. It may also be pointed out that students who need more learning opportunities should receive them.

The proposed measurement framework can also be used in investigating the implementation of a reform in different organisations (e.g. school units or classrooms). Specifically, frequency can be measured by looking at the extent to which the reform policy is implemented in a classroom or a school. As far as the focus dimension is concerned, we can investigate the extent to which teachers or schools implement a policy by following exactly what they have been asked to do or whether they are more flexible in implementing the policy in different organisation units (e.g. classrooms or schools). The second aspect of the focus dimension concerned with the number of purposes that are expected to be achieved is investigated by looking at the extent to which teachers or schools implement a reform to help them achieve the purposes mentioned by the policy-makers or whether their expectations for a reform are expanded to cover other aspects or problems of the functioning of their units. The stage dimension is measured by looking at the period during which the reform policy is implemented. It is expected that teachers and schools will try to implement the reform policy during the whole school year and not only at a certain period. Quality is measured by investigating the properties of the behaviour of teachers and schools in implementing the policy guidelines. Finally, differentiation is measured by investigating the extent to which the reform policy is implemented in such a way that more emphasis on the implementation of the reform is given to teachers and students who need the reform more. For example, a reform focused on realistic teaching in mathematics is expected to be implemented more frequently in those schools and classrooms that have high percentages of students with learning difficulties. It may also be pointed out that the reform is implemented in such a way that students or teachers who need the reform more should receive it more than others.

We would finally like to mention that although an integrated aspect of the development of an evaluation system is the development of its meta-evaluation mechanisms, only rarely are such meta-evaluation mechanisms built in. However, those evaluators who may like to develop a meta-evaluation mechanism to help them improve the quality of their evaluation studies could consider the possibility of building this mechanism around the five measurement dimensions of the dynamic model. This is also reflected in the fact that the factors concerned with the evaluation of either school or national policy have been described in relation to these five dimensions (see Chapter 7). The development of such a mechanism can help the evaluators generate data that will help the various stakeholders increase the impact of the reform on student achievement. For example, looking at the quality dimension of the evaluation of the reform will help policy-makers identify not only the psychometric properties of the evaluation (and improve them) but also the extent to which data gathered from evaluation help them make decisions on how to improve the reform and its impact on effectiveness.

Searching for non-linear relations

Evaluators should be aware that according to the dynamic model, non-linear relations between the functioning of a factor and student achievement may exist. This implies that the impact of a reform policy concerned with the provision of support to teachers and schools to improve the functioning of a factor (e.g. the quality of teaching, the quantity of teaching, aspects of the learning environment of the school) may not be linear. For example, for those factors for which an inverted-U relation with achievement is identified, teachers and schools should be aware of the optimal point of the factors. In this way, they will manage to maximise the impact of a reform by making use of its guidelines up to the optimal point. Beyond this point the implementation of the reform will not help them produce better results at student level.

Suggestions concerning the statistical analysis of multilevel data on the implementation of the reform policy and student achievement can be made. These are similar to those mentioned in the first section of this chapter, which refer to the implications of the dynamic model for research and indicate the need to include in the multilevel analysis not only the impact of the factor but also the impact of powers of the factor.

A framework for conducting evaluation studies in line with the dynamic model

This last part of the section concerned with the implications of the dynamic model for evaluation is an attempt to propose a possible theoretical framework for conducting reform evaluations (see Figure 10.2), incorporating the elements of the

Reformulate the questions of stakeholders by taking into account:

- The main characteristics of the dynamic model (e.g. multilevel structure, factors at different levels, measurement dimensions)
- The theory underlying the reform

Designing the evaluation plan:

- Summative evaluation: looking at short- and long-term effects on student outcomes
- Formative evaluation: looking at the implementation of the reform:
  - Use the dynamic model to examine variation in the implementation
  - Evaluate the behaviour of teachers, students, and other stakeholders
  - Search for learning opportunities offered to students, teachers, and other stakeholders

Design of the evaluation study/collecting and analysing data:

- Use multilevel approach
- Develop instruments based on the theoretical framework of educational effectiveness
- Conduct longitudinal or group randomisation experimental studies

Reporting to policy-makers, practitioners, and other stakeholders

Make use of the findings of the study for the development of the evaluation framework based on the dynamic model

Figure 10.2 An evaluation framework inspired by the dynamic model.

dynamic model discussed above. Acknowledging the contribution of different factors identified in previous studies as predictors of the effective implementation of a reform, we considered it imperative to include those factors in the proposed model. Yet it should be stressed that future studies need to be conducted to shed more light on the relative contribution of each factor to predicting the effectiveness of the reform under study.

The following observations arise from Figure 10.2. First, we recommend that evaluators need to reformulate the research questions that policy-makers may have in relation to a reform process. In doing so, the theory upon which the reform is based and the main characteristics of the dynamic model are taken into account. This implies that the multilevel structure of education and the factors operating at different levels should at least be considered. For example, a reform programme looking at the reduction of class sizes could examine its impact on quality of teaching, and especially on the eight classroom-level factors, before investigating the impact of the reform on student outcomes. The reformulation of the evaluation questions of the stakeholders could be the starting point for designing the evaluation plan. This plan is expected to look not only at the summative aspect of evaluation but also at the formative one. The latter is closely related to the implementation of the reform. Given that we expect some variation in the way the reform is implemented, we propose that evaluators need to focus their attention on the behaviour of those expected to make use of the reform. Data concerning the impact of the reform on teachers' and students' behaviour as well as on the behaviour of other stakeholders may help us identify factors associated with the effective implementation of the reform. The dynamic model may be of use to search for the impact of such factors and may also provide suggestions as to how the reform can be redesigned and provide further support to those who need it. Rather than discussing issues related to the existence of prescribed plans for implementing the reform, we propose that we need to examine how teachers use and modify these plans to meet student needs and promote learning. Furthermore, instead of placing so much emphasis on students' reactions towards a reform, we consider it important to examine what learning opportunities students are provided by participating in the reform.

Furthermore, the model proposed here suggests that beyond examining students' progress in terms of learning outcomes, we need to collect longitudinal data for both teachers and students. Namely, we suggest that it is worth examining both the short-term and the long-term effects of the reforms on students, since there is evidence that reforms and intervention programmes may not have enduring effects on student learning (Kyriakides and Creemers, 2006a; Plewis, 2000). The model also suggests that evaluators could examine whether teachers improve their practices through the years as a consequence of implementing the reform (that is, the reform itself could be considered a force able to bring change in teachers' practices).

The proposed framework does not aim to provide a comprehensive model for evaluating educational reforms. Rather, it aims to incorporate different theoretical frameworks into a single model, acknowledging the fact that each theoretical framework could illuminate different aspects of the reform. It is also argued that the dynamic model could have an important role in this process. However, further research is needed to refine and elaborate this framework, especially since the framework did not arise from empirical evidence, or the results of evaluation studies. Again, we underline the fact that the evaluation framework is offered as a set of hypotheses that need to be further tested; we believe, though, that it provides a framework for developing a dynamic rather than a static model of evaluating educational reforms.

Chapter 11

Implications for policy

Introduction

In Chapter 2 the difficulties of using EER to improve policy and practice were illustrated. One of the aims of establishing the dynamic model is to establish better links between EER and policy-making. This chapter is concerned with possible ways of using the dynamic model for improving educational policy. These include the development of an evidence-based model for building educational policy. Obviously, this approach will only be adopted by policy-makers if they share the value assumptions of the dynamic model, and especially its interest in improving teaching and learning. The fact that policy-makers may not be interested only in the improvement of teaching and learning should be acknowledged. However, this should not be seen as an obstacle in using the model to improve policy, especially if policy-makers can see the benefits to society of improving teaching and learning. In the past, policy-makers in most countries attempted to improve standards using procedures that are not scientifically valid. For example, accountability systems were simply based on the fact that there are more and less effective schools and on the view that exercising pressure on the less effective schools will help them to improve standards. However, this assumption was never tested and it is not supported by any of the theoretical models of educational effectiveness. Misuse of findings of effectiveness studies by policy-makers was seen as the failure of EER, but what is supported here is that results of a study cannot be used for building policy unless their relation with the theoretical framework upon which the study is based is also examined. For example, results of an evaluation of a reform which indicates that the reform has no impact on student achievement may not necessarily imply that the reform should be terminated, but might provide feedback on how the reform policy could be improved. But in order for such suggestions to be provided, a valid model that explains what makes teachers and schools effective should exist. It is therefore supported that the development and testing of the dynamic model might help policy-makers identify priorities for building policy on improvement. For example, a study investigating the effect size of different aspects of quality of teaching upon student achievement may reveal what the main concerns of policy-makers on a national policy on quality of teaching should be. Similarly, a study on the direct and/or indirect effect of effectiveness factors on student achievement might reveal the implications of a policy intervention for the functioning of any effectiveness factor and, ultimately, for student outcomes. However, limitations for using EER for the development of educational policy are, first of all, acknowledged. Thus, the first section of this chapter will refer to the political dimension of introducing a reform policy in education which helps us identify difficulties of using research and education theory for building policy.

The political dimension of reforming education

Shipman (1985) points out that there are many obstacles hindering research and educational theory from influencing policy-making. This is usually attributed to the political dimension of introducing a reform policy in education (Kyriakides and Demetriou, 2005b). The view of schools as mini-political systems with diverse constituencies and the term 'micropolitics of education' have emerged in a clearly articulated form in the research literature within the past 30 years (Hoyle and Skrla, 1999). Micropolitics recognise divergence of interests, multiple sources of power, and the potential for – if not constant presence of – conflict (Ball, 1987; Blase, 1993). Such a lens allows for the possibility that coalitions and conflict may occur both across and within organisations such as schools (Firestone and Fisler, 2002). Thus, the development and adoption of a reform policy is not just a technocratic affair, though it is determined by political influences. Codd (1995) defines educational policy-making as an exercise of power and control directed towards the attainment or preservation of some preferred arrangements for school and society. Power and the attendant capacity to make decisions are the substance of politics. Thus, the implementation success of a policy is a function of two important variables: the content of the policy, and the institutional context in which the policy is implemented. Constituencies nowadays have the ability not only to resist governments' policy will but also to induce that will. Therefore, the political dimension of introducing a reform policy, meaning the feasibility study of policy resistance groups, conducted when a reform is proposed, is a flashpoint and is taken into account in our attempt to draw implications of the dynamic model for policy.

Using the dynamic model to develop an evidence-based approach to building educational policy

In this chapter it is taken into account that policy-makers have their own agenda which is not necessarily fully determined by empirical facts. However, in view of rational decision-making, policy-makers are expected to take into account empirical validated knowledge about the political issues at stake. In this context it is argued here that the dynamic model can help policy-makers develop an evidence-based approach for building educational policy. This is attributed to the fact that the model refers to two overarching factors at the context level that are concerned not only with the evaluation but also with the establishment of a national policy on teaching and the school learning environment. The development and testing of the dynamic model can help policy-makers identify priorities for improvement, and thereby choose among alternative options for changing educational policy. In this book the importance of making use of the knowledge base of educational effectiveness to improve policy and practice is stressed. In the context of policy-making at national level, in the first part of this section it is argued that policy-makers and other stakeholders should recognise the importance of the effectiveness factors and focus their attention on introducing reform policies that are likely to improve the functioning of these factors, which will directly and/or indirectly influence student achievement. It is important to note here that some systems are centralised, to a lesser or greater degree. This implies that the context-level factors may operate at either national or regional, or even local level. Irrespective of the organisation of the educational system, the focus is not on the level at which policy is expected to be established or on the people who are expected to develop this policy but on the content of the policy and actions taken to implement it. This implies that the school level is embedded in a context (either regional or national) that is expected to provide support to the schools by contributing to the improvement of their learning environment and their teaching practice. In this chapter we use the term 'national policy', but, depending on the situation, this term could refer not only to national but also to the regional or even the local level.

As it will be argued in the second part of this section, the role of policy-makers at each level should also be reconsidered. It is important to consider improvement of teaching and learning as the ultimate aim of policy-making. Although policy-makers might have their own agenda, and the above assumption might be questioned, the dynamic model is based on this value assumption, and improvement of learning is seen as the major function of policy-making in education. This is in line with our attempt to draw implications of the dynamic model for the evaluation of a reform policy, since evaluation is treated as a systematic form of research investigating the impact of a reform policy on student achievement and identifying ways of maximising this impact (see Chapter 10). However, the description of the context level of the dynamic model (see Chapter 7) supports the idea that the actions that have to be taken at the policy level in order to improve effectiveness are much broader than evaluating reform policies. Policy-makers are also supposed to make choices about different priorities for improving the effectiveness of the system and about alternative solutions and means to meet the general aims of education. Thus, implications of the dynamic model for building educational policy will be discussed in this section.

Implications of the dynamic model for establishing reform policies concerned with teaching practice and the learning environment of the school

The dynamic model reveals the importance of the components of educational policy at the school and system levels. It is argued that aspects of policy concerned with the learning environment of the schools and the teaching practice are the most critical factors affecting effectiveness at levels above the classroom. Thus, use of the dynamic model is not restricted to establishing an evidence-based model in building educational policy concerned with the factors of the model that are associated with student learning outcomes. The use of such a model may also reveal that priorities for building policy on improvement should be related to the factors of the model operating at the system level as these are described in Chapter 7. Thus, reform policy could be focused on factors directly and/or indirectly affecting teaching practice, such as maximisation of the quantity of teaching time or improvement of the quality of teaching. Reform policies can also attempt to improve, either directly or indirectly, the learning environment in schools. For example, a reform policy concerned with the establishment of school networks to allow collaboration among teachers of different schools should have as its ultimate goal the improvement of the learning environment of the schools and/or the improvement of teaching practice. These suggestions are based on the assumption that policy-makers should develop reform policies that make sure that policy at system level has a positive impact on school level and, through that, on teaching. Emphasis on teaching and establishing the learning environment of the school is essential, since these two overarching factors are concerned with learning both inside and outside the classroom, from which not only the students but also other stakeholders (e.g. teachers and parents) can benefit.

This implies that policy-makers should realise that their role is to create conditions to support learning at school and classroom levels (see Chapter 7). However, in order to achieve this aim, an evidence-based approach is recommended, since such an approach helps policy-makers generate evidence that can help policy-makers and other stakeholders identify which of these conditions are able to support learning. Obviously, we are aware that the introduction of a reform policy is not just a technocratic affair, since stakeholders may express negative opinions about those aspects of the reform policy that might reduce their professional power. This implies that most of the time it is difficult to reach consensus among the main stakeholders about a proposed reform policy, albeit it is crucial when successful. However, research into the use of EER to establish policy reveals that consensus could be reached if policy-makers established procedures to ensure clear understanding among stakeholders of both the theoretical assumptions of the proposed policy and the types of concerns they have with regard to the reform (see Kyriakides et al., 2007). Thus, an evidence-based approach to building policy could be very useful for those in charge of mapping out policy for probing teachers' and other stakeholders' scopes when a change is impended. This probing will help track down the zone of acceptance for the various stakeholder groups. It may also help policy-makers find ways of diminishing stakeholders' concerns and 'forcing' them to accept some changes in educational policy that might not work to their advantage as a group, though legitimate and capable of contributing to the improvement of educational effectiveness.

Implications of the dynamic model for the role of policy-makers

The implications of the dynamic model for identifying priorities for improving policy presented above reveal that not only can the model help policy-makers establish an evidence-based approach to policy-making, but also it may help them reconsider their role in the process of improving education. Learning at the student level is expected to be the main concern of policy-makers. This means that, irrespective of the nature of a reform, policy-makers are expected to identify ways to make better use of the available resources of education to improve learning. Therefore, policy-makers' attempts to introduce a reform policy should emerge from their interest in helping teachers and schools achieve the main aims of education. This can be achieved through reforms of policies that are associated with the factors of the model, directly and/or indirectly. Examples of reforms that are directly associated with the factors of the model have already been provided, whereas an example associated with a reform policy on issues that are not directly related to the model will now be given.

Let us examine, for example, the discussion that takes place in different countries regarding the reduction of class size. Such a reform is usually of interest to teachers and their trade unions. However, not only policy-makers but also the other stakeholders should take into account that simply reducing class sizes does not mean that there will automatically be an increase in the educational standards of a country (Bosker, 2006). The importance of reducing class sizes should mainly be examined with regard to how such a reform could improve teaching practice. More specifically, policy-makers and teachers should realise that reducing class sizes will not automatically improve teaching and learning unless teachers make use of this reform to improve the learning environment of their classrooms by giving more opportunities for student–student and student–teacher interactions. If class size reduction is used for improving the function of these two aspects of the learning environment of the classroom, then such a reform may contribute to the improvement of the effectiveness status of the schools.

Understanding the impact of a reform on student achievement is therefore essential for both the content of a reform and the process of disseminating it. In the above example, policy-makers who are planning to reduce class sizes are expected to ensure that class size reduction will ultimately affect student achievement. In order to achieve this purpose, policy-makers should make sure that teachers understand that the main reason for reducing class sizes is to provide them with support in improving the learning environment of the classroom and, through that, to raise national standards. However, helping teachers understand the reasons why a reform has been introduced does not necessarily mean that the implementation of the reform will lead to improvement of standards. Teachers may also need professional support to discover ways to implement the reform so that the functioning of specific effectiveness factors will be improved. In the above example, helping teachers realise that the reduction of class sizes should be seen as a means of helping them improve the learning environment of their classroom does not mean that they will be able to implement the reform effectively. Training and other professional support could be provided to teachers to help them find specific ways of improving this important classroom-level factor.

Therefore, the above example helps us realise that not only policy-makers but also all other stakeholders, especially teachers, should see any reform as a way to improve student achievement gains directly or to improve them indirectly through the improvement of specific effectiveness factors included in the dynamic model. Moreover, the class size example reveals that, in part, designing a reform should be concerned not only with the dissemination process of the reform but also with the training of teachers in order to help them implement the reform in such ways that the functioning of specific effectiveness factors will be improved.

Using the measurement framework of the dynamic model to build a national policy

In this section we draw implications of the proposed measurement framework for the design and the evaluation of educational policy. Given that the national policy concerned with teaching and the learning environment of schools is considered one of the main factors of the dynamic model at the context level, it will be shown in what follows that the characteristics of any reform policy could be examined in relation to the five dimensions of measuring the effectiveness factors. In this way, policy-makers may identify areas for improving the national policy and, ultimately, the effectiveness of the educational system.

FREQUENCY

As far as the frequency dimension is concerned, policy-makers could realise that the intensity of policy guidelines concerned with teaching and the school learning environment is an issue that should be taken into account in designing a reform policy. For example, looking at the number of aspects associated with teaching practice covered by the national policy, one might draw conclusions about the need to expand the content of the policy on teaching. Since this context-level factor refers not only to the national policy but also to the actions taken to improve teaching, policy-makers could also examine the types of actions they take in order to provide support to schools, or teachers, or students in relation to quantity of teaching, quality of teaching, and provision of learning opportunities. Such investigation may help them identify strengths and weaknesses of the policy in terms of a quantitative way of evaluating it. This measurement dimension should not be underestimated, since it reveals the emphasis given to teaching and the learning environment of the school by policy-makers, and important messages to the various stakeholders arise from it. Obviously, the other four measurement dimensions should also be taken into account.

STAGE

Using the stage dimension to measure policy for teaching at the system level, policy-makers can identify the extent to which the national policy is flexible. Flexibility can also be seen as an essential characteristic of a proposed reform policy. In addition, the stage dimension is concerned with the extent to which there is time consistency in the attempts of policy-makers to improve the national policy. This implies that policy-makers are expected to make decisions that take into account the current situation of the system. The existence of time consistency in policy-makers' actions to improve teaching and the learning environment of the school is an issue that needs to be considered.

FOCUS

On the other hand, the focus dimension implies that policy-makers should examine each reform in relation to its specificity and in relation to the number of purposes that are addressed by the reform. According to the dynamic model, there is expected to be a curvilinear relation between these two aspects of the focus dimension of national policy and student achievement. Therefore, studies looking for such relations may help policy-makers identify optimal points of the specificity dimension of the focus dimension of this factor. As a consequence, the design of a reform policy could be based on the findings of these studies, since the main purpose of the reform could be concerned with the functioning of this factor, especially how to reach its optimal points.

QUALITY

As far as the quality dimension is concerned, the dynamic model is based on the assumption that policy-makers should examine the properties of the national policy guidelines on issues associated with teaching and the learning environment of the school. The properties of the actions taken by them for improving teaching and the school learning environment should also be examined. More specifically, policy-makers should identify the extent to which policy guidelines are clear, concrete, and in line with the literature. Moreover, the extent to which support is provided to teachers and/or schools to implement the policy should be examined. Therefore, this dimension of measuring national policy can be used for building a reform policy and can help policy-makers generate criteria for evaluating not only the content of a proposed reform but also its dissemination process.

DIFFERENTIATION

Finally, the differentiation dimension is concerned with the extent to which further support is provided by the system to teachers or schools who need it more. This dimension implies that the dynamic model supports the idea that policy-makers should give special emphasis to the provision of equal opportunities to students (see also Kyriakides and Creemers, 2006b). Moreover, policy-makers should identify the extent to which schools manage to reduce the variance in student outcomes compared to prior achievement. Thus, two dimensions for measuring the effectiveness of reform policies can be used concerning its implication on both the quality and the equity of the educational system. It can also be argued that this dimension of the model as well as findings of studies investigating differential teacher and school effectiveness (e.g. Campbell *et al.*, 2004; Kyriakides, 2004a; Nuttall *et al.*, 1989; Sammons *et al.*, 1993; Thomas *et al.*, 1997) help policy-makers evaluate the goals of education and discover whether some groups of students or schools are being systematically disadvantaged in their rate of learning in comparison to other groups.

At the level of the classroom, it is, of course, important that students are treated as individuals rather than as representing stereotypical groups so that the promotion of learning for all students is encouraged. However, at the level of the school or the system, if groups of students are systematically being disadvantaged, issues for educational policy at the system level should be raised. More specifically, the dynamic model implies that findings of research on differential effectiveness may help policy-makers raise questions about the appropriateness of the national policy on equal opportunities.

It should, however, be acknowledged that the effective implementation of any reform policy on equal opportunities that a system or a number of schools may introduce is likely to be influenced by various cultural factors (Kyriakides, 2004a). This argument is in line with the fact that one of the context factors included in the dynamic model refers to the wider educational environment. Nevertheless, policy-makers should realise that the argument that schools are very complex organisations justifies the importance of constructing an evidence-based model for building policy at both the national and the school level. It is argued here that for this reason, data resulting from research into differential school effectiveness as well as data from studies testing the importance of the differentiation dimension of the dynamic model should be provided to schools to monitor what is happening (Fitz-Gibbon, 1996) and identify cultural factors that affect their effectiveness. Thus, the development of any national policy on educational equality and its evaluation could be based on 'value added' data, and thereby an 'evidence-based' approach to introducing and evaluating national policy should be followed. At the same time, the value added feedback may be used to encourage not only the system but also individual schools to identify apparent areas of strengths and weaknesses to formulate provisional hypotheses about the factors that may have influenced both student achievement in specific outcomes of schooling and the reduction of unjustifiable differences among groups of students.

Establishing links between the dynamic model and policy on teacher and school evaluation

Beyond establishing an evidence-based approach to building national policy for education, we shall argue in this section that the dynamic model may help policy-makers establish teacher and school evaluation systems. Currently, researchers in the area of educational effectiveness attempt to identify theoretical links among school and teacher effectiveness research, staff development, and teacher and school improvement (Teddlie *et al.*, 2003). Although it has been noted that in most countries many of these links are underdeveloped (Reezigt *et al.*, 2003), findings from effectiveness studies and theoretical models of educational effectiveness could form a foundation upon which valid teacher and school evaluation systems could be built (Kyriakides and Campbell, 2003). In this context, a number of cognate research projects have been conducted (e.g. Kyriakides *et al.*, 2006b; Teddlie *et al.*, 2006). Moreover, policy-makers in at least one country have invited researchers to make use of the knowledge base of EER in order to design new teacher and school evaluation systems (Kyriakides *et al.*, 2007). Therefore, this second section of the chapter is an attempt to identify ways of using the dynamic model in building reform policy on school and teacher evaluation.

There are three main aspects that should be considered in order to develop comprehensive teacher and school evaluation systems: the *evaluation purposes*, the *evaluation criteria*, and the *sources for collecting relevant data* (Ellett *et al.*, 1996). Regarding the purposes of a teacher evaluation system, these might include licensing and credentialling, tenure, self-assessment, and professional development (Stronge, 1997). These specific purposes refer to two more general functions of the evaluation system: accountability and improvement. The accountability purpose reflects the need to determine the competence of teachers in order to ensure that services delivered are effective, and typically has been viewed as summative in nature. The improvement purpose reflects the need for professional growth and development of the individual teacher, and typically has been considered to be formative in nature (Beerens, 2000).

The dual character of teacher evaluation, as described above, is practically impossible to achieve with a single evaluation system, since the determination of the evaluation purposes influences the design of the evaluation instruments, their administration, as well as the interpretation of their results (Harlen and James, 1997; Kyriakides and Campbell, 2003; Black and Wiliam, 1998). However, McGreal (1988) argues that a comprehensive teacher evaluation system should be rooted in the two broad purposes of evaluation, since it should be oriented towards both outcome and improvement. Similar arguments can be made about the need to establish both formative and summative school evaluation systems (e.g. Hopkins, 1995; Kyriakides and Campbell, 2004; MacBeath, 1999; Patton, 1991). Therefore, it is imperative to establish different mechanisms for formative and summative teacher and school evaluation.

Since summative and formative functions of evaluation are based on different value assumptions, different criteria might be used for conducting each type of teacher and school evaluation. However, for teacher and school evaluation systems to serve both purposes, there must be a rational link between them (Stronge, 1995) that must not allow the summative function of evaluation to dominate the formative, as the experiences of many countries reveal (Ellett *et al.*, 1996). It is argued in this chapter that this link cannot be established unless the criteria for both formative and summative evaluation are based on the same theoretical framework of what constitutes effective teachers and schools. Moreover, we believe that policy-makers should generate criteria for both summative and formative teacher and school evaluation based on the dynamic model. For example, the eight classroom-level factors and the way these factors are measured through the proposed measurement dimensions can help policy-makers generate criteria concerning the generic teaching skills that help teachers to be effective. Similarly, looking at the description of the school-level factors could generate criteria for school evaluation.

In terms of the data sources, evaluators should employ a multidimensional approach (e.g. Danielson and McGreal, 2000; Gastel, 1991), as comparisons of various sources will increase the internal validity of the evaluation system (Cronbach, 1990). Moreover, the involvement of all constituencies in the evaluation process fosters participatory policies that mitigate stakeholders' criticism of the evaluation (Kyriakides and Demetriou, 2005b). As far as the implications of the dynamic model are concerned, policy-makers should take into account not only the suggestions for testing the validity of the dynamic model presented in Chapter 10 but also the methods and research instruments of studies used to test the validity of the model (see Chapter 8). In this way they will be able to establish procedures to test the psychometric properties of the instruments that will be developed. As is argued in this book, particular emphasis on the construct and the interpretive validity should be given in order to improve the quality of the evaluation data. As far as the interpretive validity is concerned, the main question that a meta-evaluation system should raise about the quality of the various evaluation mechanisms refers to the impact of the proposed evaluation systems. It is considered important for policy-makers not only to build teacher and school evaluation mechanisms that are in line with the knowledge base of educational effectiveness, as reflected in the dynamic model, but also to find out whether teachers and schools make use of the evaluation data and improve their effectiveness (see also Chapter 12).

Making better use of comparative studies to build reforms of national policy

Since 1959 the IEA has undertaken a large number of comparative studies in different subjects. The ultimate goal of these studies has been to isolate those factors related to student learning that could be manipulated through policy changes in the curriculum, resource allocation, or instructional practice (Martin, 1996; Yang, 2003). It has been expected that information that arises from such investigations could help policy-makers, curriculum specialists, and researchers better understand the performance of their educational systems (Martin *et al.*, 2000; Mullis *et al.*, 2000). Thus, the weaknesses and strengths of educational systems at micro or macro level could be identified, and intervention programmes attempting to improve educational effectiveness could be developed (Schmidt and Valverde, 1995). In this context, this last section of the chapter refers to the lessons that policy-makers can draw from the dynamic model in their attempt to make use of the findings of comparative studies in designing reform policies in education.

However, it is first of all important to note that the globalisation of the economy and the relation between economic growth and education is increasing the interest in education and the results of educational research, in particular comparisons between countries with respect to educational outcomes. This can be seen in the media attention given to publications about international studies on educational achievement. The results of this kind of study may impose pressure on education within countries (Mortimore, 2001). However, this pressure that arises from the results of international studies can result in a simplistic application of knowledge relating to one educational system to another educational system. Thus, many effectiveness researchers have become concerned about the oversimplified potential transfer of educational policies that has already been going on between countries (Creemers, 2006; Reynolds *et al.*, 2002; Campbell and Kyriakides, 2000). The 'importation' of educational policies from one country with one context to another country of different contextual conditions is, of course, something that has had a long history. For example, in North America, Stevenson's (1992) cross-cultural comparisons of Taiwan and the United States generated simplistic suggestions that the United States should adopt levels of children's time in school and the like that were characteristic of the Pacific Rim (see Reynolds and Farrell, 1996). After the publication of the results of the PISA study, several ministers of education of European countries decided to visit Finland to find out how the Finnish system operates and to 'borrow' some characteristics of an educational system that the study found to have the best results in terms of student learning. This simplistic approach of making use of the results of a study reveals the importance of conducting studies on the basis of a strong theoretical framework and of helping stakeholders understand the results by making use of that framework. If results are simply reported to the press, policy-makers may be led to believe that results achieved in one country can be replicated in another country by a simplistic transplant of some factors, which might then be imported without any detailed knowledge of possible contextual factors that might explain how factors that work in one country may be ineffective in another country. However, such an approach may not help us improve the educational policy of a system. What is needed is not the borrowing of policies but the conducting of secondary analyses of these studies and the identification of those characteristics of the educational systems that explain variation in achievement within and across countries (see Chapter 4). Such an approach may allow us to build an evidence-based model in introducing reform policies (see Chapter 10).

In Chapter 10 it was mentioned that international studies are usually concerned with school- and classroom-level factors. It is therefore difficult for policy-makers to make any use of these studies to identify factors at the context level that explain variation in student achievement. This chapter supports the view that we could also use the dynamic model in creating a data bank illustrating differences across countries in the functioning of context-level factors included in the dynamic model. For example, a content analysis of educational policies in different countries using the measurement framework of the dynamic model could be conducted. It would then be possible to link the data emerging from this analysis with the results of the comparative studies and identify the extent to which differences in the functioning of the context-level factors are associated with student achievement. Such an approach may allow us to make use of comparative studies in identifying not only generic contextual factors but also the major strengths and weaknesses of an educational system. Thus, the dynamic model can help policy-makers better understand the results of comparative studies and build an evidence-based approach to designing reform policies.

In this chapter, various possibilities of using the dynamic model to generate an evidence-based approach in designing reform policies have been illustrated. It is also suggested that the dynamic model may contribute to a reconceptualisation of the role of policy-makers. But the extent to which policy-makers will adopt these suggestions mainly depends on the way the resistance of different stakeholders to changing policy is manipulated. Policy-makers are expected to establish procedures to ensure clear understanding among stakeholders of the theoretical assumptions of the dynamic model and the relation of the proposed policy with the knowledge base of educational effectiveness. In addition, the types of concerns stakeholders may have regarding a reform could be identified. Such an approach may help policy-makers find ways of diminishing stakeholders' concerns and 'forcing' them to accept some changes in educational policy that might not work to their advantage as a group, even though these may be legitimate and contribute in the improvement of student learning.

Chapter 12

Implications for the improvement of educational practice

Introduction

An important constraint of the existing approaches of EER is the fact that the process as a whole does not contribute significantly to the improvement of school effectiveness. Although in 1989 an International Congress for School Effectiveness and Improvement (ICSEI) was established, together with the journal *School Effectiveness and School Improvement*, and projects attempting to establish links between effectiveness and improvement research were undertaken (e.g. the Effective School Improvement project), there are still problems in the relation between effectiveness and improvement. The question persists of how to apply the effectiveness knowledge base in practice – in other words, how to obtain valid and useful information about school improvement from studies of educational effectiveness (Creemers and Kyriakides, 2006a).

Scepticism has, however, been expressed about the possibilities of a merger between school effectiveness and school improvement. Creemers and Reezigt (1997) argue that there are intrinsic differences between the school effectiveness tradition, which is ultimately a programme for research with its focus on theory and explanation, and the school improvement tradition, which is a programme for innovation focusing on change and problem-solving in educational practice. At least in the early stages, in school effectiveness circles it was expected that a more or less 'simple' application of school effectiveness knowledge about 'what works' in education would result in school improvement. In school improvement circles this was seen as simplistic and mechanistic, and it was thought it would not work in schools. Schools have to design and invent their own solutions for specific problems and improvement in general. Nevertheless, researchers in the area of school effectiveness and improvement (e.g. Creemers and Reezigt, 1997; Reynolds *et al.*, 1993) advocated further linkage between school effectiveness and school improvement, for their mutual benefit. It is argued that effectiveness research and theory can provide insights and knowledge to be used in school improvement. For example, the dynamic nature of the proposed model can be tested by research on school improvement. Longitudinal studies on school improvement can also provide new insights and new possibilities for effective factors, which can be analysed further in EER. In recent years there have been examples of productive cooperation between school effectiveness and school improvement, in which new ways of merging the two traditions, or orientations, have been attempted (see Creemers and Reezigt, 2005; Gray *et al.*, 1999; MacBeath and Mortimore, 2001; Reynolds and Stoll, 1996; Stoll *et al.*, 1996; Reynolds *et al.*, 2000).

However, it can be argued that there are still tensions between educational effectiveness, theory, and research on the one hand and school improvement on the other. Probably this will remain the case, but the tensions between the two have also led to further clarification about what is at stake. The development of a knowledge base about educational effectiveness certainly needs to be expanded, but it has to be acknowledged that school improvement is more than just application of the available knowledge base. It needs intermediate goals and careful research and evaluation about how the ultimate goals, such as student performance and the characteristics of the school and classroom levels (the so-called effective characteristics), are related to the objectives of the improvement policies. In this context this final chapter of the book is an attempt to draw out implications of the dynamic model for improvement.

One of the main reasons for establishing the dynamic model is concerned with the need to develop a theoretical model that can provide a knowledge base upon which improvement efforts can be based. Moreover, in our attempt to define the school- and system-level factors of the dynamic model, it is not only the school policy concerning teaching and the school policy concerning the learning environment of the school that are treated as effectiveness factors. Emphasis is also given to the actions taken to improve teaching and to the actions taken to improve the learning environment of schools (see Chapter 7). This implies that the dynamic model assumes that effective schools are always in a process of improving and/or maintaining the quality of the teaching and the quality of their learning environment. These essential characteristics of the dynamic model reveal that the improvement of teaching practice and the improvement of the learning environ- ment of the school are the major functions of an effective school. Therefore, implications can be drawn from the proposed dynamic model for improving practice. It can also be claimed that if the dynamic model cannot be used for improving practice, then the establishment of the dynamic model, which is a less parsimonious model than the current models of educational effectiveness, can be questioned. Obviously, it has to be acknowledged that just introducing the model is not enough to bring about change. What really matters is that research on the use of the model for improving practice is conducted. Therefore, this chapter refers to our expectations of how the model can be used for improving practice, but research is needed to find out whether those expectations are feasible. Such research may contribute to the expanding of the knowledge base of EER in order to cover issues concerned with ways of using EER for improving practice. Moreover, evaluation of improvement efforts that are designed according to the dynamic model (see Chapter 10) may contribute not only to the further development and empirical validation of the dynamic model but also to the identification of ways of using the model for improving practice.

Strategies for school improvement

There are many strands of educational and social scientific theory that can be used to explain the process of school improvement arising from curriculum theories (e.g. Campbell, 1985; Fullan, 1991; Simons, 1998; Snyder *et al.*, 1992), organisational theories (e.g. Fairman and Quinn, 1985; Mintzberg, 1979), organisation learning theories (Morgan, 1986), and even micro-economic theory and public choice theory, which emphasise incentives and consumer-controlled accountability (Scheerens and Demeuse, 2005). These theories point out the importance of using specific strategies and taking into account specific factors for establishing improvement culture at the school level such as shared vision, autonomy used by schools, staff stability, and ownership (Reezigt and Creemers, 2005). The creation of a climate conducive to improved effectiveness is seen as essential for schools attempting to introduce interventions that will help them become more effective. For school improvement to occur, characteristics of the school culture must be favourable. Schools, for example, must have shared goals and feel responsible for success. Other requirements are collegiality, risk-taking, mutual respect and support, openness, and a willingness to engage in lifelong learning. However, research supports the idea that those schools which manage to establish a climate of trust, openness, and collaboration are among the most effective (Freiberg, 1999; Reynolds *et al.*, 2002). It can be claimed that there is something highly tautological in the argument, so that it offers no help in getting from the former state to the latter.

The dynamic model acknowledges the importance of the school climate, and for this reason not only actions that are taken for the purpose of improving teaching are treated as factors of effectiveness but also the actions taken towards improving the learning environment of the school are seen as essential characteristics of effective schools. It is also assumed that teachers should be considered an essential lever of change, because change is explicit in their classrooms and daily practices, but for effective school improvement, individual teacher initiatives are not enough. Teachers can succeed in achieving major changes in their classrooms with strong effects on student outcomes, but they cannot be expected to have a lasting impact on the school as an organisation. Improvement efforts initiated by one teacher will generally disappear (e.g. when the teacher changes schools) unless the school as an organisation sustains the efforts. This important notion is problematic for educational systems that have no strong tradition of school-level improvement, even when teacher improvement activities may occur (Kyriakides, 2005b). However, it is not supported that all improvement activities necessarily concern all members of a school staff. In practice, this will not happen very often.

At the same time, it is argued here that we should not take the culture of a school as the starting point of an improvement effort, but we should try to use the knowledge base of EER in order to identify needs and priorities for improvement. The improvement of school culture might be a welcome effect of an effective improvement effort but at the same time the determined outcomes, in this case the improvement of the factors in the dynamic model, should be achieved. For this reason the next section will refer to the importance of using a theory-driven approach in our attempt to improve school effectiveness, and the dynamic model is treated as one of the main theoretical models of educational effectiveness upon which we can draw to build comprehensive school reform programmes. Taking into account that in Chapter 10 we drew out implications of the dynamic model for the establishment of a theory-driven approach in evaluation, it can be argued that the dynamic model can contribute to the establishment of a theory-driven approach in both introducing and evaluating improvement efforts.

Before we move to the identification of possible implications of the dynamic model for building a theory-driven approach in school improvement, we should like to explain the dynamic character of our model, which reveals some of the main assumptions of the model about the process of improvement. It is first of all important to note that the school and system factors of the dynamic model refer to the development of policy and the actions taken for improving teaching and the learning environment. It is expected that these actions will influence classroom-level factors and/or student achievement (that is, they have both direct and indirect effects). However, their influences are mainly seen in relation to the changes that occur in the classroom-level factors that are directly associated with improvement of student achievement. Moreover, the development of a policy is seen as a reaction to what teachers and schools define as weaknesses in the functioning of their schools. Therefore, the development of a school policy in one aspect (e.g. absentee-ism) is not a necessary condition for a school to be effective. For example, if a school does not face any problem regarding teacher absenteeism, there is no reason for this school to take actions to improve its policy on teacher absenteeism. The dynamic model assumes that only changes in aspects of policy that evaluation reveals to be problematic will contribute to the improvement of the effectiveness status of schools. The conceptualisation of the school- and system-level factors by the dynamic model also reveals the importance of using 'stage' as a measurement dimension of effectiveness factors. In this way the dynamic model refers to ways of changing the effectiveness status of schools and does not simply describe factors associated with student achievement at a certain point of time, as static models usually try to do. Furthermore, it reveals the importance of conducting longitudinal studies to investigate the impact of changes in the school factors concerning policy regarding teaching and learning environment upon changes in the functioning of classroom-level factors and upon the effectiveness status of schools, as well as the impact of changes in the system factors upon changes in school and classroom factors, and ultimately upon student outcomes.

A theory-driven approach to school improvement: the contribution of the dynamic model

The goal of any science is the production of cumulative knowledge. In the first chapter of this book it is argued that there seems to be little sustained and systematic theoretical development in the area of educational effectiveness. The development of the dynamic model is seen as a reaction to the major weaknesses of the current models of educational effectiveness. Thus, our attempt to establish a synthesis of empirical evidence concerned with the impact of effectiveness factors upon student achievement is expected to generate more than simply a guide to the field. It is expected to provide a useful road map for practitioners, and indeed there are hints that it has, in part, been an absence of educational effectiveness theory that has hindered the take-up of effectiveness knowledge by practitioners in schools (Reezigt and Creemers, 2005). We would therefore argue that the dynamic model can be used in policy and practice for improvement. As is shown below, the dynamic model may contribute to the establishment of a theory-driven approach in school improvement.

Using the dynamic model to improve school effectiveness through a school self-evaluation approach

In defining the school-level factors of the dynamic model, findings of various studies concerning the impact of school evaluation upon student achievement were taken into account. Specifically, it is supported that school evaluation mechanisms should provide empirical data to help stakeholders identify the strengths and weaknesses of their schools and design intervention programmes to improve their effectiveness status. Commitment to gathering evidence is therefore seen as one of the major value assumptions of the dynamic model. In modern education systems, practice is expected to be informed by evidence (DfEE, 1998). The gathering of empirical data is important because it reflects the value of scientific rationality (Cohen *et al.*, 2000). Members of the school are therefore expected to express commitment to values of objectivity and a readiness to alter their practice in the light of evidence (Fitz-Gibbon *et al.*, 1990; Visscher and Coe, 2002). Organisations' members are also expected to regard the duty of gathering empirical data as part of their mission. This assumption reveals the need for involving schools' stakeholders, especially teachers, in the process of gathering empirical data on the effectiveness of their schools and thereby identifying the factors that render schools effective (Teddlie and Reynolds, 2000). Moreover, the importance of evaluative feedback is particularly strong, in that it is expected to contribute to individual learning (Beerens, 2000) and organisational development (Hopkins, 1989; Nevo, 1995; Stufflebeam and Shinkfield, 1990). For this reason, school self-evaluation (SSE) is seen as one of the most important vehicles in relation to using the dynamic model for establishing improvement in schools. A brief description of SSE will now be given, and ways of using the dynamic model to establish SSE mechanisms and improve effectiveness will be discussed.

It can be claimed that the essence of a successful organisation in the modern world is the search for improvement and that effective self-evaluation is the key to it. Devos (1998) argues that SSE should be seen as 'a process mainly initiated by the school to collect systematic information about the school functioning, to analyse and judge this information regarding the quality of the school's education and to make decisions that provide recommendations' (pp. 1–2). In another definition, SSE is described as an evaluation of the school as a whole, carried out for and by the school community, for improvement purposes (Boud and Donovan, 1982).

The overarching goals for SSE are twofold: to improve the quality of the organisation and to improve teaching and learning (Kyriakides and Campbell, 2004). Improving the quality of the organisation includes such matters as social relations between members of the organisation, organisational climate, and culture (Freiberg, 1999), the nature of decision-making (Hoy and Miskel, 2001), and the responsiveness of the school as an organisation to external and internal change forces (Fullan, 1993). Improving teaching and learning is more clear-cut. It involves concepts of teacher effectiveness and school effectiveness, and decisions about how these concepts are appropriately measured within the school setting (Fitz-Gibbon, 1996; Goldstein, 2003). As a consequence, the dynamic model could be seen as a useful research tool upon which SSE mechanisms and interventions that search for ways of improving teaching and learning can be based.

Establishing clarity and consensus about the aims of SSE: the contribution of the dynamic model

The first step in SSE is based on the assumption that it is important to start with a clear understanding of your destination and how you are going to reach SSE. It could be considered as 'a purposeful task analysis' (Wiggins and McTighe, 1998, p. 8), which suggests a planning sequence. Moreover, commitment to collaborative work needs to be established. However, Fullan (1991) points out that people have different perceptions of change. It is hence difficult to reach consensus among the participants in SSE, albeit crucial in its success. Therefore, it is important to establish procedures to ensure clear understanding among stakeholders as to the aims of SSE (MacBeath et al., 2000). At this point, the dynamic model can be a useful tool for helping stakeholders realise that the ultimate aim of SSE should be to improve student achievement across the school and not to attach blame to any individual. This implies that measures of student achievement before the implementation of an intervention, and at the end of it, should be collected. Using methods that assess value added, the impact of interventions on student achievement gains should be identified.

Collecting evaluation data and design strategies for improving effectiveness

Moreover, the factors included in the dynamic model help stakeholders design strategies for improving student achievement. More specifically, the definition of the factors at the school and classroom levels, especially their five measurement dimensions, can be used first of all for designing instruments that will help schools collect data about the functioning of the factors. Research instruments of studies investigating the validity of the dynamic model may also be helpful. Based on the results that emerge from measuring the function of the school- and classroom-level factors, strengths and weaknesses of schools could be identified. Moreover, stakeholders will identify priorities for improving the functioning of specific factors and/or grouping of factors. Finally, strategies for improving these factors could be established.

However, research has shown that the involvement of students, parents, and the wider community is a crucial factor determining the success of participatory models of evaluation (Hopkins, 2001; Kyriakides, 2005b; McTaggart, 1997). This may be only partly explained by raised levels of understanding of aims among participants, and therefore, parallel to any intervention in improving the functioning of specific factors or grouping of factors, efforts should be made to ensure active participation of the various stakeholders in SSE.

Using the model to design improvement programmes

This subsection places more emphasis on how the dynamic model can be used to design improvement programmes at a single school through an SSE approach, or even at a network of schools supported by a central agency (e.g. a local education authority or a professional association, such as an association of teachers of mathematics). It is claimed that the dynamic model may help us define the objectives of school improvement efforts, since it refers to factors that are changeable and associated with student learning outcomes. Although these factors operate at different levels, the dynamic model supports the view that least effective schools should focus their attention on the school-level factors and develop interventions and improvement efforts that will not only improve the functioning of these factors but eventually promote quality of teaching and ultimately raise student achievement. This is due to the fact that school-level factors are expected to influence classroom-level factors rather than the other way around. Therefore, designing improvement efforts that focus on the classroom-level factors alone may improve the teaching practice of individuals but may not necessarily improve the learning environment of the school. In such a case, teachers who may manage to improve the aspects of teaching practice addressed by a specific improvement effort will need at some stage some other type of support. But in the event that the reform does not succeed in improving the learning environment of the school, such support may not be available when needed, and the long-lasting effect of this reform of teaching practice could be questioned.

Moreover, a specific feature of the dynamic model is that making use of the proposed dimensions of measuring effectiveness factors gives more precise directions to design an improvement effort. At the same time, it helps each individual school and/or stakeholders (e.g. teachers) identify how the intervention should be implemented. Finally, it helps stakeholders identify ways of monitoring the implementation of the intervention. In order to show how the measurement framework can be used in designing an improvement effort, we provide below an example concerned with actions taken by a network of schools in order to establish close relations with parents and the wider school community.

Since the *frequency* dimension is a quantitative way of measuring the functioning of partnership policy, schools should identify the number of aspects concerning partnership that should be taken into account in building a policy, as well as how many and how frequently activities concerning each aspect of partnership policy should be implemented.

The *focus* dimension concerns the specificity of the policy guidelines that have to be developed and the specificity of the types of activities that are taken for improving the relations of schools with the parents and the wider school community. The dynamic model implies that in designing an intervention, answers concerned with the specificity of the reform policy should be given. For example, we could identify the extent to which policy guidelines on partnership and/or the actions taken for improving partnership are in line with any of the five types of partnership proposed by Epstein (1992). The second aspect of the focus dimension concerns the purpose(s) that are expected to be achieved. Therefore, we should make explicit whether the policy or a specific task refers to a single purpose (e.g. only dealing with a specific problem) or to multiple purposes.

The *stage* dimension is measured by identifying the period when the policy is established and whether the policy is flexible. Stakeholders are expected to design guidelines that are flexible. Moreover, the attempts of the school to improve partnership should be based on results of a previous evaluation of the partnership policy in order to establish continuity in their attempt to improve this aspect of the school policy.

As far as the *quality* of this factor is concerned, the stakeholders are expected to design the reform in such a way that the guidelines given to stakeholders are clear, concrete, and in line with the literature. During the implementation of the intervention, we should also examine the support given to teachers and students to implement the policy on partnership.

Finally, *differentiation* is measured by investigating the extent to which the reform is designed in such a way that further support is given to teachers and/or students who will gain more benefits from the establishment of close relations of the school with parents and the wider community. At the same time, the different needs of groups of parents (e.g. parents of different socio-economic status) are taken into account in implementing the reform policy. Moreover, different improvement strategies are used for parents whose backgrounds and values concerning learning differ.

Another significant characteristic of the dynamic model that has implications in designing improvement efforts has to do with the fact that some of these factors are expected to be related in a non-linear way to student achievement. This implies that different priorities for professional development for each teacher, and/or different priorities for improvement for each school, can be identified. These will be based on the fact that the effects of the improvement of a factor on student outcomes depend on the stage each individual teacher or school has currently reached. For example, a teacher who attempts to improve his or her orientation skills may succeed in improving student outcomes more than by attempting to improve his or her skills in teaching-modelling. A completely different interpretation may be made for another teacher, depending on that teacher's current situation. Similar interpretations may be made concerning attempts to improve a specific aspect of the learning environment of a school. Thus, the priorities of improvement have to be related to the current situation of the specific schools and teachers involved. The dynamic model is based on the assumption that improvement efforts require adaptation to the needs of each individual addressed by them. Specifically, since some of the effectiveness factors are expected to have a curvilinear relation with student achievement, the impact of an intervention programme attempting to improve a specific aspect of the learning environment of the school (e.g. relations of the school with parents) will depend on what the current situation is. Therefore, data collected through validation studies of the dynamic model may help stakeholders identify those dimensions that constitute the major weaknesses of the system and therefore design relevant intervention programmes for improving its effectiveness.

Finally, the dynamic model assumes that some factors at the same level are related to each other. It is therefore considered important to specify grouping of factors. This implies that different profiles of schools can be developed, illustrating the needs of the schools across factors related to each other. Therefore, specific strategies addressing a grouping of factors could be established in each school.

Using the dynamic model to establish a developmental evaluation strategy

In this section it is argued that the dynamic model may help stakeholders establish a developmental evaluation strategy in their attempt to improve the effectiveness status of their schools. It is important to note that according to the dynamic model, and especially the stage dimension of the evaluation factors, a continuous model of school evaluation is expected to exist in order to allow schools to adopt their policy decisions on the needs of different groups of school stakeholders (see Chapter 7). Moreover, according to the quality dimension, emphasis is placed on the interpretive validity of school evaluation systems, and therefore the extent to which evaluation data help stakeholders improve the policy is examined. It can therefore be claimed that the dynamic model supports the position that a developmental evaluation strategy may contribute to the improvement of the effectiveness status of schools.

For example, a developmental evaluation strategy of school policy and actions taken to improve the relations of a school with parents can be used. In such a case, the evaluation process is expected to follow a linear sequence that starts with the development of a plan for school policy on partnership, from which priorities and targets will emerge, with associated performance indicators. At the next stage, evaluation questions that followed on from the targets and performance indicators will be established, to provide the criteria for data collection. The data will then be analysed and fed back into the formative process of evaluation. In this way, stakeholders will be able to find out what is happening during the implementation of the school policy on partnership.

This strategy for improving effectiveness has a number of significant features. The evaluation process is expected to assist in the implementation and development of a school policy, since the establishment of targets and performance indicators may specify the developmental process of the partnership policy. Moreover, evaluation data may be related, through the evaluation questions, to the aims of the policy. As a consequence, a logical chain of action that relates aims to targets, to evaluation questions, and to particular information sources can be established. However, it has to be acknowledged that although the evaluation process is presented here as linear, it is very likely to be less tidy in practice. Once the evaluation process is under way, different working groups of stakeholders (e.g. coordinators of partnership policy, teachers of different subjects) may implement parts of the policy at different rates (Kyriakides, 2005b). However, it should be possible to identify the extent to which there is a gap between the implementation of a reform policy and the design of an intervention. Thus, the results of formative evaluation may help stakeholders to take decisions on how to improve the quality of school policy or on how to provide additional support to those working groups that may need it.

Beyond the fact that the school-level factors included in the dynamic model provide strong support for the use of this strategy to improve effectiveness, the model can be treated as a tool from which criteria of school effectiveness may arise. Teachers and other stakeholders could be encouraged to draw their own meanings concerning what makes a school and a teacher effective by considering the knowledge base of educational effectiveness provided by the dynamic model. Such an approach may contribute not only to the professional development of teachers but also to the establishment of criteria for school and teacher effectiveness and the identification of the specific aims of their intervention. Moreover, the proposed measurement framework of effectiveness factors could help stakeholders establish targets and performance indicators, and thereby specify the developmental process of a reform policy. Research is, however, needed to investigate the impact that the use of the dynamic model may have on improving teaching practice through building a developmental evaluation strategy for any improvement effort on the part of schools.

Using the dynamic model to maintain the quality of schools

School and teacher effects are increasingly viewed as a set of ongoing processes in which both schools and teachers fall along a set continuum of development (e.g. Kyriakides and Creemers, 2006a; Slater and Teddlie, 1992; Teddlie and Reynolds,

2000). In order to study change over time, it is necessary to study teachers and schools longitudinally (i.e. over the course of a number of years). The dynamic model seems to take this need into account, as this is reflected not only in the use of 'stage' as a measurement dimension of effectiveness factors but also in its conceptualisation of effectiveness factors at the level of school and at the level of the context of education. More specifically, the *stage* dimension implies that longitudinal studies are needed to identify the effect of the functioning of factors upon student achievement over time. Similarly, the capacity of schools or educational systems to improve their policy regarding teaching and their policy regarding the learning environment of the schools is considered to be an essential characteristic of an effective school or an effective educational system. Therefore, not only the policy but also the extent to which the evaluation of policy informs the development of policy is seen as an effectiveness factor. As a consequence, in this chapter, the implications of these two characteristics of the dynamic model for the establishment of a theory-driven approach to improvement of practice are looked at.

However, it should also be acknowledged that the assumption that effectiveness is a stable characteristic of a school over time is not justified by the dynamic model. On the contrary, it is claimed that fluctuations or changes in results over time may reflect 'real' improvement or a 'real' decline in school or teacher performance, as well as any random variations (Kyriakides and Creemers, 2006a). Changes in results may be explained by planned or naturally occurring school or teacher improvement or by unchanged school policies and teacher practices in a changing context, or by both. Slater and Teddlie (1992) assume that effective schooling is a dynamic, ongoing process. It is also argued that it is easier for a school to improve than for it to maintain a standard of excellence. Moreover, the dynamic model assumes that effective schools or educational systems are expected to change in order to remain effective as their contexts change; they must therefore adapt their schooling to the changing context. Similarly, ineffective schools may be pushed by the community and local school boards to improve. This idea is consistent with the contingency theory (Donaldson, 2001; Mintzberg, 1979) and can be seen as one of the main assumptions upon which the dynamic model is based. Therefore, the dynamic model reveals that the process of improving effectiveness is one that should take place in all schools, irrespective of how effective they are. Moreover, it implies that schools that are among the most effective should take action to remain effective. The actions needed were described in Chapter 7 and define the characteristics of effective schools, but research is also required to search for the stability over time of the impact of these factors on effectiveness rather than on stability in effectiveness of schools and teachers. Such an approach could help us to test the generalisability of the dynamic model by identifying the extent to which the proposed effectiveness factors operate similarly from one period to another and explain variation in the effectiveness status of schools as well as the ability of a school to remain effective over time.

Search for improvement of outcomes

Mostly, studies of school improvement and school change are not concerned with the outcomes themselves so much as with the inputs, the processes, and the context of the school and of education in general, and the elements within that (Fullan, 1991). This is reflected in the fact that a review of evaluation studies of comprehensive school reform programmes revealed only a very small number of studies investigating the impact of these reform programmes on student learning, and most of the evidence found was based on qualitative data (Mijs *et al.*, 2005). But, according to EER, the success and the failure of school change are affected by the combined influence that all these improvement efforts have on student outcomes (Hargreaves, 1995; Hopkins, 1996; Reynolds *et al.*, 1993). Even when the effectiveness of different components is improved, the question remains as to whether or not a particular change induces improved student outcomes. Therefore, using the dynamic model to establish a theory-driven approach in school improvement implies that the main question of improvement studies is to identify characteristics of reform programmes that are associated with the improvement of student outcomes in terms of either the quality or the equity dimension of measuring effectiveness.

The dynamic model assumes that the ultimate criteria of an effective improvement programme are concerned with the impact of the programme on student learning. Reform programmes not only are expected to address the needs of teachers or headteachers but also should help students achieve better results. In the previous chapter we gave an example of how a policy on reducing classroom sizes should be evaluated. Similarly, any effort to improve the school climate and establish, for instance, better relations among teachers should not only be expected to improve the school climate; the implementation of this programme should also help schools improve student outcomes. A climate of trust among teachers may make teachers feel better in their workplace, but what is more important is to find out whether the improvement in the school climate also gives the opportunity to teachers to exchange ideas on how to improve their teaching practice and ultimately contribute to the improvement of student achievement gains. By considering student outcomes as the ultimate criterion of any intervention, stakeholders will design strategies that are more likely to affect learning. Such strategies may also contribute to the improvement of school culture, since the ability of a school to improve its outcomes may provide support to teachers and other stakeholders. Actually, studies investigating the criterion consistency of school effectiveness reveal that those schools which help students achieve the cognitive aims of schooling are very likely to improve the well-being of their students and teachers. Finally, evaluation studies focused on the impact of improvement efforts on student achievement gains will help us generate a knowledge base of school improvement. Such studies may also help us understand the reasons why some schools remain ineffective over time. The factors included in the dynamic model are expected to provide a framework for analysing the obstacles that a school is facing in its attempt to improve effectiveness. Therefore, empirical evidence as well as the dynamic model could help stakeholders identify priorities for improvement and establish improvement programmes.

Expanding the agenda of EER by introducing a dynamic approach to effectiveness

The paucity of studies investigating the impact of comprehensive school reform programmes on student achievement says something about the state of the art of research on school improvement. In this final section of the chapter it is argued that researchers in the area of EER should attempt to expand the research agenda of their field. It is important not only to identify characteristics of interventions that are associated with the improvement of the effectiveness status of schools but also to establish dynamic models that are able to explain changes in the effectiveness status of schools, teachers, and even students. Because students enter schools to learn and develop their cognitive, affective, and psychomotor skills, it can be argued that researchers in the area of EER should be concerned with the measurement of changes on student outcomes and should identify how these changes are related to supporting activities in classrooms and schools. If Dewey was correct in his idea that education is change, it follows that educative activities influence children by changing their developmental paths. For example, a new model for reading instruction is not intended merely to add an increment to a child's reading achievement at a single point in time. Rather, the set of activities that constitute the programme is implemented over a period of time for the purpose of modifying the growth trajectory of each child. In this view, the essential dependent variable for studies attempting to establish models of educational effectiveness should be the multivariate representation of the individual growth curve (Bryk and Raudenbush, 1987; Rogosa and Willett, 1985). Even as the children are changing by virtue of their experience in school, the structures, functions, and compositions of the schools they attend are also changing. Indeed, the sources and consequences of this kind of change should constitute the object of a study of effective school improvement efforts.

At present there are two fields in the area of effectiveness and improvement, and they use different research paradigms. The first is concerned with the search for characteristics that make schools and teachers effective, whereas the second is focused on change in educational practice. At the beginning of this chapter it was claimed that mutual benefits could emerge from establishing links between school effectiveness and school improvement. However, there are still tensions between the two fields, and this will probably remain the case, since the two fields are based on different value assumptions and use different methodological approaches. At the end of this chapter it will be claimed that the tensions between the two fields have also led to identification of the importance of establishing dynamic rather than static models of effectiveness. Such models may be used for improving practice and may also contribute to the expansion of the research agenda of EER. It is probably time for researchers in the area of effectiveness to 'cross the road' and conduct research on school improvement. Such studies may reveal factors that explain changes in the effectiveness status of schools. In this way it would be possible to establish a knowledge base concerning effective school improvement efforts. Such an attempt will help researchers realise that models of educational effectiveness can only be tested through longitudinal studies that are either naturalistic in character (e.g. cross-sectional studies or case studies) or experimental. Although such studies will not only help us identify the importance of establishing a dynamic model but also expand the agenda of EER, in the current phase the emphasis should be on developing and testing the dynamic model rather than on investigating the impact that the use of the model may have on improv-ing effectiveness. However, in this chapter it is argued that the dynamic model can help us establish links between EER and improvement practices through its contribution to the establishment of a theory-driven approach in improving practice.

Main conclusions to emerge from Part IV of the book

Part IV of this book has discussed the implications of the dynamic model and of the empirical evidence collected so far regarding research and evaluation, policy, and practice. The main arguments will be summarised in this final section of the chapter.

It is argued that the dynamic model has received sufficient support from the research presented in Part III to justify continuing research aimed at testing the dynamic model, and developing it further. The dynamic model could be tested and expanded by means of four types of studies: longitudinal studies, quantitative syntheses of effectiveness studies, international comparative studies, and experi-mental studies. Important issues that need attention in longitudinal studies are the multidimensional approach and especially the measurement of the five dimensions in relation to the specific factors. The multilevel structure of the model induces research questions, for example, on the relation between the factors operating at different levels. Furthermore, research on the non-linear relations between the factors, measured through the five dimensions and student outcomes, needs to be taken further and to become more detailed. Especially important for testing the dynamic model on the context level are international comparative studies, since they provide results that can be used for expanding the model and testing how generic it is. Furthermore, these international studies will increase the variation in the factors, which will be beneficial for research on the other levels of the model. In this respect, secondary analysis of international data sets is also recommended. As far as the use of experimental studies is concerned, the group randomisation approach is supported, and it is argued that such studies could not only test the validity of the model but also find out whether it can be used for improving educational practice.

The dynamic model also provides an opportunity to develop a theory-driven approach to educational evaluation. This approach may result in an improvement of evaluation approaches by reframing the evaluation questions and supporting the design and implementation. We also present an evaluation framework that makes use both of the features of the dynamic model and of the theoretical orientations upon which a reform is based. This evaluation approach could contribute to the testing and the development of the dynamic model.

Although the features of the dynamic model have not been tested completely, the nature of the model, supported by the evidence provided by the studies reported in Part III of the book, offers educational policy and practice many ways to use the model. It is argued that the dynamic model can help policy-makers to develop an evidence-based approach for building educational policy that ultimately seeks to promote student achievement. The two overarching context-level factors point to the establishment and evaluation of a national policy on teaching and the school learning environment. Related to these factors and their dimensions, different options for changing national policy, depending on the context and the content of the reform policy, are given. The dynamic model could also be helpful in the analysis of comparative studies concerning reform policies in a variety of countries, and the effects of these policies. Such an approach may contribute to a more elaborated use of policies and reform initiatives from other countries in an evidence-based policy-making approach.

In this last chapter it has been argued that the dynamic model can also help to improve educational practice. A theory-driven approach to improvement is recommended. The model can contribute to the establishment of such an approach, since knowledge in the field about 'what works in education and why' is offered. Moreover, the current knowledge base is expanded by the attempt of the dynamic model to refer not only to effectiveness factors but also to their dimensions, and to emphasise the importance of searching for a non-linear relation between some factors and student achievement. This provides possibilities for educational practice to improve teaching and the school learning environment directly, or even indirectly.

School self-evaluation using the dynamic model as a tool can serve as an important instrument to improve the school factors. Furthermore, the dynamic model can also be used for the theory-driven evaluation of school improvement. The dynamic model promoting a theory-oriented approach to school improvement might also be able to relate effectiveness and improvement, because the model is more closely related to educational practice through the dimensions and the non-linear relations included in the theory.

Apart from the contribution to the theory and research on educational effectiveness, which is our core business, we like to argue, and we hope that, the dynamic model can promote the improvement of education, because that is, ultimately, the aim we all share.

References

Aitkin, M. and Longford, N. (1986). Statistical modelling issues in school effectiveness studies. *Journal of the Royal Statistical Society, Series A (General), 149* (1), 1–43.

Aleamoni, L.M. (1981). Student rating of instruction. In J. Millman (ed.), *Handbook of teacher evaluation* (pp. 110–145). London: Sage.

Alker, H.R. (1969). A typology of ecological fallacies. In M. Dogan and S. Rakkan (eds), *Quantitative ecological analyses in the social sciences* (pp. 69–86). Cambridge, MA: MIT Press.

Allport, G. (1937). *Personality: a psychological interpretation.* New York: Holt.

Altiere, M.A. and Duell, O.K. (1991). Can teachers predict their students' wait time preferences? *Journal of Research in Science Teaching, 28* (5), 455–461.

American Educational Research Association (AERA), American Psychological Association (APA), and National Council on Measurement in Education (NCME) (1999). *Standards for Educational and Psychological Testing.* Washington, DC: American Psychological Association).

Amit, M. and Fried, M.N. (2002). Research, reform, and times of change. In L.D. English (ed.), *Handbook of international research in mathematics education* (pp. 355–381). Mahwah, NJ: Lawrence Erlbaum.

Anderson, L.W. (1995). Time, allocated and instructional. In L.W. Anderson (ed.), *International Encyclopedia of Teaching and Teacher Education* (2nd edn, pp. 204–207). Oxford: Elsevier.

Anderson, L.W., Evertson, C.M. and Brophy, J.E. (1979). An experimental study of effective teaching in first-grade reading groups. *Elementary School Journal, 79* (4), 193–223.

Andrich, D. (1988). A general form of Rasch's Extended Logistic Model for partial credit scoring. *Applied Measurement in Education, 1* (4), 363–378.

Aparicio, J.J. and Moneo, M.R. (2005). Constructivism, the so-called semantic learning theories, and situated cognition versus the psychological learning theories. *Spanish Journal of Psychology, 8* (2), 180–198.

Armento, B. (1977). Teacher behaviors related to student achievement on a social science concept test. *Journal of Teacher Education, 28*, 46–52.

Askew, M. and William, D. (1995). *Recent Research in Mathematics Education 5–16.* London: Office for Standards in Education, 53.

Atkin, J.M. (1998). The OECD study of innovations in science, mathematics and technology education. *Journal of Curriculum Studies, 30* (6), 647–660.

Bage, G. (1997). How can we teach history through television? *Journal of Educational Media, 23*, 204–214.

Ball, S. J. (1987). *The micro-politics of the school: towards a theory of school organization.* London: Methuen.

Bamburg, J. D. (1994). *Raising expectations to improve student learning.* Urban Monograph Series, CS: North Central Regional Educational Lab, Oak Brook, IL.

Bandura, A. (1996). Regulation of cognitive processes through perceived self-efficacy. *Developmental Psychology, 25* (5), 729–735.

Bandura, A. (1997). *Self-efficacy: the exercise of control.* New York: W.H. Freeman.

Barber, B. (1986). Homework does not belong on the agenda for educational reform. *Educational Leadership, 43* (8), 55–57.

Baumert, J. and Demmrich, A. (2001). Test motivation in the assessment of student skills: the effects of incentives on motivation and performance. *European Journal of Psychology of Education, 16* (3), 441–462.

Beaton, A.E., Mullis, I.V.S., Martin, M.O., Gonzalez, E.J., Kelly, D.L., and Smith, T.A. (1996). *Mathematics achievement in the middle school years: IEA's Third International Mathematics and Science Study.* Chestnut Hill, MA: Boston College, TIMSS International Study Center.

Beerens, D.R. (2000). *Evaluating teaching for professional growth.* Thousands Oaks, CA: Corwin Press.

Bennett, N., Desforges, C., Cockburn, A., and Wilkenson, B. (1981). *The quality of pupil learning experiences* (interim report). Lancaster, UK: University of Lancaster, Centre for Educational Research and Development.

Bennetts, T. (2005). The links between understanding, progression and assessment in the secondary geography curriculum. *Geography, 90* (2), 152–170.

Bentler, P.M. (1989). *EQS: structural equations program manual.* Los Angeles: BMDP Statistical Software.

Bentler, P.M. (1990). Comparative fit indexes in structural models. *Psychological Bulletin, 107,* 238–246.

Bereiter, C. and Scardamalia, M. (1989). Intentional learning as a goal of instruction. In L.B. Resnick (ed.), *Knowing, learning, and instruction: essays in honor of Robert Glaser* (pp. 361–392). Hillsdale, NJ: Lawrence Erlbaum.

Berends, M. (2000). Teacher-reported effects of new American school designs: exploring relationships to teacher background and school context. *Educational Evaluation and Policy Analysis, 22* (1), 65–82.

Bickman, L. (1985). Improving established statewide programs: a component theory of evaluation. *Evaluation Review, 9* (2), 189–208.

Black, P. and Wiliam, D. (1998). *Inside the black box: raising standards through classroom assessment.* London: King's College London School of Education.

Blase, J. (1993). The micropolitics of effective school-based leadership: teachers' perspectives. *Educational Administration Quarterly, 24,* 143–163.

Bledsoe, K.L. and Graham, J.A. (2005). The use of multiple evaluation approaches in program evaluation. *American Journal of Evaluation, 26* (3), 302–319.

Blickle, G. (1996). Personality traits, learning strategies and performance. *European Journal of Personality, 10,* 337–352.

Bloom, B.S. (1976). *Human characteristics and school learning.* New York: McGraw-Hill.

Bloom, B.S., Englehart, M., Furst, E., Hill, W. and Krathwohl, D. (1956). *Taxonomy of educational objectives: the classification of educational goals: Handbook I. Cognitive domain.* New York: David McKay.

Bloom, H.S. and Riccio, J.A. (2005). Using place-based random assignment and comparative interrupted time-series analysis to evaluate the jobs-plus employment program for public housing residents. *Annals of the American Academy of Political and Social Science, 599* (1), 19–51.

Boekaerts, M. (1997). Self-regulated learning: a new concept embraced by researchers, policy makers, educators, teachers, and students. *Learning and Instruction, 7* (2), 161–186.

Boekaerts, M. (1999). Self-regulated learning: where we are today? *International Journal of Educational Research, 31,* 445–456.

Borich, G.D. (1992) *Effective teaching methods,* 2nd edn. New York: Macmillan.

Bos, K. and Kuiper, W. (1999). Modelling TIMSS data in a European comparative perspective: exploring influencing factors on achievement in mathematics in grade 8. *Educational Research and Evaluation, 5* (2), 157–179.

Bosker, R.J. (1990). Theory development in school effectiveness research: in search for stability of effects. In P. van de Eedem, J. Hox, and J. Hauer (eds), *Theory and model in multilevel research: convergence or divergence?* (pp. 77–98). Amsterdam: SISWO.

Bosker, R.J. (2006). Class size and cognitive effects. Paper presented at the AERA Annual Conference, San Francisco.

Boud, D.J. and Donovan, W.F. (1982). The facilitation of school-based evaluation: a case study. *Journal of Curriculum Studies, 14* (4), 359–362.

Brandsma, H.P. (1993). *Basisschoolkenmerken en de kwaliteit van het onderwijs* [Characteristics of primary schools and the quality of education]. Groningen: RION.

Brookhart, S.M. (1997). Effects of the classroom assessment environment on mathematics and science achievement. *Journal of Educational Research, 90* (6), 323–330.

Brookhart, S.M. (2004). Classroom assessment: tensions and intersections in theory and practice. *Teachers College Record, 106* (3), 429–458.

Brookover, W.B., Beady, C., Flood, P., Schweitzer, J., and Wisenbaker, J. (1979). *School systems and student achievement: schools make a difference.* New York: Praeger.

Brophy, J. (1986). Teacher influence on student achievement. *American Psychologist, 41* (10), 1069–1077.

Brophy, J. (1992). Probing the subtleties of subject matter teaching. *Educational Leadership, 49,* 4–8.

Brophy, J. and Evertson, C. (1976). *Learning from teaching: a developmental perspective.* Boston: Allyn & Bacon.

Brophy, J. and Good, T.L. (1986). Teacher behavior and student achievement. In M.C. Wittrock (ed.), *Handbook of research on teaching* (3rd edn, pp. 328–375). New York: Macmillan.

Brown, B.W. and Saks, D.H. (1986). Measuring the effects of instructional time on student learning: evidence from the beginning teacher evaluation study. *American Journal of Education, 94,* 480–500.

Brown, M.W. and Mels, G. (1990). *RAMONA PC: user manual.* Pretoria: University of South Africa.

Bryk, A.S. and Raudenbush, S.W. (1987). Application of hierarchical linear models to assessing change. *Psychological Bulletin, 101* (1), 147–158.

Bryk, A.S. and Raudenbush, S.W. (1992). *Hierarchical linear models: applications and data analysis methods.* Newbury Park, CA: Sage.

Bryk, A.S. and Weisberg, H.I. (1977). Use of the nonequivalent control group design when subjects are growing. *Psychological Bulletin, 84,* 950–962.

Busato, V., Prins, F., Elshout, J., and Hamaker, C. (1999). The relationship between learning styles, the Big Five personality traits and achievement motivation in higher education. *Personality and Individual Differences*, *26*, 129–140.

Byrne, B.M. and Goffin, R.D. (1993). Modeling MTMM data for additive and multiplicative covariance structures: an audit of construct validity concordance. *Multivariate Behavioral Research*, *28* (1), 67–96.

Campbell, D.T. and Fiske, D.W. (1959). Convergent and discriminant validation by the multitrait–multimethod matrix. *Psychological Bulletin*, *56*, 81–105.

Campbell, R.J. (1985). *Developing the Primary School Curriculum*. London: Cassell.

Campbell, R.J. and Kyriakides, L. (2000). The National Curriculum and standards in primary schools: a comparative perspective. *Comparative Education*, *36* (4), 383–395.

Campbell, R.J., Kyriakides, L., Muijs, R.D., and Robinson, W. (2003). Differential teacher effectiveness: towards a model for research and teacher appraisal. *Oxford Review of Education*, *29* (3), 347–362.

Campbell, R.J., Kyriakides, L., Muijs, R.D., and Robinson, W. (2004). *Assessing teacher effectiveness: a differentiated model*. London: RoutledgeFalmer.

Carew, D.K., Parisicarew, E., and Blanchard, K.H. (1986). Group development and situational leadership: a model for managing groups. *Training and Development Journal*, *40* (6), 46–50.

Carroll, J.B. (1963). A model of school learning. *Teachers College Record*, *64*, 723–733.

Case R. (1993). Theories of learning and theories of development. *Educational Psychologist*, *28* (3): 219–233.

Cattell, R. and Butcher, H. (1968). *The prediction of achievement and creativity*. Indianapolis: Bobbs-Merrill.

Cazden, C.B. (1986). Classroom discourse. In M.C. Wittrock (ed.), *Handbook of research on teaching* (pp. 432–463). New York: Macmillan.

Chamorro-Premuzic, T. and Furnham, A. (2003). Personality predicts academic performance: evidence from two longitudinal university samples. *Journal of Research in Personality*, *37*, 319–338.

Chen, H.T. and Rossi, P.H. (1987). The theory-driven approach to validity. *Evaluation and Program Planning*, *10* (1), 95–103.

Cheng, Y.C. (1993). Profiles of organizational culture and effective schools. *School Effectiveness and School Improvement*, *4* (2), 85–110.

Cheng, Y.C. (1996). *School effectiveness and school-based management: a mechanism for development*. London: Falmer Press.

Child, D. (1964). The relationships between introversion–extraversion, neuroticism and performance in school examinations. *British Journal of Educational Psychology*, *34*, 187–196.

Choi, J.I. and Hannafin, M. (1995). Situated cognition and learning environments: roles, structures, and implications for design. *Educational Technology Research and Development*, *43* (2), 53–69.

Clapham, M.M. (1998). Structure of figural forms A and B of the Torrance tests of creative thinking. *Educational and Psychological Measurement*, *58* (2), 275–283.

Clark, C., Gage, N., Marx, R., Peterson, P., Stayrook, N., and Winne, P. (1979). A factorial experiment on teacher structuring, soliciting and reacting. *Journal of Educational Psychology*, *71*, 534–552.

Clauset, K.H. and Gaynor, A.K. (1982). A systems perspective on effective schools. *Educational Leadership*, *40* (3), 54–59.

Codd, J.A. (1995). Educational policy as a field of philosophical enquiry. Paper presented to the Annual Conference of Philosophy of Education Society of Great Britain, Oxford, September.

Cohen, D., Manion, L., and Morrison, K. (2000). *Research methods in education* (5th edn). London: RoutledgeFalmer.

Cohen, J. (1988). *Statistical power analysis of the behavioral sciences* (2nd edn). New York: Academic Press.

Coleman, J.S., Campbell, E.Q., Hobson, C.F., McPartland, J., Mood, A.M., Weinfeld, F.D., and York, R.L. (1966). *Equality of Educational Opportunity.* Washington, DC: US Government Printing Office.

Collins, A., Brown, J.S., and Newman, S.E. (1989). Cognitive apprenticeship: teaching the crafts of reading, writing and mathematics. In L.B. Resnick (ed.), *Knowing, learning, and instruction* (pp. 453–495). Hillsdale, NJ: Lawrence Erlbaum.

Cook, T.D. and Campbell, D.T. (1979). *Quasi-experimentation.* New York: Rand McNally.

Cook, T.D., Murphy, R.F., and Hunt, H.D. (2000). Comer's school development program in Chicago: a theory-based evaluation. *American Educational Research Journal, 37* (2), 535–597.

Cooley, W.W. and Lohnes, P.R. (1976). *Evaluation research in education.* New York: Wiley.

Costa, A.L. (1984). Mediating the metacognitive. *Educational Leadership, 42* (3), 57–62.

Costa, P.T. Jr and McCrae, R.R. (1997). Longitudinal stability of adult personality. In R. Hogan, J. Johnson, and S. Briggs (eds), *Handbook of Personality Psychology* (pp. 269–290). San Diego, CA: Academic Press.

Cousins, J.B. and Earl, L.M. (1992). The case for participatory evaluation. *Educational Evaluation and Policy Analysis, 14* (4), 397–418.

Cousins, J.B. and Leithwood, K.A. (1986). Current empirical research on evaluation utilization. *Review of Educational Research, 56* (3), 331–364.

Creemers, B.P.M. (1994). *The effective classroom.* London: Cassell.

Creemers, B.P.M. (2002). From school effectiveness and school improvement to effective school improvement: background, theoretical analysis, and outline of the empirical study, *Educational Research and Evaluation, 8* (4), 343–362.

Creemers, B.P.M. (2006). The importance and perspectives of international studies in educational effectiveness. *Educational Research and Evaluation, 12* (6), 499–511.

Creemers, B.P.M. (2007). Combining different ways of learning and teaching in a dynamic model of educational effectiveness. *Journal of Basic Education, 17* (1).

Creemers, B.P.M. and Kyriakides, L. (2005a). Establishing links between educational effectiveness research and improvement practices through the development of a dynamic model of educational effectiveness. Paper presented at the 86th Annual Meeting of the American Educational Research Association, Montreal, April.

Creemers, B.P.M. and Kyriakides, L. (2005b). Developing and testing theories of educational effectiveness: testing the validity of the school level factors of the dynamic model. Paper presented at the EARLI 2005 conference, Nicosia (Cyprus), August.

Creemers, B.P.M. and Kyriakides, L. (2006). A critical analysis of the current approaches to modelling educational effectiveness: the importance of establishing a dynamic model. *School Effectiveness and School Improvement, 17* (3), 347–366.

Creemers, B.P.M. and Reezigt, G.J. (1996). School level conditions affecting the effectiveness of instruction. *School Effectiveness and School Improvement, 7* (3), 197–228.

Creemers, B.P.M. and Reezigt, G.J. (1997). School effectiveness and school improvement: sustaining links. *School Effectiveness and School Improvement, 8*, 396–429.

Creemers, B.P.M. and Reezigt, G.J. (1999a). The role of school and classroom climate in elementary school learning environments, In H.J. Freiberg (ed.), *School climate: measuring, improving and sustaining healthy learning environments* (pp. 30–48). London: Falmer Press.

Creemers, B.P.M. and Reezigt, G.J. (1999b). The concept of vision in educational effectiveness theory and research. *Learning Environments Research, 2*, 107–135.

Creemers, B.P.M. and Reezigt, J.G. (2005). Linking school effectiveness and school improvement: the background and outline of the project. *School Effectiveness and School Improvement, 16* (4), 359–371.

Creemers, B.P.M., Scheerens, J., and Reynolds, D. (2000). Theory development in school effectiveness research. In C. Teddlie and D. Reynolds (eds), *The International Handbook of School Effectiveness Research* (pp. 283–298). London: Falmer Press.

Cronbach, L.J. (1975). Beyond the two disciplines of scientific psychology revisited. *American Psychologist, 30*, 116–127.

Cronbach, L.J. (1990). *Essentials of psychological testing* (3rd edn). New York: Harper & Row.

Cronbach, L.J., Gleser, G.C., Nanda, H., and Rajaratnam, N. (1972). *The dependability of behavioral measurements: theory of generalizability scores and profiles*. New York: Wiley.

Danielson, C. and McGreal, T.L. (2000). *Teacher Evaluation to Enhance Professional Practice*. Alexandria, VA: Association for Supervision and Curriculum Development.

Darling-Hammond, L. (2000). Teacher quality and student achievement: a review of state policy evidence. *Education Policy Analysis Archives, 8* (1): http://epaa.asu.edu/epaa/v8n1/.

Datnow, A., Borman, G., and Stringfield, S. (2000). School reform through a highly specified curriculum: implementation and effects of the core knowledge sequence. *Elementary School Journal, 101* (2), 167–191.

Datnow, A., Hubbard, L., and Mehan, H. (2002). *Extending educational reform: from one school to many*. New York: RoutledgeFalmer.

Datnow, A., Borman, G., Stringfield, S., Overman, L.T., and Castellano, M. (2003). Comprehensive school reform in culturally and linguistically diverse contexts: implementation and outcomes from a four-year study. *Educational Evaluation and Policy Analysis, 25* (2), 143–170.

De Corte, E. (2000). Marrying theory building and the improvement of school practice: a permanent challenge for instructional psychology. *Learning and Instruction, 10* (3), 249–266.

De Jong, R., Westerhof, K.J., and Kruiter, J.H. (2004). Empirical evidence of a comprehensive model of school effectiveness: a multilevel study in mathematics in the 1st year of junior general education in the Netherlands. *School Effectiveness and School Improvement, 15* (1), 3–31.

De Leeuw, J. and Kreft, G.G. (1986). Random coefficient models for multilevel analysis. *Journal of Educational Statistics, 11*, 57–85.

DeFruyt, F. and Mervielde, I. (1996). Personality and interests as predictors of streaming and achievement. *European Journal of Personality, 10*, 405–425.

Delandshere, G. (2002). Assessment as inquiry. *Teachers College Record, 104* (7), 1461–1484.

Delors, J. (1996). *Learning: the treasure within: report to UNESCO of the International Commission for Education*. Paris: UNESCO.

Demetriou, A., Kazi, S., and Georgiou, S. (1999). The emerging self: the convergence of mind, personality, and thinking styles. *Developmental Science*, *2*, 387–422.

Demetriou, A., Kyriakides, L., and Avraamidou, C. (2003). The missing link in the relations between intelligence and personality. *Journal of Research in Personality*, *37* (6), 547–581.

Demetriou, D. (forthcoming). Using the dynamic model to improve educational practice. Unpublished doctoral dissertation, University of Cyprus.

den Brok, P., Brekelmans, M., and Wubbels, T. (2004). Interpersonal teacher behaviour and student outcomes. *School Effectiveness and School Improvement*, 15 (3–4), 407–442.

Devos, G. (1998). Conditions and caveats for self-evaluation: the case of secondary schools. Paper presented at the Annual Meeting of the American Educational Research Association, San Diego, CA, 13–17 April (ERIC Document Reproduction Service no. ED421493).

DfEE (1998). *Evaluation matters*. London: The Stationery Office.

Diseth, A. (2003). Personality and approaches to learning as predictors of academic achievement. *European Journal of Personality*, *17*, 143–155.

Donaldson, L. (2001). *The contingency theory of organizations*. Thousands Oaks, CA: Sage.

Douglas, J.W.B. (1964). *The home and the school*. London: MacGibbon & Kee.

Dowson, M. and McInerney, D.M. (2003). What do students say about motivational goals? Towards a more complex and dynamic perspective on student motivation. *Contemporary Educational Psychology*, *28* (1), 91–113.

Doyle, W. (1986). Classroom organization and management. In M.C. Wittrock (ed.), *Handbook of Research on Teaching* (3rd edn, pp. 392–431). New York: Macmillan.

Doyle, W. (1990). Classroom knowledge as a foundation for teaching. *Teachers College Record*, *91* (3), 347–360.

Driessen, G.W.J.M. and Mulder, L.W.J. (1999). The enhancement of educational opportunities of disadvantaged children. In R.J. Bosker, B.P.M. Creemers, and S. Stringfield (eds), *Enhancing educational excellence, equity and efficiency: evidence from evaluations of systems and schools in change* (pp. 37–64). Dordrecht: Kluwer Academic Publishers.

Driessen, G. and Sleegers, P. (2000). Consistency of teaching approach and student achievement: an empirical test. *School Effectiveness and School Improvement*, *11* (1), 57–79.

Duckworth, K. (1983). *Specifying determinants of teacher and principal work*. Eugene, OR: Center for Educational Policy and Management, University of Oregon.

Duke, D. (2004). *The challenges of educational change*. Boston: Allyn & Bacon.

Dunne, R. and Wragg, E.R. (1994). *Effective teaching*, London: Routledge.

Edmonds, R.R. (1979). Effective schools for the urban poor. *Educational Leadership*, *37* (1), 15–27.

Eisner, E. (1993). Forms of understanding and the future of educational research. *Educational Researcher*, *22* (7), 5–11.

Elberts, R.W. and Stone, J.A. (1988). Student achievement in public schools: do principles make a difference? *Economics Education Review*, *7*, 291–299.

Ellett, C.D. (1997). Classroom-based assessments of teaching and learning. In J.H. Stronge (ed.) *Evaluating teaching: a guide to current thinking and best practice* (pp. 107–128). Thousand Oaks, CA: Sage.

Ellett, C.D. and Walberg, H.J. (1979). Principal competency, environment and outcomes. In H.J. Walberg (ed.), *Educational environment and effects* (pp. 140–167). Berkeley, CA: McCutchan.

Ellett, C.D., Wren, C.Y., Callendar, K.E., Loup, K.S., and Liu, X. (1996). Looking backwards with the Personnel Evaluation Standards: an analysis of the development and implementation of a statewide teacher assessment system. *Studies in Educational Evaluation, 22* (1), 79–113.

Elshout, J. and Veenman, M. (1992). Relation between intellectual ability and working method as predictors of learning. *Journal of Educational Research, 85,* 134–143.

Emmer, E.T. and Evertson, C.M. (1981). Synthesis of research on classroom management. *Educational Leadership, 38* (4), 342–347.

Emmer, E.T. and Stough, L.M. (2001). Classroom management: a critical part of educational psychology, with implications for teacher education. *Educational Psychologist, 36* (2), 103–112.

Emmer, E.T., Evertson, C.M., and Anderson, L.M. (1980). Effective classroom management at the beginning of the school year. *Elementary School Journal, 80* (5), 219–231.

Entwistle, N. and Smith, C. (2002). Personal understanding and target understanding: mapping influences on the outcomes of learning. *British Journal of Educational Psychology, 72* (3), 321–342.

Epstein, J.L. (1992). School and family partnerships. In M. Alkin (ed.), *Encyclopedia of educational research* (2nd edn, pp. 1139–1151). New York: Macmillan.

Evertson, C.M. and Harris, A.H. (1992). What we know about managing classrooms. *Educational Leadership, 49* (7), 74–78.

Evertson, C.M., Anderson, C., Anderson, L., and Brophy, J. (1980). Relationships between classroom behavior and student outcomes in junior high math and English classes. *American Educational Research Journal, 17,* 43–60.

Fairman, S.R. and Quinn, R.E. (1985). Effectiveness: the perspective from organisation theory. *Review of Higher Education, 9,* 83–100.

Fan, X. and Chen, M. (2001). Parent involvement and students' academic achievement: a meta-analysis. *Educational Psychology Review, 13* (1), 1–22.

Ferrari, M. and Mahalingam, R. (1988). Personal cognitive development and its implications for teaching and learning. *Educational Psychologist, 33* (1), 35–44.

Firestone, W.A. and Fisler, J.L. (2002). Politics, community, and leadership in a school–university partnership. *Educational Administration Quarterly, 38* (4), 449–493.

Firestone, W.A. and Herriott, R.E. (1982). Prescriptions for effective elementary schools don't fit secondary schools. *Educational Leadership, 40,* 51–53.

Fitz-Gibbon, C.T. (1996). *Monitoring education: indicators, quality and effectiveness.* London: Cassell-Continuum.

Fitz-Gibbon, C.T. (1997). *The Value Added National Project: Final Report: Feasibility studies for a national system of value added indicators.* London: School Curriculum and Assessment Authority.

Fitz-Gibbon, C.T., Tymms, P.B., and Hazlewood, R.D. (1990). Performance indicators and information systems. In D. Reynolds, B.P.M. Creemers, and D. Peters (eds), *School Effectiveness and Improvement.* Groningen: RION.

Flanders, N. (1970). *Analyzing teacher behavior.* Reading, MA: Addison-Wesley.

Flavell, J.H. (1979). Metacognition and cognitive monitoring: a new area of cognitive-developmental inquiry. *American Psychologist, 34* (10), 906–911.

Flay, B.R. (2000) Approaches to substance use prevention utilizing school curriculum plus social environment change. *Addictive Behaviors, 25*, 861–885.

Fond Lam, J. (1996). *Tijd en kwaliteit in het basisonderwijs* (Time and quality in primary education). Enschede: University of Twente.

Foy, P. and Joncas, M. (2000). Implementation of the sample design. In M.O. Martin, K.D. Gregory, and S.E. Stemler (eds), *TIMSS 1999 technical report: IEA's repeat of the Third International Mathematics and Science Study at the eighth grade.* Chestnut Hill, MA: Boston College.

Fraser, B.J. (1991). Two decades of classroom environment research. In B.J. Fraser and H.J. Walberg (eds), *Educational environments: evaluation, antecedents and consequences* (pp. 3–29). Oxford: Pergamon Press.

Fraser, B.J. (1995). Students' perceptions of classrooms. In L.W. Anderson (ed.), *International encyclopedia of teaching and teacher education* (2nd edn, pp. 416–419). Oxford: Elsevier.

Fraser, B.J., Walberg, H.J., Welch, W.W., and Hattie, J.A. (1987). Syntheses of educational productivity research. *International Journal of Educational Research,* 11, 145–252.

Freiberg H.J. (ed.) (1999) *School climate: measuring, improving and sustaining healthy learning environments.* London: Falmer Press.

Fullan, M. (1991). *The new meaning of educational change.* New York: Cassell.

Fullan, M. (1993). *Change forces: probing the depths of educational reform.* London: Falmer Press.

Gage, N.L. (1963). Paradigms for research on teaching. In N.L. Gage (ed.), *Handbook of research on teaching* (pp. 94–141). Chicago, IL: Rand McNally.

Gage, N.L. (1977). *The scientific basis of the art of teaching.* New York: Teachers College Press.

Garaigordobil, M. (2006). Intervention in creativity with children aged 10 and 11 years: impact of a play program on verbal and graphic-figural creativity. *Creativity Research Journal, 18* (3), 329–345.

Gastel, B. (1991). A menu of approaches for evaluating your teaching. *BioScience, 41* (5), 342–345.

Gettinger, M. (1991). Learning time and retention differences between nondisabled students and students with learning disabilities. *Learning Disability Quarterly, 14* (3), 179–189.

Ghaith, G. and Yaghi, H. (1997). Relationships among experience, teacher efficacy, and attitudes towards the implementation of instructional innovation. *Teaching and Teacher Education, 13* (4), 451–458.

Gijbels, D., Van de Watering, G., Dochy, F., and Van den Bossche, P. (2006). New learning environments and constructivism: the students' perspective. *Instructional Science, 34* (3), 213–226.

Glaser, R. (1976). Components of a psychology of instruction: toward a science of design. *Review of Educational Research, 46*, 1–24.

Glasman, N.S. and Biniaminov, I. (1981). Input–output analyses of schools. *Review of Educational Research, 51*, 509–539.

Glass, G.V. (1976). Secondary and meta-analysis of research. *Educational Researcher, 11*, 3–8.

Goldberg, L.R. (1993). The structure of the phenotypic personality traits. *American Psychologist, 48* (1), 26–34.

Goldstein, H. (1997). The methodology of school effectiveness research. *School Effectiveness and School Improvement, 8* (4), 369–395.

Goldstein, H. (2003). *Multilevel statistical models* (3rd edn) London: Arnold.

Goldstein, H., Rasbash, J., Plewis, I., Draper, D., Browne, W., Yang, M., Woodhouse, G., and Healy, M. (1998). *A user's guide to MLwiN.* London: Institute of Education.

Good, T.L. and Brophy, J.E. (1986). School effects. In M.C. Wittrock (ed.), *Handbook of research on teaching* (3rd edn, pp. 570–602). New York: Macmillan.

Goodson, J.R., McGee, G.W., and Cashman, J.F. (1989). Situational leadership theory: a test of leadership prescriptions. *Group and Organization Studies, 14* (4), 446–461.

Gorard, S., Rees, G., and Salisbury J. (2001). Investigating the patterns of differential attainment of boys and girls at school. *British Educational Research Journal, 27* (2), 125–139.

Graber, K. (2001). Research on teaching in physical education. In V. Richardson (ed.), *Handbook of research in teaching.* Washington, DC: American Educational Research Association.

Grant, C.A. and Sleeter, C.F. (1986). Race, class and gender effects. *Review of Educational Research, 56,* 219–230.

Gray, J., Hopkins, D., Reynolds, D., Wilcox, B., Farrell, S., and Jesson, D. (1999). *Improving schools: performance and potential.* Buckingham, UK: Open University Press.

Gray, J., Jesson, D., Goldstein, H., Hedger, K., and Rasbash, J. (1995). A multilevel analysis of school improvement: changes in schools' performance over time. *School Effectiveness and School Improvement, 6* (2), 97–114.

Gray, J., Peng, W.J., Steward S., and Thomas S. (2004). Towards a typology of gender-related school effects: some new perspectives on a familiar problem. *Oxford Review of Education, 30* (4), 529–550.

Greenwood, C.R. (1991). Longitudinal analysis of time, engagement, and achievement in at-risk versus non-risk students. *Exceptional Children, 57* (6), 521–535.

Grigorenko, E.L. and Sternberg, R.J. (1995). Thinking styles. In D.H. Saklofske and M. Zeidner (eds), *International Handbook of Personality and Intelligence* (pp. 205–229). New York: Plenum Press.

Grigorenko, E.L. and Sternberg, R.J. (1997). Styles of thinking, abilities, and academic performance. *Exceptional Children, 63* (3), 295–312.

Guiton, G. and Oakes, J. (1995). Opportunity to learn and conceptions of educational equality. *Educational Evaluation and Policy Analysis, 17,* 323–336.

Haanstra, F. (1994). *Effects of art education on visual-spatial ability and aesthetic perception: two meta-analyses.* Amsterdam: Thesis Publishers.

Hallinger, P. and Heck, H.R. (1998). Exploring the principal's contribution to school effectiveness: 1980–1995. *School Effectiveness and School Improvement, 9* (2), 157–191.

Hambleton, R.K. and Sireci, S.G. (1998). Future directions for norm-referenced and criterion-referenced testing. *International Journal of Educational Research, 27* (5), 379–394.

Hanushek, E.A. (1986). The economics of schooling: production and efficiency in public schools. *Journal of Economic Literature, 24,* 1141–1177.

Hanushek, E.A. (1989). The impact of differential expenditures on student performance. *Educational Research, 66* (3), 397–409.

Hargreaves, D.H. (1995). School culture, school effectiveness and school improvement. *School Effectiveness and School Improvement, 6* (1), 23–46.

Harlen, W. and James, M. (1997). Assessment and learning: differences and relationships between formative and summative assessment. *Assessment in Education, 4* (3), 365–379.

Harnischfeger, A. and Wiley, D.E. (1976). The teaching learning process in elementary schools: a synoptic view. *Curriculum Inquiry, 6,* 5–43.

Harris, A. (2001). Building the capacity for school improvement. *School Leadership and Management, 21* (3), 261–270.

Harris, D. (1940). Factors affecting college grades: a review of the literature. *Psychological Bulletin, 37,* 125–166.

Harskamp, E.G. (1988). *Een evaluatie van rekenmethoden* (An evaluation of arithmetic curricula) (dissertation). Groningen, The Netherlands: RION.

Hayes, M.T. and Deyhle, D. (2001). Constructing difference: a comparative study of elementary science curriculum differentiation. *Science Education, 85* (3), 239–262.

Heck, R.A. and Marcoulides, G.A. (1996). School culture and performance: testing the invariance of an organizational model. *School Effectiveness and School Improvement, 7* (1), 76–106.

Heck, R.H. and Thomas, S.L. (2000). *An introduction to multilevel modeling techniques.* Mahwah, NJ: Lawrence Erlbaum.

Hedges, L.V. (1987). How hard is hard science, how soft is soft science? The empirical cumulativeness of research. *American Psychologist, 42,* 443–455.

Hedges, L.V., Laine, R.D., and Greenwald, R. (1994). Does money matter? A meta-analysis of studies of the effects of differential school inputs on student outcomes (An exchange: Part 1). *Educational Researcher, 23* (3), 5–14.

Hersey, P. and Blanchard, K. (1993). *Management of organizational behavior: utilizing human resources* (6th edn). Englewood Cliffs, NJ: Prentice-Hall.

Hextall, I. and Mahony, P. (1998). *Effective teachers effective schools.* London: Biddles.

Hopkins, D. (1989). *Evaluating for school development.* Milton Keynes: Open University Press.

Hopkins, D. (1995). Towards effective school improvement. *School Effectiveness and School Improvement, 6* (3), 265–274.

Hopkins, D. (1996). Towards a theory for school improvement. In J. Gray, D. Reynolds, C. Fitz-Gibbon, and D. Jesson (eds), *Merging traditions: the future of research on school effectiveness and school improvement* (pp. 30–50). London: Cassell.

Hopkins, D. (2001). *School improvement for real.* London: RoutledgeFalmer.

Hopkins, D., Ainscow, M., and West, M. (1994*). School improvement in an era of change.* London: Cassell.

Houtveen, A.A.M., van de Grift, W.J.C.M., and Creemers, B.P.M. (2004). Effective school improvement in mathematics. *School Effectiveness and School Improvement, 15* (3), 337–376.

Hoy, W.K. and Miskel, C.G. (2001). *Educational administration: theory, research and practice* (6th edn). New York: McGraw-Hill.

Hoy, W.K., Tater, J.C., and Bliss, J.R. (1990). Organizational climate, school health, and effectiveness: a comparative analysis. *Educational Administration Quarterly, 26* (3), 260–279.

Hoyle, R.J and Skrla, L. (1999). The politics of superintendent evaluation. *Journal of Personnel Evaluation in Education, 13* (4), 405–419.

Hunter, J.E. and Schmidt, F.L. (2004). *Methods of meta-analysis: correcting error and bias in research findings* (2nd edn). Thousand Oaks, CA: Sage.

Huttner, H.J.M. and van den Eeden, P. (1995). *The multilevel design: a guide with an annotated bibliography, 1980–1993.* Westport, CT: Greenwood Press.

Jackson, D.N. (1969). Multimethod factor analysis in the evaluation of convergent and discriminant validity. *Psychological Bulletin, 72*, 30–49.

Jencks, C., Smith, M., Acland, H., Bane, M.J., Cohen, D., Gintis, H., Heyns, B., and Michelson, S. (1972). *Inequality: a reassessment of the effects of family and schooling in America.* New York: Basic Books.

Jesson, D. and Gray, J. (1991). Slant on slopes: using multilevel models to investigate differential school effectiveness and its impact on pupils' examination results. *School Effectiveness and School Improvement, 2* (3), 230–247.

Johnson, B. (1997). An organizational analysis of multiple perspectives of effective teaching: implications of teacher evaluation. *Journal of Personnel Evaluation in Education, 11*, 69–87.

Johnson, D.W. and Johnson, R.T. (1993). Cooperative learning and classroom and school climate. In B.J. Fraser and H.J. Walberg (eds), *Educational environments: evaluation, amendments and consequences* (pp. 55–75). Oxford: Pergamon Press.

Johnson, R.B. (1998). Toward a theoretical model of evaluation utilization. *Evaluation and Program Planning, 21* (1), 93–110.

Jordan, K.F. (1977). Program improvement through school evaluation. *Educational Leadership, 34* (4), 272–275.

Kagan, J. and Kogan, N. (1970). Individual variation in cognitive processes. In P.A. Mussen (ed.), *Carmichael's manual of child psychology*, vol. 1 (pp. 1273–1365). New York: Wiley.

Kane, M.T. (2001). Current concerns in validity theory. *Journal of Educational Measurement, 38* (4), 319–342.

Karweit, N.L. (1994). Can preschool alone prevent early learning failure? In R.E. Slavin, N.L. Karweit, and B.A. Wasik (eds), *Preventing early school failure* (pp. 58–78). Boston, MA: Allyn & Bacon.

Kavanaugh, M.J., MacKinney, A.C., and Wolins, L. (1971). Issues in managerial performance: multitrait–multimethod analyses of ratings. *Psychological Bulletin, 75*, 34–49.

Kelly, A.V. (1989). *The curriculum: theory and practice.* London: Paul Chapman Publishing.

Kenny, D.A. and Kashy, D.A. (1992). Analysis of the multitrait–multimethod matrix by confirmatory factor analysis. *Psychological Bulletin, 112* (1), 165–172.

Kim, K.H. (2006). Can we trust creativity tests? A review of the Torrance Tests of Creative Thinking (TTCT). *Creativity Research Journal, 18* (1), 3–14.

Kline, P. (1994). *An easy guide to factor analysis.* London: Routledge.

Kline, P. and Gale, A. (1977). Extraversion, neuroticism and performance in a psychology examination. *British Journal of Educational Psychology, 41*, 90–94.

Knuver, J.W.M. (1993). *De relatie tussen klas- en schoolkenmerken en het affectief functioneren van leerlingen* (The relationship between class and school characteristics and the affective functioning of pupils). Groningen: RION.

Knuver, J.W.M. and Brandsma, H.P. (1993). Cognitive and affective outcomes in school effectiveness research. *School Effectiveness and School Improvement, 4* (3), 189–204.

Kogan, N. (1983). Stylistic variation in childhood and adolescence: creativity, metaphor, and cognitive style. In P.H. Mussen (ed.), *Handbook of child psychology*, vol. 3 (pp. 630–706). New York: Wiley.

Kohnstamm, G.A. and Mervielde, I. (1998). Personality development. In A. Demetriou, W. Doise, and K.F.M. van Lieshout (eds), *Life-span developmental psychology* (pp. 399–445). London: Wiley.

Konu, A., Lintonen, T.P., and Autio, V.J. (2002). Evaluation of well-being in schools: a multilevel analysis of general subjective well-being. *School Effectiveness and School Improvement, 13* (2), 187–200.

Košir, K. (2005). The influence of teacher's classroom management style on pupils' self-regulative behavior. *Studia Psychologica, 47* (2), 119–143.

Kraiger, K., Ford, J.K., and Salas, E. (1993). Application of cognitive, skill-based and affective theories of learning outcomes to new methods of training evaluation. *Journal of Applied Psychology, 78* (2), 311–328.

Krasne, S., Wimmers, P.F., Relan, A., and Drake, T.A. (2006). Differential effects of two types of formative assessment in predicting performance of first-year medical students. *Advances in Health Sciences Education, 11* (2), 155–171.

Kumar, D.D. (1991). A meta-analysis of the relationship between science instruction and student engagement. *Educational Review, 43* (1), 49–61.

Kyriakides, L. (1997). Primary teachers' perceptions of policy for curriculum reform in Mathematics. *Educational Research and Evaluation, 3*, 214–242.

Kyriakides, L. (1999a). The management of curriculum improvement in Cyprus: a critique of a 'centre–periphery' model in a centralised system. In T. Townsend, P. Clarke, and M. Ainscow (eds), *Third millennium schools: a world of difference in school effectiveness and school improvement* (pp. 107–124). Lisse: Swets & Zeitlinger.

Kyriakides, L. (1999b). Research on baseline assessment in mathematics at school entry. *Assessment in Education: Principles, Policy and Practice, 6* (3), 357–375.

Kyriakides, L. (2002). A research-based model for the development of policy on baseline assessment. *British Educational Research Journal, 28* (6), 805–826.

Kyriakides, L. (2004a). Differential school effectiveness in relation to sex and social class: some implications for policy evaluation. *Educational Research and Evaluation, 10* (2), 141–161.

Kyriakides, L. (2004b). Investigating validity from teachers' perspective through their engagement in large-scale assessment: the Emergent Literacy Baseline Assessment project. *Assessment in Education: Principles, Policy and Practice, 11* (2), 143–165.

Kyriakides, L. (2005a). Extending the comprehensive model of educational effectiveness by an empirical investigation. *School Effectiveness and School Improvement, 16* (2), 103–152.

Kyriakides, L. (2005b). Evaluating school policy on parents working with their children in class. *Journal of Educational Research, 98* (5), 281–298.

Kyriakides, L. (2006a). Introduction: international studies on educational effectiveness. *Educational Research and Evaluation, 12* (6), 489–497.

Kyriakides, L. (2006b). Using international comparative studies to develop the theoretical framework of educational effectiveness research: a secondary analysis of TIMSS 1999 data. *Educational Research and Evaluation, 12* (6), 513–534.

Kyriakides, L. and Campbell, R.J. (2003). Teacher evaluation in Cyprus: some conceptual and methodological issues arising from teacher and school effectiveness research. *Journal of Personnel Evaluation in Education, 17* (1), 21–40.

Kyriakides, L. and Campbell, R.J. (2004). School self-evaluation and school improvement: a critique of values and procedures. *Studies in Educational Evaluation, 30* (1), 23–36.

Kyriakides, L. and Charalambous, C. (2005). Using educational effectiveness research to design international comparative studies: turning limitations into new perspectives. *Research Papers in Education, 20* (4), 391–412.

Kyriakides, L. and Creemers, B.P.M. (2006a). Using different approaches to measure the school and teacher long-term effect: a longitudinal study on primary student achievement in mathematics. Paper presented at the Conference of ICSEI, Fort Lauderdale, FL, January.

Kyriakides, L. and Creemers, B.P.M. (2006b). Using the dynamic model of educational effectiveness to introduce a policy promoting the provision of equal opportunities to students of different social groups. In D.M. McInerney, S. Van Etten, and M. Dowson (eds), *Research on sociocultural influences on motivation and learning*, vol. 6: *Effective schooling*. Greenwich CT: Information Age Publishing.

Kyriakides, L. and Demetriou, D. (2005a). Using international comparative studies for establishing generic and differentiated models of educational effectiveness research: the PISA study. Paper presented at the ICSEI 2005 Conference, Barcelona, January.

Kyriakides, L. and Demetriou, D. (2005b). Introducing a teacher evaluation system based on teacher effectiveness research: an investigation of stakeholders' perceptions. Paper presented at the 86th Annual Meeting of the American Educational Research Association, April.

Kyriakides, L., and Pashiardis, P. (2005). Generating school performance indicators through self-evaluation: a complementary way of building the capacity for school improvement. Paper presented at the ICSEI 2005 Conference, Barcelona, January.

Kyriakides, L. and Tsangaridou, N. (2004). School effectiveness and teacher effectiveness in physical education. Paper presented at the 85th Annual Meeting of the American Educational Research Association. San Diego, CA, April.

Kyriakides, L. and Tsangaridou, N. (in press). Towards the development of generic and differentiated models of educational effectiveness: a study on school and teacher effectiveness in physical education. *British Journal of Educational Research.*

Kyriakides, L., Campbell, R.J., and Gagatsis, A. (2000). The significance of the classroom effect in primary schools: an application of Creemers' comprehensive model of educational effectiveness. *School Effectiveness and School Improvement, 11* (4), 501–529.

Kyriakides, L., Campbell, R.J., and Christofidou, E. (2002). Generating criteria for measuring teacher effectiveness through a self-evaluation approach: a complementary way of measuring teacher effectiveness. *School Effectiveness and School Improvement, 13* (3), 291–325.

Kyriakides, L., Charalambous, C., Philippou, G., and Campbell, R.J. (2006a). Illuminating reform evaluation studies through incorporating teacher effectiveness research: a case study in Mathematics. *School Effectiveness and School Improvement, 17* (1), 3–32.

Kyriakides, L., Demetriou, D., and Charalambous, C. (2006b). Generating criteria for evaluating teachers through teacher effectiveness research. *Educational Research, 48* (1), 1–20.

Kyriakides, L., Pashiardis, P., and Antoniou, A. (2007). Building a national reform policy on evaluation based on educational effectiveness research: the methodology of the ATHENA project. Paper presented at the ICSEI 2007 Conference, Portorož, Slovenia, January.

Lamb, S. (1996). Gender differences in mathematics participation in Australian schools: some relationships with social class and school policy. *British Educational Research Journal, 22* (2), 223–240.

Lamberts, P.C. and Abrams, K.R. (1995). Meta-analysis using multilevel models. *Multilevel Modelling Newsletter, 7* (2), 17–19.

Lassibille, G. and Gomez, L.N. (2000). Organization and efficiency of educational systems: some empirical findings. *Comparative Education, 36* (1), 7–19.

Leinhardt, G., Weidman, C., and Hammond, K.M. (1987). Introduction and integration of classroom routines by expert teachers. *Curriculum Inquiry, 17* (2), 135–176.

Leithwood, K. and Jantzi, D. (2006). Transformational school leadership for large-scale reform: effects on students, teachers, and their classroom practices. *School Effectiveness and School Improvement, 17,* 201–227.

Levenberg, I. and Sfard, A. (1996). When change becomes the name of the game: mathematics teachers in transition to a new learning environment. In L. Puig and A. Gutierrez (eds), *Proceedings of the 20th Conference of the International Group for the Psychology of Mathematics Education,* vol. 3 (pp. 249–256). Valencia: University of Valencia.

Levine, D.U. and Lezotte, L.W. (1990). *Unusually effective schools: a review and analysis of research and practice.* Madison, WI: National Center for Effective Schools Research and Development.

Lewis, C. and Tsuchida, I. (1997). Planned educational change in Japan: the case of elementary science instruction. *Journal of Educational Policy, 12* (5), 313–331.

Lingard, B., Ladwig, J., and Luke, A. (1998). School effects in post-modern conditions. In R. Slee and G. Weiner, with S. Tomlinson (eds), *School effectiveness for whom? Challenges to the school effectiveness and school improvement movements* (pp. 84–100). London: Falmer Press.

Lloyd, G.M. and Wilson, M. (1998). Supporting innovation: the impact of a teacher's conceptions of functions on his implementation of a reform curriculum. *Journal for Research in Mathematics Education, 29* (3), 248–274.

Lounsbury, J.W., Sundstrom, E., Loveland, J.M., and Gibson, L.W. (2003). Intelligence, 'Big Five' personality traits and work drive as predictors of course grade. *Personality and Individual Differences, 35,* 1231–1239.

Lugthart, E., Roeders, P.J.B., Bosker, R.J., and Bos, K.T. (1989). *Effectieve school-kenmerken in het voortgezet onderwijs. Deel 1: Literatuurstudie* (Effective schools characteristics in secondary education. Part I: Literature review). Groningen: RION.

Ma, X. (1999). Dropping out of advanced mathematics: the effects of parental involvement. *Teachers College Record, 101* (1), 60–81.

MacBeath, J. (1999). *Schools must speak for themselves: the case for school self-evaluation.* London: Routledge.

MacBeath, J. and Mortimore, P. (2001). *Improving school effectiveness.* Buckingham, UK: Open University Press.

MacBeath, J., Schratz, M., Meuret, D., and Lakobsen, L. (2000). *Self-evaluation in European schools.* London: RoutledgeFalmer.

MacDonald, B. (1991). Critical introduction from innovation to reform: a framework for analysing change. In J. Rudduck (ed.), *Innovation and change: developing involvement and understanding.* Milton Keynes: Open University Press.

McDonnell, L.M. (1995). Opportunity to learn as a research concept and policy instrument. *Educational Evaluation and Policy Analysis, 17,* 305–322.

McGreal, T.L. (1988). Evaluation for enhancing instruction: linking teacher evaluation and staff development. In S.J. Stanley and W.J. Popham (eds), *Teacher evaluation: six prescriptions for success* (pp. 1–29). Alexandria, VA: Association for Supervision and Curriculum Development.

McTaggart, R. (1997). *Participatory action research.* New York: Albany.

Madaus, G. and Pullin, D. (1991). To audit and validate 'high stakes' testing programs. In R.G. O'Sullivan (ed.), *Advances in program evaluation*, vol. 1A: *Effects of mandated assessment on teaching* (pp. 139–158). Greenwich, CT: JAI Press.

Marsh, H.W. and Byrne, B.M. (1993). Confirmatory factor analysis of multitrait–multimethod self-concept data: between-group and within-group invariance constraints. *Multivariate Behavioral Research, 28* (3), 313–349.

Marsh, H.W. and Hocevar, D. (1985). Application of confirmatory factor analysis to the study of self-concept: first- and higher-order factor models and their invariance across groups. *Psychological Bulletin, 97*, 562–582.

Marsh, H.W. and Parker, J.W. (1984). Determinants of student self-concept: is it better to be a large fish in a small pond even if you don't learn to swim as well? *Journal of Personality and Social Psychology, 47* (1), 213–231.

Marshall, S.P. (1995). *Schemas in Problem Solving*. New York: Cambridge University Press.

Martin, M.O. (1996). Third International Mathematics and Science Study. In M.O. Martin and D.L. Kelly (eds), *TIMSS technical report*, vol. 1 (pp. 1.1–1.19). Boston, MA: Boston College (IEA).

Martin, M.O., Mullis, I.V.S., Gonzalez, E.J., Gregory, K.D., Smith, T.A., Chrostowski, S.J., Garden, R.A., and O'Connor, K.M. (2000). *TIMSS 1999: International Science Report*. Boston, MA: International Study Center at Boston College (IEA).

Marzano, R.J. and Marzano, J.S. (2003). The key to classroom management. *Educational Leadership, 61* (1): 6–13.

Marzano, R.J., Hagerty, P.J., Valencia, S.W., and DiStefano, P.P. (1987). *Reading diagnosis and instruction: theory into practice*. Englewood Cliffs, NJ: Prentice-Hall.

Maslowski, R. (2003). *School culture and school performance: an explorative study into the organisational culture of secondary schools and their effects*. Enschede: Twente University Press.

Meehl, P.E. (1978). Theoretical risks and tabular asterisks: Sir Karl, Sir Ronald and the slow progress of soft psychology. *Journal of Applied Psychology, 46*, 806–834.

Messick, S. (1996). Bridging cognition and personality in education: the role of style in performance and development. *European Journal of Personality, 10*, 353–376.

Meuret, D. and Morlaix, S. (2003). Conditions of success of a school's self-evaluation: some lessons of a European experience. *School Effectiveness and School Improvement, 14* (1), 53–71.

Mijs, D., Houtveen, T., Wubells, T., and Creemers, B.P.M. (2005). Is there empirical evidence for school improvement? Paper presented at the ICSEI 2005 Conference, Barcelona, January.

Miller, S. (1984). *Experimental design and statistics* (2nd edn). London: Routledge.

Ministry of Education (1994). *The New Curriculum*. Nicosia: Ministry of Education.

Mintzberg, H. (1979). *The structuring of organizations*. Englewood Cliffs, NJ: Prentice-Hall.

Monk, D.H. (1992). Education productivity research: an update and assessment of its role in education finance reform. *Educational Evaluation and Policy Analysis, 14* (4), 307–332.

Monk, D.H. (1994). Subject matter preparation of secondary mathematics and science teachers and student achievement. *Economics of Education Review, 13* (2), 125–145.

Morgan, G. (1986). *Images of organizations*. Beverly Hills, CA: Sage.

Morgan, H. (1997). *Cognitive styles and classroom learning*. Westport, CT: Praeger.

Mortimore, P. (2001). Globalisation, effectiveness and improvement. *School Effectiveness and School Improvement, 12* (1), 229–249.

Mortimore, P., Sammons, P., Stoll, L., Lewis, D., and Ecob, R. (1988). *School matters: the junior years.* Wells, UK: Open Books.

Muijs, D. (1997). Predictors of academic achievement and academic self-concept: a longitudinal perspective. *British Journal of Educational Psychology, 67,* 263–277.

Muijs, D. and Reynolds, D. (2000). School effectiveness and teacher effectiveness in mathematics: some preliminary findings from the evaluation of the Mathematics Enhancement Programme (Primary). *School Effectiveness and School Improvement, 11* (3), 273–303.

Muijs, D. and Reynolds, D. (2001). *Effective teaching: evidence and practice.* London: Sage.

Mullis, I.V.S., Martin, M.O., Gonzalez, E.J., Gregory, K.D., Garden, R.A., O'Connor, K.M., Chrostowski, S.J., and Smith, T.A. (2000). *TIMSS 1999: International Mathematics Report.* Boston, MA: International Study Center at Boston College (IEA).

Murphy, J.F., Weil, M., Hallinger, P., and Mitman, A. (1982). Academic press: translating high expectations into school policies and classroom practices. *Educational Leadership, 40* (3), 22–26.

Murray, D.M., Feldman, H.A., and McGovern, P.G. (2000). Components of variance in a group-randomized trial analysed via a random-coefficients model: the Rapid Early Action for Coronary Treatment (REACT) trial. *Statistical Methods in Medical Research, 9* (2), 117–133.

Nevo, D. (1995). *School-based evaluation: a dialogue for school improvement.* Oxford: Pergamon Press.

Noble, T. (2004). Integrating the revised Bloom's taxonomy with multiple intelligence: a planning tool for curriculum differentiation. *Teachers College Records, 106* (1), 193–211.

Nunnally, J.C. and Bernstein, I.H. (1994). *Psychometric Theory* (3rd edn). New York: McGraw-Hill.

Nuthall, G. and Church, J. (1973). Experimental studies of teaching behaviour. In G. Chanan (ed.), *Towards a science of teaching* (pp. 9–25). London: National Foundation for Educational Research.

Nuttall, D., Goldstein, H., Prosser, R., and Rasbach, J. (1989). Differential school effectiveness. *International Journal of Educational Research, 13,* 769–776.

Oakes, J. and Lipton, M. (1990). Tracking and ability grouping: a structural barrier to access and achievement. In J.I. Goodlad and P. Keating (eds), *Access to knowledge: an agenda for our nation's schools* (pp. 187–204). New York: College Entrance Examination Board.

Opdenakker, M.C. and Van Damme, J. (2000). Effects of schools, teaching staff and classes on achievement and well-being in secondary education: similarities and differences between school outcomes. *School Effectiveness and School Improvement, 11* (2), 65–196.

Opdenakker, M.C. and Van Damme, J. (2006). Differences between secondary schools: a study about school context, group composition, school practice, and school effects with special attention to public and Catholic schools and types of schools. *School Effectiveness and School Improvement, 17* (1), 87–117.

Oser, F.K. (1992). Morality in professional action: a discourse approach for teaching. In F.K. Oser, A. Dick, and J.L. Patry (eds), *Effective and Responsible Teaching: The New Synthesis* (pp. 109–125). San Francisco: Jossey-Bass.

Oser, F.K. (1994). Moral perspectives on teaching. In L. Darling-Hammond (ed.), *Review of Research in Education 20* (pp. 57–127). Washington, DC: American Educational Research Association.

Pajares, F. (1999). Current directions in self-efficacy research. In M. Maehr and P.R. Pintrich (eds), *Advances in motivation and achievement* (pp. 1–49). Greenwich, CT: JAI Press.

Pajares, F. and Miller, M. (1994). Role of self-efficacy and self-concept beliefs in mathematical problem solving: a path analysis. *Journal of Educational Psychology, 86* (2), 193–203.

Pajares, F. and Schunk, D.H. (2001). Self-beliefs and school success: self-efficacy, self-concept, and school achievement (pp. 239–266). In R. Riding and S. Rayner (eds), *Perception.* London: Ablex Publishing.

Paris, S.G. and Paris, A.H. (2001). Classroom applications of research on self-regulated learning. *Educational Psychologist, 36* (2), 89–101.

Patton, M.Q. (1991). *Qualitative evaluation and research methods.* London: Sage.

Peterson, P., Wilkinson, L.C., and Hallinan, M. (eds) (1984). *The social context of instruction: group organization and group processes.* New York: Academic Press.

Pines, A.L. and West, L.H.T. (1986). Conceptual understanding and science learning: an interpretation of research within a source-of-knowledge framework. *Science Education, 70* (5), 583–604.

Pintrich, P.R. (1999). The role of motivation in promoting and sustaining self-regulated learning. *International Journal of Educational Research, 31*, 459–470.

Plewis, I. (2000). Evaluating educational interventions using multilevel growth curves: the case of Reading Recovery. *Educational Research and Evaluation, 6* (1), 83–101.

Polettini, A.F.F. (2000). Mathematics teaching life histories in the study of teachers' perceptions of change. *Teaching and Teacher Education, 16*, 765–783.

Pollard, A., Broadfoot, P., Croll, P., Osborn, M., and Abbott, D. (1994). *Changing English primary schools? The impact of the Education Reform Act at Key Stage 1.* London: Cassell.

Ponte, J.P., Matos J.F., Guimaraes, H.M., Leal, L.C., and Canavarro, A.P. (1994). Teachers' and students' views and attitudes towards a new mathematics curriculum: a case study. *Educational Studies in Mathematics, 26*, 347–365.

Popham, W.L. (1997) Consequential validity: right concern – wrong concept. *Educational Measurement: Issues and Practice, 16* (2), 9–13.

Prawat, R.S. (1989a). Teaching for understanding: three key attributes. *Teaching and Teacher Education, 5* (4), 315–328.

Prawat, R.S. (1989b). Promoting access to knowledge, strategy, and disposition in students: a research synthesis. *Review of Educational Research, 59*, 1–41.

Preskill, H., Zuckerman, B., and Matthews, B. (2003). An exploratory study of process use: findings and implications for future research. *American Journal of Evaluation, 24* (4), 423–442.

Purkey, S.C. and Smith, M.S. (1983). Effective schools: a review. *Elementary School Journal, 83* (4), 427–452.

Ralph, E.G. (2004). Developing managers' effectiveness: a model with potential. *Journal of Management Inquiry, 13* (2), 152–163.

Ralph, J.H. and Fennessey, J. (1983). Science or reform: some questions about the effective schools model. *Phi Delta Kappan, 64* (10), 689–694.

Rao, S.P., Collins, H.L., and DiCarlo, S.E. (2002). Collaborative testing enhances student learning. *Advances in Physiology Education, 26* (1), 37–41.

Raudenbush, S.W. (1994). Random effects models. In H. Cooper and L.V. Hedges (eds), *The handbook of research synthesis* (pp. 301–323). New York: Russell Sage.

Raudenbush, S.W. and Bryk, A.S. (1985). Empirical Bayes meta-analysis. *Journal of Educational Statistics*, *10*, 75–98.

Raudenbush, S.W. and Bryk, A.S. (1986). A hierarchical model for studying school effects. *Sociology of Education*, *59*, 1–17.

Raven, J. (1991). The wider goals of education: beyond the three R's. *Educational Forum*, 55 (4), 343–363.

Redfield, D. and Rousseau, E. (1981). A meta-analysis of experimental research on teacher questioning behavior. *Review of Educational Research*, *51*, 237–245.

Reezigt, G.J. and Creemers, B.P.M. (2005). A comprehensive framework for effective school improvement. *School Effectiveness and School Improvement*, *16* (4), 407–424.

Reezigt, G.J., Guldemond, H., and Creemers, B.P.M. (1999). Empirical validity for a comprehensive model on educational effectiveness. *School Effectiveness and School Improvement*, *10* (2), 193–216.

Reezigt, G.J., Creemers, B.P.M., and de Jong, R. (2003). Teacher evaluation in the Netherlands and its relation to educational effectiveness research. *Journal of Personnel Evaluation in Education*, *17* (1), 67–81.

Resnick, L.B. (1987). *Education and Learning to Think.* Washington, DC: National Academy Press.

Reusser, K. (2000). Success and failure in school mathematics: effects of instruction and school environment. *European Child and Adolescent Psychology*, *9*, 17–26.

Reynolds, A.J. and Walberg, H.J. (1990). *A Structural Model of Educational Productivity.* De Kolb: Northern Illinois University.

Reynolds, D. (1993). Linking school effectiveness knowledge and school improvement practice. In C. Dimmock (ed.), *School-based management and school effectiveness* (pp. 185–200). London: Routledge.

Reynolds, D. (2000). School effectiveness: the international dimension. In C. Teddlie and D. Reynolds (eds), *The International Handbook of School Effectiveness Research* (pp. 232–256). London: Falmer Press.

Reynolds, D. (2006). World class schools: some methodological and substantive findings and implications of the International School Effectiveness Research Project (ISERP). *Educational Research and Evaluation*, *12* (6), 535–560.

Reynolds, D. and Farrell, S. (1996). *Worlds Apart? A Review of International Studies of Educational Achievement Involving England.* London: HMSO for Ofsted.

Reynolds, D. and Stoll, L. (1996). Merging school effectiveness and school improvement: the knowledge base. In D. Reynolds, R. Bollen, B. Creemers, D. Hopkins, L. Stoll, and N. Lagerweij (eds), *Making good schools: linking school effectiveness and school improvement* (pp. 94–112). London: Routledge.

Reynolds, D., Hopkins, D., and Stoll, L. (1993). Linking school effectiveness knowledge and school improvement practice: towards a synergy. *School Effectiveness and School Improvement*, *4*, 37–58.

Reynolds, D., Teddlie, C., Hopkins, D., and Stringfield, S. (2000). Linking school effectiveness and school improvement. In C. Teddlie and D. Reynolds (eds), *The International Handbook of School Effectiveness Research* (pp. 206–231). London: Falmer Press.

Reynolds, D., Creemers, B., Stringfield, S., Teddlie, C., and Schaffer, G. (eds.) (2002). *World class schools: international perspectives on school effectiveness.* London: RoutledgeFalmer.

Riding, R. and Cheema, I. (1991). Cognitive styles: an overview and integration. *Educational Psychology*, *11*, 193–215.

Rink, J. (2003). Effective instruction in physical education. In S. Silverman and C. Ennis (eds), *Student learning in physical education: applying research to enhance instruction*. Champaign, IL: Human Kinetics.

Robson, C. (1993). *Real world research*. Oxford: Blackwell.

Rogosa, D.R. and Willett, J.B. (1985). Understanding correlates of change by modeling individual differences in growth. *Psychometrika*, *90*, 726–748.

Rogosa, D.R., Brand, D., and Zimowski, M. (1982). A growth curve approach to the measurement of change. *Psychological Bulletin*, *90*, 726–748.

Rohrbeck, C.A., Ginsburg-Block, M.D., Fantuzzo, J.W., and Miller, T.R. (2003). Peer-assisted learning interventions with elementary school students: a meta-analytic review. *Journal of Educational Psychology*, *95* (2), 240–257.

Rosas, S.R. (2005). Concept mapping as a technique for program theory development: an illustration using family support programs. *American Journal of Evaluation*, *26* (3), 389–401.

Rosenholz, S.J. (1989). *Teachers' workplace: the social organization of schools*. New York: Longman.

Rosenshine, B. (1971). Teaching behaviors related to pupil achievement: a review of research. In I. Westbury and A.A. Bellack (eds), *Research into classroom processes: recent developments and next steps* (pp. 51–98). New York: Teachers College Press.

Rosenshine, B. (1976). Classroom instruction. In N.L. Gage (ed.), *The psychology of teaching methods: the seventy-fifth yearbook of the National Society for the Study of Education* (pp. 335–371). Chicago, IL: University of Chicago Press.

Rosenshine, B. (1983). Teaching functions in instructional programs. *Elementary School Journal*, *83* (4), 335–351.

Rosenshine, B. and Furst, N. (1973). The use of direct observation to study teaching. In R.M.W. Travers (ed.), *Second Handbook of Research on Teaching*. Chicago, IL: Rand McNally.

Rosenshine, B. and Stevens, R. (1986). Teaching functions. In M.C. Wittrock (ed.), *Handbook of Research on Teaching* (3rd edn, pp. 376–391). New York: Macmillan.

Rosenthal, R. (1994). Parametric measures of effect size. In H. Cooper and L.V. Hedges (eds), *The Handbook of Research Synthesis* (pp. 231–245). New York: Russell Sage.

Rowan, B., Bossert, S.T., and Dwyer, D.C. (1983). Research on effective schools: a cautionary note. *Educational Researcher*, *12* (4), 24–31.

Rutter, M., Maughan, B., Mortimore, P., Ouston, J., and Smith, A. (1979). *Fifteen thousand hours: secondary schools and their effects on children*. Cambridge, MA: Harvard University Press.

Sammons, P., Nuttall, D., and Cuttance, P. (1993). Differential school effectiveness: results from a reanalysis of the Inner London Education Authority's Junior School Project data. *British Educational Research Journal*, *19* (4), 381–405.

Sammons, P., Hillman, J., and Mortimore, P. (1995). *Key characteristics of effective schools: a review of school effectiveness research*. London: Ofsted and Institute of Education.

Savery, J.R. and Duffy, T. M. (1995). Problem based learning: an instructional model and its constructivist framework. *Educational Technology*, *35* (5), 31–38.

Sax, G. (1997). *Principles of educational and psychological measurement* (4th edn). Belmont, CA: Wadsworth.

Schaffer, E., Nesselrodt, P., and Stringfield, S. (1994). The contributions of classroom observations to school effectiveness research. In D. Reynolds, B.P.M. Creemers, P.S. Nesselrodt, E.C. Schaffer, S. Stringfield, and C. Teddlie (eds) *Advances in school effectiveness research and practice* (pp. 133–152). Oxford: Pergamon Press.

Scheerens, J. (1992). *Effective schooling: research, theory and practice.* London: Cassell.

Scheerens, J. (1993). Basic school effectiveness research: items for a research agenda. *School Effectiveness and School Improvement, 4* (1), 17–36.

Scheerens, J. and Bosker, R.J. (1997). *The foundations of educational effectiveness.* Oxford: Pergamon Press.

Scheerens, J. and Creemers, B.P.M. (1989). Conceptualizing school effectiveness. *International Journal of Educational Research, 13,* 691–706.

Scheerens, J. and Demeuse, M. (2005). The theoretical basis of the effective school improvement model (ESI). *School Effectiveness and School Improvement, 16* (4), 373–385.

Scheerens, J., Glas, C., and Thomas, S. (2003). *Educational evaluation, assessment and monitoring: a systemic approach.* Lisse: Swets & Zweitlinger.

Schmidt, F.L. and Hunter, J.E. (1977). Development of a general solution to the problem of validity generalization. *Journal of Applied Psychology, 62,* 529–540.

Schmidt, W. and Valverde, G.A. (1995). *National policy and cross-national research: United States participation in the Third International Mathematics and Science Study.* East Lansing: Michigan State University, Third International Mathematics and Science Study.

Schmidt, W., Jakwerth, P., and McKnight, C.C. (1998). Curriculum sensitive assessment: content *does* make a difference. *International Journal of Educational Research, 29,* 503–527.

Schmidt, W., McKnight, C.C., Valaverde, G.A., and Wiley, D.E. (1997). *Many Visions, Many Aims,* vol. 1: *A cross-national investigation of curricular instructions in school mathematics.* Dordecht: Kluwer Academic.

Schmitt, N. and Stults, D.M. (1986). Methodology review: analysis of multitrait–multimethod matrices. *Applied Psychological Measurement, 10,* 1–22.

Schmuck, R.A. (1980). The school organization. In J.H. McMillan (ed.), *The social psychology of school learning.* New York: Academic Press.

Schon, D.A. (1971). *Beyond the stable state.* Harmondsworth, UK: Penguin.

Schunk, D.H. (1991). Self-efficacy and academic motivation. *Educational Psychologist, 26* (3), 207–231.

Schwartz, W. (1995). *Opportunity to learn standards: their impact on urban students* (ED389816). New York: Eric Clearinghouse on Urban Education.

Scriven, M. (1994). Duties of the teacher. *Journal of Personnel Evaluation in Education, 8,* 151–184.

Shadish, W.R., Cook, T.D., and Campbell, D.T. (2002). *Experimental and quasi-experimental designs for generalized causal inference.* Boston, MA: Houghton Mifflin.

Shavelson, R.J., Webb, N.M., and Rowley, G.L. (1989). Generalizability theory. *American Psychologist, 44* (6), 922–932.

Shaw, K.M. and Replogle, E. (1996). Challenges in evaluating school-linked services: toward a more comprehensive evaluation framework. *Evaluation Review, 20* (4), 424–469.

Shepard, L.A. (1989). Why we need better assessment. *Educational Leadership, 46* (2), 4–8.

Shipman, M.D. (1985). Ethnography and educational policy-making. In R.G. Burgess (ed.), *Field methods in the study of education*. London: Falmer Press.

Shuerger, J.M. and Kuma, D.L. (1987). Adolescent personality and school performance: a follow-up study. *Psychology in the Schools, 24*, 281–285.

Siedentop, D. and Tannehill, D. (2000). *Developing teaching skills in physical education* (4th edn). Mountain View, CA: Mayfield.

Siedentop, D., Tousignant, M., and Parker, M. (1982). *Academic learning time – physical education: coding manual* (2nd edn). Columbus: Ohio State University.

Silverman, S. and Skonie, R. (1997). Research on teaching in physical education: an analysis of published research. *Journal of Teaching in Physical Education, 16*, 300–311.

Simons, H. (1998). Evaluation and the reform of schools. In *The evaluation of educational programmes: methods, uses and benefits*. Report of the Education Research Workshop held in North Berwick, UK, 22–25 November (pp. 46–64). Amsterdam and Lisse: Swets & Zeitlinger.

Simons, R.J., van der Linden, J., and Duffy, T. (2000). New learning: three ways to learn in a new balance. In R.J. Simons, J. van der Linden, and T. Duffy (eds), *New learning* (pp. 1–20). Dordrecht: Kluwer Academic.

Sirin, S.R. (2005). Socioeconomic status and academic achievement: a meta-analytic review of research. *Review of Educational Research, 75* (3), 417–453.

Slater, R.O. and Teddlie, C. (1992). Toward a theory of school effectiveness and leadership. *School Effectiveness and School Improvement, 3* (4), 247–257.

Slavin, R.E. (1983). When does cooperative learning increase student achievement? *Psychological Bulletin, 94* (3), 429–445.

Slavin, R.E. (1986). Best-evidence synthesis: an alternative to meta-analytic and traditional reviews. *Educational Researcher, 15* (9), 5–11.

Slavin, R.E. (1987a). A theory of school and classroom organization. *Educational Psychologist, 22* (2), 89–108.

Slavin, R.E. (1987b). Mastery learning reconsidered. *Review of Educational Research, 57* (2), 175–213.

Slavin, R.E. (1987c). Ability grouping and student achievement in elementary schools: a best-evidence synthesis. *Review of Educational Research, 57*, 293–326.

Slavin, R.E. (1996). *Education for All*. Lisse: Swets & Zeitlinger.

Slavin, R.E. (2002). Evidence-based education policies: transforming educational practice and research. *Educational Researcher, 31* (7), 15–21.

Slavin, R.E. and Cooper, R. (1999). Improving intergroup relations: lessons learned from cooperative learning programs. *Journal of Social Issues, 55* (4), 647–663.

Slee, R. and Weiner, G. with Tomlinson, S. (eds) (1998). *School effectiveness for whom? Challenges to the school effectiveness and school improvement movements*. London: Falmer Press.

Smith, L. and Sanders, K. (1981). The effects on student achievement and student perception of varying structure in social studies content. *Journal of Educational Research, 74*, 333–336.

Snijders, T. and Bosker, R. (1999). *Multilevel analysis: an introduction to basic and advanced multilevel modeling*. London: Sage.

Snow, R.E. (1973). Theory construction for research on teaching. In R.M.W. Travers (ed.) *Second Handbook of Research on Teaching* (pp. 77–112). Chicago: Rand McNally.

Snyder, J., Bolin, F., and Zumwalt, K. (1992). Curriculum implementation. In P.W. Jackson (ed.), *Handbook of Research on Curriculum* (pp. 402–435). New York: Macmillan.

Soar, R.S. and Soar, R.M. (1979). Emotional climate and management. In P. Peterson and H. Walberg (eds), *Research on teaching concepts: findings and implications*. Berkeley, CA: McCutchan.

Sosniak, L.A. (1994). The taxonomy, curriculum, and their relations. In L. Anderson and L.A. Sosniak (eds), *Bloom's taxonomy: a forty-year retrospective: ninety-third yearbook of the National Society for the Study of Education, part II* (pp. 117–118). Chicago, IL: University of Chicago Press.

Sosniak, L.A. (1999). Professional and subject matter knowledge for teacher education. In G.A. Griffin (ed.), *The Education of Teachers: ninety-eighth yearbook of the National Society for the Study of Education, part I* (pp. 185–204). Chicago, IL: University of Chicago Press.

Spencer, M.B., Noll, E., and Cassidy, E. (2000). Monetary incentives in support of academic achievement: results of a randomized field trial involving high-achieving, low-resource, ethnically diverse urban adolescents. *Evaluation Review, 29* (3), 199–222.

Squires, D.A., Hewitt, W.G., and Segars, J.K. (1983). *Effective schools and classrooms: a research based perspective*. Alexandria, VA: Association for Supervision and Curriculum Development.

Stacy, A.W., Widaman, K.F., Hays, R., and DiMatteo, M.R. (1985). Validity of self-reports of alcohol and other drug use: a multitrait–multimethod assessment. *Journal of Personality and Social Psychology, 49*, 219–232.

Stenmark, J.K. (1992). *Mathematics assessment: myths, models, good questions and practical suggestions*. Reston, VA: National Council of Teachers of Mathematics.

Sternberg, R.J. (1988). Mental self-government: a theory of intellectual styles and their development. *Human Development, 31*, 197–224.

Sternberg, R.J. (1994). Allowing for thinking styles. *Educational Leadership, 52* (3), 36–39.

Stevenson, H. (1992). Learning from Asian schools. *Scientific American*, December, 32–38.

Stevenson, H.W., Chen, C., and Lee, S.Y. (1993). Mathematics achievement of Chinese, Japanese and American children: ten years later. *Science, 259*, 53–58.

Stoll, L., Reynolds, D., Creemers, B., and Hopkins, D. (1996). Merging school effectiveness and school improvement: practical examples. In D. Reynolds, R. Bollen, B. Creemers, D. Hopkins, L. Stoll, and N. Lagerweij (eds), *Making good schools* (pp. 113–147). London and New York: Routledge.

Stringfield, S. (1994). A model of elementary school effects. In D. Reynolds, B.P.M. Creemers, P.S. Nesselrodt, E.C. Schaffer, S. Stringfield, and C. Teddlie (eds), *Advances in School Effectiveness Research and Practice* (pp. 153–187). Oxford: Pergamon Press.

Stringfield, S. (1995). Attempting to enhance students' learning through innovative programs: the case for schools evolving into high reliability organizations. *School Effectiveness and School Improvement, 6* (1), 67–96.

Stringfield, S.C. and Slavin, R.E. (1992). A hierarchical longitudinal model for elementary school effects. In B.P.M. Creemers and G.J. Reezigt (eds), *Evaluation of educational effectiveness* (pp. 35–69). Groningen: ICO.

Stronge, J.H. (1995). Balancing individual and institutional goals in educational personnel evaluation: a conceptual framework. *Studies in Educational Evaluation, 21*, 131–151.

Stronge, J.H. (1997). Improving schools through teacher evaluation. In J.H. Stronge (ed.), *Evaluating teaching: a guide to current thinking and practice* (pp. 1–23). Thousand Oaks, CA: Corwin Press.

Stufflebeam, D.L. and Shinkfield, A.J. (1990). *Systematic evaluation*. Boston, MA: Kluwer-Nijhoff.

Sztajn, P. (2003). Adapting reform ideas in different mathematics classrooms: beliefs beyond mathematics. *Journal of Mathematics Teacher Education, 6*, 53–75.

Taggart, B. and Sammons, P. (1999). Evaluating the impact of a raising school standards initiative. In R.J. Bosker, B.P.M. Creemers, and S. Stringfield (eds), *Enhancing educational excellence, equity and efficiency: evidence from evaluations of systems and schools in change* (pp. 137–166). Dordrecht: Kluwer Academic.

Taylor, A. and MacDonald, D. (1999). Religion and the five factor model of personality: an exploratory investigation using a Canadian university sample. *Personality and Individual Differences, 27*, 1243–1259.

Teddlie, C. (1994). The integration of classroom and school process data in school effectiveness research. In D. Reynolds, B.P.M. Creemers, P.S. Nesselrodt, E.C. Schaffer, S. Stringfield, and C. Teddlie (eds), *Advances in school effectiveness research and practice* (pp. 111–133). Oxford: Pergamon Press.

Teddlie, C. and Reynolds, D. (2000). *The International Handbook of School Effectiveness Research*. London: Falmer Press.

Teddlie, C. and Stringfield, S. (1993). *Schools make a difference: lessons learned from a 10-year study of school effects*. New York: Teachers College Press.

Teddlie, C., Reynolds, D., and Sammons, P. (2000). The methodology and scientific properties of school effectiveness research. In C. Teddlie and D. Reynolds (eds), *The International Handbook of School Effectiveness Research* (pp. 55–133). London: Falmer Press.

Teddlie, C., Stringfield, S., and Burdett, J. (2003). International comparisons of the relations among educational effectiveness and improvement variables: an overview. *Journal of Personnel Evaluation in Education, 17* (1), 5–19.

Teddlie, C., Creemers, B.P.M., Kyriakides, L., Muijs, D., and Fen, Y. (2006). The International System for Teacher Observation and Feedback: evolution of an international study of teacher effectiveness constructs. *Educational Research and Evaluation, 12* (6), 561–582.

Thomas, S. (2001). Dimensions of secondary school effectiveness: comparative analyses across regions. *School Effectiveness and School Improvement, 12* (3): 285–322.

Thomas, S., Sammons, P., Mortimore, P., and Smees, R. (1997). Differential secondary school effectiveness: comparing the performance of different pupil groups. *British Educational Research Journal, 23* (4), 451–470.

Thorndike, E.L. (1920). Intelligence examination for college entrance. *Journal of Educational Research, 1*, 329–337.

Tobin, K. (1987). The role of wait time in higher cognitive level learning. *Review of Educational Research, 57* (1), 69–95.

Torres, R.T. and Preskill, H. (2001). Evaluation and organizational learning: past, present, and future. *American Journal of Evaluation, 22* (3), 387–395.

Townsend, T., Clarke, P., and Ainscow, M. (eds) (1999). *Third millennium schools: a world of difference in school effectiveness and school improvement*. Lisse: Swets & Zeitlinger.

Trautwein, U., Koller O., Schmitz B., and Baumert, J. (2002). Do homework assignments enhance achievement? A multilevel analysis in 7th-grade mathematics. *Contemporary Educational Psychology, 27* (1), 26–50.

Tyack, D. and Cuban, L. (1995). *Tinkering toward Utopia: a century of public school reform*. Cambridge, MA: Harvard University Press.

Tymms, P., Merrell, C., Heron, T., Jones, P., Albone, S., and Henderson, B. (2006). The importance of districts. Paper presented at the AERA Annual Conference, San Francisco, April.

Valverde, G.A. and Schmidt, W.H. (2000). Greater expectations: learning from other nations in the quest for 'world-class standards' in US school mathematics and science. *Journal of Curriculum Studies*, *32* (5), 651–687.

van den Berg, R., and Ros, A. (1999). The permanent importance of the subjective reality of teachers during educational innovation: a concerns-based approach. *American Educational Research Journal*, *36* (4), 879–906.

van den Berg, R., Sleegers, P., Geijsel, F., and Vandenberghe, R. (2000). Implementation of an innovation: meeting the concerns of teachers. *Studies in Educational Evaluation*, *26* (4), 331–350.

van der Werf, M.P.C. (1995). *The educational priority policy in the Netherlands: content, implementation and outcomes*. The Hague: SVO.

Vaughan, M., Brighouse, T., Neill, A.S., Readhead, Z.N., and Stronach, I. (2006). *Summerhill and A.S. Neill*. Milton Keynes, UK: Open University Press.

Vermunt, J. and Vershaffel, L. (2000). Process-oriented teaching. In R.J. Simons, J. van der Linden, and T. Duffy (eds), *New learning* (pp. 209–225). Dordrecht: Kluwer Academic.

Vernon, P. (1973). Multivariate approaches to the study of cognitive styles. In J.R. Royce (ed.), *Contributions of multivariate analysis to psychological theory* (pp. 139–157). London: Academic Press.

Visscher, A.J. and Coe, R. (2002). *School improvement through performance feedback*. Rotterdam: Swets & Zeitlinger.

Walberg, H.J. (1984). Improving the productivity of America's schools. *Educational Leadership*, *41* (8), 19–27.

Walberg, H.J. (1986a). Syntheses of research on teaching. In M.C. Wittrock (ed.), *Handbook of Research on Teaching* (3rd edn, pp. 214–229). New York: Macmillan.

Walberg, H.J. (1986b). What works in a nation still at risk. *Educational Leadership*, *44* (1), 7–10.

Wang, M.C., Haertel, G.D., and Walberg, H.J. (1990). What influences learning? A content analysis of review literature. *Journal of Educational Research*, *84* (1), 30–43.

Wang, M.C., Haertel, G.D., and Walberg, H.J. (1993). Toward a knowledge base for school learning. *Review of Educational Research*, *63* (3), 249–294.

Weiss, C.H. (1997). How can theory-based evaluation make greater headway? *Evaluation Review*, *21* (4), 501–524.

Wentzel, K.R. and Wigfield, A. (1998). Academic and social motivational influences on students' academic performance. *Educational Psychology Review*, *10* (2), 155–175.

Widaman, K.F. (1985). Hierarchically nested covariance structure models for multitrait–multimethod data. *Applied Psychological Measurement*, *9*, 1–26.

Wiggins, G. and McTighe, J. (1998). *Understanding by design*. Alexandria, VA: Association for Supervision and Curriculum Development.

Wilkerson, D.J., Manatt, R.P., Rogers, M.A., and Maughan, R. (2000). Validation of student, principal and self-ratings in 360° Feedback® for teacher evaluation. *Journal of Personnel Evaluation in Education*, *14* (2), 179–192.

Wilks, R. (1996). Classroom management in primary schools: a review of the literature. *Behaviour Change*, *13* (1), 20–32.

Willett, J.B. (1988). Questions and answers in the measurement of change. *Review of Research in Education*, 345–422.

Willis, D. (1993). Learning and assessment: exposing the inconsistencies of theory and practice. *Oxford Review of Education, 19* (3), 383–402.

Witziers, B., Bosker, J.R., and Kruger, L.M. (2003). Educational leadership and student achievement: the elusive search for an association. *Educational Administration Quarterly, 39* (3), 398–425.

Wolfe, R. and Johnson, S. (1995). Personality as a predictor of college performance. *Educational and Psychological Measurement, 55,* 77–185.

Woods, P. (1994). Adaptation and self-determination in English primary schools. *Oxford Review of Education, 20* (4), 387–410.

Worthen, B.R., Sanders, J.R., and Fitzpatrick, J.L. (1997). *Program evaluation: alternative approaches and practical guidelines* (2nd edn). New York: Longman.

Wubbels, T., Brekelmans, M., and Hooymayers, H. (1991). Interpersonal teacher behaviour in the classroom. In B.J. Fraser and H.J. Walberg (eds), *Educational environments: evaluation, antecedents and consequences* (pp. 141–161). Oxford: Pergamon Press.

Yair, G. (1997). When classrooms matter: implications of between-classroom variability for educational policy in Israel. *Assessment in Education, 4* (2), 225–248.

Yang, Y. (2003). Dimensions of socio-economic status and their relationship to mathematics and science achievement at individual and collective levels. *Scandinavian Journal of Educational Research, 47* (1), 21–41.

Zhang, L.F. (2001a). Do thinking styles contribute to academic achievement beyond self-rated abilities? *Journal of Psychology, 135,* 621–638.

Zhang, L.F. (2001b). Thinking styles and personality types revisited. *Personality and Individual Differences, 31,* 883–894.

Zhang, L.F. (2002). Measuring thinking styles in addition to the measuring personality traits? *Personality and Individual Differences, 33,* 445–458.

Zhang, L.F. and Huang, J. (2001). Thinking styles and the five-factor model of personality. *European Journal of Personality, 15,* 465–476.

Zhang, L.F. and Sternberg, R.J. (1998). Thinking styles, abilities, and academic achievement among Hong Kong university students. *Educational Research Journal, 13,* 41–62.

Appendix
Studies investigating the effect of school-level factors on student achievement used for the meta-analysis reported in Chapter 9

Aksoy, T. and Link, C.R. (2000). A panel analysis of student mathematics achievement in the US in the 1990s: does increasing the amount of time in learning activities affect math achievement? *Economics of Education Review, 19*, 261–277.

Bamburg, J.D. and Andrews, R.L. (1991). School goals, principals and achievement. *School Effectiveness and School Improvement, 2* (3), 175–191.

Bosker, R.J. and Scheerens, J. (1994). Alternative models of school effectiveness put to the test. *International Journal of Educational Research, 21*, 159–181.

Bosker, R.J., Kremers, E.J.J., and Lugthart, E. (1990). School and instruction effects on mathematics achievement. *School Effectiveness and School Improvement, 1*, 233–248.

Brewer, D.J. (1993). Principals and student outcomes. *Economics of Education Review, 12* (4), 281–292.

Brown, R. and Evans, P.W. (2002). Extracurricular activity and ethnicity: creating greater school connections among diverse student populations. *Urban Education, 37* (1), 41–58.

Cheng, Y.C. (1993). Profiles of organizational culture and effective schools. *School Effectiveness and School Improvement, 4* (2), 85–110.

Cheng, Y.C. (1994). Principal's leadership as a critical factor for school performance: evidence from multilevels of primary schools. *School Effectiveness and School Improvement, 5*, 299–317.

de Jong, R., Westerhof, K.J., and Kruiter, J.H. (2004). Empirical evidence of a comprehensive model of school effectiveness: a multilevel study in mathematics in the 1st year of junior general education in the Netherlands. *School Effectiveness and School Improvement, 15* (1), 3–31.

DiPaola, M.F. and Tschannen-Moran, M. (2005). Bridging or buffering? The impact of schools' adaptive strategies on student achievement. *Journal of Educational Administration, 43* (1), 60–71.

Driessen, G. and Sleegers, P. (2000). Consistency of teaching approach and student achievement: an empirical test. *School Effectiveness and School Improvement, 11* (1), 57–79.

Durland, M. and Teddlie, C. (1996). A network analysis of the structural dimensions of principal leadership in differentially effective schools. Paper presented at the Annual Meeting of the American Educational Research Association, New York, April.

Eberts, R. and Stone, J. (1988). Student achievement in public schools: do principals make a difference? *Economics of Education Review, 7*, 291–299.

Fan, X. (2001). Parental involvement and students' academic achievement: a growth modeling analysis. *Journal of Experimental Education, 70* (1), 27–61.

Fan, X. and Chen, M. (2001). Parent involvement and students' academic achievement: a meta-analysis. *Educational Psychology Review, 13* (1), 1–22.

Farrow, S., Tymms, P., and Henderson, B. (1999). Homework and attainment in primary schools. *British Educational Research Journal, 25* (3), 323–341.

Fraser, B.J., Walberg, H.J., Welch, W.W., and Hattie, J.A. (1987). Syntheses of educational productivity research. *International Journal of Educational Research, 11*, 145–252.

Friedkin, N.E. and Slater, M.R. (1994). School leadership and performance: a social network approach. *Sociology of Education, 67*, 139–157.

Goldring, E. and Pasternak, R. (1994). Principals coordinating strategies and school effectiveness. *School Effectiveness and School Improvement, 5* (3), 239–253.

Griffith, J. (2002). A multilevel analysis of the relation of school learning and social environments to minority achievement in public elementary schools. *Elementary School Journal, 102* (5), 349–366.

Griffith, J. (2003). Schools as organizational models: implications for examining school effectiveness. *Elementary School Journal, 110* (1), 29–47.

Guay, F., Boivin, M., and Hodges, E.V.E. (1999). Predicting change in academic achievement: a model of peer experiences and self-system processes. *Journal of Educational Psychology, 91* (1), 105–115.

Hallinger, P., Bickman, L., and Davis, K. (1996). School context, principal leadership and student reading achievement. *Elementary School Journal, 96* (5), 527–549.

Heck, R. (1993). School context, principal leadership, and achievement: the case of secondary schools in Singapore. *Urban Review, 25*, 151–166.

Heck, R., Larson, T., and Marcoulides, G. (1990). Principal instructional leadership and school achievement: validation of a causal model. *Educational Administration Quarterly, 26*, 94–125.

Heck, R., Marcoulides, G., and Lang, P. (1991). Principal instructional leadership and school achievement: the application of discriminant techniques. *School Effectiveness and School Improvement, 2*, 115–135.

Hofman, R.H. (1995). Contextual influences on school effectiveness: the role of school boards. *School Effectiveness and School Improvement, 6* (4), 308–331.

Hofman, R.H., Hofman, W.H.A., and Guldemond, H. (2002). School governance, culture and student achievement. *International Journal of Leadership in Education, 5* (3), 249–272.

Hofman, W.H.A. and Guldemond, H. (1999). Social and cognitive outcomes: a comparison of contexts of learning. *School Effectiveness and School Improvement, 10* (3), 352–366.

Houtveen, A.A.M., van de Grift, W.J.C.M., and Creemers, B.P.M. (2004). Effective school improvement in mathematics. *School Effectiveness and School Improvement, 15* (3), 337–376.

Hoy, W.K., Tater, J.C., and Bliss, J. R. (1990). Organizational climate, school health, and effectiveness: a comparative analysis. *Educational Administration Quarterly, 26* (3), 260–279.

Jimerson, S., Egeland, B., and Teo, A. (1999). A longitudinal study of achievement trajectories: factors associated with change. *Journal of Educational Psychology, 91* (1), 116–126.

Karlya, T. and Rosenbaum, J.E. (1999). Bright flight: unintended consequences of detracking policy in Japan. *American Journal of Education, 107* (3), 210–230.

Kyriakides, L. (2005). Extending the comprehensive model of educational effectiveness by an empirical investigation. *School Effectiveness and School Improvement, 16* (2), 103–152.

Kyriakides, L. (2007). Investigating the generalisability of models of educational effectiveness: a study on teacher and school effectiveness in mathematics and language at pre-primary education. Paper presented at the EARLI 2007 Conference, Budapest, August.

Kyriakides, L. and Charalambous, C. (2005). Using educational effectiveness research to design international comparative studies: turning limitations into new perspectives. *Research Papers in Education, 20* (4), 391–412.

Kyriakides, L. and Tsangaridou, N. (2004). School effectiveness and teacher effectiveness in physical education. Paper presented at the 85th Annual Meeting of the American Educational Research Association, San Diego, CA.

Kyriakides, L., Campbell, R.J., and Gagatsis, A. (2000). The significance of the classroom effect in primary schools: an application of Creemers' comprehensive model of educational effectiveness. *School Effectiveness and School Improvement, 11* (4), 501–529.

Kythreotis, A. (2006). The influence of school leadership styles and culture on students' achievement in Cyprus primary schools. Unpublished doctoral dissertation, University of Cyprus.

Lee, V.E. and Bryk, A.S. (1989). A multilevel model of the social distribution of high school achievement. *Sociology of Education, 62* (3), 172–192.

Leithwood, K. and Jantzi, D. (1999). The relative effects of principal and teacher sources of leadership on student engagement with school. *Educational Administration Quarterly, 35*, 679–706.

Leithwood, K. and Jantzi, D. (2006). Transformational school leadership for large-scale reform: effects on students, teachers, and their classroom practices. *School Effectiveness and School Improvement, 17*, 201–227.

Leitner, D. (1994). Do principals affect student outcomes? *School Effectiveness and School Improvement, 5*, 219–238.

Ma, X. (1999). Dropping out of advanced mathematics: the effects of parental involvement. *Teachers College Record, 101* (1), 60–81.

Mandeville, G.K. and Kennedy, E. (1991). The relationship of effective school indicators and changes in the social distribution of achievement. *School Effectiveness and School Improvement, 2*, 14–33.

Marks, H.M. and Printy, S.M. (2003). Principal leadership and school performance: an integration of transformational and instructional leadership. *Educational Administration Quarterly, 39* (3), 370–397.

Mortimore, P., Sammons, P., Stoll, L., Lewis, D., and Ecob, R. (1988). *School matters: the junior years.* Wells, UK: Open Books.

Mudler, L. and Van de Werf, G. (1997). Implementation and effects of the Dutch educational priority policy: results of four years of evaluation studies. *Educational Research and Evaluation, 3* (4), 317–339.

Opdenakker, M.C. and Van Damme, J. (2001). Relationship between school composition and characteristics of school process and their effect on mathematics achievement. *British Educational Research Journal, 27* (4), 407–432.

Pritchard, R.J., Morrow, D., and Marshall, J.C. (2005). School and district culture as reflected in student voices and student achievement. *School Effectiveness and School Improvement, 16* (2), 153–177.

Reezigt, G.J., Guldemond, H., and Creemers, B.P.M. (1999). Empirical validity for a comprehensive model on educational effectiveness. *School Effectiveness and School Improvement, 10* (2), 193–216.

Scheerens, J., Vermeulen, C.J., and Pelgrum, W.J. (1989). Generalisability of instructional and school effectiveness indicators across nations. *International Journal of Educational Research, 13,* 789–799.

Shann, M.H. (1999). Academics and a culture of caring: the relationship between school achievement and prosocial and antisocial behaviours in four urban middle schools. *School Effectiveness and school Improvement, 10* (4), 390–413.

Sillins, H. and Mulford, B. (2004). Schools as learning organizations: effects on teacher leadership and student outcomes. *School Effectiveness and School Improvement, 15,* 443–466.

Smyth, E. (1999). Pupil performance, absenteeism and school drop-out: a multi-dimensional analysis. *School Effectiveness and School Improvement, 10* (4), 480–502.

Smyth, E. and Hannan, C. (2006). School effects and subject choice: the uptake of scientific subjects in Ireland. *School Effectiveness and School Improvement, 17* (3), 255–273.

Sterbinsky, A., Ross, M.S., and Redfield, D. (2006). Effects of comprehensive school reform on student achievement and school change: a longitudinal multi-site study. *School Effectiveness and School Improvement, 17* (3), 367–397.

Sweetland, R.S. and Hoy, K.W. (2000). School characteristics and educational outcomes: towards an organizational model of student achievement in middle schools. *Educational Administration Quarterly, 36* (5), 703–729.

Teddlie, C. and Stringfield, S. (1993). *Schools make a difference: lessons learned from a 10-year study of school effects.* New York: Teachers College Press.

van de Grift, W. (1990). Educational leadership and academic achievement in elementary education. *School Effectiveness and School Improvement, 1* (3), 26–40.

van de Grift, W.J.C.M. and Houtveen, A.A.M. (2006). Underperformance in primary schools. *School Effectiveness and School Improvement, 17* (3), 255–273.

Van der Werf, G. (1997). Differences in school and instruction characteristics between high- , average- , and low-effective schools. *School Effectiveness and School Improvement, 8* (4), 430–448.

Van Der Werf, G., Creemers, B., De Jong, R., and Klaver E. (2000). Evaluation of school improvement through an educational effectiveness model: the case of Indonesia's PEQIP project. *Comparative Education Review, 44* (3), 329–355.

Van Houtte, M. (2004). Tracking effects on school achievement: a qualitative explanation in terms of the academic culture of school staff. *American Journal of Education, 110* (4), 354–388.

Webster, B.J. and Fisher, D.L. (2000). Accounting for variation in science and mathematics achievement: a multilevel analysis of Australian Data Third International Mathematics and Science Study (TIMSS). *School Effectiveness and School Improvement, 11,* 339–360.

Webster, B.J. and Fisher, D.L. (2003). School-level environment and student outcomes in mathematics. *Learning Environment Research, 6,* 309–326.

Willms, J.D. and Somers, M. (2001). Family, classrooms, and school effects on children's educational outcomes in Latin America. *School Effectiveness and School Improvement, 12* (4), 409–445.

Index

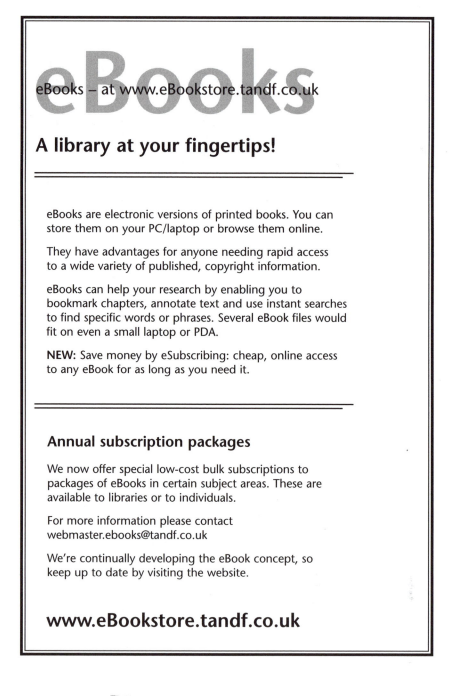